A South Carolina Upcountry Saga

A South Carolina Upcountry Saga

THE CIVIL WAR LETTERS OF
Barham Bobo Foster and His Family
1860-1863

"To live in hearts one leaves behind is not to die."

EDITED BY
A. Gibert Kennedy

The University of South Carolina Press

Publication of this book is made possible in part by the
support of the South Caroliniana Library with the assistance
of the Caroline McKissick Dial Publication Fund.

© 2019 University of South Carolina

Published by the University of South Carolina Press
Columbia, South Carolina 29208

www.sc.edu/uscpress

Manufactured in the United States of America

28 27 26 25 24 23 22 21 20 19
10 9 8 7 6 5 4 3 2 1

The Library of Congress Cataloging-in-Publication data
can be found at http://catalog.loc.gov/.

ISBN 978-1-61117-924-8 (cloth)
ISBN 978-1-64336-022-5 (ebook)

This book was printed on recycled paper with
30 percent postconsumer waste content.

To Pam, Grace, and Gibert

CONTENTS

ILLUSTRATIONS

Figures

Maps

PREFACE

In 1989 my father asked me if I wanted my great-great grandfather Barham Bobo Foster's "pockets" which contained some old papers. Being an ancestor-worshipping South Carolinian, I naturally accepted. These Civil War–era pockets were originally tied around the waist and worn inside the pants, rather like a modern money belt. As I began going through the documents in the pockets, I found they included a series of about seventy-five Civil War letters between Lt. Col. Barham Bobo Foster; his wife, Mary Ann Perrin Foster; and his sons Lewis Perrin and James Anthony.

The Civil War was a cataclysmic event that affected not only soldiers but also their families. Where the details of most family stories are now lost, this group of letters formed the core of my family's story. By compiling the letters and doing the research to discern their context, I could rebuild and preserve this story for my family and other interested persons. I felt obligated to do so.

As I learned of Lieutenant Colonel Foster's importance as an upcountry community leader, as a representative to the S.C. Secession Convention, as a signer of the Ordinance of Secession, as the organizer of a celebrated South Carolina Infantry regiment, and as a post-war leader, the scope of the project grew beyond mere family interests.

The project received a significant boon when I found another 225 letters in Rion McKissick's papers in the South Caroliniana Library at the University of South Carolina. McKissick, a beloved president of the University of South Carolina in the 1930s and 1940s, was Foster's grandson.

These letters, records, and research reveal a complex picture of the life of a Southern family living through the historical events of the American Civil War. Their words and actions were framed by Protestant religious conviction and a sense of duty to God, personal honor, state, and country—I think pretty much in that order.

There remains a small monument to James Anthony Foster and Lewis Perrin Foster in the family graveyard beside their ancestral home outside Spartanburg, South Carolina. The monument is inscribed from Thomas Campbell's *Hallowed Ground*: "To live in hearts one leaves behind is not to die." I hope that through these letters, these young men will live in the hearts of this and future generations.

I feel very fortunate to have had a chance to get to know these people. I have learned much about the family life; the military life; and the personal motives, hopes, loves, and fears of these individuals during the Civil War.

I hope that you will enjoy meeting them, also.

ACKNOWLEDGMENTS

Upon the completion of this project, I feel an immense gratitude to the many people who have encouraged and assisted me in this effort.

I especially owe a debt to those who preserved the letters and made them available to me. My father, Barham Foster Kennedy II and my grandfather Albert Gibert Kennedy enabled this study by preserving and passing to me the initial set of 75 Foster letters. Herb Hartsook and, later, Nathan Saunders at the South Caroliniana Library at the University of South Carolina in Columbia made more than 150 letters from the Rion McKissick papers available for this project. The staff of this library was always very helpful to me. Ruth Ahlers of Lafayette, Colorado, made six letters to Eunice Foster available. The late Sam Cothran and his son, Frank Cothran, generously permitted the use of letters from the "Cothran-Chiles Notes" as well as an update more than a half century later (1992). Harvey Teal of Columbia, South Carolina, provided a letter from his personal collection; it is now in the South Caroliniana Library. Another letter was found in clippings from an unknown newspaper, and I include it with gratitude to the unknown owner.

I relied upon the research of Mac Wyckoff and his *A History of the Third South Carolina Infantry 1861–65* in making sense of the movements of these soldiers in the 3rd S.C. The identification of many of the soldiers in this story would not have been possible without his earlier research. In 2008 Wyckoff published *A History of the 3rd South Carolina Regiment: Lee's Reliables*, an even more comprehensive account of this storied regiment. I have not attempted to provide a history of the 3rd S.C., but, instead, to focus on telling the family story. I strongly recommend Mac Wyckoff's books to any who seeks a military history of this storied unit. Mac gave me helpful advice when I toured the Fredericksburg battlefield.

At a roundtable discussion at the University of South Carolina Aiken in 1995, Mac admonished would-be Civil War storytellers to "Do the research." I have sought to follow his advice and I hope that I have done so.

Althea Northcross of Boston, Massachusetts, created the maps used in the book. Her precise and efficient work will greatly enhance the reader's understanding of the soldiers' engagements and movements described in these letters.

Thank you to those who read my early drafts and manuscript, for providing excellent suggestions: the late Myrna Kennedy; Barham Foster Kennedy; Jim

Arnett; James Everett Kibler; and my wife, Pamela Kennedy. The book was shaped in many ways by your wise advice.

I am grateful to those who encouraged and advised me in this project, perhaps in ways that they don't know: James Everett Kibler, Bill Brockington, Gordon Smith, Mac Wyckoff, Theresa Shackelford, and Herb Hartsook.

A project like this occurs in a context of those who advise, encourage, wait, are inconvenienced, listen, care, and love. My context is:

my wife, Pam

my children, Grace and Gibert

my parents, Barham Foster and the late Myrna Kennedy

my brothers, Perrin Kennedy and Foster Kennedy

my Sewanee Temperance League friends—You know who you are.

To live in hearts. . . .

LETTER SOURCES

The following Letters were passed down through the family to A. Gibert Kennedy and are presently in his possession.

February 25, 1856	Mary Foster to her son LPF	Spartanburg, S.C.
October 29, 1857	Mary Foster to her son LPF	Spartanburg, S.C.
January 31, 1858	LPF to his sister Sallie	South Carolina College Columbia, S.C.
April 1861	BBF to his wife	Camp Ruffin, Columbia, S.C.
April 26, 1861	LPF to his mother	Camp Ruffin, Columbia, S.C.
April 27, 1861	BBF to his wife	Camp Ruffin, Columbia, S.C.
May 7, 1861	BBF to his wife	Camp Ruffin, Columbia, S.C.
June 20, 1861	BBF to his wife	Camp Jackson, Richmond, Va.
June 22, 1861	BBF to his wife	Camp Jackson, Richmond, Va.
June 23, 1861	LPF to JAF	Manassas, Va.
June 1861	BBF to his wife	Camp Butler, Bull Run, Va.
June 26, 1861	BBF to his wife	Camp Beauregard, Bull Run, Va.
June 28, 1861	BBF to his wife	Camp Beauregard, Bull Run, Va.
July 8, 1861	LPF to his mother	Fairfax, Va.
July 9, 1861	BBF to his daughter	Fairfax, Va.
July 12, 1861	BBF to his wife	Fairfax, Va.
July 25, 1861	LPF to JAF	Vienna, Va.
July 30, 1861	BBF to JAF	Vienna, Va.
July [30], 1861	BBF to his wife	Va.
July 1861	LPF to his mother	Fairfax, Va.
August 7, 1861	BBF to his wife	Vienna, Va.
August 25, 1861	BBF to his wife	Va.
September 1, 1861	BBF to his wife	Arlington Heights, Va.
September 4, 1861	BBF to his wife	Flint Hill, Va.

September 6, 1861	LPF to his mother	Flint Hill, Va.
September 11, 1861	LPF to his mother	Flint Hill, Va.
September 13, 1861	BBF to his wife	Flint Hill, Va.
September 14, 1861	BBF to his wife	Va.
September 1861	BBF to his wife	Flint Hill, Va.
September 19, 1861	BBF to his wife	Flint Hill, Va.
September 20, 1861	LPF to his sister Jennie	Charlottesville, Va.
September 21, 1861	LPF to JAF	Charlottesville, Va.
September 24, 1861	BBF to his wife	Va.
September 25, 1861	BBF to JAF	Flint Hill, Va.
September 28, 1861	LPF to JAF	Selma, Va.
September 29, 1861	BBF to his wife	Va.
September 30, 1861	BBF to his wife	Flint Hill, Va.
October 1, 1861	BBF to his wife	Flint Hill, Va.
November 12, 1861	LPF to BBF	Centreville, Va.
November 18, 1861	LPF to BBF	Centreville, Va.
November 22, 1861	LPF to his sister	Centreville, Va.
[December (13), 1861]	BBF to his wife	Richmond, Va.
December 19, 1861	BBF to his wife	Va.
December 22, 1861	BBF to his wife	Centreville, Va.
December 26, 1861	BBF to his wife	Centreville, Va.
January 1, 1862	BBF to his wife	Centreville, Va.
January 4, 1862	LPF to his sister	Centreville, Va.
January 15, 1862	BBF to his wife	Centreville, Va.
January 22, 1862	BBF to his wife	Camp James Orr, Bull Run, Va.
February 3, 1862	LPF to his sister	Camp James Orr, Bull Run, Va.
February 20, 1862	LPF to his mother	Camp James Orr, Bull Run, Va.
February 27, 1862	LPF to his mother	Camp James Orr, Bull Run, Va.
March 21, 1862	LPF to BBF	Rapidan Station, Va.
March 25, 1862	JAF to his mother	Green Pond, S.C.
March 27, 1862	LPF to BBF	Rapidan Station, Va.
March 28, 1862	JAF to BBF	Green Pond, S.C.
April 13, 1862	JAF to his mother	Camp Gregg, Colleton Dist. S.C.
April 16, 1862	LPF to BBF	York Town, Va.
May 29, 1862	LPF to his mother	Chickahominy River, Va.
June 3, 1862	LPF to BBF	Richmond, Va.
June 7, 1862	LPF to his mother	Richmond, Va.
June 22, 1862	LPF to BBF	Camp Jackson, Richmond, Va.
June 26, 1862	JAF to his mother	Camp Jackson, Richmond, Va.
July 4, 1862	JAF to his mother	Malvern Hill, Va.

July 6, 1862	LPF to BBF	Telegraph
July 17, 1862	LPF to his sister	Camp Jackson, Richmond, Va.
August 1, 1862	JAF to BBF	Camp McLaws, Richmond, Va.
August 3, 1862	JAF to his mother	Camp McLaws, Richmond, Va.
August 9, 1862	JAF to BBF	Va.
August 15, 1862	JAF to his mother	Chafin's Bluff, Va.
August 19, 1862	JAF to his mother	Near Malvern Hill, Va.
October 17, 1862	LPF to BBF	Manchester, Va.
October 27, 1862	LPF to BBF	Berrietown, Va.
October 30, 1862	LPF to BBF	Berrietown, Va.
November 16, 1862	LPF to BBF	Culpepper, Va.
December 2, 1862	LPF to his sister	Fredericksburg, Va.
May 28, 1863	SAF to her sister Jennie	Millway, S.C.
July 26, [1894]	Eunice Foster to BBF	Home

Ruth Ahlers of Lafayette, Colorado, generously made the following letters available for this book.

July 14, 1861	LPF to Eunice Foster	Fairfax, Va.
August 4, 1861	LPF to Eunice Foster	Vienna, Va.
August 10, 1861	LPF to Eunice Foster	Vienna, Va.
August 18, 1861	LPF to Eunice Foster	Flint Hill, Va.
August 29, 1861	LPF to Eunice Foster	Flint Hill, Va.
October 31, 1861	Sallie Foster to Eunice Foster	Home

The following letters are reprinted from the "Cothran-Chiles Notes" and an update after more than a half century (1992). The late Sam Cothran of Aiken, South Carolina, made the letters available to the editor. His son, Frank Cothran, generously gave permission to publish the letters.

December 31, 1861	Sallie Foster to Elizabeth P. Cothran	Glenn Springs, S.C.
May 9, 1862	Sallie Foster to Elizabeth P. Cothran	Glenn Springs, S.C.
July 18, 1862	Sallie Foster to Elizabeth P. Cothran	Glenn Springs, S.C.
August 11, 1862	Sallie Foster to Elizabeth P. Cothran	Home
December 19, 1862	Eunice Foster to Sallie Foster	

The following letter was printed in a clipping from a Spartanburg newspaper. The date of publication is unknown.

| April 30, 1861 | LPF to Major Alvin Lancaster | Camp Ruffin, Columbia, S.C. |

Harvey Teal of Columbia, South Carolina, gave the following letter for use in this publication. This letter is now in the South Caroliniana Library.

| October 9, 1861 | LPF to his mother | Selma, Va. |

All other letters were generously made available for publication courtesy of the South Caroliniana Library at the University of South Carolina–Columbia.

METHODOLOGY

The letters are generally in good condition; but, they have their problems. Stains and water damage obscure the writing. Some of the paper is lost and there are holes in the text. In a letter dated October 29, 1857, Mary Ann Foster admonished her son Perrin on his penmanship:

> It took your Father, Tony and I all to read your letter and I don't know whether we all deciphered the whole contents of it or not. I saw Edwin sometime since He told me he had received a letter from you that he had a great difficulty in reading, that he could not make out all the words but had to be content with making out the sense of the letter.

There are many places where the letters are unreadable. I have followed a convention using square brackets [ ] to indicate where words have been restored or emended. Normally I have done this only where it is necessary to make sense of the sentence. Where there was a gap in the manuscript that I was unable to read or restore, I have denoted this gap with [. . .]. I have left the punctuation, capitalization, spelling, and usage as I found them in the letters. Where the letter writer has duplicated a word, (for example, "of of"), I have removed one of the duplicates. I believe that readers will grow accustomed to these anomalies after reading a few pages.

In most cases the letters are presented in chronological order. I have added commentary to provide the historical context for the letters and knowledge that would be assumed by the letter writer. I have made every effort to identify the people and events discussed in the letters and have placed this information in the footnotes. Bibliographic information is referenced and placed in the endnotes. Genealogies of the Foster and Perrin families are provided to assist the reader in identifying family members.

GENEALOGY

The letters are primarily associated with the Foster family; and centrally, with Barham Bobo Foster. Two other closely associated families are the Perrins and the Kennedys. The Perrin family became closely linked to the Fosters with the marriage of Mary Ann Perrin to Barham Bobo Foster. The children of B. B. Foster and Mary Ann maintained close ties to their cousins, who are encountered many times in the letters. The Kennedy family and the Fosters lived near each other in the Glenn Springs and Jonesville areas. Benjamin Kennedy raised a company of infantry for B. B. Foster's regiment, and after the war he married Foster's daughter Eunice.

The plus marks (+) in the genealogies identify individuals who appear in the letters.

Foster Family

+Barham Bobo Foster* (1817–1897). He married Mary Ann Perrin, the sister of Thomas Chiles Perrin, in 1837. His children were:

- +Lewis Perrin Foster (1837–1862).
- +Sarah Agnes (Sallie) Foster (1840–1918). She married Issac Going McKissick. Her son, James Rion McKissick, became the President of the University of South Carolina in 1935.
- +James Anthony (Tony) Foster (1839–1862).
- +Eunice (Nunie) Foster (1856–1928). Eunice married Captain Benjamin Kennedy in 1869. After the war, they farmed near Jonesville, S.C.
- +Jane Eliza (Jennie and Lizzie) Foster (1852–1929). Jennie married James +Andrew Thompson in 1871. They farmed in the area around Jonesville, S.C.

* Graydon, Graydon, and Davis, *McKissicks*, 162.

Perrin Family

The Perrin family* lived in the Abbeville, South Carolina, area. Samuel Perrin married Eunice Chiles and they had seven children:

1. Elizabeth Lee Perrin (1803–1874) married John Cothran.
   Eunice Cothran (1845–1851).
   +Elizabeth (Lizzie) Perrin Cothran (1843–1925) married Col. F. E. Harrison on Feb. 7, 1878.

2. +Thomas Chiles Perrin (1805–1878). He married Jane Eliza Wardlaw. Thomas Chiles Perrin was a signer of the S.C. Ordinance of Secession representing Abbeville District.
   Amanda Elizabeth Perrin (1830–1831).
   +Mary Eunice Perrin (1832–1877). She married Col. F. E. Harrison on May 16, 1861.
   +James Wardlaw Perrin (1833–1890) married Mary Livingston.
   Emma Chiles Perrin (1834–1916) married James Sproull Cothran.
   +Hannah Clarke Perrin (1836–1918).
   William H. Perrin (1838–1862) was killed in action at Gaines' Mill.
   +Lewis Wardlaw Perrin (1839–1907) married Mary Means McCaw.
   Sarah Eliza Perrin (1841–1925) married George White.
   Thomas Samuel Perrin (1845–1863) was killed in action at Chancellorsville.
   Francis (Frank) Perrin (1846) died as an infant.
   George Clopton Perrin (1850–1912).
   Robert Coalter Perrin (1852–1853).

3. Lewis Perrin (1809–1880) married Elizabeth Hinde and Mary Grant.
   Mary Eunice Perrin (1839–1874) married Achilles Perrin.
   Martha Perrin (1842–1859).
   James Hinde Perrin (1845–1877) married Mary Belcher.
   Thomas Grant Perrin (1860–1921).

4. +Mary Ann Perrin (1811–1886) married Lt. Col. Barham Bobo Foster.
   +Lewis Perrin Foster (1837–1862) was killed in action at Fredericksburg.
   +Sarah Agnes (Sallie) Foster (1840–1918) married Col. Isaac Going McKissick.
   +James Anthony (Tony) Foster (1839–1862) was killed in action at Harper's Ferry.
   +Eunice (Nunie) Foster (1845–1928) married Captain Benjamin Kennedy.
   +Jane Eliza (Jennie and Lizzie) Foster (1852–1929) married James Andrew Thompson.

* Thomas Perrin Cothran, *The Perrin Family* (Greenville, S.C.: Privately printed by the Peace Printing Company, Greenville, S.C., 1924), 17–34.

5. +Agnes White Perrin (1815–1905) married R. P. Quarles.

    Sarah B. Quarles (1836–1933) married George Galphin.

    Eunice Chiles Quarles (1839–1885) married L. R. Cogburn.

    +Thomas P. Quarles (1841–1924) married Mary Thompson McDonald.

    Susan Quarles (1844–1932) married J. H. Walker.

    James W. Quarles (1840–1910) married Dolly Coleman.

    Mary Elizabeth Quarles (1848–1929) married W. D. Sullivan.

    Richard P. Quarles (1850–1883) married Lula Neville.

6. +Samuel Perrin (1818–1880) married Emma Blocker, Julia Quarles, and Fannie Quarles.

    +Anna Isabella (Belle) Perrin (1847–1927) married Dr. John Watts.

    James B. Perrin (1850–1855).

    Louis Henry Perrin (1851–1923) married Mary Letitia Yeldell and Mary Elizabeth (Bessie) Gilchrist.

    Julia Elizabeth (Lizzie) Perrin (1853–1874) married Frank Waldrop.

    Arthur Berwick Perrin (1855–1859).

    Katherine Perrin (1857–_____).*

    Fannie Allene Perrin (1873–1874).

    Sarah Lee Perrin (1869–1892).

    Mary (May) Eunice Perrin (1866–1925) married Gaspar Loren Toole.

    Thomas C. Perrin (1864–1874) married Ann C. Smith.

7. +James Monroe Perrin (1822–1863). He married Mary Elizabeth Smith and Kitty Tillman. He was killed in action at Chancellorsville.

    Joel S. Perrin (1849–1875) married Ellen Watkins.

    Mary E. Perrin (1853–1941) married L. C. Thompson.

    Janie Perrin (1855–1940) married John S. Thompson.

    Ivy Wardlaw Perrin (1858–1938) married Rev. John Gass and Bishop T. D. Bratton.

    Eunice Chiles Perrin (1860–1885).

    James S. Perrin (1861–1924).

    Kitty Tillman Perrin (1863–1947).

* Her name spelling and birth date are uncertain. Some sources call her Catherine Emma or Emma Catherine, and give a birth date of 1859. This is the information in the 1924 Perrin genealogy.

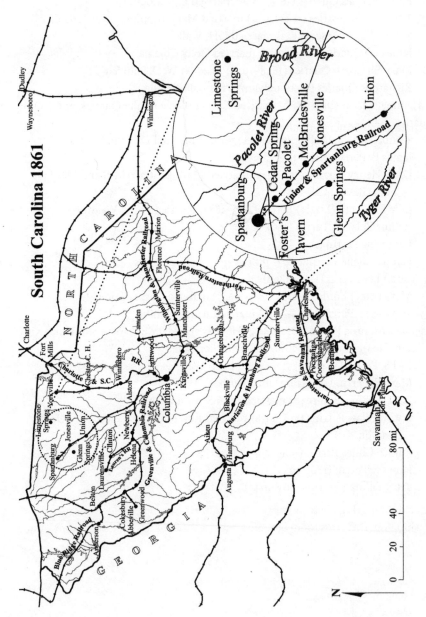

South Carolina, 1861

Introduction

Barham Bobo Foster's grandfather Anthony Foster moved from Fairfax, Virginia, to the Cross Anchor settlement in Union District, South Carolina,* in about 1792. With him came his second wife, Sarah Barham Foster; his daughter, Mary; and his living sons, John, James, Fielding, and Anthony, Jr. The McKissick family tradition says that his son, Achilles, was killed in the Revolutionary War at Bunker Hill in 1775 and another son, Joel, was killed at the Battle of Brandywine in 1777.† By the time Anthony Foster died in 1805, he had established a home and plantation in Cross Anchor. His wife, Sarah, died in 1812.

Anthony Foster, Jr. used his share of his father's estate to build Foster's Tavern in 1807 at the crossroads near Cedar Spring within the present city limits of Spartanburg. This building was both a home and a public tavern. The 1820 *Mills' Atlas* survey of Spartanburg District shows Foster's Tavern at the intersection of the road "To Union Line" and a road running southwest to northeast. These roads connected Spartanburg with Columbia; Charleston; Charlotte, North Carolina; Augusta, Georgia; and Atlanta, Georgia. Foster's Tavern is an impressive two-story structure constructed with slave-made bricks fired in a kiln built on the property. The homesite included slave cabins and a family cemetery. The cemetery was occasionally shared with unfortunate travelers who died along their journey. The tavern and Foster home place still exists at the intersection of S.C. 295 (Southport Road) and S.C. 56 (Union Road). The tavern prospered due to its location along these important stagecoach routes.

One of the most prominent guests was John C. Calhoun, who always took the same room during his trips between his home in Pendleton, South Carolina, and Washington, D.C. This room became known as "the John C. Calhoun room." Many

---

* Billy Glen Foster, *The Foster Family of Flanders, England, and America* (Bryan, Texas: Insite Publishing, 1990), 53.

† Research by B. G. Foster suggests that Achilles may have lived into 1777 and died before 1778. Further, Foster suggests that Anthony Foster's son, Joel, may have survived the war contrary to the McKissick family history. N. Graydon, T. Graydon, and Davis, *McKissicks*, 161–163.

Foster's Tavern, home of B. B. Foster, 1997. Photograph taken by the editor.

years later, when Anthony Foster, Jr.'s son Barham Bobo Foster was an old man, he explained with pride to a Dr. Lancaster that his room was "next to Mr. Calhoun's."*

On June 16, 1796, Anthony Jr. married Elizabeth Bobo. They had eleven children. The ninth child, Barham Bobo Foster, was born February 22, 1817 in the Cross Roads tavern home. Little is known of Barham Bobo's earliest years. As a young adult, B. B. Foster managed a successful plantation, so he must have had significant exposure to farm life in his youth, probably at the family plantation in Cross Anchor. Mills's *Statistics of South Carolina*, published in 1826, reported on schools in Cedar Spring, "An academy is established here, which promises well. In it are taught the Latin and Greek languages, and mathematics, besides the usual course of English studies."† This was the Word Academy, founded in 1824 as a "Latin school," with a Presbyterian minister, Reverend Porter, serving as the first teacher. Barham Bobo and his brother, Joel, attended this academy.‡ Barham Bobo Foster's daughter Eunice later wrote that as a young man her father studied medicine under Dr. R. M. Young in Spartanburg, until the health of his father, Anthony Foster, declined, at which time B. B. Foster returned home to manage the family farm.§

---

* N. Graydon, T. Graydon, and Davis, *McKissicks*, 165.

† Robert Mills, *Statistics of South Carolina* (Charleston, S.C.: Hurlburt and Lloyd, 1826), 726.

‡ J. B. O. Landrum, *History of Spartanburg County* (Atlanta, Ga., 1900, reprinted by Reprint, Spartanburg, S.C., 1985), 87.

§ Landrum, *History of Spartanburg County*, 6, 432.

The Tariff of 1824 and the Tariff of 1828, both Federal protective acts, infuriated many South Carolinians who saw the tariffs as a way of raising costs for imported British goods to promote Northern manufacturing. South Carolina leaders saw that Federal laws could as easily affect slave institutions, and the South Carolina legislature passed laws nullifying or vetoing the Tariff Acts. The Force Act of 1833 authorized President Jackson to dispatch military forces to the state to enforce the tariffs. An uneasy truce was reached when the Tariff of 1833 reduced tariffs and South Carolina repealed the nullification laws. Even at sixteen years old, Barham Bobo Foster was an ardent nullifier during the Nullification Crisis of 1833. Before he was eighteen years old he was elected captain of a local militia company.* His letters reflect a love for his home state of South Carolina and a commitment to states' rights.

On January 19, 1837, at the age of twenty, B. B. Foster married Mary Ann Perrin, the daughter of Samuel Perrin and Eunice Chiles from Abbeville. They made their home in the Cedar Spring area near Spartanburg; and, later that same year their first child, Lewis Perrin, was born. He was followed by James Anthony (Tony) in 1839 and Sarah Agnes, nicknamed Sallie, in 1840. Around 1840, the young family moved to Glenn Springs to manage the family plantation.† Eunice Elizabeth was born June 13, 1845, in Glenn Springs. In 1852, Jane Eliza (nicknamed both Jennie and Lizzie), the last child of Barham Bobo and Mary Ann Foster, was born. A son, Barham Bobo, was born in 1848 and died at the age of two. Another son, Joel, apparently died as an infant or child.

As a young man, Barham Bobo Foster prospered professionally. His plantation was productive, and he was known for using advanced farming practices of his day. He was one of the first in the Spartanburg area to use guano as a fertilizer. His neighbors teased him for subsoiling, a practice of deep tillage to prevent soil compaction, telling him "God knew which side of the ground to put on top."‡ While Foster earned his living as a successful planter, he kept a keen interest in his militia duties and in politics. He was a state militia officer, holding every rank from captain to major general; a Commission of Spencer Morgan Rice signed by Major General B. B. Foster of the 5th Division of the South Carolina Militia confirms that he was leading this unit in December 1849.§ In later years, Foster's daughter Eunice fondly remembered him drilling his men while astride his parade horse, Dinah. Before the Civil War, Foster served as a magistrate for many years.¶ He was elected

---

* Landrum, *History of Spartanburg County*, 430.

† Landrum, *History of Spartanburg County*, 430.

‡ Landrum, *History of Spartanburg County*, 430–431.

§ South Carolina Daughters of the Confederacy, *Recollections and Reminiscences 1861–1865 Through World War I, Vol. 3* (Daughters of the Confederacy, 1992), 98–99.

¶ Landrum, *History of Spartanburg County*, 431.

twice as Union County Treasurer* and he served four terms in the State House of Representatives.† He was a legislator in the State House of Representatives in the 1844–46, 1846–48, 1848–50, and 1864–65 terms. He was County Treasurer during Reconstruction.

Lewis Perrin Foster, the Fosters' oldest son, was born November 14, 1837. He received his primary education under the instruction of the Reverend Clough S. Beard at the Glenn Springs Academy in the 1840s and under Captain A. F. Edwards at the Spartanburg Male Academy.‡ In 1848 Perrin Foster's cousin, Oliver E. Edwards, boarded at B. B. Foster's home while he attended the Glenn Springs Academy, also studying under Beard.§ It seems apparent that Perrin attended the Glenn Springs Academy at about the same time. Eunice Foster reported that Perrin boarded with Simpson Bobo,¶ a prominent Spartanburg resident and Barham Bobo Foster's brother-in-law by his sister Nancy. Perrin apparently attended the Spartanburg Male Academy, located in a brick building at what is now the intersection of Henry and Union Streets in Spartanburg; he later attended the South Carolina College in Columbia and graduated in 1858.

Anthony, Sarah Agnes, Eunice, and Jane Eliza were all educated in the manner of planter's children. On January 31, 1858, Lewis Perrin wrote to his sister (probably Sallie) and said that he was glad that Anthony was placed in the St. John's School. This was the St. John's High School in Spartanburg. Sarah attended the Johnson Female University** in Anderson, South Carolina.†† Eunice was in attendance at Limestone College no later than 1861; she completed her education there. It is not clear whether Jane Eliza attended a university or college. She reached college age just about the time that her father was going through bankruptcy. In 1870 his bankruptcy proceedings were finalized; and, there may not have been any money to give her an advanced education.

---

* N. Graydon, T. Graydon, and Davis, *McKissicks*, 172.

† John Amasa May and Joan Reynolds Faunt, *South Carolina Secedes* (Columbia: University of South Carolina Press, 1960), 145.

‡ Landrum, *History of Spartanburg County*, 435.

§ Landrum, *History of Spartanburg County*, 510.

¶ Landrum, *History of Spartanburg County*, 435.

** The Johnson Female Seminary was founded by the Reverend William B. Johnson in 1848 and operated until it closed during the Civil War. In 1853, the school transitioned from a seminary to a university. Rev. Johnson was the first president of the Southern Baptist Convention. The Seminary was one of the nation's first institutions of higher learning for women. Late in the Civil War, the administration building was used as a branch of the Confederate Treasury. The building is extant. Anderson College, which opened in 1912, traces its history to this early university.

†† N. Graydon, T. Graydon, and Davis, *McKissicks*, 37.

At the start of the Civil War in April 1861, none of the Foster children were married. Perrin was twenty-three; Tony was twenty-two; Sarah Agnes (Sallie) was nineteen; Eunice (Nunie) was fifteen; and Jane Eliza was nine years old.

Benjamin Kennedy, Jr. and his family from nearby Union County were closely linked to the Foster family during and after the war years. In 1754, Benjamin's grandfather William Kennedy moved from Pennsylvania to South Carolina during Scotch-Irish immigration, along with the Brandon, Jolly, Savage, and McJunkin families. This group settled in the South Carolina Piedmont and founded the village of Unionville. Kennedy built his homestead in the Brown's Creek area a few miles east of present-day Union. William Kennedy, Sr. fought in the Revolutionary War; he served with his son, William, in Col. Thomas Brandon's Regiment at Cowpens, King's Mountain, and in other Revolutionary War engagements.

After the war, William Kennedy served in the state legislature for several terms and was a magistrate and a county judge. William Kennedy, Sr.'s last child, Benjamin, was born in 1788 and lived near Brown's Creek in present-day Union County. In 1818, Benjamin married Lucy Gibert of Abbeville. Lucy was the daughter of Pierre Gibert and Elizabeth Bienaime, who had come to America in 1764 to settle the Huguenot New Bordeaux Colony along the South Carolina side of the Savannah River. A son, John Lewis, was born to Benjamin and Lucy on October 7, 1819. Their second son, Benjamin, Jr., was born November 23, 1821, shortly after his father's death that same year.* A few years later, Lucy Kennedy moved with her two boys to Jonesville, South Carolina.†

Educated by Rev. James Hodge Saye and Abiel Foster,‡ Benjamin Kennedy, Jr. completed his studies at the Fair Forest Academy in 1843. He studied reading, spelling, writing, arithmetic, geography, English, classics in Latin, and Latin and Greek grammar. Abiel Foster declared Kennedy qualified to teach and govern a school.§

Kennedy used this education to teach school while assisting with the family farm, and he became a successful planter. He inherited enslaved people from his father, but he never bought or sold one.¶ Benjamin and his brother John built a profitable merchant mill on Harris Creek, known locally as Kennedy's Mill.** Kennedy served as a major in the state militia during the years preceding the Civil War.

---

* Albert M. Hillhouse, *Pierre Gibert, French Huguenot, His Background and Descendants* (Danville, Kentucky: Bluegrass Printing Company, 1977), 211.

† Landrum, *History of Spartanburg County*, 539.

‡ Landrum, *History of Spartanburg County*, 540.

§ Hillhouse, *Pierre Gibert*, 234.

¶ Hillhouse, *Pierre Gibert*, 234.

** Kennedy operated a gristmill and sawmill on present-day Kennedy Mill Creek which drops into Fairforest Creek in western Union County. The gristmills and sawmills are shown

The close ties between the Foster and Kennedy families strengthened during the Civil War when Benjamin Kennedy, Jr. served as a company Captain under Lt. Col. Barham B. Foster. Perrin Foster was a company Lieutenant and later a Captain of Kennedy's company. After the war, in 1869, Benjamin Kennedy married Lieutenant Colonel Foster's daughter Eunice.

The Spartanburg District

Spartanburg County is situated on the Piedmont at the foot of the Blue Ridge Mountains and was formed from erosion of an ancient mountain range. The land is generally hilly, and the clay soil is thin and stony. The county is drained by the Enoree, Broad, Tyger, and Pacolet Rivers flowing generally northwest to southeast. Although these rivers were not naturally navigable to the sea, the drop in elevation offered water power which was used to drive mills and factories.

In 1755, Governor Glen established a treaty with the Cherokees in Saluda Old Town that resulted in ceded land that included present-day Spartanburg and Union counties. These lands became part of the Ninety Six District; in 1785, the South Carolina legislature passed an ordinance establishing districts including Spartanburg; and the Constitution of 1868 changed districts to counties.

The Piedmont was opened to settlement by the 1755 treaty. The most notable migration to the area came from the Scotch-Irish. England encouraged the migration of impoverished Scottish lowlanders to present-day Northern Ireland by offering time-limited land grants. As these grants expired, rents exceeded the capacity of the farmland to yield both rent and a subsistence living. These economic pressures resulted in the immigration from Ireland to the North American colonies, with many arriving in Pennsylvania. The general path of migration was toward western Pennsylvania, down the Shenandoah Valley, and into the Carolinas. These Scotch-Irish developed a reputation for toughness, hard work, a Calvinistic religious ethic, and a willingness to fight. These traits were needed to extract a pioneer farmer's living from the stingy soil of the Piedmont.

By the Civil War, most people in the area made their living by farming. Most farming was done by small, family farms raising primarily corn, other grains, and livestock. Small amounts of cotton were raised as a cash crop. If a yeoman farmer owned enslaved people at all, it was typically one family.[*] In 1860, most slave owners in the Spartanburg District (52.6%) owned one to five people.[†] Some

---

together on the 1825 *Mills' Atlas* on the creek identified as Harris Creek. Landrum, *History of Spartanburg County*, 540.

[*] Phillip N. Racine, *Living a Big War in a Small Place* (Columbia: University of South Carolina Press, 2013), 9.

[†] Bruce W. Eelman, *Enterpreneurs in the Southern Upcountry* (Athens: University of Georgia Press, 2008), 15.

families had grown their farms sufficiently to become members of the planter class. The planters were able to farm much larger tracts using paid farm hands and the enslaved. In the Spartanburg District in 1860, 9.8% of slaveholders owned more than nineteen people.* While the upcountry planter operations were small compared to the large, wealthy lowcountry plantations, they were prosperous enough to live in comfortable houses, educate their children, and devote time to politics. Spartanburg District industries at the time included sawmills, gristmills, cotton mills, and tanneries.†

Spartanburg was the major town in the District with a population of about a thousand residents. Being the district administrative seat, Spartanburg had a courthouse and a jail. The town had merchants, doctors, tailors, bootmakers, blacksmith shops, law offices, hotels, and churches. Educational institutions included day schools, a male academy, a female academy, and Wofford College.‡ The town had the businesses, professionals, and institutions needed to support the farming community.

The town was well connected by roads and rails to other cities and towns. A road to the southwest connected Spartanburg to Greenville and Pendleton, South Carolina, and on to Atlanta, Georgia. Another road led southeast to Union, South Carolina, and from there to both the state capital, Columbia, and to Charlotte, North Carolina. A road to the north connected Spartanburg to Asheville, North Carolina. A railroad line connected Spartanburg and Union, on to Columbia where rail connections to other southern cities were available.

The Letters

The Foster family letters provide a picture of planters in the upper echelon of society in the Spartanburg District during the Civil War. Barham Bobo Foster's plantation, which primarily grew corn and cotton, was in Glenn Springs about thirteen miles south of Spartanburg. Foster owned forty-three people according to the 1860 census, up from thirteen such ten years earlier. Of these, twenty-two were over the age of ten. He possessed $10,100 of real property and $46,300 of personal property.§ The Fosters were closely associated with professional society in Spartanburg. As an example, Perrin Foster boarded with attorney Simpson Bobo, who was his uncle, while attending the Spartanburg Male Academy; and, he later studied law with the firm of Simpson Bobo, Oliver E. Edwards, and John W. Carlisle.

* Eelman, *Enterpreneurs,* 15.
† Racine, *Living a Big War,* 6.
‡ Racine, *Living a Big War,* 5.
§ Ralph Wooster, "Membership of the South Carolina Secession Convention." *The South Carolina Historical Magazine, Vol. LV* (1954), 196.

The letters cover the period of the Civil War beginning with Barham Bobo Foster's letter from the Secession Convention (December 20, 1860) through the last letter concerning the death of Perrin Foster, dated February 17, 1863. The epilogue contains letters and excerpts of letters that show how the lives of the central figures played out over the postwar period. The last letter is dated July 26, 1894.

Most of the letters were written by Lt. Col. Barham Bobo Foster and his sons, Capt. Lewis Perrin Foster and Corporal James Anthony Foster. Most of the letters were written to Mary Ann Perrin Foster and, upon his discharge in 1862, to Barham Bobo Foster. There are also letters from Foster's daughters, Sallie and Eunice, and from family friends.

The letters provide insight into many aspects of the war, beginning with B. B. Foster writing from the Secession Convention. Lieutenant Colonel Foster and his son, Perrin, give us a picture of the early organization of the 3rd S.C. Volunteer Infantry at training camps established outside Columbia in the spring of 1861. We see confidence and high spirits on their travels to the Confederate lines in Virginia. The father and son wrote home about the preparation, infantry movements, and the battle of the Confederate victory at Bull Run. Perrin took ill and was sent to recover in Charlottesville, Virginia. There is a bucolic interlude in the letters during Perrin's convalescence, when he wrote to family members about a happy, prosperous people inhabiting a beautiful countryside.

Returning to camp, the soldiers moved into Winter Quarters during the winter of 1861 to 1862. There, B. B. Foster suffered from edema, was discharged from the army, and returned home. In March 1862, Tony Foster enlisted with the 13th S.C. Volunteers assigned to the South Carolina coastal defenses; and, he camped at Green Pond. With the arrival of spring, military action resumed. Perrin Foster described their movements and engagements in the face of McClellan's advance up the Peninsula. Tony Foster obtained a transfer to join his older brother Perrin with the 3rd S.C. on the Richmond defenses. The brothers fought in the Seven Days' Battle, and they wrote vivid descriptions of the battle in their letters home. In August 1862, Perrin developed a severe abscess on his arm and was sent to Richmond to recover. While he was recovering, Confederate forces were ordered to take Harpers Ferry in preparation for Lee's movement into Maryland, a campaign that ended at Antietam. Kershaw's brigade was dispatched to take Maryland Heights, across the Potomac from Harpers Ferry; and Tony Foster was killed in action. Friends in the 3rd S.C. wrote to B. B. Foster about Tony's death. Perrin rejoined his unit in October and wrote about their subsequent movements, culminating in their defensive positions at Fredericksburg. Those are his last letters.

These letters are important in many ways. The letters reveal the thoughts of educated, well-informed people of the upcountry planter class, individuals whose letters reveal an awareness of the initial hope of the Confederate strategy (to win independence through a steadfast defense until England and France would recognize Southern independence and force the Federals to cease the war). As the war closed in on its second year we see that the letter writers became aware that this strategy would not be successful, and that the Confederacy would have to survive on its own resources.

We see a more complex relationship than some would expect between the enslaved and their owners. B. B. Foster sent messages of greeting to the enslaved at home in a friendly manner. He seemed at a loss when one of them with him at camp, Mid, slipped through the Confederate lines to freedom in the North. We see another who captured a Federal soldier, marched the prisoner to his master, and was rewarded with the prisoner's weapons.

Camp life is revealed: its tedium, constant drilling, conflict, threat of disease, camaraderie, reunions of friends and family, and a bit of humor. Women in uniform drilled their husband's companies. We hear what it is like to camp on the grounds of an earlier battlefield, where corpses in shallow graves lay exposed.

Battles are described in detail that begins to explain the physical exertion of war. We hear of Tony Foster being hit by spent balls, of the calls for help from the wounded, of the terror of being pinned under the continuous cannonade at Malvern Hill. We hear the last words of a mortally wounded young man. We can understand what it means to march over a small hill onto an exposed position at the killing ground of Fredericksburg.

We get, in short, a personal picture of life and death in the Confederate army, told by articulate, discerning writers. Their story is one of courage and duty that needs to be preserved and shared.

I think the Governor better form a company of you and
send you to Kansas. You are too full of fight.

Mary Ann Perrin Foster, February 25, 1856

There seems to be no prospect of a fight and think
there will not be any use for us soon if ever.

Lt. Col. Barham Bobo Foster, April 27, 1861

The price of human freedom has ever been human life. If we
prize the latter higher, then the other cannot be ours.

Lt. Lewis Perrin Foster, August 5, 1861

I am not as keen myself for a third sight of the elephant as I was for the first.

Private James Anthony Foster, August 1, 1862

I feel like shrieking now.

Eunice Foster, December 19, 1862

CHAPTER 1

Secession

BARHAM BOBO FOSTER TO HIS SON, PERRIN

Charleston 20th Dec 1860

My Dear Son

I merely have time to say to you that South Carolina is out of the Union without a dissenting voice. It took place at a quarter past one o'clock. I am well.

Your & C

B. B. Foster

B. B. FOSTER TO HIS WIFE

December 23, 1860
South Carolina Republic
Charleston Sunday

My Dear Wife

I went today to the Baptist Church. A fine church it is. Mr Landrum* preached a fine sermon. I shipped your sugar & coffee yesterday morning. I think you can get it certainly Thursday morning. I received Perrins letter to day the first I have received from home. I written every day but one since I left. I sent a letter containing vaxine matter. I suppose Perrin did not get it if he has received it tell him to vaxinate all the family it has taken on me and my arm is very soar. I now think I will be at home Wensday or Thursday remember me to all

your husband B B F

This will be mailed by John Green on the road.

B B F

---

* Rev. John Gill Landrum, the pastor of the First Baptist Church in Spartanburg, was a representative from Spartanburg and a signer of the Ordinance of Secession. He later served as Chaplain in the 13th S.C. Volunteer Infantry.

In the following letter we see that Tony Foster intended to follow his brother in attending South Carolina College; however, the smallpox outbreak and the war kept him from doing so.

B. B. Foster to His Daughter, Sallie

South Carolina Republic
Charleston Dec. 25th 1860

My Dear Daughter

I received your letter yesterday evening. I have written every day since I left home but one and have not received but two letters. Today is a lively time here. I never have seen such a Christmas. The streets are alive with people with a crowd of children all seem to be enjoying themselves to the fullest extent. I wish I could be at home but so it is I must stay and attend to the business of the young republic. It is believed here by the wise men that there will be no war. The commissioners started yesterday for Washington to treat with congress for our share of the public property and the forts in Charleston it is believed that all will be done in peace. The governor of Florida is here a fine looking man.* Florida will be with us in a short time. We received a dispatch from Mississippi. That state has elected secession to the convention. The election came off in Alabama yesterday. As far as heard from that state the principal cities have gone largely for secession. We will hear today by telegram from other parts of the state. It is believed that Georgia will go with us by a large majority. This convention is the ablest body I have ever seen assembled together. We was in secret session last night and will be today. I think now that I will be at home by Saturday night. I have suffered for two days with my arm. The vaxine matter took well and I now feel safe as far as small pox is concerned. The report here is that there is now in Columbia two or three hundred cases. Tell Perrin that the matter will not be apt to take under eight or nine days. He must then put it in all the negroes. I hope however to be at home. It will not do for your brother Anthony to go to Columbia now. There is no doubt but the small pox is prevailing there as an epidemic. He must studdy on and apply when the danger is over. I have visited as far as I could the principal parts of the citty. The Catholics worshiped all night last night and are still worshiping today. The convention will meet in a few minutes and I must close this letter. I will bring your music. I cannot find the piece Eunice sent for. I am sorry I cannot. It is not in the citty. She certainly gave me the wrong name your Uncle Bobo and all the delegation are well. Remember me to your mother and all the family. Tell Maj. Lancaster all is safe and he need fear no evil.

your affectionate Father
B. B. Foster

* Governor Madison Starke Perry.

In early December 1860, Barham Bobo Foster made his way from his Glenn Springs home south of Spartanburg, South Carolina, to the capital in Columbia. He was headed for the First Baptist Church on Hampton Street as the elected representative from the Spartanburg District to a convention to consider "the dangers incident to the position of the State in the Federal Union." This convention was afterward known as the South Carolina Secession Convention. The forty-three-year-old planter had served in political offices before, as a three-term member of the South Carolina House of Representatives from 1844 to 1850. He had been a nullifier† with strong views that the Federal Constitution was a compact between sovereign states; that states had the sovereign right to nullify or void Federal law; and that sovereign states had the right to secede from the Union. The State of South Carolina and President Jackson had gone to the brink of military confrontation over the right of South Carolina to nullify Federal tariffs in 1833. While both sides compromised and avoided confrontation, Jackson saw that the simmering desire to test the right of secession was unsatisfied. He predicted the "next pretext will be the Negro, or slavery question."‡*

The convention, called by Governor Pickens and legislatively empowered, opened on Monday, December 17. In his opening address the convention president-elect D. F. Jamison encouraged the assembly with Danton's revolutionary motto, "To dare! And again to dare! And without end to dare!" Later that day, a committee was appointed to draft an Ordinance of Secession. The convention was adjourned to Institute Hall in Charleston because of a smallpox outbreak in Columbia. On Thursday, December 20, the committee returned with the draft Ordinance. The members voted 169–0 to pass the Ordinance. That evening, Foster and the other members signed the Ordinance and the convention proclaimed South Carolina an independent commonwealth.

On Saturday, Foster and several other members were appointed to a committee to determine how much congressional legislation would be canceled by the secession of the state. Over the next two weeks, the convention directed actions concerning Fort Moultrie, Fort Sumter, Castle Pinckney in Charleston Harbor, Federal properties in South Carolina, and the publication of the Ordinance of Secession—and spent time reading letters of support from other Southern states. Aware of the historical importance of their actions, the convention members sent the table, chair, and other items used to ratify the Ordinance to the Legislative Library in the State House in Columbia. The convention adjourned its first session on January 5, 1861.

The second session of the Secession Convention opened on March 26, 1861, at St. Andrew's Hall in Charleston. The purpose of this session was to consider the Constitution of the Confederate States of America, which had been adopted by the

---

* May and Faunt, *South Carolina Secedes*, 3.

† May and Faunt, *South Carolina Secedes*, 145.

‡ Samuel Eliot Morison, Henry Steele Commager, and William E. Leuchtenburg, *The Growth of the American Republic. Vol. I* (New York: Oxford University Press, 1969), 434.

Constitutional Convention in Montgomery, Alabama, on February 8, 1861. On April 3 of that year, B. B. Foster, with 137 fellow delegates, voted to ordain the Constitution of the Confederate States of America. Twenty-one delegates voted against it. South Carolina joined the Confederate States of America.

On April 9, the convention granted Foster leave for military duties.

CHAPTER 2

No Prospect of a Fight

In January 1861, following adjournment of the Secession Convention, troops began to assemble and drill at a makeshift camp at the Columbia Fairgrounds.* The camp was called Camp Ruffin in honor of Edmund Ruffin,† a prominent secessionist. A camp was established at Lightwood Knot Springs, a popular resort for Columbians of the day, about four miles from Columbia along the Columbia-Charlotte railroad line. Early on, the Lightwood Knot Springs Camp was called Camp Williams, in honor of Col. James H. Williams who had been elected colonel of the Third South Carolina Infantry.‡ The camps at the Columbia Fairgrounds and at Lightwood Knot Springs were combined at the latter location and named Camp Johnson.§ A camp of instruction was maintained there through much of the conflict.¶

In the early stages of the conflict, units were very locally organized, assumed unit names of their own choice, and elected their own officers. Prominent community leaders would typically recruit soldiers from pre-war militias and through other contacts, creating a company of a hundred men. Immediately after the First Secession Convention adjourned on January 3, 1861, B. B. Foster returned to Spartanburg and raised and drilled the Blackstock Company, serving as captain.** The company took its name from the 1780 Battle of Blackstocks, a Revolutionary War engagement in present-day Union County.

Foster returned to the Second Secession Convention convening on March 26 in Charleston to consider the Constitution of the Confederate States of America.

---

* The 1872 "Bird's Eye View" map shows these grounds just north of Upper Street (present-day Elmwood Avenue) at the terminus of Wayne and Gadsden Streets.

† August D. Dickert, *History of Kershaw's Brigade* (Newberry, S. C. 1899: reprinted by Morningside Press, Dayton, 1988), 33.

‡ Dickert, *History of Kershaw's Brigade*, 33.

§ Mac Wyckoff, *A History of the Third South Carolina Infantry, 1861–1865* (Fredericksburg, Va.: Sergeant Kirkland's Museum and Historical Society, 1995), 14.

¶ John Hammond Moore, *Columbia and Richland County* (Columbia: University of South Carolina Press, 1993), 184–186.

** Dickert, *History of Kershaw's Brigade*, 100.

Foster voted to ratify the Confederate constitution on April 3 and, on the 9th, he was excused from the convention for military duty. Three days later, on April 12, 1861, South Carolina opened fire on Fort Sumter and the Civil War was underway.

Foster reported to Camp Ruffin in Columbia, bringing the Blackstock Company with him from Spartanburg. He was elected lieutenant colonel of the Third South Carolina Volunteer Regiment, and he commanded the regiment until Col. James H. Williams could report from his estates in Arkansas. The Blackstock Company became Company K of this regiment.* Leadership of this Company included Foster's future son-in-law, Capt. Benjamin Kennedy, and Foster's twenty-three-year-old son, Lt. Perrin Foster. They arrived in April 1861 to prepare for a fight that they were sure would never occur.

The letters from this period reflect the heady optimism of the self-proclaimed new republic. The authors expected there would be no fighting now that the Charleston Federal facilities at Castle Pinckney, Fort Moultrie, and Fort Sumter were in the control of the state of South Carolina. The secession leaders believed that a confident show of military preparation and force combined with a quick union with other secession states would intimidate Lincoln and the Federals into inaction. The young army settled immediately into the tasks of drilling, parading, and assigning satisfactory military positions for important people. Immediate problems of obtaining adequate uniforms and weapons were present and persistent throughout the conflict. Camp health quickly emerged as a critical issue; a great many of these hopeful young men died in the coming months and years, from typhus, pneumonia, and other camp diseases. Mercantile profiteering on the soldiers became a persistent complaint in future letters.

The authors of these letters maintained a willingness to fight with ferocity, courage, and abandon. The early brawling and drinking soon yielded to a military discipline; this discipline, combined with an attitude of frontier independence and a sense of religious purpose, characterized the fighting Confederate soldier.

B. B. FOSTER TO HIS WIFE

Head Quarters Columbia
Camp Ruffin
April 1861

I am here safely quartered in our camp at the fair grounds with about 1150 men in our Regiment. I suppose that we will go no farther for the present at least. Perrin[†] came down last night with his company. He is well and in fine spirits. I have

---

* Dickert, *History of Kershaw's Brigade*, 100.
† Lewis Perrin Foster, Col. B. B. Foster's son.

Lt. Colonel Barham Bobo Foster, 3rd S.C. Volunteers
circa 1861. From the editor's collection.

concluded not to send for Dinah* although it would be a real comfort for Perrin
to have her when he has leisure. I cannot say but am disposed to think from all that
I can learn they we will be discharged before long. There seems to be not much
prospect of a fight now. The harbor of Charleston is cleared and I think that will
be the last of it there The boys are all well. No accident has happened in camp. We

* Dinah was Lieutenant Colonel Foster's parade horse.

Mary Ann Perrin Foster. From the editor's collection.

are all well. Uncle Dicky* is here. Tell John Harmon† he may do as he likes about planting the old field new ground in cotton I had as soon have it in corn tell John if Panuch cant get work he can work him at home I had much rather keep him hired

---

* Uncle Dicky is Rev. Richard Woodruff. He was related to B. B. Foster through Foster's grandfather, Anthony Foster, Sr.

† Apparently, John Harmon ran Foster's plantation while he was in the service.

out.* I have good quarters and if I stay here I will send up for you to come down and stay awhile with us. If it was not for my family I could not be better pleased than to be commander of this camp. I felt yesterday when I was marching the Regiment from the depot through broad street that it was about the proudest day of my life. I would be prouder still if Kenedys Company† & Fergusons‡ was uniformed. our people have not done their duty to those gallant men who had turned out to defend the homes and firesides of those left behind. They are doing the drudgery and rich men left at home. I do hope some one will take it in hand and have it done yet. Perrin has went down town and left his measure and will be uniformed. all the officers will uniform themselves. The western Battallion can give the company and ought to do it 2000.00 remember me to Sallie§ Anthony⁋ and Jimy Harmon** and all the neighbors write soon direct to Lieut Col B. B. Foster Columbia SC. I hope to hear soon may god bless you all well in camp

Your affectionate husband

B. B. Foster

L. P. FOSTER TO HIS SISTER, PROBABLY SALLIE

Glenn Springs
[~April 18, 1861]††

My Dr Sister

Our first day of Camp life has passed and the 2nd began and I like it better than I expected. Our quarters are as comfortable as we could expect, much more than I thought they would be. Our men are in fine spirits and a very orderly crowd. We have but one thing which worrys us and that is the want of a uniform It is a shame that we could not bear to be here without a uniform and 14 of us have determined

---

* Hiring out the enslaved was a common practice. Often the master received a percentage of the worker's earnings. Racine, *Living a Big War*, 48.

† Captain Benjamin Kennedy commanded the Blackstock Company from Spartanburg District. The Blackstocks became Company K of the 3rd S.C.

‡ Thomas B. Ferguson brought the Cross Anchors Company from the Union and Spartanburg Districts to Columbia to become Company D of the 3rd S.C.

§ Sallie is Sarah Agnes Foster, B. B. Foster's daughter. She was twenty years old at the time of this letter.

⁋ James Anthony Foster, Lieutenant Colonel Foster's youngest son.

** James Harmon enlisted in Kennedy's Co. K in the 3rd S.C.; Harmon was mortally wounded at Chickamauga.

†† This letter is undated but the reference to Virginia's Secession (April 17, 1861) provides an approximate date.

to buy the cloth on a credit and risk getting the money from our friends at home. We sent a man to Charleston this morning to buy the cloth and trimmings, and will send it up home as soon as we can get it here and have it cut. They will probably be at Lownsville Saturday evening. You must [use] all possible haste in making them and have them made by neat sewers. We do not know whether those at home intend to let us suffer that expense or not but one thing we do think and that is that it is hard for the soldier to pay for such things alone when those whom he left behind are more interested than we are but all we are and have is at the disposal of our government and if the men at home who we know are able to uniform us and not miss the money can consciously suffer us to pay it, why we will make the best of it. I wish you would show this to Maj Lancaster, Mr. Montgomery and as many of the prominent men in the settlement and request them to take up collections and raise the money as soon as possible. We will not probably get credit for longer than 60 days so if they do anything they must act fast. What I have said hastily in this letter is not intended for those men who have subscribed liberally already. One of my college friends found out that I was here yesterday and came round last night and brought me a cot 2 large quilts and a pillow so I am faring well. I have given the cot for the present [to] one of our camp who is a little unwell. Virg has passed a resolution of secession. There has been no demonstration made here yet in honor of her. We think she does not deserve. We have no orders as yet to march. Nothing more will be done until Lincoln has time to recruit his army. He can not begin to meet us with his present army. There are a good many of my old college friends here. Cass* and Ossian Simpson† are both here. Dr. Kilgore‡ joined us this morning.

My love to all

Write to me soon

Yr affec Brother L. P. Foster

L. P. Foster to His Sister, Probably Sallie

Camp Ruffin, Columbia
April 21st 1861

My Dear Sister

My first Sunday in Camp has come and brings with it a novel scene been doing sentinel and guard duty on this day seems strange yet it is actually necessary that the camp should be under guard for there are many men here who if we were to let them go down street would get enough liquor to keep them drunk a week. Liquor

---

* Richard Caspar Simpson of Co. A, 3rd S.C.

† Ossian Freeborn Simpson of Co. A, 3rd S.C.

‡ Dr. B. F. Kilgore, from near Woodruff, South Carolina, was a South Carolina state representative during the 1854–1856 term.

Lewis Perrin Foster, 3rd S.C. Volunteers. On the back of this photo, his sister, Jennie wrote that he had brown eyes. Another inscription, believed to be by his sister, Eunice, identifies this as Lewis Perrin Foster. From the editor's collection.

is a contraband article here and if a man is caught with it he will be put under guard. The drinking men of our camp are doing well. Tom Zimmerman* looks much better than he did when he left home and I think that if he stays in camp long we can sober him. Our men will not let him have liquor at all. We have some

---

* Thomas H. Zimmerman of Co. K of the 3rd S.C., according to Augustus Dickert. This is believed to be Thomas Holman Zimmerman, the son of John Conrad Zimmerman of Glenn Springs, South Carolina.

Lewis Perrin Foster. Identified on the back by his sister,
Eunice Foster Kennedy. From the editor's collection.

very awkward and green men I have been putting some of them in the awkward
squad.* They do not like it much but there is no other way to do. Several of our
men have been sick since we came here but all have got well or nearly so. I have not
been sick a minute and am as hearty as any body. I never had such an appetite since
I can recollect. I relish this bakers bread and tough beef here more than good fare
at home, however a box occasionally from our friends would not hurt us. Some of
the other camps got theirs after Uncle Dick preached last night he had a large and

---

* "Awkward squad" is military slang for recruits who have difficulty performing military
duties. Foster had apparently formed an awkward squad to give such men additional drilling.

Sarah Agnes (Sallie) Foster as a young woman. From the editor's collection.

attentive audience. He preached again to day at 11½ o clock. He has been appointed temporarily chaplain of the regiment. We sent Col. Allen to Charleston to buy our uniforms but he could not get enough cloth in the city to make it. We went down town yesterday and bought a piece of [. . .] and trimmings and have taylors now cutting it. Dr. King* will be up with it Tuesday or Wednesday. Make mine first and send it to me immediately. The news in the papers is encouraging. Williams† has not yet come and Father is still in command. Garlington‡ has not been here since

* Likely Dr. Gideon H. King of Walnut Grove, South Carolina.

† James H. Williams, Colonel of the 3rd S.C.

‡ Lt. Col. Benjamin Conway Garlington. Garlington brought the State Guards from Laurens District to Camp Ruffin to become Company A of the 3rd S.C. He was later elected

I came here. Ashmores* or rather Sloans† regiment is here yet. We know nothing about our destination yet we training our men and getting them ready. Our labor is pretty heavy, but we do not much mind it. Is anybody getting any money for our uniforms? Our names are now pledged for the payment of the money and if they do nothing at home we must pay it. The decision is with them. Will soon remember me to the neighbors. The Woffords desire me to remember to their family.

Yr. Affec Brother

L. P. Foster

Father received your letter and we were glad to hear from you.

In these letters, we continue to see very localized loyalties, to their companies in particular and to regiments recruited and formed from their neighborhoods and districts. In the letter below, these loyalties come into conflict with Governor Pickens's thoroughly modern desire to cobble together a suitable command for a favored personage. Colonel Garlington was valiant officer, but these men had no interest in having their units broken up or their elected officers replaced to make room for him.

L. P. FOSTER TO HIS MOTHER
―――――――――

Camp Ruffin Columbia
April 22nd 1861

My Dear Mother

Another day has come and I must write to you without anything of interest to write. The business of camp life, though it may be interesting to those engaged in it is yet too monotonous to be interesting to others.

Today the two regiments were thrown together to make a call for volunteers under Davis but they say it would be most an excellent failure and stopped it. We are all willing to fight for our country but not to be entrapped by breaking up our regiment to listing with any expected gentlemen. Our men and nearly every comp in the camp have come to the conclusion that Gov Pickens‡ is just trying to fix a place for Genl Garlington and those will not be their companies that will answer the call. We prefer to go in some other way and with our eyes open if we have to go at all. So you need not fear my volunteering for the present. Say nothing of this. Several of our men have been sick but I am well. So is Father. Our uniforms will be up in a few days. I am having mine made here. Our men are lively and in fine spirits.

―――――――――

lieutenant colonel of the 3rd S.C. He was mortally wounded in the Battle of Savage's Station.

* John Durant Ashmore, Colonel of the 4th South Carolina, resigned before the unit was called into service.

† Sloan's Regiment was the 4th South Carolina.

‡ Francis Wilkinson Pickens, S.C. Governor, 1860–62.

Captain Benjamin Kennedy, 3rd S.C. Volunteers,
Company K. From the editor's collection.

Those who have wives speak of home very often. We are faring pretty ruff. A few large boxes would be very acceptable. Some of the companies here are just fed by boxes from their friends at home. I know Miss Sallie* and Hannah† would send our mess a box. Our mess consists of Capt Kennedy, Hank West,‡ Henry Cunningham,§

* Miss Sallie is likely to be Sarah Eliza Perrin, daughter of Thomas Chiles Perrin.
† Likely Foster's cousin Hannah Clarke Perrin, daughter of Thomas Chiles Perrin.
‡ Henry West of Co. K, 3rd S.C. He died of pneumonia in 1862.
§ Henry M. Cunningham of Co. K, 3rd S.C. died in Pt. Lookout Prison in 1865. He was a teacher in Glenn Springs, South Carolina.

James Henry Cunningham,* David Bray† and myself. I have not got a letter from home since I came here.

Write to me soon

Remember me to the family, John Harmon and inquiring neighbors.

All of our crowd are well except David Bray who has been a little sick but say nothing of it as it may cause his mother a great deal of uneasiness.

Yr affec Son

L. P. Foster

L. P. Foster to His Sister, Probably Sallie

Camp Ruffin Columbia
Apl 23rd /61

My Dear Sister

Since yesterday nothing of importance has transpired here. I have very little time to go into the city—yet my office requires less work than any other & I had rather have it than any. All our men are lively. Most of our men who when at home were drunkards give us no trouble here. Gabe Moore‡ has not been drunk since he came here and looks better than I ever saw him. Tom Zimmerman is doing well. One of our men went into the city yesterday & got drunk. We found it out last night about 9½ o clock and sent a corporals guard after him. They marched him up and lodged him in the guard house, where he is now, and will be until he gets all right. Uncle Dick exhorted and prayed last night. He preaches tonight. I don't know what he will do when another chaplain is appointed for he is too lazy to drill. We have some men that I fear we never can drill. We keep them in the awkward squad most of the time. Mid§ was put in the guard house yesterday for a short time for fighting another negroe, but he was not in fault and Maj Baxter¶ had him released.

I have not yet seen many of my friends in town. Col Harmon has been very kind to us. He has sent us 20 or 30 pair of very good insoles. I have not had a letter from home since I came here. You must have forgotten how to write. I shall soon petition to headquarters to detail a private sentry for the benefit of some of you. I write every day, Father has recd 2 or 3 letters from home. Our uniforms will leave here tomorrow in charge of Dr King. You must work fast and make them in a hurry.

---

* James Henry Cunningham of Co. K, 3rd S.C. died at Chickamauga in 1863.

† David S. Bray of Co. K, 3rd S.C. survived the war and was paroled at Greensboro in 1865.

‡ Likely Gabriel C. Moore of the 5th Infantry Regiment S.C.

§ Mid was enslaved. Lieutenant Colonel Foster took him to Columbia and later to Virginia as a personal servant.

¶ Maj. James M. Baxter of the 3rd S.C.

If Elias Gentry* comes to our house, send it to his wife. He wants her to make it. Tell Misses Sallie and Hannah to mark send on our uniforms and oblige these old friends LPF.

Remember me to the family John Harmon and inquiring friends.

Send the much hoped for boxes hams & e.

Yr affec Brother
L. P. Foster

L. P. FOSTER TO HIS MOTHER

Camp Ruffin Columbia
April 26th 1861

My Dear Mother,

Yours and Sallies letter came yesterday evening. I was glad to hear that things were going on so well also that Patrick was convalescent. Things are going on very well here. A call was made for volunteers in the confederate army yesterday. It met with no favor in any of the camps except the Quitman rifles and State Guards. About 50 out of each volunteered. I fear from prejudice to certain men we have acted wrong and will injure the cause of Southern rights. I have felt very much like volunteering all the time but Father opposes it and consequently I shall not do it.

Sloans regiment came down yesterday and heard the speaking genls Garlington McGowan† and Waddy Thomson‡ spake and appealed in a feeling manner to us to sustain the separation of S Carolina. The Butler Guards,§ a comp from Greenville, volunteered to a man. They may get 6 comps out of the two regs but I dont believe they will.

Dr. King and Wm Simmons left this morning for home with our uniform. They will distribute it as fast as they can. Have Elias Gentrys sent to his wife. He wants her to make it. We had some made here but they are as ruff as a meat axe. What is to be the result of all of this I cannot tell one thing I think certain that is we can not stay here much longer. This is the place to test a mans grit. If he has not the right pluck and has any infirmaty he will be sure to try to get off some of our men have and are trying to get off but there will not be enough disabled ones to injure the camp.

Father is well. Remember me to all the family and enquiring friends.

Yr affec Son
L P Foster

---

* Elias Gentry served in Co. K of the 5th S.C.

† State Militia general Samuel McGowan.

‡ Waddy Thompson of Company G of the 3rd S.C. was killed in action at Savage's Station.

§ The Butler Guards became Company B of the 2nd S.C., commanded by Capt. J. W. Cagle.

B. B. Foster to His Wife

Camp Ruffin
April 27th 1861

I did not write yesterday. I was so busy that I did not have time. nothing new since my last. a good deal of sickness in the camp nothing serious much affection which seems to yield to treatment very readily. I have a great deal of writing to do which keeps me up late at night. My health and Perrins is fine I never felt stouter. Our Regiment refused to go to Virginia and justly too Virginia passed her ordinance of secession subject to ratification of her people on the fourth Thursday in may next. she cannot confederate until her ordinance is ratified Therefore I think the marching of troops at this time to Virginia is an invasion or something of a [. . .] expedition. Therefore could not ask the Regt to be transferred and sent to Virginia. I do not wish to invade even the government of old abe. They have been whiped from our soil and waters and that I think is all that we ought to do at this time The men are improving rapidly. mustering fine King Simmons and Dicky Woodruf have gone home to raise the money and get the uniforms made I hope the ladies will take hold and do it at once Tell John Harmon that I trust to him to manage everything in my [absence] I try to think as little as possible about my business in truth I have no time for it. If we are not moved or discharged and williams gets in I shall take a furlough for awhile and go home There seems to be no prospect of a fight and think there will not be any use for us soon if ever. I confess I would like to lead my Regiment into battle if the occasion arises. Camp life produces that tendency. I feel more like I could stand a fight now than I did when I first came here. give my best respects to Mr & Mrs Lancaster tell them [. . .] Sumner stands it fine as well as any one in the camp. All our boys is now on foot and doing dut[y] except [. . .] Allen he is unwell and very lazy Thomas Ham still keeps sober and gabriel moore Thomas Zimmerman takes too much at times he has kept much straighter than I expected we hear preaching every Sunday and frequently at night the Rev Dr Breaken* preaches for us Sunday next remember me to the children all tell Tony that he must act the man and take my place at home he need have no uneasiness about a draft† before he should be drafted I would bring him here with us They have no right to put his name on the muster roll I hope all things will be soon better and we will be together again at home.

your affectionate husband
B B Foster

* Dr. J. B. O. Landrum's *History of Spartanburg County* identifies a "Breaken" family on page 254. However, it is not clear whether this Reverend Breaken is of that family.
† A draft is a system to establish compulsory military service.

L. P. Foster to His Mother

Camp Ruffin Columbia
Apl 28th 1861

My Dear Mother

I did not receive a letter from any of you yesterday or day before and have not yet but two letters from home since I came here. You have all surly forgotten to write. My second Sabbath in camp has come. It is a beautiful day but does not seem much like Sunday. The Rev. Dr Bracken preaches for today. He is said to be a fine preacher. We have had several hard rains since I came here but we are protected from the rains being in houses and under shelters. Some of our men are getting very homesick, but they seem willing to stay. They dislike staying here and having no fighting. A good many want to go to Virginia. It is said that gov claims the right to stand us anywhere in the southern confederacy, but I have no idea that he will try to exercise such a doubtful right. I am perfectly willing to go if the comp will go and would be willing to go as a private if Father seemed willing.

We are getting along very well [camp fare is] very good our mess having rec'd several boxes from home this week. Are independent of our commissary. I am looking for another box in a few days. Cousin Oliver* came down to see us yesterday evening. He is on his way from Alabama and would have gone up yesterday, but his [. . .] Duff Gary† sick. He is a recruit of one of the Laurens Comp.‡ He is said to be very dangerous this morning.

Our uniform has gone up and I hope you will all exert yourselves in making it and be sure to [mark] the names on them.

Remember me to the family.

And write to me soon

Yr affec Son L. P. Foster

N.B.§ If any letters come to Glenns for me, send them here. I am looking for one from Cousin Mary Perrin.¶

L. P. Foster

* Col. Oliver E. Edwards organized the 13th S.C.

† Duff E. Gary died on April 30, 1861. Guy R. Everson and Edward W. Simpson, Jr., *Far, Far from Home* (New York: Oxford University Press, 1994), 7.

‡ The Laurens Briars Company became Company G of the 3rd S.C.

§ NB is an abbreviation for nota bene, Latin for "note well." It is sometimes used in place of "P.S."

¶ Mary Eunice Perrin, daughter of Thomas Chiles Perrin.

L. P. Foster to His Mother

Camp Ruffin Columbia
Apl 30th 1861

My Dear Mother

I have written home every day since I came here and have rec'd only two or three letters to day. I think I shall make a demand upon the Brigade head quarters for a private sec. For Lt. Co. B. B. Foster's family. I have been in head quarters all this morning and I can tell you if you were here you have been disgusted to see a number of stout hearty men trying to get furloughs. Some of them even under the pretext of sickness. I tell you if a man has not got the pluck here he will show it soon enough. There has not been any of our men here. Some of them want furloughs and ought to have them and I think will get them. Wm. Henry Lancaster* came down yesterday evening to take Henry Burroughs place. He will be rec'd. I suppose Mr. Harmon is having Dinah well attended to. She I suppose is now in fine fix as I told him to have her covered and well attended to. I think Father will send for her soon. He will soon begin the battallion drills when he will need her. Have her well attended to. Dick ought to curry her twice a day. I have nothing of interest to write. We do not yet know our destination.

Remember me to the family and all inquiring friends. Write to me soon.

Yr affec Son
L. P. Foster

L. P. Foster to Major Alvin Lancaster[†]

Camp Ruffin
April 30, 1861

[Major Alvin Lancaster,]

. . . We rise in the morning a little after day, at reville. In about 15 minutes, the assembly is beaten, when we assemble, call the roll, and drill until 7 o'clock. At 7 we have breakfast. At 10 o'clock the assembly is again beaten, when we again assemble, call the roll and drill in the squad drill until 11:15 o'clock, when retreat is beaten and we have to get dinner, which we have at 1 o'clock. At 4 the assembly again beats, when we drill in the company until 5:15 o'clock, when the retreat is again beaten and

---

* William Henry Lancaster of Co. K, 3rd S.C. was mortally wounded at Fredericksburg.

† This letter was found in a newspaper clipping among Kennedy family papers. Based on other dates in the clipping, it appears to have been printed in the Spartanburg Journal sometime around January 1926.

we go off and prepare for dress parade, to which the assembly calls us at 6 o'clock.
At 7 we have supper. At 9, tattoo, in a half hour after which lights have to be extinguished. Every two hours during the day and night we have guard mounting, so you see our time is taken up in drilling, eating and guard mounting.

*[The letter then discusses letters from home and the death of Duff Gary, a member of one of the Laurens companies, who succumbed to pneumonia on the night of April 29 at Camp Ruffin.]**

. . . Our men are in fine spirits.

L. P. Foster

B. B. Foster to His Wife

Camp Ruffin
May 7th 1861

My Dear Wife

I write to let you know that I am well Perrin has entirely recovered and is doing well Their company is coming out marchs equal to any of them. The sickness in the camp is abating no bad cases our boys are the last one of them on foot except Thomas Zimmerman he has a spell of delerium tremens. I think he will recover from it he gives me a great deal of trouble he has men that bring him spirits and it seems impossible as long as he has money to do anything with him I have some in truth a good many hard cases to deal with it is very hard to maintain order in a camp of volunteers. We will move to the sand hills in a few days. I would say next week. I have no news from williams we think he will be here before long as soon as he comes, I am good for home until he does come I cannot leave. I am still worked very hard have no leisure stay in the camp all the time. I hope before many days to see you all. I write more particularly about Tony's coming down. remember me to my neighbors and friends remember me to the children

Your husband
B B Foster

---

* Perrin Foster refers to Duff Gary's death on the night of the 29th. However, Gary likely died early in the morning of the 30th. His gravestone marks his death as April 30. Everson and Simpson, *Far, Far from Home*, 7.

L. P. Foster to His Mother

Camp Ruffin Columbia
May 7th 1861

My Dear Mother

The time for me to write has again come and have but one item of news to write you which you have heard before this time. Uncle Thomas* came down yesterday. I have not seen him yet but Father saw him. All are well and Cousin Mary[†] is to be married the 16th. You are all invited. I have forgotten the gentlemans name to whom she is to be married. I suppose they will have a lively time about then. A Lutheran preacher named Wist preached here last night. I did not hear him. I was at head quarters and knew that he was going to preach. Those who heard him said his sermon was pretty good. Thomas Zimmerman had a very bad spell of the delirium tremens last night. I never saw a man in such a fit. He is better today. How he got the liquor we can not tell. I think he will have to be discharged for he will do no good here. He is not able to do camp duty—say nothing of this for it will give his family uneasiness for nothing. Father is bent on keeping him here and keeping liquor from him. He will put him in the guard house as soon as he is able to stand it and keep there where he can not get it until he cools off. Our men are doing well. I have written to Lockwood[‡] to make me a blue cloth uniform and may go up to the wedding but don't really think I shall.

Remember me to all and send us a box when it is convenient.

Yr affec Son

L. P. Foster

On Wednesday, May 8, Samuel Edward Burges reported going to the fairgrounds to watch the 3rd S.C. Infantry dress parade.[§] The next day the 3rd was preparing to leave for the Lightwood Knot Springs camp.

---

* Thomas Chiles Perrin, B. B. Foster's brother-in-law.

† Mary Eunice Perrin, daughter of Thomas Chiles Perrin, was married on May 16, 1861 to Francis Eugene Harrison as his second wife. Harrison served as captain of Co. D, in the South Carolina Rifles. He was wounded at Gaines's Mill, returned to the war and was promoted to colonel after Chancellorsville. Ill health forced him to transfer to the S.C. Reserves in 1864. Thomas Perrin Harrison, *The Honorable Thomas Chiles Perrin of Abbeville, South Carolina, Forebears and Descendants* (Greenville, S.C.: A Press, 1983), 20.

‡ Lockwood was apparently a shopkeeper or a tailor in the Spartanburg area.

§ Thomas W. Chadwick, ed., "The Diary of Samuel Edward Burges, 1860–1862," *The South Carolina Historical and Genealogical Magazine*, LXVIII, no. 1, January (1947), 156.

L. P. Foster to His Sister Probably Sallie

Camp Ruffin Columbia
May 9th 1861

My Dear Sister

I rec'd a letter from Annie* a few days since, containing a message from you to the effect that you rec'd no letters from me. I think I have written as many times to you as to any member of the family except Mother. I went out last night to Mr. Sims to call on the ladies.† I there met with Miss Caldwell whom you met at Glenn Springs last summer. She inquired after you. I spent the evening very pleasantly. We leave here tomorrow and march to the Lightwood Knot Spring, our advance guard went on today to prepare the camp for us. I will have a pretty long march of it as it is about 7 miles. I am glad we are leaving here for this is a crowded, dusty, dirty, and disagreeable place. I want to get away from this water. Our tents went on this morning and will be stretched this evening I suppose. They are large and roomy and will be much more comfortable than these houses, unless we had more room. Mr. Bobo was here this morning, but went up on the train. On opening my belts this morning, I found my pipes. Tell Miss L. that I am very much obliged to her for them. Though I have almost quit using tobacco, I love grist chewing and smoke very seldom. We are getting on well. All our absent men came back last night, and report all well at home. They say there was a perfect rush for the making of our uniforms. Several of them are willing. If you hear anything of them, send them on to us. Write soon.

Remember me to all the family.

Yr affec Brother

L. P. Foster

* Possibly Anna Isabella Perrin, Foster's cousin, and daughter of Samuel and Emma Blocker Perrin.

† Perrin Foster mentions the Sims family in Columbia, South Carolina, several times in the letters, including references to James Sims and Colonel Sims. On July 27, 1861, he mentions receiving a letter from Babe Sims. This was most likely Leora Amanda (Babe) Sims, the daughter of James T. Sims in Columbia. In the obituary of his wife, Rebecca Sims, James Sims is referred to as Col. James T. Sims. These references are likely to Col. James T. Sims, his wife, Rebecca, and their daughters. Louis P. Towles, *A World Turned Upside Down, The Palmers of South Santee, 1818–1881* (Columbia: University of South Carolina, 1996), 1010–1011. "Winthrop University Digital Commons @ Winthrop University, The Lantern, Chester S.C.—March 19, 1907, http://digitalcommons.winthrop.edu/cgi/viewcontent.cgi?article=101 7&context=chesterlantern1907 (accessed September 7, 2016).

The following letter describes the move from Camp Ruffin in Columbia to Camp John-son at Lightwood Knot Springs, about four miles outside of Columbia on the Charlotte railroad.* Foster refers to the Sand Hills. The Sandhills are a geographic region sepa-rating the Coastal Plain from the Piedmont. They were formed from the sand dunes of an ancient coastline.

L. P. FOSTER TO HIS SISTER, PROBABLY SALLIE

Camp Johnson
May 13th 1861

My Dear Sister

To day we reached this place. We left our camp this morning about 9 o clock and march through the streets of Columbia to the Charlotte Depot where we took the cars for this camp. I will attempt a description of it. In the first place it is situ-ated 7 miles from Columbia in the Sand Hills, the poorest country that ever human eye beheld. The over head growth is pine. The pines are very tall and large but very sparse and scattering which makes it one of the most open countries over head that I have ever seen. The under growth is very thick, it is oak and reminds me very much of the rolling mills.† This we have cut and cleared away and made a place for our tents, also for a parade ground. The soil is a perfect sand bank. You can just drive a stake as far in as you please. When we got here this morning I thought it was the saltiest and most dusty place I ever saw and some of the crowd named it Camp Misery, but we went to work and built us long brush arbors in front of our tents and now although it is not so comfortable a place as we ought to have had and might have got, yet i[t] is generally pleasant and I think far preferable to our last quarters. We have any amount of the finest kind of water. There are some hol-lows around our camp grown with as thick vegetation as you ever saw and they are luxuriant and beautiful. There are a good many hay flowers among the growth and they look very pretty. They look a good deal like the magnolia. I have just rec'd a letter from cousin Mary Perrin. They are having warm times in Kentucky. There are 10,000 Lincoln soldiers stationed in 70 miles of Cincinnatti and they threaten to demolish Covington and Newport if Kentucky secedes. They are running all the secessionist out of Cincinatti who refuse to hoist the stars and stripes. She said that

---

* This camp was near present-day Farrow Road (Highway 555), probably between Parklane Road and Interstate 20. Dickert, *History of Kershaw's Brigade*, 33.

† This likely refers to the Hurricane Rolling Mill and Nail Works owned by the South Carolina Manufacturing Company, whose agent was Simpson Bobo. Rolling Mills was also referred to as a settlement by Perrin Foster in his letter dated November 24, 1862. J. P. Lesley, *Iron Manufacturer's Guide to the Furnaces, Forges and Rolling Mills of the United States* (New York: John Wiley Publisher, 1859), 245.

she could see a dozen of the infamous flags floating in their town from her window while she was writing, that they are just surrounded with abolitionists. They are going in to the interior of the State to spend the summer and if Kentucky goes with the north Uncle Lewis* is going to move south. He speaks his opinion freely and refuses to hoist a Union flag and says if he hoists any sort it will be a secession flag and if he was to do that his house would be torn down. I think from Cousin Mary's letter he will leave the infamous den of iniquity even as Lot left Sodom never looking behind him. Johnny Beard is very sick we had to leave him in Columbia. David Bray went up this morning with a sick negro of Capt. Kennedy's and will see Mr. Beard† about him. I wanted to write to some of you to get me some clothes and send me, but I will wait until next time. My health is pretty good. The health of the camp is much better than it has been.

   Write to me soon

Remember me to the family Your affec
Brother L. P. Foster

The next two letters illustrate petitions typically submitted to Confederate leaders of the time.

JAMES. L. HILL TO B. B. FOSTER

———

Hills Factory May 15th 1861
Spartanburg S.C.
Col. B. B. Foster

Dear Sir

   I received a letter from my son William‡ a few days ago he is very anxious to serve in your regiment, you are aware that he rightfully belongs to you, and I much rather he would serve under you than where he is. If there is any possible chance of obtaining him I hope that you will make the application as soon as it is convenient.

   He wrote to me saying that you could not have him released and that I was the only one that could release him by petitioning to the governor certifying that he is not 21 years old. I suppose some one has so informed him. My impression is that you can get him. Please make the application and if you fail please inform me soon and you will oblige your friend.

---

* Lewis Perrin, B. B. Foster's brother-in-law.

† Mr. Beard, frequently referred to in the letters, was the father of James Clough Beard and John W. N. Beard. Both sons were in Kennedy's Blackstocks Co. K of the 3rd S.C. James died of disease at home in 1864. Johnny Beard survived the war.

‡ William A. Hill served as a sergeant with the Gilchrist's Company, South Carolina Heavy Artillery, also known as Gist Guard Artillery.

N.B. Direct your letter to J. L. Hill*
Glenn Spring.

J. L. H.

J. S. Birge to B. B. Foster

Frog Level† *May 18th 1861*
Col. B. B. Foster Columbia, S.C.

Dear Sir

After my last respects to you up to this date I suppose no one to be regularly emplaced to carry boxes to any from your Camp to the depot and being a poor man greatly in want of business I appeal to you for your influence I also wish to establish a regular line every day for the purpose of conveying all mail matter to and from the companies passengers to and from the places & I furthermore wish to get permission to establish a lemonade stand inside of your lines and will be governed by any law the officers may require of me & feeling confident that I could gain entire satisfaction I am yours very respectfully

J. S. Birge

Perrin Foster was apparently granted a brief leave to visit his relatives in Abbeville.

L. P. Foster to His Mother

Abbeville
May 19th 1861

My Dear Mother

I am afraid that you have been uneasy from not receiving a letter from me for the last two or three days. I got here Thursday evening and since then have had not chance to write. I found all of our friends well and full of life in anticipation of the festival their approaching and which came off that night in the presence of a large and gay crowd of ladies and gentlemen. Cousin Mary looked better than I ever saw her. Her "Old Man"‡ is quite [different] in appearance from what I would have thought Cousin Mary would have fancied. He is very slender and 6 ft 2 or 3 inches high and by no means fine looking, yet he has a very pleasant and striking

* James Hill owned a cotton factory on the north side of the Tyger River in Spartanburg District. The family business started operations in 1816–1817 and was in business until 1866. Landrum, *History of Spartanburg County*, 158–160, 718.

† Prosperity, South Carolina, was originally named Frog Level. The name was changed in 1873.

‡ Francis Eugene Harrison.

appearance. He is an intelligent man and I like him very much. Both of them seem well pleased and quite at home. He had a very pleasant party and the finest supper I ever saw. Just any amount of champaign and other wines, brandy and other liquors [. . .] fruit especially strawberries of the finest kind in every kind of preparation in short every thing you could call for. On Friday we had a dining party here which was one of the most boring and finest affairs I ever saw. I would like to describe it if I had time. This ended the parties. We had a concert last night where we saw many ladies, so I have had quite a fine time. I have seen all the friends in the village. Aunt Quarles* has been very unwell for a day or two with sick headache. Laura† & Lizzie Cothran‡ Sue Quarles§ Belle Perrin were up here and are here now except Sam. All the friends in Hard Labor are all well. I shall go down Monday morning. I have about got well of my dysentery Uncle James⁵ looks well. Cousin Emma** was the prettiest lady here by far. James A. Wardlaw†† came near dying this morning he has paralasis & I suppose cannot live long. Excuse the hasty manner in which I have written. Remember me to the family.

Yr affec Son
L. P. Foster

L. P. Foster to His Sister, Probably Sallie

Camp Johnson
May 21st 1861

My Dear Sister

I arrived here safe yesterday evening. I found your letter here & was glad to hear from you. I wrote to Mother from Abbeville all about the wedding. Mr. Zimmerman and son also Maj Wofford‡‡ came down yesterday. They are here yet from what they say you all must hear some awfull tales about us. I found Father right unwell

---

* Agnes White Perrin Quarles was B. B. Foster's sister-in-law. She was married to R. P. Quarles.

† Likely Laura Bobo.

‡ Elizabeth Perrin Cothran.

§ Susan Quarles, daughter of Agnes White and R. P. Quarles.

⁵ James Monroe Perrin was B. B. Foster's brother-in-law. Cothran, *Perrin Family*, 32.

** Emma Chiles Perrin.

†† James A. Wardlaw is apparently related to Jane Eliza Wardlaw, wife of Thomas Chiles Perrin. The exact relationship is unknown.

‡‡ Believed to be Maj. Joseph Llewellyn Wofford who entered the Civil War in the service of the Spartan Rifles (Capt. Joseph Walker's Company) and was attached to the 5th S.C. Later he was in Col. Oliver E. Edwards's 13th S.C. Wofford suffered an incapacitating wound at Fredericksburg and left the service. Landrum, *History of Spartanburg County*, 234–235.

yesterday. He had little billious* attack, but is much [better] today and I think will be well by tomorrow. Do not be uneasy about him at all for I have written the truth and you have I expect heard a thousand and one reports about him. Cousin Oliver has been out here for several days but has now gone to Char. A great many of our friends come out to see us. We are doing well, our tents are very comfortable and pleasant. The health of the regiment is pretty good. They have not yet got over the effects of drinking the spout water in Columbia but I hope soon will. Gen'l Bates† also was here yesterday evening. The crops up in Abbeville look pretty well. They are in good fix, but the corn and cotton are both very small. They have scarcely left the ground. So if Johns corn and cotton is small he need not despair. Miss Sallie Norwood‡ asked about you at the wedding. She is quite a belle in Abbeville.§

All our friends are vexed at your not coming. They never seemed to look for me at all but were looking for you. I rec'd a letter from Cousin Mary Perrin¶ today. They are well. She thinks there is doubt about the secession of Ky. She and Jennie speak of coming to see us in the fall. The Misses Simms will be out to see us this evening.

I have nothing of interest to write. Write to me soon. Remember me to the family

Yr affec Brother
L. P. Foster

L. P. Foster to His Mother

Camp Johnson
June 4th 1861

My Dear Mother

We arrived here safely yesterday evening. Father wrote to you as soon as he got here telling you he stood the drive. He stood it pretty well, better then I expected.

---

* Biliousness was a complex of symptoms comprising nausea, abdominal discomfort, headache, and constipation—formerly attributed to excessive secretion of bile from the liver.

† General Bates was likely Gen. B. F. Bates, one of the Spartanburg leaders who, on December 6, 1860, elected B. B. Foster, John G. Landrum, Benjamin F. Kilgore, James H. Carlisle, Simpson Bobo, and William Curtis as delegates from Spartanburg to the Secession Convention.

‡ This might be Sallie M. Norwood, daughter of Dr. Wesley C. Norwood and Jane Pickens Miller. Sallie Norwood died at age 23 on October 29, 1869.

§ "Person Sheet," http://homepage.mac.com/bfthompson/Miller_family/pso2_378.html (accessed July 20, 2004).

¶ Probably Perrin's cousin, Mary Eunice Perrin, the daughter of Lewis Perrin and Elizabeth Hinde. Mary Eunice Perrin married Achilles Perrin. An Achilles Perrin was an early editor of the Cynthiana Democrat newspaper in Kentucky. The connection is plausible but not confirmed.

He was considerably fatigued when he got to Columbia but not sick. He remained in Columbia until 5 O clock, then came out here but did not stay long. He was afraid of the noise of the camp and went back to the city. Dr. Kilgore* came out this morning. He said he was doing very well. I think from what he Dr. Kilgore says He is better than when he left home. Col Williams came yesterday morning and was gladly rec'd. The reg will all go. I think Father will now go back home until he gets strong. He may go in the course of two or three days. As soon as he sees what is to become of his reg. which is as yet doubtfull. I am apprehensive that we will not go to Virg. now. I fear the gov. is working against us, though others better informed than we all think we will. If we go it will probably be the last of this week or the first of next. Since I came back I feel much better than I have in several weeks. I drilled this morning and feel as well as I ever did. I think I am now well for good. The crowd on the cars yesterday was very [. . .] 4 or 5 trains crowd yet no accident. I hope will not take my absence so much to heart. The knowledge of your being always uneasy and distressed on my acc't is the worst thin[g] I have to contend with. Were it not for that my duties though arduous would be very pleasant for I consider that I am engaged in one of the noblest works that man ever engaged in & feel that I would be not only committing a sin but disgracing my self and family did I not go and fight the battles of my country. I will write to you as often as I can and do all in my power to lighten your uneasiness about us. So far as my sickness is concerned you must not be uneasy a moment. I have drilled 5 hrs this morning and feel perfectly well.

Jenkins† reg. will march in a few days. It is a splendid reg. All well armed and equipped. The health of the camp is much better than when we left. We have no bad cases and very little sickness.

Dick Springs and cousin Mary are here. I have no news

Write to me soon

Yr affec Son

L. P. Foster

L. P. Foster to His Sister, Probably Sallie

Columbia

June 8th 1861

My Dear Sister

Your letter came yesterday evening I was glad to get it as I have not rec'd one before since I came back and think from home comes to me laden with much

---

* Dr. Benjamin F. Kilgore enlisted in Co. K of the 3rd S.C. at the start of the war. Shortly afterwards he was transferred to the 13th S.C. as assistant surgeon. In 1862 he replaced L. C. Kennedy as the full surgeon. Landrum, *History of Spartanburg County*, 447–449.

† Micah Jenkins of the 5th S.C.

pleasantness. I have been quite well since I left home and think I am now in a good way to fatten up. I came here from the camp yesterday evening to Mr Sims. The family are well and as kind as can [be]. Every characteristic which can make one hospitable and kind seems to enter into all of their characters. They have treated both father and me more like relations than otherwise. I never can forget their kindness. They have made me a beautiful pr of shoulder straps make me a very nice haversack and mark my oil cloth. There was no news in the camp when I left. Every thing was quiet. When we will move to Virg I can not tell but think in the course of a very few days. Our men are getting uneasy as fast as they can. You will learn soon that there have been several little fights in Virginia our men were always victorious but in the last lost 500 stands of arms.* This is so far I hear it was from a private letter

Remember me to all the family

Write soon Yr affec brother

L. P. Foster

L. P. FOSTER TO HIS SISTER, PROBABLY SALLIE

Camp Johnson
June 11th 1861

My Dear Sister

I would not write home this evening if it were not merely to keep you from being uneasy about me for I have very nearly nothing to write. I know no more about when we will leave now than when I last wrote. I [asked] Gen'l Williams† about it last night. He told me that he thought there was no doubt about our going but as far as when he could not tell. I think it will take us 10 days yet to get ready. They took our old guns to day and will bring us others this evening or tomorrow. We have no drill this evening as we have no guns. Mr James Sims went on to Virg this morning. He intended going with our regiment but was so restless he could not wait for us. Cousin Oliver also went on. I did not get to see him. Our Reg are in fine health there being but few sick men. The remnant who did not volunteer have gone home. They were discharged last night and started this morning. How they were rec'd in Columbia I can not say but the remnant of Sloans reg started home yesterday morning and the ladies hissed them while passing through the street and a lady threw a petty coat out of a window at them. A considerable take off. Mind that no mistake gets out from this as it was the remnant of Sloans and not our regiment.

---

* This might refer to the Battle at Philippi in western Virginia. On June 3, 1861, Gen. Thomas A. Morris routed sleeping Confederates in an early morning attack. The Federals referred to this engagement as The Philippi Races.

† This is likely Col. James H. Williams of the 3rd S.C. He did not hold the rank of General.

I am looking for Father this evening. Mr. Zimmerman is here and said he would come to day. He came down for Tom who looks very much cut at being rejected by the mustering officer. Has since gone back to Limestone.* Write me soon.

> Your affec Brother
>
> L. P. Foster

P.S. Remember me to all the family.

L. P. FOSTER TO HIS MOTHER

Camp Johnson
June 14th 1861

My Dear Mother

I write by Mr. Beard to explain the bundle which he carries. It consists of 3 of my photographs and one of Capt Kennedy, which he gave me. They are said by my friends to be fine. Take one of them for yourself and give one to Ed.† And if you all think one at home is enough give the other to Anna Bobo.‡ Keep Capt Kennedys for me I would be glad if Tony would get me a case or frame for it when he goes to the village for if left out I think they will soon spoil. We will leave tomorrow at 12 o clock. We are getting very well fixed to go. We draw our pay today. Some have already drawn. If Mrs Sims or any of the family come up the country you must seek them out and treat them with every kindness which is in your power for they have treated Father and I both like brothers. Our men are all delighted at the idea of going to Virg. We will have a fine time going on. We go on the Manchester road.§ Sloans regiment will start at 8 o clock. Father went out to Mrs Sims last night and has not come back yet. We have very hot weather and pretty warm drilling. We are now ready in service our sentinels load their guns at night & are instructed to shoot any one attempting to pass unless he will halt at command which makes things very quiet indeed. When we will arrive in Richmond it is hard to tell but think in about

---

* This may refer to either the Limestone Springs Female Academy or the Limestone Springs Hotel. The original hotel is now part of Limestone College and is named Cooper Hall.

† Edwin Henry Bobo, son of Simpson and Nancy Foster Bobo. He served in Company E of Holcomb's Legion.

‡ Anna Bobo was Foster's cousin, the daughter of Simpson and Nancy Foster Bobo.

§ During the Civil War, Manchester was located southeast of Columbia near present-day Wedgefield near Sumter, South Carolina. Manchester was an important railroad station, connected by rail to Columbia and being the terminus of the Wilmington and Manchester Railroad. The town is now abandoned; a state park of the same name preserves the memory of the community. "Guide to the Ghost Towns of South Carolina," http://freepages.history .rootsweb.com/~gtusa/usa/sc.htm (accessed March 10, 2005).

6 days. I will write every chance I get on the way. Father is improving he looks very well. You need not write to me any more here but write to me at Richmond directing to Lt. L. P. Foster

Care Lt. Col. B. B. Foster
3rd Reg. SCV
Richmond Virg
Remember me to all the family & write soon to yr affec son. L. P. Foster
P.S. Yesterday we had no drill it be fast day.* I spent the day at Mr. Sims. Miss Bobo and I went to the B.C. We all fasted

L. P. foster

Father and I will send a trunk of clothes home as we have more than we can manage.

The Third Infantry Regiment was created from Laurens, Union, Spartanburg, Newberry, and Lexington District volunteer companies. After organization and training in Columbia, the regiment was assigned to the Manassas defenses. Assigned to Gen. Luke Bonham's Brigade, the regiment saw action at First Manassas. The Third spent the winter of 1861–1862 near Centreville, Virginia. In January 1862, Gen. Joseph B. Kershaw replaced Bonham as brigadier general. Traveling in the spring of 1862 to the defense of Richmond on the Peninsula, the Third, in Kershaw's Brigade, was engaged in the Seven Days Battle at Savage's Station and Malvern Hill. Later that year, they were in the Maryland campaign, taking Maryland Heights under Gen. Lafayette McLaws and fighting at Antietam. In December they fought at Marye's House at Fredericksburg. The next year, Kershaw's Brigade was on Lee's right flank at Gettysburg. In September, the brigade was assigned to support Gen. Braxton Bragg in Tennessee. Traveling quickly by train, they arrived in time to fight at Chickamauga. They continued to see action in Tennessee, fighting in Knoxville and wintering in East Tennessee. Returning to Virginia in spring of 1864, the brigade fought at the Battle of the Wilderness, the Battle of Spotsylvania Court House, the Siege of Petersburg, and the 1864 Shenandoah Valley Campaign. In January 1865, Kershaw's Brigade took the train to South Carolina to oppose Sherman in his march through the Carolinas. The Third's last major action was at Bentonville, North Carolina, in March. The Third surrendered on April 26 in Greensboro, North Carolina, and was paroled May 2–3.

* Thursday, June 13, 1861, was declared by Jefferson Davis to be a day of fasting and prayer. *Overton and Jesse Bernard Diaries #62-z*, Southern Historical Collection, Wilson Library, University of North Carolina at Chapel Hill. Folder 3, June 14, 1861, http://blogs.lib.unc.edu/civilwar/index.php/page/141/ (accessed August 10, 2016).

CHAPTER 3

Bull Run

"We soon saw the Elephant"

The Ordinance of Secession in Virginia was provisionally passed on April 17, 1861, and the Commonwealth formally voted to secede on May 23. The Confederate Congress designated Richmond as the capital of the Confederacy on May 21, defiantly placing the capital near the hostile frontier of the new country. If war actually broke out, the battle lines would be drawn in northern Virginia in defense of Richmond. Regiments throughout the South poured into Richmond by rail; some were ordered to Gen. Joe Johnston in the Shenandoah Valley and some down the Peninsula guarding Richmond. Most went to Gen. Beauregard along the banks of Bull Run.

Bull Run formed a natural defensive line between the Union forces in Washington and land approaches to Richmond, connecting the Bull Run Mountains to the Potomac River. This steep-banked, slow-moving creek resisted easy crossing except at established fords. The Confederate command established a defensive line along the south bank of Bull Run with concentrated positions at the fords. The important railroad center at Manassas Junction, just below Bull Run, enabled the quick transfer of forces and supplies from Richmond to the south and from the Shenandoah Valley to the west.

Ordered to the defense of Virginia, the Third South Carolina Infantry left Camp Johnson June 15th, traveling by railroad cars to Manchester, South Carolina, and thence to Wilmington, North Carolina. On the 17th they were in Petersburg, Virginia, and in Richmond on the 18th. They stayed at Camp Jackson* on the western side of the city for a few days, leaving Richmond at 5:00 in the evening on the 22nd for Manassas Junction. In towns along the way, the soldiers were celebrated by the citizenry; ladies showered the soldiers with flowers and snatched their palmetto buttons. The enthusiasm for the new Confederacy and the confidence of the soldiers' ability to defend it are evident in these letters.

---

* Camp Jackson in Richmond was a training camp located at the site of the present William Byrd Park. "Winder Hospital," http://www.mdgorman.com/Hospitals/winder_hospital.htm (accessed August 10, 2016).

L. P. FOSTER TO HIS MOTHER

Richmond Virg.
June 18th 1861

My Dear Mother

We are here safe and sound. I wrote you a note yesterday from Petersburg giving you a sketch of our trip up to that place but as it was very meager I shall allude to it again. The country from Columbia to Petersburg is one of the poorest looking countries I ever saw being entirely small lands with the exception of the cypress swamps which are very dense and fragrant nearly all of the way. Between Kingville and Sumpter* the R. R. runs through swamp most of the way we were running on one trestle there for near a half hour. Sumpter is a very small place. I could not see much of it as we passed it after dark. Florence is also a small town on the road. Also Marion. The crops all through this poor land are very fine. In S.C. the corn was grown waste high to as high as my head. I saw many large plantations containing hundreds of acres which seemed planted entirely with corn. The cotton also looks fine being about half as high. The wheat was in most places cut until I got in this state where the crops are not yet ripe but look finely. So between here and home there must be a plenty of provisions. This state seems to be planting corn almost altogether. I have not seen a tobacco patch since I came here. The chief staple between Columbia and Petersburg seems to be the resin. Almost all of the pines are blazed and at every little place on the road you see quantities of it and many distills for it.

Our going here was almost like a triumphal procession being saluted by every person whom we met whether white or black. We got to Wilmington a little before night Sunday. Just before getting there we passed through some of the prettiest rice fields I ever saw and crossed the Cape Fear River on a fine steamboat. We were detained there all night. It is one of the ugliest places I ever saw. [. . .] a very large and business place. At Edgeton we were very kindly rec'd and the ladies gave us a great many things to eat. Also a quantity of lint and bandages. Miss Mary May was the fair donor she was very pretty. At Goldsborough we faired well. I there saw Cousins Madora, Anna & Willie.† Anna well fixed. She is in a pretty place and has a fine house and lot. Dr. Davis seemed very clever. Willie and all looked well except Madora. She looks very badly and is getting very gray. She seems care worn and not at all herself. At Hallifax we were kindly rec'd. But at Weldon we found it hard

---

* Kingsville was an important railroad junction southeast of Columbia. Sumpter refers to Sumter, South Carolina.

† Cousins Madora, Anna, and Willie were likely related to the Fosters through the Oliver Edwards family. The subsequent reference to Dr. Davis indicates that the surname is likely Davis.

to get any thing to eat. It is quite a small dirty place. Petersburg is a small town. The number of Lincolns army is much smaller than I thought being about 80,000 ours about 12500 in Virg. Virg has 15000 or more in the field. She could get many more but has not arms for them. These men put all confidence in S. Carolinians. They beg us for our palmettos. The gents and boys come beg us to give them our buttons. Write to me soon at this place

Your affec son. L. P. Foster

B. B. FOSTER TO HIS WIFE

Camp Jackson
Near Richmond Virginia
June the 20th 1861

My Dear Wife,

We have arrived here safe and pitched our camp and commenced drilling vigorously. Our men are in fine health and spirits and very anxious for the conflict. I hear much less said about fighting here than I did in Carolina. There are troops from all quarters of the confederacy and I have no means of ascertaining the number it is a powerful army They are coming in every train our arms have been victorious in every engagement. I think our officers Davis & Boreguard* are wide awake and perfectly cool. They know their business and will attend to it properly We have no information as to when we will be moved nor where to. I think we will be placed with the ballance of the Carolina Regiments I felt quite large marching at the head of the Third Regiment through the streets of Richmond The ladies throwing their Bokas† at me and cheering us on. Our trip here was disagreeable. our train was so long they were afraid to run fast. no accident happened after Williams‡ was killed at the Wateree Bridge. I have sent Perrin into the citty to day and ordered a Richmond Paper to be sent to you I send you a slip from the morning paper They compliment us highly we have a splendid Regiment and I think god willing we will do our duty friends need have no uneasiness we know where we came from and if we are called into action we will make a struggle worthy of carolinians They stand high here.

Perrins health seems as good as it ever was. he looks as well as you have ever seen him. Johny Beard has improved very much in fact we have no sickness that I know of and as for myself I never felt better have fattened. We have fine water and two blankets and a comfort is not too much cover almost as cool as it was when we were on the Blue Ridge I feel anxious about you all it could be permitted to see

---

* Jefferson Davis and Brigadier General P. G. T. Beauregard.

† Bouquets.

‡ Private N. J. D. Williams was killed while standing on a boxcar as it passed under the Wateree bridge. Wyckoff, *Third South Carolina*, 15.

you all occasionally. I would be delighted with camp life whenever an opportunity offers I will come home and see you all you must not expect letters too often we have all our time taken up and the chance for mail facilities will not be good when we leave here we are doing everything up in military order and I am sure that our men will soon be prepared for action Remember me to all my neighbors The boys from our Region are all well and doing well Remember me to all the children and Mr Harmon I hope you are all well we have not heard from Tony May the Lord bless and preserve you all and allow us to meet again is my prayers

Yr affectionate husband B B Foster

L. P. Foster to His Sister, Probably Sallie

Camp Jackson
Richmond Virg
June 21st 1861

My Dear Sister

I have written to mother once and Father twice we got here. In my last I told you of my trip here. Since we got here we have had perfect order in our camp. Our sentinels march with loaded guns every night. I was Lieut of the guard day before yesterday and was up all night that night drilling my sentinels. One of them came so near shooting a man that it made cold chills run over me. The man was a man of Capt. Garlingtons camp. When he approached the line the sentinel halted him twice.

I went in the Virg convention a few minutes. It is a very ornery looking body of men. I looked a long time but in vain for some things like greatness but was compelled to turn to the statue in the square to know that Virg had been the mother of great men. The churches are also very large and fine. The steeples seem to rival each other in reaching heavenward. The penitentiary is a very large and dismal looking building. I did not go in it. There are too many big strapping fellows loafing about here doing nothing. Too many fine gentlemen going with ladies. Too many can boast fair skin soldiers, too many office seekers for the place to be interesting at present except as made so by the ladies and art. There seems not to be a spark of patriotism in any of the business circles, they charge us enormous prices for everything. The ladies seem very interesting. They will speak to a palmetto boy any where they meet him, come up to our camp, walk all through it beg us for our palmetto and even for the buttons on our coats. I was walking across the parade ground day before yesterday evening and while passing a carriage one of the ladies said to come and speak to [her]. As I was not anticipating such a thing so walked on pretending not to hear her, but yesterday I dressed up, got some palmettos from my trunk and went in search of the same carriage. I was standing on the old field when it drove up. They saw me about 50 yds off and bowed to me. So I walked presented my palmetto talked a good while and had a nice time. Who they were I know not. The ladies here are too bold. They look like they would kiss the whole party if they could. I saw one entertain a crowd of 40 or 50 yesterday evening with a dissertation on S. Carolina. She being the center, the others crowded around you cannot confuse them at all.

I expect we will leave here to night or tomorrow for a camp near Manassas. The lines there are getting pretty warm. No regular fighting, but armies in 8 miles of each other and skirmishes frequently. Col. Gregg had a little fight the other day. He attacked a detachment trying to plant themselves at Vienna.* The[y] soon fled. 10 of their men being killed none of ours. Our men capturing a whole train of baggage, stores, arms, ammunition & e. There are reported fights at Harpers Ferry and Yorktown but are not confirmed.† Believe nothing but what comes strait we can not get the truth here. Write to me soon I have not heard from home since I came here. Father is well.

All of our men are in fine spirits.

All our neighbors well.

Yr affec Brother

L. P. Foster

I made a slight mistake in writing this on two sides of paper. Too late to correct.

LPF

An unusual passage in the following letter refers to two women in an Alabama regiment who wore uniforms and led drills.

B. B. FOSTER TO HIS WIFE

Camp Jackson
Near Richmond
June 22nd 1861

My Dear Wife

We are still here in fine health and spirits. as to the men in this part of Virginia they do not seem to exhibit much hospitality and many of them but little patriotism yet they have a large number of soldiers in the field. we are charged the most

---

* On June 17, 1861, Colonel Maxcy Gregg and his 1st S.C. engaged Federals repairing a railroad and captured a train and its stores. He was later promoted to brigadier general and was killed in action at Fredericksburg.

† Along the Potomac, there was a skirmish at Conrad's Ferry on June 17 and another at Edwards Ferry on the 18th. At the time, Gen. Joseph Johnston was evacuating Harpers Ferry. Perhaps that is what Foster refers to. I find no reference to any action at Yorktown at this time.

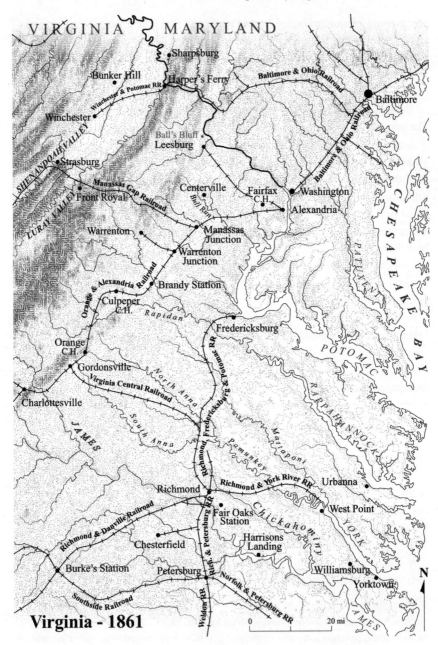

Virginia, 1861.

extravagant prices for everything we have to buy Col Williams bought a pair of shoes in the city yesterday paid eight dollars and a half for them every about in that ratio. I must say the thing is quite different with the Ladies they [are] kind and exceedingly clever fond of the soldiers. and seem anxious to make them feel at home men are packing up to leave this for Manassas Junction under the command of Boriguard Just what we want. It is all a mistake about our troops evacuating Harpers Ferry* we are still in possession they had a fight there yesterday† Held a good muster and took several prisoners among them a Lieut Col of the Pensylvania Regiment They are now in Richmond Prisoners of war sent up last night when our men began to press them they gave way and finally run. I am of opinion that there will be but little fighting until after the 4th of July I never have seen such preparations so many soldiers cannons flying artillery and every description of weapons of warfare there are two ladies here in the alabama regiment wives of captains they drill their husbands companies and wear uniforms what do think of that, there is a regiment here from Mississippi. They are looking for Brother Anthony‡ here every day, I have now comparatively but little to do and am getting fat again this is a delightful climate Perrin is standing it fine. I now believe he will get stouter than he ever has been, there is less talk here and less excitement about the war than there is where you are no one seems to be alarmed in the slightest the truth is the telegraph dispatches are by no means reliable, they do not wait for official reports and they report at least half that there is no foundation for there is no doubt but there will be fighting at some of the points in this state one day it is thought that it will be at harpers ferry next day rumors at Alexandria it is impossible to tell or form any correct opinion there is large preparation making at Washington Citty they [say] Abes men think we are after that place. I do not think so we will not cross the confederate border. There is said to be thirty two thousand southerners and western troops where we are going. I am anxious to see so large an army together it will be a grand show we have not heard a word from home since we left Camp Johnson still direct to Richmond until otherwise directed we will make arrangements to have them forwarded. all our magnificent boys are well except Chris Birch§ he is sick with typhoid but not supposed to be dangerous we sent in to town to the hospital yesterday he

---

* Gen. Joseph Johnston began evacuating Harpers Ferry on June 15 and moved to Winchester, Virginia. General Patterson moved into Harpers Ferry and then returned his forces to the Maryland side of the Potomac, so there was no significant action at Harpers Ferry.

† William C. Davis, *Battle at Bull Run* (Garden City, N.Y.: Doubleday, 1977), 83.

‡ Brother Anthony was B. B. Foster's brother, Anthony.

§ Christopher F. Burch of Company K survived this round of typhoid but died in Richmond before the end of 1862, according to Wyckoff.

has been slightly unwel for some days. remember me to my dear children and my neighbors one and all may the good Lord preserve you all is my constant prayer

your affectionate husband

B B Foster ·

At this point, a brief explanation of Civil War–era fighting tactics might be helpful. To successfully prosecute a Civil War battle generally required a commander to succeed in concentrating superior numbers of soldiers delivering concentrated firepower onto a critical point in an opponent's position. Saying this is easy. It is a very difficult matter to move tens of thousands of soldiers quickly down a narrow wagon road, spread them out in organized, controlled units on a line of battle and advance them in a manner that permits concentrated fire. Maintaining command and control in battle was at best difficult in the smoke, fire, and confusion of battle; losses in company, regiment, and brigade officer ranks often resulted in complete loss of control. The continual drilling described in these letters was a way of ensuring control during battle.

A Civil War army was typically positioned in a line of battle along a naturally strong position that provided advantages of cover, movement, or firing concentration. Facing the enemy, soldiers on a commander's right constituted his right flank, and those on his left, his left flank. Firing into a facing line of soldiers, bullets had a chance of hitting an enemy beyond the first line or rank of soldiers, as deeply as the enemy ranks were arranged. If a commander were able to flank his enemy by positioning his infantry perpendicular to the enemy line of battle, he could concentrate a superior fire on the small number of enemy soldiers who could turn and fire to the left or right. Further, the commander could fire down the enemy line of battle, greatly increasing the effectiveness of his fire. This is termed an enfilade fire.

Armies had great difficulty knowing enemy positions. Cavalry units provided the eyes of an army. Ranging across the countryside, they probed and identified the position, boundary, and strength of the enemy force. At a shorter range, pickets* were advance forces who guarded the edges of an army, providing early detection of the enemy. An interesting example of the difficulty these armies had in knowing each other's positions is revealed in L. P. Foster's letter of July 20, 1861. McDowell's army of 34,000 was marching a few miles in front of the Confederate positions and a large Union reconnaissance force was sent south, engaging the Confederates at Blackburn's Ford on July 18. On the 20th, Foster wrote of the Union army, "They have gone out of sight."

As the war progressed, defensive infantry positions increasingly included the use of breastworks that allowed soldiers to take cover behind mounds constructed by ditch digging. Depending on the situation and the amount of time available to the defenders, these could be very elaborate earthworks or quickly dug earth berms and rifle pits.

---

* At times, the Fosters use the French word *piquet*.

Additional protection could be provided by constructing an abatis, a dense array of sharply pointed sticks that greatly slowed down advancing troops and created a killing zone. Later in the war, trench warfare, in the manner used so effectively in World War I, was innovated.

A variety of artillery had different uses. Solid shot and rifled shells could knock down defensive works. Shells containing fused explosives could be fired into enemy ranks, exploding and sending fragments into soldiers. Spherical case shot with a fused bursting charge exploded, scattering balls (shrapnel) among enemy troops. Canister and grape shot were packages of balls sprayed into ranks of soldiers in the manner of a shotgun. Powder and the selected projectile were rammed into the cannon barrel, the powder bag was pricked through the vent hole, and a friction primer placed into the vent hole. A roughened wire slider pulled by lanyard ignited the primer and powder, firing the cannon. Captured cannons were frequently disabled by "spiking" them: a tapered steel pin was driven into the vent hole and hammered flush, rendering the cannon useless unless the pin was laboriously drilled out.

The 3rd S.C. left Richmond by rail at 5:00 pm on June 22, 1861, for Manassas Junction. On June 23rd, the 3rd S.C. marched to Camp Beauregard at Mitchell's Ford, on Bull Run, between the Manassas Junction rail center and the towns of Centreville, Fairfax Court House, and Alexandria. The Federal lines were just beyond Fairfax Court House, and Beauregard—expecting the main Federal thrust at this place—had fortified the Bull Run crossing, manning it with South Carolinians and other units.

Accounts of women serving in the Civil War as nurses is common and frequently mentioned in these letters; however, women serving as soldiers is rarer. Foster finds this unusual; but, he limits his letters to basic descriptions. Women are noted as serving openly in positions of leadership. Women in the war were typically disguised as men.

L. P. FOSTER TO HIS BROTHER ANTHONY FOSTER

Manassas Junction
June 23rd 1861

Dear Brother

We left Camp Jackson yesterday evening about 5 o clock and marched through the streets of Richmond 3 miles to the depot and the cheers of both ladies and gentlemen. I never have seen just so many handkerchiefs in my life. The ladies of Richmond are fully alive to the cause. The[y] would come to our camp whilst there and go all about our tents talking to any of us without an introduction, and beg us all the time for palmetto even for the buttons of our coats. Some girls caught holt on mine last night before we left and I thought they would have pulled them off whether or no. We left Richmond about 9 o clock last night and passing over one of the prettiest countries I ever saw got here to day about 10 o clock. The clover and wheat fields are very fine. I never saw any wheat to compare to it. It is all sown in drills, and cut by horse power. The Southern feeling in the country is much stronger than I expected to see it when at Richmond, I think being right in the country but there are a good many at Richmond who will not do. The[y] came out to see us all along the road and at every depot sent negroes to carry water for us. I passed Hanover C.H. the place of the Henrys. Patrick Henry and Henry Clay both being born in two and a half miles of it. We had a splendid view of the Blue Ridge all of the way & can see it now. I thought I saw crowds of soldiers when in Richmond but I never saw many in comparison to what are here. There are troops all through this country. Several regiments are here now Several have moved lower down. They are very fine look- ing fellows. This place is well fortified there are batteries on every side. Most of the S Carolina troops are at fairfax C.H. near enough the enemy to march by the rap of their drums. We will leave here tonight and march nine miles to Bulls run. Where

Lewis Perrin Foster, circa 1861. From the editor's collection.

James Anthony Foster, circa 1861. From the editor's collection.

will encamp and fortify ourselves. There are said to be about, well I hardly know what number to say accounts are different but over 40,000. there are crowds here from Loisana, The finest equipped troops that I have seen any where at all. A portion of a reg came in today with 2 ladies with them, one their flag bearer. She was dress[ed] after the Turkish costume in the same cloth as the soldiers. I saw one also in Richmond bring in an Alabama comp. She was said to be a fine drill officer and was acting as first Lieut. We leave here soon. I have not time to write more—know we are all very well this water agrees with one Finally we do not expect a fight right off not in ten days. My love to all

Your Affec Brother
L P Foster

B. B. Foster to His Wife

Camp Butler*
Prince William County
Virginia near Bulls Run

My Dear Wife

We are now stationed at this place the main road leading from Alexandria to Manassas Junction The grand junction of all the Rail Roads from all points in this state. This is said to be the stand point where the forces will be concentrated provided our men in advance of us should be driven back by the Lincoln troops we are well fortified here and will have a battallion of artillery attached to our Regiment tomorrow we are 230† miles from Richmond and within 18 miles of Alexandria I think from our breast works we can easily whip 10000 men with our Regiment you all think that we are in great danger and must be uneasy about us. it ought not to be so we feel just as safe here as we do at home and I believe that we will never have any more fighting unless Davis determines to push the war into yankeedom They have no idea of advancing uppon us. I am uneasy about you all have not heard since we arrived here I left directions for our letters to be forwarded to us we are comfortable here a fine camp cool water good shade good butter and plenty of every thing to live on I hope we will stay here and not be moved again. I am tired of moving so much we are all well direct your letters to B. B. Foster Lieut Col 3rd Regt SC Volunteers Manassas Junction Prince William County Virginia remember me to the children May God bless and preserve you all

your husband B. B. Foster

L. P. Foster to His Mother

Camp
June 24th 1861

My Dear Mother

I wrote to you yesterday from Manassas giving you the points of my travel that far. We left there last night about dark and marched to this point, a distance of four miles over the dustiest road I ever saw in my life. We marched slowly and all stood it finely. I did not feel at all fatigued when I got here. We did not stretch our tents but just lay down on our blankets and went to sleep. To day we are busy fixing up. We

---

* The Fosters initially referred to this position as Camp Butler; however, a few days later they corrected themselves and began to refer to it as Camp Beauregard.

† Manassas is about 100 miles from Richmond, but the letter clearly states "230"; the reason for the discrepancy is unclear.

are on a creek called Bulls Run a very clean pretty stream. This place was considered by Genl Boureguard as a very important point being on the road from Alexandria to Manassas. He has had breastworks thrown up here every where around the foot of the hill in rear of which our tents overlooking a pretty little valley. We are about 10 miles from Fairfax which is very near the enemies Camp. We are ordered to hold this point until relieved by some of the regiments which will probably be soon. Col. Jenkins, ours, and two Mississippi regiments have been thrown in the same brigade which will be one of the finest in the army. Col. Jones now genl Jones* commands the brigade. He passed here this morning. I did not see him. I have heard this morn that Virg has seceded. It is thought to be so. Whether it is or not I cannot say. When any fight will have any fight unless it be a skirmish I cannot tell.† This seems to be a fine place. We can get any am't of fine cut line.

I never have seen such soldiers than I have of the confederate army. Most of them volunteers for 2 years or the war. They seem resolute and determined to do or die. They never seem to doubt their success and I don't think such men can be whipped at all. I don't think the enemy will try to hold Alexandria against us unless reinforced. I should not be surprised to hear that they had burnt the town and left at any moment. Several of the northern states are petitioning for peace. What the July congress may bring forth I can not tell but think they are evidently badly cowed. I saw two live yankee prisoners yesterday at Manassas which I mentioned on the back of yesterdays letter. One a searg't the other a corporal both taken by our troops at the same time they being well armed. He having a double barrel shot gun. The capt of the same comp was taken and sent to Richmond. We are all well and much pleased. I saw the Spartanburg Rifles‡ this morning. They were left here to hold this place until we came. They leave this evening. I have not seen a letter from any of you since I left Columbia. Write soon directing to Lieut L. P. Foster

3rd Regiment SCV

Manassas Junction

Virginia

I think we are in Fairfax County

Remember me to all,

Yr affec Son L. P. Foster

P.S. We are about 30 miles of Washington and not very more than 20 from the Potomac.

L. P. Foster

* Brig. Gen. D. R. Jones.

† Foster seems to have lost his thread of thought.

‡ Foster is likely referring to the Spartan Rifles, which organized just before the outbreak of war and became Company K of Col. Micah Jenkins's Fifth South Carolina Infantry.

B. B. Foster to His Wife

Camp Boreguard
Prince William County
Virginia June 26th 1861

I am still here nothing new or of much interest had taken place since I last wrote you We are all well and disappointed we expected to have a little brush but I think that there is about as much chance for a fight here as there would be at Glenn Springs* we are rather hard pressed for nicknack plenty of strong food there is such an army here that the good things are cut out. I have not heard a word from home since we left Columbia I am uneasy about you all I trust in god & believe all will be for the best I wrote yesterday and have nothing of much interest to write remember me to the children and all the neighbors may the Lord bless and protect you all

your affect husband
B B Foster

In the letter below, we have the first instance of the use of the name, "Army of the Potomac" in the letters. This name may be confusing because people are most familiar with the Federal Army of the Potomac, which was formed by Gen. George McClellan in July 1861 and was the Federal Army in northern Virginia through the rest of the war. As the Confederates massed their forces in northern Virginia, they named their army the Army of the Potomac. This Confederate army was renamed the Army of Northern Virginia in March 1862.

L. P. Foster to His Mother

Camp Boureguard
June 27th 1861

My Dear Mother,

You will see from the heading of this that the name of our camp has been changed since I last wrote. We have not moved, but when we came here not knowing that this camp had been reg'mtly named we called it Camp Butler, but had to fall back on its original name.

We have written home every day since we came here and have not rec'd a line from any of you. We know you have written but suppose there must be some derangement in the mails. Father is a little uneasy about Tony as you said in yr last letter that he was unwell. How is he. Has Nunie† gone back to Limestone. I would

---

* Glenn Springs, South Carolina, was the Foster family farm site.

† Nunie was Perrin Foster's sister Eunice. She was sixteen years old and attending Limestone College in Gaffney, South Carolina.

write but don't [know] whether she is there or not. We are all well and having a very fine time, but have despaired of having any fight. The Yankees have been claimed perfectly surprised by our mustering such an army into service in so a short time. Scott* doubtless started his army to Richmond via Alexandria but before got to Alexandria found it met by a very powerfull army. We ourselves even are surprised at our progress. The Army of the Potomac which is under the command of gen'l Boureguard and which now numbers about 30,000 men is I dare surpassed by none in the world and from the few engagements which already taken place have found that to reach Richmond with their present army is as impossible as to march it across the Sea and since taking fright have commenced to retreat. They have moved from Falls Church which was their advance post back to Alexandria where they have fortified themselves strongly and may make a desperate struggle but I have no idea that such will be the case. They must know that unless they are powerfully reinforced they can not meet us and I think that they will burn Alexandria and retreat beyond the river, to which they seem to have moved all their forces. I may be mistaken and we will not be surprised by anything. Nothing can exceed the vigilance of our sentinels and pickets. We have pickets who scour this country every day from here to as near the enemy as they can venture. We have had no fight lately that is our army. This is the poorest country I ever say so far as inhabitants are concerned. The land seems to be good but the people are "poor shoats." I have not seen a white woman since I left Manassas.

There are some Yankees and any quantity of free Negroes through here, but most [of] the women seem to have left. There are crowds of my friends in the army, relations and college friends here. Will Anthony† came here this morning. He is just from Miss. He is a sort of independent volunteer going to fight when and where he pleases. He looks very old. His beard is perfectly white and very long, but his life is the same. He says all are well. Tom Quarles‡ stopped here a little while last night. He was going after the mail for Bacons regiment of which he is a member. He is stationed about 10 miles from here at Fairfax. Dr. Hearst§ and Wade Cothran¶ are there. George Shuford** is about 2 miles from here in a Miss Regiment which

---

* Winfield Scott was the Union general-in-chief at the time.

† Possibly W. L. Anthony of Co. A, Eleventh Mississippi Infantry Regiment.

‡ Lt. Thomas P. Quarles of Co. C. in the 7th S.C., Col. Bacon's Regiment, in Kershaw's Brigade. Quarles was Lewis Perrin Foster's cousin, the son of Agnes White and R. P. Quarles. Agnes White Quarles was B. B. Foster's sister-in-law.

§ Dr. J. W. Hearst of Co. C, 7th S.C.

¶ Capt. Wade Elephare Cothran of Co. C. in the 7th S.C. of Kershaw's Brigade. Cothran was related to Lewis Perrin through marriages between the Cothrans and Perrins.

** George Shuford of Co. H in the Seventeenth Mississippi Infantry.

Eunice (Nunie) Foster as a young woman. From the editor's collection.

is in our Briggade. The brigade* is composed of Col Jenkins, Ours & 17th & 18th regiments of Miss troops. Our Brigadier gen'l is named Jones. Will Wardlaw[†] is in Col Greggs Regiment so I meet friends every where. Write to us Remember me to all.

* The Third Brigade of the Army of the Potomac.

† Will Wardlaw is likely related to Foster through his aunt Jane Eliza Wardlaw Perrin, wife of Thomas Chiles Perrin.

Yr affec Son L. P. Foster

B. B. Foster to His Wife

Army of the Potomac Camp Boreguard
Mitchels ford Prince William
County Virginia June 28th 1861

My dear wife

I received your letter this evening dated the 24th last. I had begun to get very restless not hearing word from home untill yesterday Since we left Columbia. Perrin received a letter from Tony yesterday. I am rejoiced to know that you were all well and that the money had reached you. I wrote you several times to pay no attention to anything you hear or read in the newspapers Harpers Ferry has never been evacuated. There was some fighting there in which our men were victorious. Fair fax court house is still held by our troops they had a fight there and our men were victorious without the loss of but one man Philipi* is still ours Col Bacons Regt is encamped at Fair fax right on the Battleground not one inch of ground has been given up but the enemy has been driven before us and as we advance they recede our men are killing some of them every day yesterday one of old Abes sentinels was shot dead on his post and the two others arrested and brought into Greggs camp The pickets gather them every day or two I saw Thomas Quarls yesterday he looks† Dr Hearst is at fair fax we are anxious to advance our hope to do so soon our camp is well fortified we have a Battallion of Artillery with our Regt among their pieces There is six rifle cannon I now have no idea of a fight this side of the Potomac they will not advance uppon us. We have a grand Regt second to none in the service no trouble with our men Thomas Zimmerman is perfectly sober he has not drank a drop since he left Columbia and looks better than I ever saw him I am afraid he will break over. our men and officers are keen for a fight we have drilled and trained and we now want to show our hand Brother Anthony is here he looks well. his whiskers is about eight or ten inches long and white as snow he looks ancient he is with me and intends to stay with me our next door friends are all well george shuford is in one of the Missipi Regiments stationed about two and a half miles from us. There are men here from all parts of the Confederacy Kentucky has men here doing fine service. I must think the Virginians are not doing just right yet she has about 40,000 men in the field and as many more ready if they could get arms many of them about us are abolitionist if they dare own it. our scouts of Cavalry

---

* On June 3, 1861, a Federal force surprised and routed Confederates at Philippi, West Virginia. This was the first major land engagement in the Eastern theater.

† The sentence is incomplete. He probably meant to say that Thomas Quarles looks well.

are scouring the country day and night and those that have subversive notions are afraid to cheep they know they would be hung this is however the cold part of the state settled mostly with yankees L. Edwards* is here he looks well I saw Ligg today our friends are here all times one of our Regiment died last night with congestion of the brain They are now about to bury him and I must close this letter the mail agent will start in a few minutes the dead man† belongs to Capt Nunnamakers‡ company he lived in the dutch fork remember me kindly to the children and all the neighbors may god keep you all is my prayers

your affectionate husband
B B Foster

*Early in the morning of the 30th, the 3rd S.C. was ordered to march forward to Fairfax Court House and establish a position about a mile north of the courthouse, with only J. E. B. Stuart's cavalry between the Federal and the Confederate armies.§ The 3rd S.C. had been ordered forward to replace Maxcy Gregg's 1st S.C. whose enlistment had expired.¶ A reorganization put the 3rd S.C. and other regiments under General Luke Bonham establishing a brigade.** They stayed at Fairfax Court House until the large Federal advance of July 17 forced an orderly retreat to Mitchell's Ford.*

L. P. FOSTER TO HIS SISTER, PROBABLY SALLIE

Fairfax C.H.
June 30th 1861

My Dear Sister

You may be somewhat astonished at the heading of this letter. This morning at 4 o clock the drum beat for the men to get up and prepare to leave Camp Boreguard for this place. Genl Boreguard having ordered Col. Williams to report at this place to Genl Bonham for the purpose of taking the place of Col. Greggs Regiment whose time of service expired today. We left our camp between 9 and 10 o clock and passing over a distance of 11 miles arrived here before about 2 o clock. The day was cool and it rained most of the time making the march less tiresome. The men seemed to stand it finely. No one seeming to be much fatigued. We passed several regiments on the way at their encampments and any amount of piquets. I did not

---

* Lacey L. Edwards, of Company G, was killed in action at Savage's Station.

† This was Private W. Walter Hipp. According to Wyckoff, he was the first man in his company to die.

‡ Captain Nunnamaker led Company H of the 3rd S.C.

§ Dickert, *History of Kershaw's Brigade*, 46.

¶ Everson and Simpson, *Far, Far from Home*, 23.

** Wyckoff, *Third South Carolina*, 19.

have to march all of the way. Uncle Anthony & Mr. Sims hired a two horse waggon for themselves and I rode a part of the way with them. Our regiment will now be the advance regiment & we feel proud of our place, as we regard it a great [. . .] over pickens, who has done all he could [. . .] in the dark from the beginning. There a crowd of troops around here Col Kershaws and Col. Cashs* regiments are very near us also some artillery and Virginia Cavalry. Genl Boreguard seems to be moving his forces in this direction as soon as he can. The nearest posts of the enemy are 8 miles from us which is quite near. We are now in a few yards of the place where Capt Marr† was killed in the engagement which took place here some time since. Although we are very near the enemy I have no idea that we will have a fight soon. Davis will not fight until he sees the presidents message. There may in the near time be little skirmishes between the cavalry shouts but they will not amount to much. Many think that congress will not sustain Lincoln and the war will end. I think the chances for peace are very good. The main body of the enemies troops are stationed farther on some 16 miles at Alexandria. On day before yesterday 6 Virginia soldiers encountered 56 of Lincolns. The sit[e] we reinforced by 8 more & that fourteen killed 17 of the 56 wounded several and put the rest to flight. The enemy captured two Lt of the Virg cavalry this evening. They [. . .] with a strong force of infantry. [. . .] made their escape. Two more [. . .] did not get in until late Thursday.

I have met a good many of my friends since I got here I have not yet seen any of our relations Will try later in the morning.

Uncle Anthony says to be remembered to you and says that if these Yankees don't kill him he may come by with us and see you all when the war is over. If you do not hear from us so afterward you need not be surprised. Manassas Junction will still be our post office and it is 15 miles off. I have nothing more of interest to write. Remember me to all. Yr affec Brother L. P. Foster

N.B. Still direct to Manassas Junction

L. P. FOSTER TO HIS MOTHER

Fairfax C.H.
July 1st 1861

My Dear Mother

I have sent one letter home this morning but write again to caution you from telling any thing that I have written or may write from being published or getting where it may get in papers as I have written very unreservedly about our affairs

---

* Col. E. B. C. Cash of the 8th S.C.

† Capt. John Q. Marr, Co. K (Warrenton Rifles), Seventeenth Virginia Infantry, was killed in a skirmish at Fairfax Court House on June 1, 1861.

& would be cashered* should anything get out. A youn[g] man here wrote to the editor of the Mercury† about our matters and genl Boreguard threatened to hang him if he could find him out. Remember me to all & write soon directing to Manassas. I fear that our writing will be stopped from the imprudent act of that young man.

Yr affec Son L. P. Foster

The following letter includes an account of a Union soldier. And it is worth noting an enslaved person who was given the soldier's arms as a reward. Perhaps more remarkable to the modern reader is that he was walking around armed with a pistol in the first place, and there is not the first hint that there was anything unusual about that. The relationships between Civil War–era Southern blacks and whites were more varied and complex than has often been portrayed.

L. P. FOSTER TO HIS MOTHER
───────────

[July 1861]‡
Advance Forces Army of the Potomac
Fairfax C.H.

My Dear Mother

I rec'd your letter yesterday & Father rec'd on this morning. Why you do not get our letters I can not tell. One or the other of us writes every mail which is almost every day. I was glad to hear you were all well. To§ did right in refusing to merge his Comp with Farrows.¶ Tell him to stick to it. What are his intentions about the matter. Is his comp forming merely for drill or immediate service. In either case I could give him much advise which would benefit him as I know something about men. & tactics and an officer must know both well or he can do nothing at all. Tell him to send me 4 swords instead of two. The additional ones are for Cap't Kennedy & Lt. R. M. Smith.** Tell him to use as much haste as possible and get me one that

---

* Cashiered: dismissed from service, typically dishonorably.

† The *Charleston Mercury.*

‡ This letter is undated but from the content and address, it was probably written in July 1861.

§ James Anthony "Tony" Foster, Lewis Perrin Foster's brother.

¶ Major T. Stobo Farrow of the 13th S.C.

** Lt. Robert M. Smith of Co. K, 3rd S.C. Frequently referred to as Dr. Robert Smith. He studied medicine under Dr. Gideon H. King of Walnut Grove, South Carolina, and graduated from the Atlanta Medical College. Discharged due to illness, he later joined the 2nd Regiment S.C. Cavalry. He lost his right arm at the shoulder due to a wound suffered at the battle on John's Island, South Carolina, in 1864. Landrum, *History of Spartanburg County,* 281.

is good marking my name on a cord attached to it. Please make a cover for mine. He can put them in a very small box and send them to Columbia by some one who can send them by Adams* express to Father's address. I have no news to write. We are ready to receive the enemy in whatever manner or direction they may come. Some think they will advance others that they will not. It is hard for me to think that an enemy in whose courage I have not the slightest confidence who never yet have stood the swords from our men will advance upon us at such a place as this. Yet I can not tell what a day may bring to light. I only wish they may come if they intend to fight us at all. As I think we can interest them a while here. I have just returned from blockading so[me] roads. I have not rested a Sunday since I left So. Ca. I have not worked from choice but from necessity. We have preaching this evening. If I am not called up on duty I intend hearing it. It will be the first sermon I have heard since I left Columbia, not having had an opportunity. It is true that we are in advance of the other reg's but have not changed our position and the farthest regiment of our brigade is not much more than ½ a mile from us. So you need not be uneasy about us on that account. The long roll can call all to any one camp. Tell Tony that John W. W.† says I owe him a puppy. When we left Richmond we left Christopher Burch very sick with typhoid. Fever. We have heard that he is dead and I suppose it must be true. We regret very much to loose him & sympathize with his relations. I don't [know] whether he was buried at Richmond or sent home. None of us could be there to see about him being near 200 miles from him. Dick Gist‡ is here in our tent now. Uncle Anthony had toothache yesterday for the first time in his life. He had it pulled. I suppose Carries Old Man did not come the night of the wedding but made the trip the next day. I expect she had a lonesome night. A Negro belonging to a soldier of gen'l Johnsons Division captured a yankee armed with an Enfield rifle, pr pistols & knife. The Negro had a pistol. The Negro ordered him to ground arms which he did and then marched him to his master. They even tried to get him to take him to the guard house but he said his master must have him. They gave the Negro the arms and it is said he is quite a lion in the camp. Father is field officer of the day today.

Will Orrs reg§ come on? Can they get arms for it. If it comes uncle Tony will come with it. The climate is much cooler than ours. I have very little use for summer clothes. It is always cold enough at night for a soldier to sleep under one blanket & I suppose you all would have three over you.

---

* Adams and Co. was a shipping company in Columbia, South Carolina.
† Probably John Wesley Wofford in Co. K, 3rd S.C.
‡ Richard Valerius Gist of Col. Micah Jenkins's 5th S.C.
§ Orr's First South Carolina Rifles.

Remember me to all the family & enquiring friends. Write often.

yr affec Son

L. P. Foster

L. P. FOSTER TO HIS MOTHER

Advance Forces Army of the Potomac, Fairfax C.H.
July 6th 1861

My Dear Mother,

As Father wrote yesterday I scarcely know what to write. Sam Means* & Mr. Renwick came here this morning and joined our Comp. Does Ed say anything of coming. When I left home I thought he would be with us soon. I meet a great many of my old friends here. Our relations were well when I saw them last. Our piquets members of Capt Davidsons† comp have just sent in a prisoner—an Irish soldier & I suppose a deserter from the way he talks. The piquets of Capt. Walkers‡ comp took a finely mounted trooper day before yesterday who had been in the service for 10 years. He pretended to be a deserter. We have not drilled any since we came here but have been busy throwing up breast works. Our men work hard and cheerfully and will soon have our camp well fortified. You would be astonished to see the work they have done in the last three days. I was on piquet guard the other night was pretty near the enemies camp but I saw no one. When I sleep soundly not more than 2 or 3 miles from their out posts but with my sword and pistol on my side & gun in my arms. Col Jackson a few days since attacked Cadwalladers§ column of 15000 men at Sheperdstown with between one & three thousand men. He killed 50 took 75 prisoners and lost none. Since then gen'l Johnston has attacked the same column at Martinsburg with 15,000 men.¶ We do not know the particulars,

---

* Sam Means is frequently mentioned in the Foster letters, usually in context of obtaining and delivering uniforms and other supplies to members of the 3rd S.C. This is believed to be Samuel Clowney Means.

† Capt. Samuel N. Davidson of Co. B, 3rd S.C.

‡ Capt. Tandy Walker of Co. F, 3rd S.C.

§ Foster refers to Jackson's sharp skirmish at Falling Waters or Hoke's Run on July 2 and Johnston's movements at Martinsburg on July 3. Gen. George Cadwalader US Army advanced into the Shenandoah through Harpers Ferry in July 4. The Federals under Brig. Gen. Robert Patterson intended to keep Gen. Joseph E. Johnston's forces occupied in western Virginia during the upcoming attack on Manassas Junction. Johnston intended to keep the Federals in the Shenandoah Valley and maintain his ability to move quickly to Manassas to help counter a Federal attack there.

¶ Davis, *Battle at Bull Run*, 84–85.

but know that he achieved a brilliant victory. There is a report here which we are disposed to credit, that he has taken Cadwallader & 600 men prisoners and has the others surrounded. It may not be so, but seems to meet with credence. When I last wrote I did not think there would be any fighting soon for I did not think the enemy would advance upon us & I saw that our authorities were waiting for the U.S. Congress to extend to their same friendly morsel, but day before yesterday their forces at Falls Church advanced two miles nearer as for some reason or other & now the chances for a fight are good unless the[y] are taken with their usual running fit. They are said to be 4 or 5 thousand strong and it is folly for them to come here with any such force unless they just wish to throw themselves in our power. Yesterday many thought the day of battle had come. An old citizen followed by several couriers came in and reported that one of our piquet guards had been attacked. No one seemed at all excited but went to fixing their arms with great deliberation. We were not called out. You can not excite Col. Williams. He sent some men out to see what was the matter. Some cowardly Yankees had slipped up on our advance piquet and shot at him from a thicket 4 or 5 times. They did not hurt him but shot a hole through his hat. He thought they were in 15 or 20 paces of him but could not see them owing to the thick bushes. They made their appearance no more. I went to sleep last night and slept all night, but would not have been surprised to have heard our drum at any moment. Our piquets give no account of their advancing any further. I hear that our friends in Spartanburg are expecting us to be cut all to pieces—such friends know nothing of our strength. Believe nothing that you see in the news papers. The editors can not get any thing from the army for if a volunteer were to permit any thing which he might write concerning our army to be made public he would be hanged. So don't believe them and don't expose my letters. We are all in fine spirits & feel confident of success should an engagement take place which is very uncertain. Remember me to all. The boys of our neighborhood all well. Write soon.

Yr affec Son
L. P. Foster

L. P. FOSTER TO HIS MOTHER

Advance Forces, Army of the Potomac, Fairfax C.H.
July 8th, 1861

My Dear Mother,

I have not time to write much as I have to go on the village guard tonight & it is now late. I am afraid that I alarmed you unnecessarily in my last letter. When I wrote it I thought the time of fighting was about come. Was sleeping several nights with my clothes on & arms by my side, but will not be so easily fooled hereafter. I have learned to take false alarms cooly and to make allowances for the excitement of men. The yankees have not advanced on us any more. It is now very doubtful whether they even advanced at all or not. I am now doubting whether there will be any fight here or not. We are getting most too many men here and most too well prepared for them yet they may come. When they practice in Alexandria or on Arlington heights we can hear every cannon distinctly. I was on pickett yesterday, we got a good race after a yankee, but the woods being very dense, he got away from us. I saw Lincoln's message yesterday, a lady brought some papers down from Alexandria to some of the brig soldiers under her clothes. We have nothing to hope from it. He calls for 400,000 men and four hundred millions dollars. Says states cannot remain neutral, which we hope will drive Kentucky, Maryland, and Missouri out of the union. It is merely a scare crow to frighten weak minded men. He can neither raise the men or money. I have heard nothing from Johnsons* command since I wrote. Some think he has had a fight & some think not. Believe nothing you see in the news papers. We cannot even get the truth here from our couriers. They lie to you for nothing. So be quiet!

I meet some old friends every day and this place seems now more to me like S.C. than Virg. from the fact that I meet so many friends from the former state. Send us some Spartanburg papers some times. We never see ours at all. We are all well. Remember us to the family and write soon.

Yr Affec Son,

L. P. Foster

B. B. Foster to His Daughter, Probably Sallie

Army of the Potomac
Fair Fax Court House Virginia
July 9th 1861

My Dear Daughter

I received a letter from your mother and Perrin received one from you yesterday. I assure you I felt relieved. I have no doubt you will get ours we write regularly. When we receive them they come all together and you will probably get them in the same way. it must be the neglect of post masters. If you all knew how we enjoyed ourselves here you would not be uneasy about us. we live rough but have plenty of it for instance yesterday our Brigadier and his staff eat with us we have mutton chickens molasses & coffee Mid is the cook and a right good one at that. it is true

---

* This may refer to Joseph E. Johnston's action at Harpers Ferry. Johnston evacuated Harpers Ferry on June 15, considering the town indefensible. His deceptive movements kept Patterson's force from playing a role at Manassas.

that we are in an enemies country. and have a strong force to contend with, yet we feel about as secure as if we were at home we think they are afraid to attack us. and if they do we are prepared to receive them our fortifications will be completed this evening and they are very strong. behind them there is but little danger. our men all seem to be anxious for a fight. occasionally our pickets have some skirmishing with them but they will not stand a fire They run every time I think however in a large body they would fight, If I had you all out here I would rather be here than not in this part of the country there is nothing to attract attention but the army. I have not been in a house since I came here they are yankees mostly but few native virginians. I hope you will all enjoy yourselves at home and suffer no uneasiness about us we are not in the hands of our enemies. The God of Battles governs all things I have confidence to believe we are engaged in a glorious cause & that we will be sustained. I have nothing to regret by coming here. I think I done right. I want to warn you not to pay any attention to anything you see published in the papers They scarcely ever publish the truth especially the telegraph dispatches. There is no confidence in them I feel sure of that. I saw the carolinians saying the big battle was to be fought here the fourth of July Instead of a battle it was as quiet a day as we have had since we left home nothing like a fight. your uncle Anthony is here as active as a ten year old boy tell Mr Harmon he must do the best he can for me tell your brother Tony he must help him all he can, tell Jennie* she must learn her book and take good care of the sheep. all the boys Johny Jimy Beard Henry Barnett† Lancaster the Smith‡ boys are well and making fine soldiers Kenedys company is a bragg company remember me to your mother & sisters and Tony and all the neighbors may God bless & preserve you all

B B Foster

The engagement at Big Bethel Church described in the letter below was a very small engagement by later standards, but was the first significant infantry combat. On the lower end of the Virginia Peninsula, near the Federal Fort Monroe, Confederates built an artillery battery near the Big Bethel Church. On June 10, the Federals under Brig. Gen. Ebenezer Pierce launched an attack by 2400 men against a defending force of 1200 led by Col. John Magruder. The planned, coordinated attack of four separate regiments failed in execution and the result was a rout of the attacking Federals. The

---

* His youngest daughter, Jane Eliza, then nine years old.

† William Henry Barnett was in Kennedy's Co. K. He died in Richmond in 1863 of disease.

‡ Probably A. S. Smith, Benjamin. M. Smith, and Elijah F. Smith; all in Co. K. Benjamin M. Smith died of disease in Richmond in 1862. The other two survived the war. There is some confusion on Elijah Smith's middle initial. Dickert and Landrum say it is an "F." Wyckoff says it is an "E."

humiliation of this defeat contributed to the Union pressure to quickly launch a major offensive against the Confederates at Manassas.

L. P. Foster to His Brother

Advance Forces Army of the Potomac Fairfax C.H.
July 11, 1861

Dear Brother

Father wrote home yesterday & I suppose gave you all the news. We are just here in a state of suspense waiting for our enemy to attack us who are too cowardly to advance on us. The[y] have to get a new set of men and officers & more of them before they can carry on an aggressive war. The men they now have are too much cowed. Their officers are not fitted for their places. In the fight which took place at Bethel some time since they used every kind of ammo known in this country for 2 ½ hrs and hurt but one man & he would not have been hurt they not shot off a limb from a tree which fell on him which shows they are neither shots nor tacticians.

Our army is well drilled and equal to any in the world. We are now strongly fortified here and ready for them. Every thing seems to be waiting for the start of a battle which we think is soon be tried between the Federal Genl's Cadwalader & patterson & our genl Johnson* at Winchester. What a day may bring forth we can not tell but feel that we are prepared for any thing. Our piquets catch a stragler every now and then. Our men are in fine spirits & anxious for a fight. How are my puppies? What kind of a one did you save for me & yourself? Are there any left?

We hear through Elijah Smith that you fellows are raising a company. I suppose ready for drill. If you are, drill from the start by Hardee.† We have drilled by Hardee since we got in the C.S.A. Write to me about it & I can give you much usefull information. If you get an office see to one thing. That your non commissioned officers are well selected much depends on them & most of all on the C. Sergt. He should be a good scribe and as good an officer as the Capt. I suppose your company have a notion of joining the army. I think the quota of S.C. is here but if you should think of such a thing let me know it before you tender yr comp. If you have an opportunity send me two large swords like Fathers select a good one for me short pretty short and heavy grind it well about half way down. If you can not get a chance to send it here get some one to take them from Spartanburg & deliver them to the agent of the Adams & Co. express in Columbia to be sent to me at Manassas. Let

* General Joseph E. Johnston.

† Hardee's Rifle and Light Infantry Tactics by William Joseph Hardee was a common military reference manual at the time.

them send to Lieut Col. B. B. Foster 3rd Reg. S.C.V. Manassas Junction Virg as they will be apter to come to him than to me. Use haste if possible. One like Fathers will do but I prefer a shorter one. No news to write.

Remember me to all & tell Ed either to write to me & come on. I have written to him twice.

Yr affec Brother

L. P. Foster

The other sword is for John Col[e].* He is layed up now with a carbuncle on the hip. Select good blades.

B. B. FOSTER TO HIS WIFE
_____

Army of the Potomac
Fairfax Court House
July 12th 1861

My Dear Wife

I write so often that I hardly know what to write about. We have been looking for old Abe to send down his forces uppon us here until we have almost given him out. and no fight yet. Our men have some little skirmishing. I mean the advanced pickets. almost every day we bag some of them. One of Capt Garlingtons men had a hole shot through his hat a few days ago whilst he was searching a thicket that is the nearest they have come to getting any of our men. We are now in fine condition for a fight our fortifications are all complete the cannons planted and all the embankments prepared for our men to stand behind and fight and I do believe that they need not come unless they bring about fifteen to twenty to one our men have worked hard and have thrown up works that will save them from almost any force. I now think that we will have to fight. There is no hope from the Northern congress and think as we have it to do the sooner the better our Regiment is all anxious for the fray and I believe they will stand and make a glorious fight. I am afraid that Christopher Birch is dead we left him in the hospital sick the surgeon wrote to Kendy† that he thought he would not live a day This is the last we have heard from him. Our Regiment is in good health some sick of course but not one of our neighbors sons except J. Y. Worford‡ he has a carbuncle but is mending

I feel confident in all the providence of our heavenly Father that we will be victorious and hand down to our children the glorious liberty which was entrusted to us by our fathers remember me kindly to the children all the neighbors. Montgomerys

---

* John A. Cole of Co. B, 3rd S.C.

† Benjamin Kennedy, Captain of Co. K.

‡ J. Y. Wofford of Co. K, 3rd S.C.

Bobo Lancaster & may the lord preserve you all is my prayer your affectionate husband

B.B. Foster

L. P. FOSTER TO HIS SISTER, EUNICE

Advance Forces, Army of the Potomac
Fairfax C. H.
July 14th 1861

My Dear Sister

I wrote to you a few days since, but have rec'd no answer from you as yet. I have but little news to communicate. We are now ready for the yankees & will interest them better than they have been interested lately. We can give them a good fight let them [come] in any way or manner. Some think they are coming down on us some of these days, but it is hard for me to think that our enemy in whose courage I have no confidence will advance on us at such a place as this. I only wish they would come. If they would we would learn them a lesson they would never forget. I have been on a working party to day blockading some roads. I have not rested a Sunday since I left S.C. I have not worked from choice but from necessity. I have not heard a sermon since I left So. Ca. Our chaplain preaches this evening and I shall hear him if I am not called off on duty. Our guard and working is very heavy now but I am able to stand it. I think I am as well now as I ever was & do not lack much of being as heavy. Father is Field Officer of the day to day. A negro over a[t] Winchester belonging to a soldier in Gen'l Johnson's division captured a yankee soldier having an enfield rifle, pr pistols and knife. The negro had a pistol. He carried him to his master. They tried to get him to take him to the guard house, but he said his master must have him. They gave the negro his arms and he is quite a lion in the camp now.

I suppose you had a fine time at Carries wedding, I hear her old man did not come on the night appointed, but had the thing fixed up the next day. He must be a slow coach or he would have come at the appointed time. I [have] no more to write & not much time. I have merely written to let you know we are well. Don't believe the reports you see in the papers.

My respects to my friends.
Your affec Brother,
L P Foster

"Forward to Richmond! Forward to Richmond!" chanted Horace Greeley's New York Tribune, reflecting, or perhaps creating, the mounting pressure on the Federals to quickly move against the Confederacy. The rising calls to march against Richmond, the

apparent impunity with which the Confederacy was creating itself, the sting of the rout at Big Bethel Church, the highly publicized killing of Col. Elmer Ellsworth* when he cut down the Confederate flag at a tavern in Alexandria all contributed to a demand that decisive military action be taken quickly against the Rebels.

In July, Gen. Irvin McDowell commanded 40,000 Union soldiers near Washington. Across the Potomac, eight miles along the banks of Bull Run, General Beauregard had about 25,000 available men. Gen. Joe Johnston had an additional 10,000 Confederates in the Shenandoah Valley facing 14,000 Federals under Gen. Robert Patterson. McDowell's objective was to take the railroad junction at Manassas, cutting off a critical rail link to Confederate forces in the Shenandoah and positioning the Federal army for movement against Richmond. To maintain his advantage in numbers, he needed Patterson to keep Johnston's army occupied in the Shenandoah and unable to assist Beauregard. The Federal battle plan was to march from Arlington through Fairfax and Centerville† along the Warrenton Turnpike and engage the Confederates at a weak point along Bull Run.

Beauregard established his defensive line along Bull Run, concentrating his defenses at fords and bridges along the steep-banked creek. His left flank was positioned at Sudley Ford. His center was at Mitchell's Ford. Blackburn's Ford, about a mile to the right, was heavily defended. The right flank was anchored at McLean's Ford. Most of Beauregard's forces were massed on his right flank so that when the Federals attacked, he could launch a wheeling attack by the Confederate right on the Union left flank.

On July 17th, McDowell's Federals advanced in force on Fairfax Court House from the East on Flint Hill Road, nearly cutting off and capturing Foster's company on picket at a barricade on the Alexandria Road several miles in advance of Fairfax.‡ The picket companies returned quickly to the Confederate forces at Fairfax and retreated to Mitchell's Ford on Bull Run.

The following day, McDowell sent reconnaissance forces toward Blackburn's Ford that were heavily engaged and repulsed by James Longstreet's forces positioned there. Heavy skirmishing also took place at Mitchell's Ford where the 3rd S.C. was positioned. The heavy fighting revealed that the Confederates were positioned at these fords in considerable force, causing McDowell to revise his plans to cross Bull Run at Sudley Springs Ford and to attack Beauregard's left flank. The first major battle of the Civil War was about to begin.

---

* In April 1861 Elmer Ellsworth raised the 11th New York Volunteer Infantry Regiment, calling them the Fire Zouaves because they were recruited from New York firefighting volunteers. Zouave units in the Civil War wore distinctive uniforms based on the uniforms of the French Zouaves in North Africa.

† Later Centreville.

‡ Wyckoff, *Third South Carolina*, 22.

L. P. Foster to His Mother

July 19th 1861
Bulls Run Near Manassas Junction

My Dear Mother

I snatch a moment to write you a few lines. As I know that after our last two days work many false reports will reach you. The enemy advanced on Fairfax day before yesterday morning about 10,000 strong as we supposed. Our comp was 4 miles in advance of our camp on piquet duty and came very near being cut off before we could reach the camp had to double quick most of the way 3 or 4 thousand came in the road not two minutes after we past. When we got to our reg. I was thrown in to line of battle. No one seemed at all excited, although we could see their lines plainly extending for miles, but our genls seeing they were about to come in our own rear and cut us off and as I believe it being a scheme of Bouregard to draw them here, ordered a retreat. Our men obeyed most reluctantly. I never hated any thing worse, yet know it was for the best. Some then came to me and said they would rather die than retreat. We retreated in perfect order to this place in quick and double quick time which being a march of 15 or 16 miles was hard on our comp. Some of them threw their knapsacks away but all made the trip. I stood it I think as well or better than any man in the comp. Had my gun and accoutrements on. They advanced on us yesterday morning here & we soon saw the Elephant.* Our men open first with the artillery about 1 o clock which they continued for several hrs when they tried to force our lines. Our men repulsed them and threw them in confusion with great loss. We know not how many of the enemy were killed, but know that over one hundred were killed & think from the continuous work of the waggons hauling off the dead that their loss was great. Our loss was 8 killed No So. Ca. was hurt. No S.C. regiment was in it but Kershaws & it but a short time. The attack was not our posts. They threw several shells pretty near us. Our men stood the music finely. We are all now with heads up ready for them, have a fine place & have no doubt about whipping them if they come which we are not certain of as they were out of sight yesterday evening. We have had but 4 or 5 reg engaged yet. I could write you many interesting things about the battle if I had time. Father and I are well. Our neighbors are all safe and unhurt and ready for a fight. We are in fine spirits and doubt nothing. I know our cause is just & god will be with us. He has been with us and has protected us. To 12 o clock last night I had not slept two hours since Tuesday nights but we slept from that time to night and till Friday this noon. Do not doubt our success. If you could be here & see with determination the countenances of our men are stamped you would not. You must think that god is

* To "see the elephant" was a Civil War expression meaning to experience a battle.

with us. Let Mr. Smith William Beards* mother as well as all our mens neighbors who have children here know what I have written about them. We will do our duty. Remember me to all the family and friends. Yr affec Son

L. P. Foster

This note was included with L. P. Foster's letter of July 19, 1861, probably from Sallie to Eunice. It was obviously added after the Battle of First Manassas on July 21.

My Dear Sister

This is the last account we have had from Brother and Father. R. V. Gist telegraphed to Columbia that the 3rd Regiment was entirely safe and as he belongs to that Regiment I believe the dispatch correct. You have heard no doubt of the great and glorious victory of the Confederacy at Manassas. There is great rejoicing here but great anxiety to hear particularly about our friends. We are all well. Nothing here.

Your Devoted Sister

L. P. Foster to His Mother

Bulls Run 3 miles from Manassas Junction
July 20th 1861

My Dear Mother

I wrote to you yesterday telling you how we came here also of the battle on Thursday.† We are here yet the enemy have not advanced on us. We are here awaiting their approach but I don't much think they will come on us here again. They have gone out of sight. Our piquets have had several little fights since I wrote in which we have always whipped them and never lost but one man a Louisianian killed by his own comp. The amount of our loss which I gave you was correct but the loss of the enemy must have been 5 or 6 times as great as I gave—as late as yesterday evening there were seventy of their dead bodies on the field. No one can tell what number they lost but they must have lost a very large number for the force in action, I would say between 500 and 1000 many say the latter number. Our men captured two of their cannons which they spiked and left on the field. They also hauled away many loads of guns, knapsacks, coats and other baggage. We have taken a good many prisoners. I can not tell how many. A Negro belonging to one of the Louisianian regiments took an officer prisoner yesterday. He came along the road with him waving his handkerchief. We are all well & in the finest of spirits &

---

* William F. Beard, Company A, 3rd S.C.

† Battle of Blackburn's Ford, July 18th, 1861. About 83 Federals and about 68 Confederates died there.

confident of success not matter what may turn up. I can only say we are all ready & will whip them if they come. The day in which they come will be memorable.

Some of the men have just come from the battle field with a load of baggage among other things a letter describing the hard times of friends at home & a ladies ambrotype. I have not been on the field of carnage. I have not had time to leave my comp nor have I had much anxiety to see it. I have writing conveniences here. All of our baggage is off with our Q.M. We have a regular soldiers life now. Sleep on our arms in line of battle. Father is well. Remember me to all. Tell our neighbors their relations are well. Write to us.

Yr affec Son

L. P. Foster

The next letters describe the aftermath of the devastating Union defeat at First Manassas on July 21, 1861. The Union attack across Bull Run Creek took place at three locations. On the left end of the Confederate line, the Union forces crossed Sudley Ford, meeting Confederate forces at Matthews Hill. The center attack took place at the famous Stone Bridge along the Warrenton Turnpike. The attack on the Confederate right took place late in the day at Blackburn's Ford. The Confederate cavalry commander, Colonel Jeb Stuart, was able to keep Patterson confused and occupied in the Shenandoah, allowing Johnston's 10,000 soldiers to join Beauregard's defensive forces at Bull Run. With forces more evenly matched and the Confederates able to fight from a defensive position, the inexperienced Confederate boys defeated the likewise-inexperienced Federal boys on Henry Hill. The retreating Union soldiers found themselves in a traffic jam at the bridge over Cub Run as the army supply wagons became entangled with the wagons of sightseeing Washingtonians. Feeling trapped between this jumble of wagons on the bridge and the victorious rebels, the retreat became a panicked rout, equipment was tossed aside, and soldiers fled toward the safety of Washington. The Federals finally established defensive positions at the bridges leading across the Potomac as tired, dirty, disorganized, whipped troops flooded into the streets of Washington. The Union army suffered 2,896 killed, wounded, or captured; the Confederates suffered 1,982 casualties.

Foster's Third South Carolina was positioned perhaps ¼ mile west of Mitchell's Ford along Bull Run, Mitchell's Ford being about ¾ mile to the west of Blackburn's Ford. The 3rd S.C. saw only minor fighting during this battle, mostly in receiving diversionary fire. At 5:00 p.m. on the 21st, the 3rd S.C. crossed Bull Run at Mitchell's Ford following the Union retreat along a ravine to the left of the road between Mitchell's Ford and Centreville. The regiment was ordered to return that evening to their fortified positions along Bull Run. The next day, the regiment was ordered to advance and collect abandoned munitions, returning to their original positions on July 22.*

---

* Wyckoff, *Third South Carolina*, 24–25.

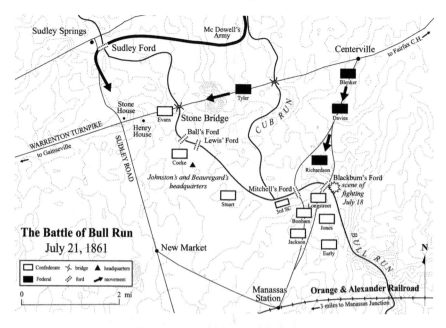

The Battle of Bull Run, July 21, 1861.

B. B. FOSTER TO HIS WIFE

Sunday, July 21st, 1861
My Dear Wife

This letter as you see is written in yankee paper. This has been a glorious day for southern troops this morning Sunday we were attacked at Bulls Run by fifty thousand of Abes troops and after six hours hard fighting almost without cessation both with cannon and small arms we routed them horse foot and dragoon killing thousands of them taking 42 of their cannon and lots of prisoners we pursued them miles until dark Our men mustered down and returned to camps it is impossible to tell but it is believed that five to six thousand of them have been killed or wounded

Thursday was the first battle* we whipped them then badly we lost 8 killed and almost 40 wounded. This morning they came reinforced and we ruined them Bull Run has been a dear place for them. Our loss was severe today No one knows precisely I would suppose at least three hundred killed and five hundred wounded Our regiment was held in the works until late in the evening We were ordered to leave the works and charge the enemy They fled before us and we could not get near enough to fire upon them we to[ok] a good many [prisoners] they left waggon

---

* The Battle of Blackburn's Ford on July 18, 1861.

loads of blankets oil cloths sugar coffee and hospital stores They threw shell at us in the works all day but it so turned out that not a man in our regiment was hurt or touched I feel thankful to god that this grand army after two days fighting has been routed and cut up our boys are all well send word all around that their people may know they are well and unhurt No such a battle has ever been fought on this continent before We only had about 20,000 men in the fight They played uppon us with their rifled cannon and mortars from 9 oclock until ½ passed five They were driven by a charge of the Infantry They could not stand still. I am well and hearty gaining flesh fast and Perrin has mended beyond all expectations He is within seven pounds of his heaviest weight Anthony is well remember me to my dear children and my neighbors allow nothing to be published that I have written May god bless and preserve you all Write to me often and account of the farm place that green hay [. . .] made of the yanky that [. . .] toward [. . .] pasture [. . .] purpose [. . .] to receive them. I think we will have peace awhile until they can collect another army

your affectionate
Husband B.B.F

L. P. FOSTER TO HIS MOTHER

Bull Run Near Manassas Junction
July 22nd 61

My Dear Mother

The great battle Waterloo of the Western Continent had been fought. The army of the Federals [. . .] routed and driven beyond the Potomac in the wildest confrontation. God has given us a victory which will occupy many pages of future history and strike wonder in many a mind. Not one of the 3rd reg has been touched. I wrote to [you] the other day giving you an account of the battle fought on Thursday* in which the Enemy tried to force our right wing the account which I gave was correct except the enemies loss was much greater than I thought, being about 970 men. On Sunday morning activated by an unholy and ferocious design having been reinforced by Patersons† division of 30,000 men & 20,000 from Washington under gen'l Scott in person. They tried to force our left wing which was at first weak. About 7 oclock they opened a heavy cannon fire on our whole line from the hills a mile and a half off. A great many shell along our lines but hurt none of our reg. Several fell very near me and one exploded in 15 steps of me. They also shot

---

* The Battle of Blackburn's Ford on July 18, 1861.

† Union Major General Robert Patterson failed to keep Joseph Johnston's forces occupied in the Shenandoah; their arrival at Manassas was a key element of the Confederate victory there.

many rifle cannon balls. The shell made such an awful noise that our men at first pretty quiet and dodged them but soon got used to the wushe and were very lively, but if I never hear another I shall always remember the sound. About 10 oclock [they] advanced on our left wing with almost their entire force & opened a most terrific [fire]. That point was then weak being defended principally by Col Hamptons Legion & Col Sloans reg. They stood returned the fire & repulsed the enemy joining bayonets with them until reinforcements came. They suffered very severely from the heavy cannon fire and the small arms. Col Hamp. loosing some 20 men & Col Sloan some 50. When the reinforcements came the battle was still more terrific. There being an incessant fire of musketry & cannon for near five hours. You can form no conception of it unless you had been here. At last the Enemy gave away loosing all their cannons & horses and leaving wound and dead, throwing away guns and knapsacks & in the wildest confusion. Many were killed in the flight. They tried to rally their men 4 or 5 times but failed and finaly beat the retreat to collect them in order but could get no one in ranks. Every one seeming to try to save his life. Our loss is estimated now at from 5 to 6 hundred killed and from 1000 to 1500 wounded. That of the Enemy by thousands—from 2 to 7 thousand killed & no estimate of the wounded. We took all their cannon 63 in number some 20,000 guns. Any quantity of blankets oil cloths and every thing which is taken with an army. [. . .] reg was given the post where all thought the Enemy would advance, but they [. . .] came near us and we were not allowed to leave it consequently did not fire a single gun. Col. Kershaws men were [. . .] of it & lost a few men. The virginians fought to the death. Never consider them cowardly again. Large details were all day yesterday taking the dead from the field burying & taking care of the wounded. The wounded of the enemy were still on the field last night suffering. Men who went on the field say the sight was awfull but could not be helped. Our regiment was detailed yesterday to pick up baggage on their retreat and I did not see the battlefield, but such a route of baggage of every kind I never saw & cannot describe. They seemed to throw every thing away. We all got plenty of provisions & feasted over good fires it being a very rainy day & got good oil cloths blankets & ct. I slept under yankee blankets last night. I am well. Father says he is as well as he has been in 10 years. So don't be uneasy & consider yr questions answered. I can not write any more as [. . .] some where immediately. Remember me to all. Several [. . .] prisoners of the Enemy [. . .] taken & they fled beyond the Potomac. None of ours been taken but escaped.

Yr affec Son L. P. Foster

As the Union forces retreated across the Potomac into Washington, the Confederate forces advanced toward the Union capital. On July 23, the 3rd S.C. advanced to Centreville; they marched through the night to the railroad station at Vienna on the 24th, *about halfway between Manassas and Alexandria.* The next day they settled into tearing up the track to prevent its use by the Federals. Soon the sky was blackened with the smoke from the burning heart pine and chestnut railroad ties.†*

L. P. Foster to His Brother, Tony Foster

Vienna, 9 miles from Alexandria
July 25th 1861

My dear Brother,

I have written you a good many things about the battle, and you will learn all from the papers before this reaches you. We left the scene of carnage day before yesterday evening. Marched almost all night got here yesterday morning sun up. When we left our men were not even done burying the enemies dead. They ran off and left all their dead and wounded. You cannot imagine the havoc of all kind of stores they left on the road we marched over it last night our men have not near taken care of all of them yet. It was the most complete rout I ever heard of the yankees are clean gone home near as. I did not go on the battle field. Father did and saw most awful sight he ever saw in his life. Men and horses lying in piles everywhere. It extended over 8 miles. As we came on night before last we found a dead horse and dead yankee 10 miles from the battle field. We have taken over twenty prisoners here and they are scattered all about trying to make their way back to Washington I merely write to let you know that father and I are perfectly well. What will be our next break I can tell. Mail about to start & no other chance quick to Manassas.

Yr affec Brother
L.P. Foster

L. P. Foster to His Sister, Probably Sallie

Advance Forces Army of the Potomac
Vienna 10 miles from Washington
July 27th 1861

My Dear Sister

I rec'd your letter day before yesterday. Was glad to hear that the health of the settlement was so good. We have much for which to be grateful. It seems to me more than any people ever had before. The victory at Bullrun seems to me to have been a special intercession of providence in our favour. How 15000 thousand troops could gain such a victory of an army the finest equipped & well drilled of such size as that of the enemy was I am not able to see. I [do] not mean to say that we had

---

* Everson and Simpson, *Far, Far from Home*, 37.
† Dickert, *History of Kershaw's Brigade*, 72.

only 15000 troops in our army but only that many engaged. The army of the enemy must numbered 100000 men of that number 60000 must have been engaged in the fight. The fight was an utter surprise to them. Their leaders had told them they would have no fight that the rebels would retreat before them and they would be retarded but a few hours at Manassas and proceed with the numerous crowd of fashionable ladies and gentlemen who followed them to Richmond & have a grand frolic. Our men knew it must be a death struggle and therefore prepared themselves to conquer or die. Our leaders Davis and Bouregard led their soldiers animated them and scorned to order them where they feared to go themselves while Scott remained at his camp. Bouregard had two horses shot from under him, lead Hamptons Legion after Col Hampton* was wounded & Lt. Col Johnson† killed in four successive charges. I will not enter details now. You have seen all in the papers before now. None of our friends hurt. John White‡ was wounded in the leg by a musket ball, also in the breast by a piece of shell both very slight. He is able to follow his regiment. His reg was not in the main fight but charged a battery on the right wing & took two pieces. From the clothes shoes guns ammunition and baggage of all kinds which they left behind them it must have been the finest equipped army that ever went into the field. Bill Roebuck§ in Col Hamptons legion was shot through the left arm and in the stomach, the ball not breaking the bone or entering the cavity of the stomach so his wound is not dangerous. It was done in the last charge. Nearly all of Ellsworths Zouaves were killed. They had red shirts and our men could see them well. After the fight the field was red with them. It is said that not more that 160 of them were saved. The Zouaves and regulars fought hard, very hard killed many of our men. They were the strength of their army. Shermans¶ men also fought bravely dying almost to a man around their cannons. The citizens here say they were several [days] passing through this place and most of them were wounded & without any gun, stragling through the woods enquiring for Arlington Heights. The amt of baggage of all kinds taken by our men is immense. We have taken a great many prisoners. They all say they never volunteered to invade Virginia but to protect Washington and were forced to come over the river. They are with some exceptions a horrid looking set. Intelligent men say the countenances of their men dead on the battle field were quite different from those of ours, theirs having a haggard look as of fear. When they were retreating citizens along the road

---

* Colonel Wade Hampton commanded a cavalry unit named Hampton's Legion.
† Lt. Col. B. J. Johnson of Hampton's Legion.
‡ John White—Possibly John Warren White of Company K (Spartan Rifles) in the 5th S.C.
§ Private W. P. Roebuck was in Company D of the Gist Rifles in the Hampton Legion. O. Lee Sturkey, *Hampton Legion Infantry C.S.A.* (Wilmington, N.C.: Broadfoot Publishing, 2008), 335.
¶ William Tecumseh Sherman.

say they were cursing Lincoln and Scott & swearing they would go home & remain there that they had been deceived by them.

The Battle field extended over some 8 miles of country & Father says was the most horrible spectacle he ever saw. Our men were not near done burying the enemies dead on Wednesday. They were digging wholes and throwing them in several in a grave. They could do no better as there was so many of them. It is said that 5 or 6 hundred horses were killed. Sam Means leaves here in a few days & goes through N.C. to get goods for our winter uniforms. When he gets home with it get mine. Get Lockwood to cut it & if you are busy to make it please. Make me two or three pants heavy and flannel drawers as many under shirts of same, as many other shirts of same woven soft worsted gray if you can get it. Don't be afraid of getting them two heavy casimir will not be too heavy. It is pretty cool here now 2 or 3 pr wool socks, my scarf & please nit me & pr of very long over socks & tell Tony to keep the whole shoe covered with leather enough to go over a No. 6 ½ shoe. Also a heavy pr leggings with buttons on sides. A long list I fear giving you much trouble but if I should have to stay here this winter I will need them & can not tell whether I will need them & can not get them here. Send them by Sam Means.

Remember me to the family and all my friends. Father is perfectly. He seems to be in as good health as he ever was but not quite so fleshy. Everyone looses their surplus flesh here. I had none and at or near my usual weight. I was very well. I rec'd a letter from Miss Babe Sims last night in which she said Miss Pattie Thornwell spoke of in high terms to your liking seems to be mutual. Tell Sam & John to write to me. Has Toney sent the swords I wrote for. Write soon

Yr affec son
L. P. Foster

Uncle Anthony begs to be remembered to all of you

As observed earlier, Confederate soldiers wanted to serve and fight with their friends and neighbors, not mixed together in units formed from conscripts. Lieutenant Colonel Foster advises Tony how he can exit South Carolina and enlist with his family in the 3rd S.C.

B. B. Foster to His Son, Tony Foster

Advanced Forces Army of the Potomac
Vienna Virginia July 30th 1861

My Dear Son

Yesterday we received letters one from your mother one from Sallie and one from Eunice. No one knows but me how delightful it is to receive a letter from the loved ones at home. I have no doubt but you have seen a full account of the late glorious victories of the southern troops over the yankees. It cannot be described as it really was. The route was complete, and the destruction awful. Sallie sent in her letter the proclimation of governor Pickens. I think situated as we are your first duty is to your mother and sisters but if a draft should occur I have no hesitation in saying that you are not to stand a draft but to apply to Bobo at the store for money to bear your expenses take the carrs to Columbia then take the Charlotte Road to Richmond. There obtain from the provo martial a pass to Manassas. There apply to general beaureguard for a pass to join the third Regiment (ours) take your chance with us. you will have to pass out of South Carolina as a citizen and not as a volunteer. I sincerely hope you will not have this to do. I think the full quota from our immediate family has been already furnished. I know something of war it is a hard life to live you could stand it and if I thought it was necessary to our success I would say come every one that could shoulder a gun. but we have already men enough to drive the yankees from confederate soil and that with but little loss, if well managed. if they had have attacked us on our front at Bull Run there would not have been enough of them left alive to have carried back the news and we would not have lost twenty men they possess low cunning mixed with a large portion of cowardice the regulars fought well and the Ellsworth Zouaves fought desperate nearly all of them were killed dead on the field I saw the Zouaves piled on one another on the field there was from eight to ten acres of land well spotted with them. our boys are all well as usual we left at centerville Henry Barnet at the hospital he had a cold not dangerous but not able for the march. When we will leave here I am not able to say. If it turns out that you had to come you must have a uniform coat two pair of pants two pair of drawers and two shirts a good hat and real good pair of thick soled water proof shoes. and bring no more you will not be allowed any more. two flannel shirts you can go into Kenedys company and serve the remaining of the 12 months and then be discharged with us tell Mr Norman* when he is done laying by to clean up the stubble land clear out the fence corners. The sixth of August I expect to be paid off If so I will send money home write soon

your father
B B Foster

The following letter was included in the envelope with the letter to his son on July 30, 1861.

B. B. FOSTER TO HIS WIFE.

My Dear Wife

I wrote to Eunice yesterday just before getting her letter let her know that I desire her to keep at school. The day before I wrote to Sallie to day to Tony. Samuel

---

* Mr. Jno. Norman—apparently a foreman on Foster's plantation.

Means leaves in the morning for home his business is to have the uniforms made for Kenedys company The boys have worn their uniforms badly the whole Regiment is to be uniformed alike field officers and all. I want Lockwood to make my coat. I prefer the white buttons if he can get them if not cut the yellow buttons from the old uniform and use them let him cut the pants I want two pair made and a vest of the same. I also want two flannel shirts and two pair drawers good coarse strong two pair of good cotton socks and get Mr Norman to put soles to my own socks and send them that is all I want. I had hoped that I would be able to come home but the order is against it and I cannot come we have routed the yankees completely and such destruction of an army has never been heard of on this continent they have fled in every direction I think we will have some rest for awhile now. Thousands of volunteers are daily pouring in from the south and west we have more than double the force now that we had when the great battle was fought The yankees had over one hundred thousand men and I am certain that we did not have more than twenty thousand men engaged in the fight all told we had more than that number twice told on the field but was not engaged only holding the breast works and held as the reserve when we were ordered out the yankees were in full flight and they pulled the string for Washington scattering everything as they went. I had no idea myself but it is supposed that the property they left behind which fell into our hands cost the old government at least from two to three millions of dollars we captured sixty two pieces of the first order of cannon twenty rifled cannon of the first order they threw shot and shell all along our line of breast works passing just over our heads and striking the embanks for six hours and strange to say not a man was hurt John Beard and Jimy are well and getting along very well they are fine boys. I hope the people will do up the uniforms for the blackstock company in first rate order the cloth will be sent. I expect to draw money the 6th of August if I do I will send you three hundred dollars remember me to the children Norman and the negroes and all my neighbors may god bless and preserve you all is my prayer

your affect. hus

B B Foster

P.S. I send Jenny a bible with a yankees name on it taken from the yankees or left by them in camp.

L. P. Foster to His Mother

Advance Forces Army of the Potomac Vienna
Aug 1st 1861

My Dear Mother

We have written to home to you every day or two since the fight but has been now nearly a week since we got a letter from any of you. With what we have written you and you have seen in the papers you have learned about the fight. Since then things have remained perfectly quiet. No enemy are near us & they are under their present strength & confusion afraid to come near us. Their out post are not far on this side of the chain bridge* if on this side at all, which doubtful. I was on pickett duty night before last in 5 miles of the Potomac & in hearing of the great falls of the Potomac, but not so near the chain bridge, the native Virginians out at our post were kind to us and sold us provisions and fruit very reasonably—good plumbs & some pretty good peaches were among the purchased articles. Whenever we strike a yankee born near we find one who will skin us our money is all they want. I got a Botimore paper of the 27th July out there & saw the yankee account of the battle. They have given a horrible account of the whole affair but pretty accurate. They say our men fought desperately not like men but demons. Theirs acted cowardly. That our strength and bravery can no longer be doubted. Scott and the cabinet have had a muss. Scott tendered his resignation but withdrew. Cammeron† resigned and such says report the northern mind is evidently much dampened out account of the battle. Instead of uniting them it has made their breaches widen, so that it seems to be doubtfull whether Scott can raise another army at all or not. Their congress is wrangling a[s] bad as ever. Their great cause of uneasiness seems to be that England will recognize our independence and their credit abroad and at home be ruined. What is to be the result of the whole affair I cannot say but think one thing certain. That is, that Scott is a man of too much ambition to allow the last act of his life to be one of ignominy if he can help himself—hence will make a death struggle if he can get the army & means. Where we are to go from here, when we are to leave what part we are to play in the game are all known to Gen'l Boreguard, & he keeps his own secrets.

We have lost some great and valuable men, but their lives were demanded in a great and holy cause. They were paid as the price of liberty and their names shall ever live in our memories as fresh as now. That they should have fallen in the first great battle seems sad but is not the part of a finite mind to judge of the means which god employs to accomplish his ends. It is not for us to say that it would have been better had their lives been spared, but we should thank god for the result leaving the means employed to his own wisdom. Several of my college friends were wounded, but not killed. Lieut Depass‡ with whom Sallie was acquainted of Col Kershaws reg was shot in the§ and his skull was badly fractured but even then had

---

* The Chain Bridge, located near the Little Falls of the Potomac, was one of the major bridge approaches across the Potomac between Virginia and Washington.

† Secretary of War Simon Cameron did not resign but was replaced in January 1862 by Edwin Stanton.

‡ W. J. DePass of Co. E. 2nd S.C.

§ The sentence is incomplete. Likely should read, " . . . was shot in the head and his skull badly fractured."

to be removed from the field by force. My old precepton prof Venable* was struck by three spent balls none hurting him. Many men in Kershaws reg were struck by spent balls, but none hurt by them. Mr. McMaster was struck in the mouth by one but not hurt. God was with us. Just as Kershaws regiment was leaving their trenches for the field of battle Mr. Monardy† their chaplain held prayer with each comp. The loss of that regiment was remarkably small. I wrote to you that Father had been sick. He was right sick with something cholic one day but has got better. Our relations are all well & safe. You need not be uneasy about Father. He had just such a spell as I have often seen him have at home. He is up and about, but we won't let him do duty yet. There is a good deal of measles in the army. Some in our regiment some in our camp we sent Sam Means home with instructions about our uniforms gave him a letter for you. All the letters we get bring cheering news. Farm the crops. Tell Tony to get me a black soft hat let it be high like one Ed Bobo had, a regular slouch.

No news. Mr Renwick will carry this.

Remember me to all & write soon.

Yr affec son,

L. P. Foster

P.S. Let the sock you send me be dark colored.

In the following letter, we see that Perrin Foster's mother was quite concerned. I have felt the same when my children have traveled to distant places and forgotten to contact me to say they arrived safely. Not much has changed in this regard.

L. P. Foster to His Brother

Advance Forces, Army of the Potomac
Vienna Aug 4th 1861

My Dear Brother

I wrote home yesterday and did not intend to write today but rec'd mothers letter giving us bricks for not telegraphing the effect of each musket or cannon

---

* Charles Scott Venable was a professor of Mathematics and Astronomy at South Carolina College in the years before the Civil War. He enlisted in the Confederate army and rose to rank of Lt. Colonel. He served as R. E. Lee's aide from 1862 until the surrender at Appomattox. Venable returned to teaching at the University of Virginia. He died in 1900 and is buried in the University Cemetery. Venable Hall at the University is named for him. Precepton, associated with precepts, is a term used in the study of logic. Edwin L. Green, *A History of the University of South Carolina* (Columbia, S.C.: The State Company, 1916), 66.

† Elias J. Meynardie was the chaplain of the 2nd S.C. from April 9, 1861–November 30, 1861. He was later assigned as chaplain of the 20th S.C. Mac Wyckoff, *A History of the Second South Carolina Infantry: 1861–65* (Wilmington, N.C.: Broadfoot Publishing, 2011), 541; Dickert, *History of Kershaw's Brigade*, 576.

shot during the engagement and concluded to write a few lines in our defense, the reasonableness of which you will see at once. While an engagement is going on every officer has his post if he leaves it he will surely be court marshaled. While an engagement is going on no one is allowed to send a dispatch and generally not wire a letter. After the engagement he has enough to do to employ all of his time, taking care of his men and the spoils. Now although we did not fire a gun at Bull-run yet we were being shot at all the time and had to stay right at our post after the battle. Sunday evening we were ordered to charge the reserve in front raised a yell and started but they run before we got in two miles of them. We were until late at night getting back to our camp, but when we got there we sent Gist off to Manassas to telegraph home that all were safe. You see we were 4 miles from the telegraph. You say that Father should always put his name to the dispatch. If he were to do so without permission of the gen'l command he would be very apt to be court marshaled. If every man in such times were allowed to telegraph what a medley of confusion would exist. What chance would there be to get near the tele-graph office. You see that every man in a battle has his post and must stay at it. It is strange what ideas folks have of it. They write to know about particular friends as if we could tell immediately all about them. Now you will immediately see how absurd this is when I tell you line on the day of the fight was 7 or 8 miles in length. It is hard even to tell who falls in your comp until after the battle where your role is called your missing looked after. We are now 20 miles from any telegraph in our possession. I think you all were bent on some of us getting killed and it took about 20 confirmations to give any credit to a dispatch. Now just here after let the Yankees kill us before you write our obituary and be sure you don't have us dead before we are for we are pretty hard to hit now having practiced charging for two days. I have no news to write except what you get in the papers. You know nearly as much about the army as I do, as the different brigades have but little to do with each others. Tell Maj L. that if he will get me a furlough of 40 days I will try to write a meager description of the late engagement for him. It would take half of that time and all the conflicting rumors to get the truth of what I did not see. Crowds of S.C.s have come over here to see after their children & friends. No sign of a fight soon just resting in our oars doing but drilling and guard duty. All friends well except Tom Z. He is a little unwell but up. Father is officer of the day and gone to headquarters. We have preaching by our chaplain this evening at 4 o clock. He has prayer writing every night. Tell mother I wrote about winter clothes. I did not get a yankee sword. If any thing happens very strange go to Glenn Springs and telegraph immediately.

    All in fine spirits. If we stay here this winter all will need flannel under clothes.
Write to me soon.
Remember me to all.

Yr affec Brother
L. P. Foster

L. P. Foster to His Sister, Eunice

Advance Forces Army of the Potomac
Vienna Aug 4th 1861

My Dear Sister,

Your very interesting letter came this evening. I am glad to see you so trusting, so willing to rely upon a just god for the end of this merciless war. Would that the last lingering doubt might be removed from your mind & your faith be perfect. What little faith we have! How we distrust the goodness of god, even in his kindest acts. If he takes the life of a few in freeing a whole nation from a bondage worse than death, should we murmur? Are we Christians or patriots if we are or are not willing that our friends should be sacrificed on the altar of freedom? When he afflicts for our good without faith we considering the present evil & forgetting the future good which may arise from those few hrs of trouble, murmur and complain of our hard lot.

"Faith builds a bridge across the gulf of death to break the shock blind nature cannot shun, and lands thought smoothly on the farther shore."* God was surely with us in the battle such small numbers in the open field could never have triumphed such a strong and well drilled army. You have before this time rec'd our last letters telling you about the fight & that none of our reg or of yr friends were touched. I am glad to hear you say that you wish us to stay here until our work is finaly ended, for of all things a great work half finished is the worst botch. It stands as a stupendous monument of the weakness of its builders You say truly he would be a poor soldier who would be willing to turn back now after so much has been done and our proud flag floats over the soil forever we have driven the ruthless invaders and retrace his steps down the glorious path he has had & to allow by that act the whole to be darkened in ignominy, rather let us enter the path on until in glorious brightness it shall rival the [. . .] track in the strong vault & become bright spots indicative of the glory of our country, on either side even as the start on either side of the nations track, not that we would be vainglorious but show forth the love of our country & the justness of our cause. Where our next move will be I cannot tell nor can I tell where the enemies will move will be Only know we have run them back to their fortifications on the Potomac & many to their northern, there to recount our brave deeds & never return again. Scotts army is very much crippled & many think he cannot raise another. The last victory and stampede having very much intimidated both their fighters and creditors. However this I cannot tell. Great confusion exists everywhere north, even in their congress & cabinet & great dissatisfaction in their army. Their volunteers are going home to a man, many it is said becoming mutinous. It is reported and believed here that when Scott returned

---

* Quotation from "Night Thoughts" by Edward Young (baptized 1683–died 1765).

from Bullrun to Washington he resigned his office on acct of some grouse with the cabinet, but withdrew his resignation. It is also reported that many of the officers who were engaged in the battle at Bullrun are now under arrest for their cowardly conduct. I think Scott is to[o] ambitious to allow the last act of his life to be one of ignominy and will make one more effort, a death struggle. If they should be routed again, then the war must close for they will lack both men and means to carry it on. I doubt they can give us battle in this direction soon. There may [be] a fight in western Virg where govn Wise* is stationed, one is daily expected. He is a great man and will whip them if they come on him. I know our dist must be terribly excited yet there is not need of it as I don't think a single man from the dist was killed. We are well. Father was right unwell in the first of the week with some like cholic, but is now up and seems very well, says he never felt better, when he was unwell some of the ladies came in from the country to see him and brought him quite a number of nice things. The Misses Swinks came to see him several times. They live in six miles of Washington. They sent me some tomatoes the other day and to day gave me a very nice cake, some tomatoes & cucumbers. They seem to be quite smart and accomplished, of first circle, fully alive to the cause and as kind as people could be. I saw them sitting by a sick soldiers bed today waiting over him and distributing deliveries among the sick. We have a goodeal of measles in camp. None of our comp have them & will not have. They will only act [. . .], If the Misses Swink did not live so near the enemies army I would certainly call to see them. You see they are heroines or they would not dare come in our camp while so near Lincolns army. But it is getting late. All our relations are well. One thing I must tell you just as Col. Kershaws regiment was starting to the battle field, Mr. Maynardy their chaplain held prayer with every comp, but 3 or 4 of that reg killed in the fight. Remember to all my friends.

Yr affec Brother
L P Foster

P. S. I was glad to hear that Miss May had done so well. Father says it is his wish that you should remain at Limestone. L P Foster

L. P. FOSTER TO HIS MOTHER

———

Advance Forces Army of the Potomac
Vienna Aug 5th 1861

My Dear Mother

We rec'd a letter from you day before yesterday & one yesterday from Nunie. Yours I could see was written under evident excitement. Nunies in a very trusting

---

* Brigadier General Henry A. Wise, commander of provisional forces in the Kanawha Valley of Virginia.

hopeful spirit. Why will you be so uneasy about us? Your believing we are here in gods service. A service from which we must reap a rich harvest. Then when he takes us away from you a little while, that thereby good may result to the whole nation that we may assist in rolling back the tide of abolition soldiery which threatens us & place civil liberty on a firm basis, should you not be willing to trust us to his care & not distrust his wisdom and goodness [even] while he is working the very thing for which we long, our freedom. If perchance it requires some of our lives to accomplish this great work should they not be willingly given both by our selves and friends. If our patriotism stops at the point where our lives or the lives of our friends are demanded the great work must even now crumble & the stupendous pile of unfinished work be a monument of our weakness and folly. The price of human freedom has ever been human life. If we prize the latter higher then the other cannot be ours. Why our letters have not reached you I can not tell. We have written several since the fight. The night after the first fight* we telegraphed to the guardian† that the third regiment was unhurt & the day after the second‡ did the same thing. Was this not explicit enough? You can form no idea of the perfect impossibility there exist during a battle of getting any accurate account. Those men who now form one part of the line to another are gen'l so excited that they have to stir about to keep folks from thinking they are scared & no confidence is to be put in what they say-besides you cannot leave your post even for something to eat until the battle was over but had we have written sooner than we did it would have been detained at Manassas, there being an embargo on letters. I have no news to write. Father has got well again. He had something like cholic, was in bed one day and moping for 2 or 3. Whilst he was unwell the ladies of the country came in to see him, brought him plenty of nice things. Two Misses Swincks came to see him several times. I saw them yesterday sitting by the bed of a sick soldier Mr. John Jones§ and waiting on him in the kindest manner and sending delicacies to others. They sent me some tomatoes several days ago, and yesterday a nice cake, some cucumbers & more tomatoes. I think them intelligent and refined, intend to give them some palmettos today. They come in every day to see some soldiers sick with measles. None of our comp have them and won't if they will be prudent. What will be our next work I can not tell, nor what will be the next work of the Yankees. I am satisfied that there will be no Yankees here soon some think there will be no more fighting, that old Abes army is two much crippled to carry on the war & his credit is gone. How this is I can not tell, but believe that if they can raise an army they will carry on the war, commencing in the valley of virg between the Cumberland

* The Battle of Blackburn's Ford, July 18th.
† *The Daily Southern Guardian*, a Columbia, South Carolina, newspaper.
‡ First Manassas, July 21st.
§ Possibly John S. B. Jones of Co. B, 3rd S.C.

& Allegheny Mts. Thence on to Memphis. They will try to over run Wise but they will learn some things. If you get this before Sam Means leaves please send me 6 or 7 grid letter papers & 4 or 5 packs of envelopes. They are very scarce here we fare pretty well, have had 4 or 5 kinds of vegetables for two days.

All of our relations are well.

Write soon. Remember me to all.

Yr affec son L. P. Foster

Within the Democratic Party in the North, there was a faction of Democrats called Peace Democrats—and later called Copperheads—who supported a negotiated peace with the Confederacy. In the following letter, Perrin Foster refers to this split in Northern sentiment. I find no reference in congressional daily summaries between the Battle of Bull Run and this letter to indicate a peace vote taking place.

L. P. Foster to His Sister, Probably Sallie

Advance Forces Army of the Potomac
Vienna Aug 6th 1861

My Dear Sister,

Tomorrow is mail day and I wrote merely to let you know that we are well. I have nothing stirring to write. I see in the papers that New Jersey has refused to furnish her quota of the last call for troops. This drop may create a wave. McClellan* has superceeded Scott virtually which will detract many of the souths friends from the man. He is said to be a fine officer great excitement north. They are very much split-peace party in congress lacked 23 votes of carrying their party. There is a conservative element north which will cripple their efforts very much—yet what they will do we can not tell. We are just staying here awaiting orders. Many think the war ended.

We have any quantity of measles in our brigade. None in our comp. None will ever have if our men will act prudently. I mentioned a Miss Swink in a former letter. She still continues her kindness to our men stays with the sick all of the time. Has not been at home in 4 or 5 days. She is nursing John Jones who is very sick with typhoid fever—she sits up with him every night. She brings in ice & quantities of good things for the sick every day for the sick—I believe she would work herself to death. Her sister is but like her—the misses Williams are of the same stamp. Miss Swink sends us some vegetables almost every day. To know her & see her kindness is to esteem as one of the most usefull of her sex. True virginians are not very plenty in this country but where you strike one you find a heart fully alive to our

---

* Gen. George B. McClellan.

cause ready to do anything to advance it. They are warm hearted and ready to give every thing to the cause.

We have no bad cases of sickness in our reg. nothing much but measles. I am stout and in as good health as I ever was in my life. Father is well—looks much better than when he left home last. Tom Quarles is unwell. Their surgeon thinks he is taking the measles, but I think he has bad cold & will be well in a few days.

We have some fruit tin [. . .] but it cant last long. There are too many mouths to fill. Everything here much later than home corn just beginning to silk.

Aaron Smith is here—came yesterday evening—reports good health in the country. Has Ed started yet. We could take several men in our camp.

Remember me to all.

Write soon.

Yr affec Brother

L. P. Foster

The relationship between Lieutenant Colonel Foster and Mid appears to be complex. Mid first is mentioned in the Foster letters on February 25, 1856, when he was whipped by Mr. Gentry, ran off, and was still missing days later. Mrs. Foster sounded disapproving and offended at Gentry's actions; Foster was described as "worried" and irritated, of a partial mind to sell him. Mid returned and stayed with the family.

Mid accompanied Foster to Camp Ruffin in Columbia, South Carolina, and to Virginia, where he handled camp chores, cooking, and errands. However much Foster cared for Mid, though, Foster overestimated Mid's happiness living as his slave. A few weeks later, Mid undertook the dangerous journey through the Confederate pickets and sharpshooters to freedom in the North. Foster was concerned about Mid surviving the dash through the lines; but apparently, he did so—and made his way to freedom.

B. B. FOSTER TO HIS WIFE

Advanced forces Army of the Potomac
Vienna Va August 7th 1861

My dear wife

I received your letter yesterday. I was delighted to know that you had at last received our letters relieving your anxiety about us. we did all we could to relieve you at the earliest possible moment. tell Jennie Dinah was not hurt. a cannon ball struck the ground close by her and ploughed the ground for twenty yards. a shell from a rifled cannon fell in about twenty yards of her but did not from some cause burst. one of the boys picked it up. you desire to know how I felt. did you expect an honest answer, I hardly know how I did feel. when the shot and shell from the most dangerous weapon of warfare was flying thick all about you for hours. and we did not have the pleasure of returning the fire. Just had to stay there and take the chances. I did feel relieved when we were ordered out to charge the enemies reserve. they however fled before we got in reach of them and left every thing behind them. they fired their grape shot at us as we were pursuing them, but fortunately for us they threw them above our heads. I think I had my courage screwed up to the stand point. we are now in advance of the forces. some of you wished to know where mid was. I sent him back with the waggons to save our baggage. he laid down and went to sleep many of the negros left the waggons and ran back to Manassas Mid was not alarmed he has had thousands of chances to be free he choses to stay with us. I think more of him than I ever did. he could not be induced to leave us. he does all of our cooking and does it well washes everything but our shirts and sometimes washes them, and irons them I have no fault to find of him. we are now living well a young lady Miss Martha Swink one of the first families in this county sends us vegetables every day beans tomatoes cucumbers and potatoes Irish. This lady brings in ice and something for the sick every day. John Jones* from greenville is very sick and I am afraid he will die he is the youngest son of old george Jones who lived at Spartanburg. This lady has not left him in five days day nor night and seems determined to remain with him until he recovers or dies She never saw him before. She has a boy that comes in the camp every day with a horse waggon loaded for the sick she takes out their clothes washes and mends them. she insisted on my sending I did so my shirts some of them were worn collars and risbands† they came back neatly done up with new collers and risbands, this looks like Carolina ladies, she is the first one I have seen since I left Carolina our soldiers would die by her, her father and mother and sister comes in every other day.

They all seem anxious to do especially for the sick, our Regiment is suffering awfully from the measles none have died from it we have very nearly two hundred cases. one company of 88 men paraded yesterday fourteen men Benjamin Smith‡ is very unwell but not dangerous he has cold and seems to be weak. Henry Barnet has come up with us still unwell, William Bearden§ and all the ballance are well as usual Aron Smith is here. Perrin is as stout and looks as well as you ever saw him he stands it fine. I am well but have not regained my flesh and never will while I have so much to think of and do. I am still of opinion that there will be no more fighting to do at this place for some time. remember me to Gannin Mr Harmon and all my neighbors tell Majr Lancaster he owes me a letter. I have not heard from him in sometime I rely uppon him to keep the settlement straight untill I come back tell

* John S. B. Jones of Company B. He survived his illness and was present in the unit as late as June 30, 1864.

† Wristbands.

‡ Benjamin M. Smith of Company K, 3rd S.C.

§ William Bearden of Company K. 3rd S.C.

him he must stop that thing that is going on at Mrs Beardens. Remember me to the children may the Lord bless and preserve you all is my prayer.

your affectionate husband

B B Foster

NB. I wish to be remembered to the Montgomerys tell Joe to come out and see us. I have written to Eunice at Limestone twice since the fight we now have mail but three times a week and you cannot expect to hear so often tell Sallie to cheer you

Anthony is well and hearty

L. P. FOSTER TO HIS MOTHER

Advance Forces Army of the Potomac Vienna
Aug 10th 1861

My Dear Mother

It is not my regular time to write but I have a chance to send a letter by hand & therefore use it. Nothing of importance has occurred since I last wrote. Father and I are well. My friends say I look better than they ever saw, that they can hardly believe I am the Foster that left Columbia. I never felt stouter & more ready to run from the yankees in my life. The health of our reg is bad, the health of the brigade is bad. Principally measles we have a good many sick. No dangerous cases in our reg & but five in the brigade. We have no measles in our comp but several sick from colds diarhaea and the like. Our neighbors well except Benjamin Smith. He is unwell but able to be up. Also Wm. Barnett had a breaking out which some thought measles but nothing more than roseola.* They will I think soon be stout and I would say nothing to their folks about it. Night before last we thought the time for another fight had come. Some of the enemies cavalry having advanced nearer than usual. I was on picket duty had to watch all night, but saw nothing. So if you hear we are expecting a fight you may attribute it to that false alarm. This was what I saw as to the sickness of our brigade will not do for the public. You need not fear that Father and I will get sick as we have had measles. You may recollect when I had them. The ladies here have been very kind to our sick and Miss Swink in particular has spared neither labor nor expense in making them comfortable. I wrote of John Jones sickness in a former letter. He is better. The sickness the surgeons say is decreasing. measles mild & get well fast. I only fear that it will be some time before those who have had measles can with safety stand the fatigue of the camp. We had a hard rain yesterday evening. I marched in it 4 miles coming from our post of picket guard. This is the muddiest slickiest slipperiest place in wet weather that you ever saw. There is just lime enough in the soil to make it slippery but you know soldiers soon learn to care but little for rain. This very pleasant today. Have had some very bad

---

* Roseola is a viral disease marked by high fever and a characteristic rash.

weather. We live well here get quality vegetables and goodeal of fruit—peaches very good makes as fine as you ever saw any where.

The yankee government as you know is very much split up. Many think peace will result from necessity many petitions for peace are being sent to their Congress. Some from New York. Men in congress now openly denounce the war. Three months since, it would have been called treason. What is to be the result can not say. Remember me to all. Write soon.

Yr affec Son L. P. Foster

L. P. FOSTER TO HIS SISTER, EUNICE

Advance Forces Army of the Potomac
Vienna
Aug 10th 1861

My Dear Sister

As I have a chance to send a letter to Manassas by hand to day, I have concluded to write to you. We do not hear from you as often as we hear from home. Why don't you write? Father and I are well. My friends say I look better than they ever saw me. I never felt better and more like whipping the Yankees. But that article called Yankees has suddenly become quite scarce in this vicinity. With the exception of a little false alarm night before last caused by some of the enemies cavalry coming a little nearer us than usual every thing has been perfectly [quiet] since the fight. The Yankees seem to have given up the idea of invasion and gone to fortifying themselves along the Potomac and even as far back as Philadelphia, quite a change seems to have been made in their program lately. I think the idea of a grand ball a[t] Richmond has been given over for a more convenient season at least. The weather is too hot down south for the present. You have seen in the papers that the Lincoln gov. is very nearly split up. Numerous petitions have been sent by the citizens of different N. States to their congress for an adjustment of the present difficulty in a peaceable way. Congressmen now openly denounce the war as unconstitutional before the USC* and such a thing 3 months since would have been considered treasonable. Many think that this want of unanimity at the north must of necessity bring about peace by some. I only hope it may for although I have as little fear of the yankees as most men yet I prefer being at home to this place. This is the slipperiest place in the weather that you ever saw. There's just enough lime in the soil to make it slick. We had a hard rain here yesterday evening. I marched 4 miles in it, coming from our post on picket guard but you know a soldier soon learns to care very little about rain. I can sleep in it if it don't beat too hard.

The health of our reg is not very good. We have a good many cases of measles in the army here. They are mild and the sick get well fast. The ladies here treat the

---

* United States Congress.

sick very kindly sit by their beds night and day nursing them. Miss Swink is especially kind spares neither labor or expense in contributing to their comfort. We are all gratefull to them and will ever remember their kindness. I have no news to write you. We have had some very warm weather. We live very well here, get a good many vegetables, finest tomatoes I ever saw, fine butter, fine milk and pretty good fruit, so we are doing pretty well. We are now camped in the woods in a cool shady place. I suppose your play time over & school commenced again. I hope you will have a fine school.* Don't think this war should disturb the female schools.

But I must close. Remember me to friends.

Write soon

yr affec Brother

L P Foster

According to Rion McKissick,[†] the Bull Run battlefield map was hand drawn by a man named Bearden in Company K of the 3rd S.C. This was most likely Lt. William Bearden; however, it could have been E. M. Bearden or Glenn Bearden. All three were in Co. K and were in service at the time of First Manassas. The 3rd S.C. was positioned on the left flank of the North Carolina units shown to the left of Mitchell Ford marked as Williams's Regiment in Bonham's Brigade. As described in Lieutenant Colonel Foster's letter of July 21, the 3rd S.C. pursued the retreating Federals across Mitchell's Ford in the area marked, "Bonham Sunday." This map is likely the map referenced in Foster's letter.

B. B. FOSTER TO HIS DAUGHTER SALLIE

Advanced Forces Army of the Potomac
Vienna
August 11th 1861

My Dear Sallie,

I have no news to write nothing new has taken place since I last wrote. Quite a number of our men are sick from the measles and sent back to Manassas. The 9th eighty three men. They have the old style red measles. Henry Barnett was sent back to recruit. He has been sick and quite feeble was not mending we sent him back to where he could be more comfortable. I think he will soon be able to take his place. All the others of our neighborhood are well except Wm. Henry Lancaster he was sent back to Culpeper to have the measles and we do not know where he is now but think he went on to Richmond in company with Thad Borroughs[‡] and Theodore

---

* Eunice Foster was at the Limestone Female Academy in Limestone Springs at the time.

† Rion McKissick, "Letter to A. G. Kennedy, October 20, 1935." In possession of A. G. Kennedy, III.

‡ Thaddeus C. Burroughs of Co. K, 3rd S.C.

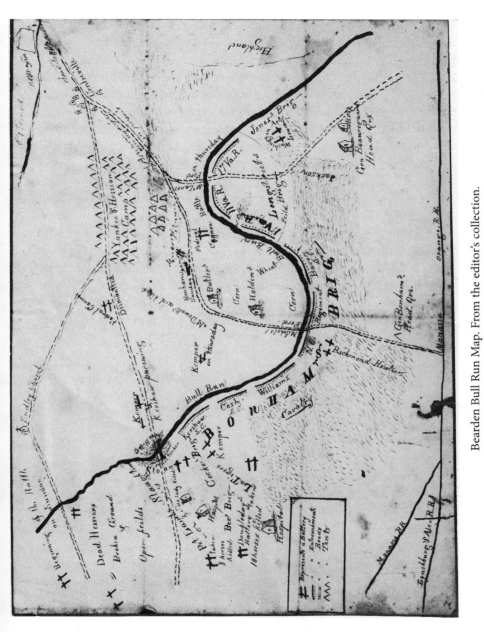

Bearden Bull Run Map. From the editor's collection.

West.* They went back three weeks ago we wrote down to find out but have not heard yet. Our pickets had a fight with the enemy yesterday about four miles from Alexandria. Captured three Yankees, four of our foot pickets whipped and actually put to flight yesterday evening a whole company of the Yankees and afterwards our cavalry captured the trio above named. I am still of opinion that we will not get a fight at this place. Boureguard keeps all his plans to himself we know nothing from him until we are ordered to move. He hardly lets his right hand know what his left does. He is a great man. I have full confidence in him. I send you an imperfect sketch of the great fight Sunday and Thursday you can see the position we occuppied. You asked how I felt. I must confess that it was not comfortable we had to hear the shot and shell from the enemys cannon and had not chance to reach them with small arms and when we were ordered to advance upon the enemys reserve I felt relieved for I wanted to get out from the shot and shell but fortunately for us the enemy flew without giving us a fight our boys raised the shout when we left the entrenchment. They took fright I suppose and left, we pursued nearly to Centerville but could not catch them. We took a good number of prisoners and returned to camp. The prisoners were trying to get back from the battlefield and fell into our hands. Johnny and Jimmy† & Elijah‡ are well. I would be pleased to see Mr. Beard and Mr. Barnett,§ but tell your mother not to come she would not feel easy here. God knows I be pleased to see any of you but this is not the place for females. My love to your mother and all the children. Tell Jennie I think of her often and will bring her something nice. God bless you all.

B. B. Foster

Do not allow this map to be published you can show it to your friends.

On August 14, Beauregard concentrated his troops at a new camp at Flint Hill, a few miles from Fairfax Court House.¶

L. P. FOSTER TO HIS SISTER, EUNICE

———

Advance Forces Army of the Potomac
Flint Hill Church
Aug 18th 1861

My Dear Sister

I must acknowledge that it required considerable effort to write to you this evening. I do not think that I am predisposed to laziness, but a kind of mental apathy

---

* Theodore J. West of Co. K, 3rd S.C.

† James Clough Beard and John W. N. Beard.

‡ Elijah F. Smith of Co. K, 3rd S.C.

§ Mr. Barnett, father of William Henry Barnett.

¶ Dickert, *History of Kershaw's Brigade*, 73.

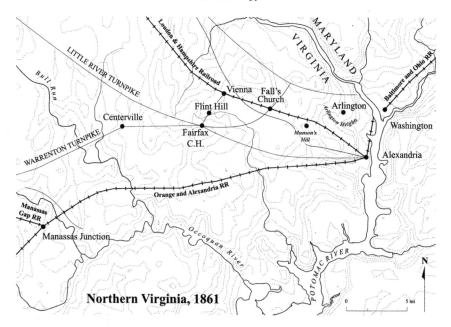

Northern Virginia, 1861.

or lethargy resulting I suppose from the five days rest which we have had makes every effort of mind burdensome so you may judge from this preliminary that the dish about to be set before you will not be very palatable. As I am here in an army upon which hangs the hopes and safety of our young confederacy, an army which has so recently passed through scenes of the most soul stirring nature and which now being situated in less than 25 miles of the federal capital may be attacked at any moment, you doubtless imagine that each day brings with its as it were a series of shining events which you would read with interest, but not so. No place is possessed of more monotony and less excitement than a military encampment. Tis true that reports reach us almost every day which to one unaccustomed to camp life would seem startling but we have learned to credit nothing unless from a source to which falsehood could not be attributed. Since they are merely heard and if repeated only to create wonderment in some credulous mind. You are now ready to think we are having quite a dull time, time what would be considered dull in an army. There being nothing to excite us, but what you would consider dullness we can find plenty of good friends and associates here with whom to pass our idle moments. (and you know no one enjoys the society of good friends than yr brother) you could scarcely come into our camp with [out] hearing the merry laugh from some lively group, to which some fellow is recounting [. . .] of a jocund nature. We scarcely ever see a lady when at Vienna we saw them right often, but they never come here. There is one old lady in a house near our tent. I think I shall have to go and take a look at her every now and then. We have much to make us sad not withstanding our vivacity.

We can stand our labor privations and exposure without a murmur, yes joyfully, but when we see so many of our friends sick it is hard even for the bronsed face soldier to restrain a sigh or tear. I do not think the sickness of our reg as great as it has been yet we have a good many cases yet, primarily measles. We have 5 cases in our comp and about 23 to have them. None of your immediate friends have them except Tom Quarles. He has them in the hospital at Culpepper C. H. where he will be well cared for. The measles are generally very mild. We have some cases of Typhoid fever but not many have dangerous here. As to those in the hospitals beyond Manassas I cannot say no[t] having heard from them lately.

There are no signs of a fight soon. Every thing perfectly quiet & but for the array of tents and soldiering no one would think this country was to be the scene of war. I don't think we will have any fighting here soon. McClellan will not risk a general engagement until he has raised a very powerfull army and had it thoroughly drilled and equipped. This will take some time since his army was greatly diminished by the fight and going home of the 3 mo volunteers. What is to be the end of all of it I yet have no idea. I know I am in the discharge of my duty and am willing to await the result. Cousin Ed* is here will be pleased. We will [be] very glad to see him. I can assure you, I know no one whom I would have welcomed more heartily. I wish Tony could come, but can not bear the idea of having mother left alone. I fear it would be more than she could stand. Have any of you heard any thing of Uncle Lewis. I have not heard from any of them since I came to Virg. I wrote to Cousin Mary† but I suppose my letters being from the C.S.A. was intercepted by some yankee P. M. between here and Newport. I rec'd one letter from Cousin Laura Hunt. Our friends all well except Virgil‡ and Carr§ Bobo. Both were sick with Typhoid fever. They were in the army at Corinth Miss. But were sent home sick. David Bobo⁵ and the Shufords are in the 18th Miss reg in 4 miles of this place. It is in gen'l Jones Brig. I have not seen them yet. I have heard that Cousin Berryman Edwards** was in the army, but have not seen him, if here. I suppose he is in Col. Blandings reg.†† I saw Capt Bill Foster‡‡ the other day. He was as funny as ever mocking Wm. Scrugs

---

* Edwin Henry Bobo.

† Probably Mary Perrin who lived in Kentucky.

‡ Virgil A. Bobo served in Company F of the 12th Mississippi Regiment.

§ Kerr B. Bobo served in Company F of the 12th Mississippi Regiment.

¶ David B. Bobo is identified as being in Company F of the 12th Mississippi Regiment in the National Park Service Soldiers and Sailors system. Foster could be in error or Bobo might have been attached to the 18th Mississippi at the time.

** Berryman (or Berriman) W. Edwards was in Micah Jenkins's 5th S.C., units of which were later reorganized into the 9th S. C. Infantry.

†† Col. J. D. Blanding commanded the 9th S.C. Infantry.

‡‡ Capt. William Moultrie Foster (later Major) of the 9th S.C. Infantry. He raised a company at the start of the Civil War, which became Co. C. of the 9th Reg. S.C. Landrum, *History of Spartanburg County*, 286–287.

and old Dr. Curtis* yet. We have very wet bad weather yet but don't care much from it, having long since become accustomed to it.

You take the proper vein in going back to school. You know not what a train of circumstances may bring forth. When you may be deprived of yr earthly goods, hence should store your mind well with usefull. It will enable you to accept such a crisis more successfully than any thing else. Labor bestowed on the mind can not be taken from us so long as reason is left. Every other good resulting from our labor may. Hence you should cultivate that with which you can make yourself easy in life and from which you can not be separated. It is truly possible that there will be enough soldiers to make husbands for all you ladies. So you will have to be very sharp or you won't be a chosen bird. This crowd of soldiers will be the worst marrying set you ever saw should they all be spared to get home. I think almost every fellow has his eye on someone of the many fair ladies left behind. I know [. . .] has. But enough of this. I wish I could have been at your examination, but did not have my crop quite plowed over so could come over this time. If I catch up with my work you may look for me bye & bye.

Remember me to my friends, Cousin sends best love. Write very often as nothing [gives] me more pleasure than to receive yr letters. They are generally a long coming. Direct as you did your last which was rec'd a few days ago since for Manassas Junction. I will get them quicker from Manassas than any other place.

Yr affec Brother
L P Foster

L. P. Foster to His Mother

Advance Forces Army of the Potomac
Flint Hill Church
Aug 19th 1861

My Dear Mother

Father wrote home yesterday giving you every thing interesting but as I have an opportunity to send a letter by Mr. Mayfield† our chaplain who goes home today, I will write you. I suppose you have quite a stir a shaking among the dry bones just at this time. You fear a draft I do not men will not be held by a capt so long as to bring

---

* Likely Dr. William Curtis, a founder of Limestone College.

† W. D. Mayfield, a Baptist minister from Newberry, South Carolina, was the regimental chaplain until his resignation on May 15, 1862. He was associated with the community of Martins' Depot in July of 1862 per the State Convention of the Baptist Denomination in South Carolina. *Minutes of the Forty Second Anniversary of the State Convention of the Baptist Denomination in S.C.* (Columbia, S.C.: E. R. Stokes, 1862), p. 176 (Call No. 4384, Rare Book Collection UNC-CH. http://docsouth.unc.edu/imls/scbc1862/scbc1862.html) Accessed August 10, 2016).

on a draft when they see there is no chance of raising to comp of their choice they will join some other. I am only glad that the spirit is up I would not have Spartanburg behind in this brightest of glorious works for I believe the future historian will record this as the finest army ever raised or its deeds the most patriotic. When the end will come I have no idea. Don't suffer myself to think much about it but that it will crown our efforts with success I have not a doubt nor do I think any one here entertains the slightest doubt. Our success in the battle of Bull Run & Manassas plains against such fearfull odds has inspired our men with contempt for them and the almost universal belief that god was the author of that days fortune. That there must have been a special inference of providence or the battle would have been lost and now they would expect victory no matter what kind of army they had to meet. Why should not this faith render our army as irrisistable as it did Cromwells or even more so, since less of superstition and more genuine faith works in our army. I do not think we will have a fight soon at any rate there are no appearances of it. McClellan will not risk all soon. As brave as he may be, he is not brave enough to rush up us with the present U.S.A.

I don't think we have quite as many cases of sickness as when I last wrote, but many yet. I heard through a letter from J. H. Wofford* from Richmond that James Johnson† and Thad Burrow‡ had both been discharged by the surgeon Gen'l. The former having a disease of the heart & the latter having lost the use of one arm. How it is I don't see. In the first place I never heard Johnson complain of anything like heart disease nor Burrow of any think like rheumatism or parallasis and again don't see how the surgeon Gen'l could discharge them without Col. Williams permission, however it may be so. T. H. West§ had measles and was doing well. Nothing more from Wm. Barnett since Father wrote. Nothing from Lancaster. My impression that he is behind at town frolicking. Col. Williams is going to send some one in search of him and some other sick men soon. I have not uneasiness about him myself. S. Z. Shurbutt⁋ about well of measles. S. M. Lanford** James Riddle†† James Roundtree.‡‡ All have measles here. Rest of our neighbors pretty well. Tom Quarles still at Culpepper. Dr. Hearst has just returned from a visit to the sick at Culpepper. Says Tom is sitting well. Uncle Anthony still nursing John Jones who is getting well. We have very wet and muddy weather. No news at all. I saw Capt Bill Foster the other day. He was very lively & still making fun. Do you know whether Cousins Benjamin

---

* John Henry Wofford of Co. K, 3rd S.C.
† James A. Johnson of Co. K, 3rd S.C.
‡ Thaddeus C. Burroughs of Co. K, 3rd S.C.
§ Thomas H. West of Co. K, 3rd S.C.
⁋ S. Z. Shurbutt of Co. K, 3rd S.C.
** Lt. Seaborn M. Lanford of Co. K, 3rd S.C.
†† James M. Riddle of Co. K, 3rd S.C.
‡‡ James (Joseph) R. Rountree of Co. K, 3rd S.C.

and Augustus* are in the army or not? I hear that B. is but not A. I thought he had more spirit but anger is by no means indicative of a bold, patriotic spirit. Father has bought him another fine mare a beautiful horse calls her Fannie. I am sorry that Sam Means could not get our cloth, but not at all surprised. I wanted him to go through the virg. Factories first but Capt Kennedy thought otherwise, and as I had had something to do with the getting up of our old uniforms which turned out to be a grand humbug I concluded to hold my peace. If I were in his place I should try Augusta & Savannah. He will never get enough in as small a place as Shelby. Make me two pants instead of out of what ever he gets on as near like it as you can get if he don't get enough & if he gets more do the best you can. He has my measure. I find my pants on hand are not of much from hence one pr not enough. You said in your last which came day before yesterday that you would have to make our shirts of white flannel. If you can get any other color at all it will be better. Please get me also two heavy nit under shirts. Mr. Bobo had some when I left home. If you can get colored goods for my over shirts it will be better. I expected Sam Means to have gotten it. You need not be afraid of getting it too heavy. Any kind heavy cassimir made according to directions I gave in a previous letter. You may think two sets of undershirts besides my over shirts too much but I fear this winter worse than yankees. I suppose you got the letter sent by Sam Means had sent a letter by him containing $5.00 for his wife to be left at the office of Glenns but I must close. Is our Batallion doing nothing for Capt. Kennedys comp because we can nurse our sick in some sort of manner and make out with bad shoes & clothing now is no proof that the cold of winter will never come. There will be suffering here this winter unless something is done by individual efforts. The confederacy is too young to bear every expense besides she can not get the material. Remember me to the family and write soon and often,

yr affec son L. P. Foster

B. B. Foster to His Wife

*Advanced Forces Army of the
Potomac August 25th 1861*

My Dear Wife,

Your letter to Perrin and came yesterday. I was rejoiced to know that you were all well and had at least a prospect for bread. Tell Mr. Harmon he must give the hogs all the hops and take special care of them. I feel sure that nut will be very scarce and hard to get. Anthony had gone home his wife is very sick. I advised him to go. Edwin is here and well. Perrin is well. There is now only about four hundred of our Regiment able for duty. The ballance sick principally measles and there is still more

---

* Cousins Benjamin and Augustus—Augustus may be Augustus Edwards, brother of Col. Oliver E. Edwards; Benjamin may be an Edwards brother or another relative.

to have them. We are in bad fix for active service at this time. Furgusons company has but twenty men for duty and all the commissioned officers of that company is sick and the orderly seargeant commands. Wm Henry Lancaster is here he came in yesterday. looks as well as I ever saw him. He says he staid at Charlottesville. Henry Barnett is at Charlottesville. He has been very sick but is improving. He is in charge of the South Carolina hospital and will be well attended too. The Smith boys are all here and well as usual. The Woffords* all well. Jolly Bobo† is much better and doing duty. Let Rufus Lancaster‡ know that his son is here. I have no doubt but you will here worse rumors before long than the undermining of Arlington Heights, such a thing had never been thought of here. We had an alarm here yesterday. The news reached us that the enemy were advancing and there was quite a stir for a few hours it proved to be for the most part false. The yankees about a hundred and fifty of them was foraging and got lost and found inside of our pickets were fired uppon. They took to their [. . .] and left all sorts of rumors will go out from this. This day Longstreets Brigade took posession of Falls Church. The pickets have been shooting at one another there for some time but little damage done. Our men killed a few of them without any loss on our side. I have no idea what old Beauregard intends to do. I feel sure he will do right, and pay no attention to the thousand and one rumors which I hear daily in the camp. I am in need of pants. I hope you have succeeded in getting for me a piece of jeans for coat and pants. The cloth Means give you is too light for service. Remember me to Harmon and Sam and all the children neighbors generally I hope Mitchel will stay away. Mich is well and doing well. I am getting your letters regular now. Tell Jennie and Sally I hope they enjoy themselves well now. I feel like we will all be together again may the Lord preserve you all.

Your husband

B B Foster

L. P. FOSTER TO HIS MOTHER

Advance Forces Army of the Potomac
Flint Hill Church
Aug 29th 1861

My Dear Mother

I rec'd a letter from Sallie also one from Nunie yesterday evening and was glad to hear that all were well. We have heard wondrous things from home lately. It seems that the evil spirit has left old Abes government (it's usual abode) for a time

---

* The Woffords in Co. K included John Henry Wofford, John Wesley Wofford, John Young Wofford, William B Wofford, and William Thomas Wofford. All had enlisted in April 1861.

† Jolly Bobo was probably J. P. Bobo in Co. D of the 3rd S.C.

‡ Rufus Lancaster was doubtlessly the father of William Henry Lancaster of Co. K.

to work evil in your midst. I hear that Dr. Winsmith* has challenged Genl Edwards[†] for the adroit and insidious manner in which he brought about the defeat of his son on Sullivan's Island. Now this is a miserable subterfuge. The man who has suffered ambition to make him point to himself habitation on the dizzy heights of fame which he can never reach is sure to have this life embittered by many a humiliating failure, as the crippled serpent he drags himself along his tortuous path, and vents the keen resentment of his embittered & foiled soul upon all who dare oppose or approach him. But disappointment is not the only pain which such men feel, envy with a thousand hideous speeches torments his sinfull soul till instead of praying his god to bless his fellow man he is ready to curse each blessing rec'd by his neighbors and hate the god which bestowed them. No man has been a more complete vassal to a groveling ambition than Dr. Winsmith. It has subjected him to failures of a very humiliating nature, which have embittered his soul and left him a prey for envy and hatred.

Gen'l Edwards has obtained certificate from the comp signed by every man in it showing he never spoke to a single one of the on the subject of the election. If I were in Edward's place I should hush his mouth or break it. He came to the 5th Reg not since and reports there that Gen'l Edwards went home after the fight and reported to the people that he had planned every movement in which the 5th Reg was engaged & claimed all the credit as due to himself. Some [in] the 5th are disposed to believe him and are abusing Edwards but by far the longer party are [. . .] Winsmith especially so the Morgan Light Infantry. Bless him for asserting that Gen'l Edwards could influence him in casting their votes. Lt. Col Legg[‡] I hear has written a piece for the Spartan[§] concerning it. I suppose Sam Means left home day before yesterday. I fear he will not get all the things. We could have waited a while longer for him. We rec'd a Col from the western part of our district which helped our comp very much. There is still much sickness in our Reg. A good many of our comp have 7 had the measles. They are very mild indeed and rarely confine them more than four days.

Mr. Barnett is at Culpepper with Henry.[¶] Father rec'd a letter from Henry this morning saying that he had intermittent fever that his brothers were there and anxious to come here to see us but the Sec of War would not grant him a pass to

---

* Dr. John Winsmith was a physician and planter in the Glenn Springs area. This is a challenge to a duel. Eelman, *Enterpreneurs*, 15.

    † This is Col. Oliver E. Edwards of Micah Jenkins's 5th S.C. The reference to his being a General is likely due to Edward's election as Brigadier General of the 9th Brigade, South Carolina Militia in 1854. Landrum, *History of Spartanburg County*, 510.

    ‡ Lt. Col. G. W. H. Legg of the 5th S.C.

    § Carolina Spartan newspaper.

    ¶ William Henry Barnett and his father.

come farther. There is something wrong about it. [. . .] Everything is uncertain it is impossible to tell what a day may bring forth. We all well. Wet rainy weather. Mud enough.

Remember me to all and write soon. yr affec son

L. P. Foster

L. P. FOSTER TO HIS SISTER, EUNICE

Advance Forces Army of the Potomac
Flint Hill Church
Aug 29th 1861

My Dear Sister,

This evening is too rainy to be out hence I am confined to the large merits of our tent, say 10 ft by 10 ft, but its quite a comfortable place for me. I have passed many a very pleasant hour in it & neither scorn its narrow limits nor its open front. This is a way of living for which I have considerable fancy, so much like nature itself, not so much house for fixing up & play the gentleman. Not so much affectation as in the warm nicely furnished parlor. More of usefulness, less idleness. I some times think I would like the profession of arms very much, most as much as law. It is true many condemn it as demoralizing and slothful in time of peace, but is not necessarily so, else god never would have made it the duty of any man be a soldier. The field is one full of danger and wild excitement but at the same time one in which the noblest duties of man are accomplished, duties for which his fellow man will praise him more than for any other. Your letter came last night. I was glad to hear from you. Glad especially to hear that your spirit was not drooping, but that a Christian hope still pointed to brighter and better days and you cheerfull and lively. Tis marry and simple for one to allow apprehension of evil from me[re] specters of imagination to blight and wither the soul, to cloud the sky of joy and shut a cloud of gloom over ones brow, through which hope can see no bright spot. Tis true your friends lives may be thrown in dangerous positions, may meet the end of life, but is not such the case in time of peace do not friends die every yr. Were we not created with the hope of a joyous abode beyond the earth to which there is no approach except by death. The greatest uneasiness we suffer is on this subject. Oft does the mind [. . .] to have scenes and shudder as it imagines you all sitting in the little family circle unhappy on our account. If we could but know that that the smile of joy and pleasure still played on all your cheeks. That each was radiant with the bright beam of hope and as cheerful as of yore where we each sat around the cheerful fireplace was occupied and the sheath of contentment and happiness fall from heart to heart. Then no feeling of a gloomy nature could crowd itself upon us, but conscious of a full discharge of duty our hearts would know little of pain.

I heard nothing of gen'l Beauregards coming near being taken prisoner. You have and will hear many false reports concerning the fight. The various reports in the papers have disgusted me not a little.

You were hard on Mauldin, but you are right. He is not acting his part, not worthy of the respect of the [. . .] he would back. No young man now has a right to give his time to employ peace and quiet to his soul, but he is an effeminate kind of body whom the heavy trappings of a soldier would become but poorly. I am not sure a petticoat would suit him better and if he attains ease and leisure he should haul off his trousers and put in on, as we fight for the ladies with the best imaginable will but conclude young gentlemen of ease resting on "Otium cum dignitate"* unworthy a single amount of toil and exposure.

I am glad to know the school is increasing. I know no school save the S.C.C.† in which I feel a greater interest. It has turned out many a good soldier but few who were in college with me are not here. I meet them every day. Mr. Barnett is at Culpepper C. H. with Henry who is in the hospital there sick from intermitant fever. He wants to come here to see us but the Sec of War would not grant him a pass to go farther than Culpepper. I would like very much to see him. Every thing here now is wrapped in uncertainty. We know not what a day may [bring] forth. Our troops have advanced beyond Falls Church which throws them very near the enemy. Our pickets and theirs skirmish almost every day. Our pickets have killed 8 of them lately and taken 5 prisoners. Our Brig still remains here on the Vienna road hence is as yet out of it, but we can not tell what will be our future actions. I don't think there can be much of a battle here soon but if there is not one over in western Virg soon I shall be surprised. We will however have nothing to do with it. I hear Dr. Winsmith has challenged gen'l Edwards and the latter refused to fight him. His charge was "for his adroid and insidious management in bringing about the defeat of his son on Sulivans Island" A miserable subterfuge. He has generated his [. . .] about gen'l Edwards to the effect that he went home after the fight and told the people that he planned every action of the 5th Reg in the battle and claimed all the credit due for the same. He [. . .] has not many friends here and the men curse him oftener than bless him. He is merely trying to prevent Edwards from being made Col. of the Reg being raised in our Dist.

Cousin Ed Kups well and hearty, but seems to think much of home. He has not been here long enough to get weaned from home. We live very well now I expect as well or better than you. We have the finest butter I even saw. Also the largest tomatoes as large around as a saucer. Some pears but no watermelons. You do [. . .] to deprive yourself of such things because you think we can not get them. We buy

---

* "Leisure with dignity."
† South Carolina College.

whatever we can get to eat. Chickens 25 cts butter 25 cts peaches $4.00 per bushel. We can also get plenty of green corn. I read a novel (Ehrenstein) yesterday and day before, the first I have got a chance at since I left home. Wish I had another or something else to read.

Remember me to my Limestone friends & write soon.

Yr affec Brother

L P Foster

Eunice (Nunie) Foster was attending Limestone College at Limestone Springs near Spartanburg, with her Cousin Belle Perrin and her friend Carrie Zimmerman. Carrie is believed to be Caro Zimmerman, the sister of Thomas Holman Zimmerman and daughter of John Conrad Zimmerman. Home support for the war effort and concern at the irregular mails are evident. In December, Belle was forced out of school due to a painful attack of Dengue Fever. Strained family finances made her return to school uncertain.

EUNICE FOSTER TO HER SISTER SALLIE

Limestone Sprs

Aug 31st 1861

My Dear Sister,

I am very sorry that my not writing last week caused you so much useless uneasiness but I thought my poor note by Mrs. Clark was sufficient if I had known that Mother would feel anxious about me, or think I was sick, nothing would have prevented my writing. You surely have forgotten how fat and hearty I look, no Sister, I am not sick at all that I know of.

There is no news at all to write that will interest you. I have to study very hard, but do not mind it much, for I have books and know it is for a great advantage to me.

I am very glad you have sent Fathers and Brothers clothes, it will be a great comfort both to them and me if they have a plenty of good warm clothes this winter. I would like very much to see Father's fine horse. Why did he buy another horse? What will he do with Dinah now? I hope he will not sell her.

I received a letter from Brother this evening, he and Father are both quite well. I have to pay for all the letters I get from them now, but am so rejoiced to hear from them that I do not mind paying for their letters. Cousin Ed was also quite well and Tom Q. better.

I saw a list of the "Forest volunteers' last night was proud to see Bookters Eds and Mrs Carlisles named among them. I think they might so have volunteered because they had nothing to keep them at home.

Sister I do not get all the letters that Father and Brother write me, Father wrote Mr. Curtis the other day and said he wrote to me the day before. I have not received his letter yet. I declare it is too provoking.

I wish you would be so kind as to knit me some stockings after you finish those you are making for the soldiers. I am tired of darning these I have.

The people about home must be very stingy if they would not help the soldiers but you had better be close now for a full thread is $1.00 a day in Charleston and coffee 50 cts a pound all the coffee we drink is half rye. I like it better than without it.

I sent you some ambrosia seeds, you must take good care of them and plant them next spring.

What are you doing with yourself now a days? I wish you could come over and stay awhile with me, and help me with lessons. Please give my best love to Tony and ask him to write to me. Tell him that I am anticipating a nice time studying algebra with him this winter if he will teach me.

Has Mr. Harmon pulled fodder yet? You must give my best respects to him and other friends.

The girls felt an earth quake this morning at 5 o clock. I did and not feel it but Debbie waked up jumped out of bed and ran to the window a good many of the girls got up perhaps you felt it.[*]

Carrie is writing to you so I will close and let her tell the news. I must be sure to give her best love to you.

Write soon. Love to your and all the others

Affectionately
"Nunie"

L. P. FOSTER TO HIS FATHER

Camp Near Rocky Run[†]
Sept 1st 1861

My Dear Father

Nothing of importance to write but as we go on picket today I will write. I may not have a chance again in several days. I heard from you at Richmond through a Mr Hill from N. Carolina. We had a muster today. Our Reg seemed very full &

---

[*] On August 31, 1861 and earthquake with an epicenter in extreme southwest Virginia or western North Carolina occurred. It was felt as far to the south west as Columbus, Georgia. "Virginia Earthquake History," USGS, http://earthquake.usgs.gov/earthquakes/states /virginia/history.php (accessed August 10, 2016).

[†] Rocky Run is a watershed near Centreville, Virginia.

presented a good appearance. Inspector gen'l Holmes[*] was our mustering officer. We had a little row today in camp. A few days since Smith Jones[†] went to the commissary department to attend in person to the issuing of rations to his comp upon which some warm words were passed between him and Capt Hunt.[‡] This morning he again came to the same business and claimed the right to look at the calculations of Mr Lorrence[§] and see how he issued rations to other comps. Capt Hunt told him he could see none but his own where upon warm words again issued when Jones insulted Hunt and Hunt slapped him in the mouth. They then closed but were soon parted. Hunt not having rec'd a scratch and Smith Jones with bruised face. Smith drew his sword and attempted again to get to Hunt again. John Mayes[¶] sensing it got between them to prevent another fight. Jones told him two or three times to get out of his way when not obeying his command he struck him with his sword. Mayes returned the blow—a fight ensued but they were soon parted both somewhat bruised. Col Williams parting them in his normal cool manner took Jones sword and sent Mayes to the guard house. Hunt would have probably killed him with a musket when he struck Mayes had not Dr. Bruce[**] caught him and held him. Capt told him in the person of Col Williams that he was a rascal and demagogue. Hunt is his match in any kind of fight. I thought the thing entirely provoked by Jones and his striking Mayes an outrage. You had probably say little about it as it may get to a court martial. I hear Capt Nance[††] is not pleased with the way Jones treated Mayes. You know my opinion of Jones yet I shall not take sides in the affair.

I am well. Col Williams [. . .] to day to secure your saddle for him in case you ever let any one have it.

Remember me to all

yr affec son L. P. Foster

In late August, Beauregard decided to dislodge the Union pickets and occupy Munson's Hill and Mason's Hill overlooking Washington. The Second South Carolina under Kershaw drove the Federals from those heights and by early September, other regiments were taking turns at picket duty on these advance positions.

[*] Likely General Theophilus Hunter Holmes.

[†] Possibly B. S. Jones of Company I, 3rd S.C.

[‡] Captain James Hamilton Hunt, Commissary 3rd S.C.

[§] Captain Rufus N. Lowrance, Commissary 3rd S.C.

[¶] Most likely John B. Mayes of Co. E, 3rd S.C., although William J. Mayes of Co. K is a possibility.

[**] Jerome D. Bruce, Company E, 3rd S.C.

[††] James Drayton Nance, Captain of Company E, 3rd S.C. Later he became Colonel of the regiment.

B. B. Foster to His Wife

In front of Arlington Heights
Sept. 1 1861

After a fatigueing march we are here in sight of the great citty of Washington in a mile and a half of Arlington and in sight of Alexandria. We can see the Potomac boats lining up the river we will stay here two days more and then be relieved by others. Things are getting in close quarters but I am of opinion that there will be no serious work here The pickets fight every day none of our boys have been hurt yet There's scarcely half an hour but some one is shot at we killed several of the yankees yesterday The firing is going on whilst I am writing I feel as safe here almost as if I was at home I know you are uneasy you ought not to be our lives are not in the hands of the yankees, I am careful I feel that there is a great charge on my hands. I am in good health fattening again. Perrin has avoided a great deal of exposure by going back we left all our tents back at our camp and we have to take the weather as it comes one consolation it will be over in two mondays. I write to keep you informed of my whereabouts all the boys are in fine spirits remember me to all our friends and the children. write direct to the same place May the Lord bless and protect you all is my prayer

your affectionate husband B. B. Foster

B. B. Foster to His Wife

Flint Hill Sept. 4th 1861

My Dear Wife

I have not written in several days being very busy. I am sorry to inform you that Mid* has at last chosen the cloven foot. Last night he left for parts unknown. Took his clothes I think it altogether likely that he is in yankeedom nothing had occurred I had not even scolded at him four others in the camp left with him. I have just learned that the pickett arrested two yankees and five negro fellows this morning near the Potomac. It may not be so but I hope it is. We are boarding and got fine fare at fifty cents per day each and men are improving. Mr. Barnett is at Culpeper with Henry he is improving I am sorry that he cannot come any further. No one can come unless they have sons in the army he is with his son and they will not let him come any further There is not much prospect of active operations. Our Briggades have been advanced and seem to be closing up on Alexandria we are no longer in the advance other Briggades have been sent in advance of us and I am glad of it. It will relieve us from so much heavy duty. Perrin [ ] has more flesh than common he

---

* It is not known whether Mid made it through the Confederate lines to freedom in the North.

is stout and looks well. I have gained three lbs in ten days. I now think that I will regain my flesh. I think our regiment will soon get through with the measles they are coming back every day and seem to be getting well. I am anxious to get home once more, but I feel that my country needs my services and I must submit until the last enemy is expelled from our soil and our independence fully acknowledged. I feel that I am doing more for family even if it should be the will of our heavenly Father that I should never return than I possibly could do at home. I do intend to watch for an opportunity and if it should present itself I will come home for awhile. The Smith boys are well as usual even Beardens* son of the old lady has been sent back sick. I hear that he is better. Your letters come regular. This morning our men attacked the yankees at the bigg falls on the Potomac.† The yankees men stationed there on the other side of the river our men had three pieces of artillery with them went up last night and opened on them this morning killing many of the yankees. and driving them off the ground. We lost none nor had none hurt. Our Brigade was not in the fight. I do not know the exact amount killed, but it is certain that they are whipped we heard the fight and have seen some of our men who was in the battle Remember to the children and all the neighbors Sam and Mrs. Harmon. I am sorry for the Majors loss May the Lord bless and preserve you all is my prayer. Thom Zimmerman looks better may your way save him.

Your husband
B. B. Foster

L. P. Foster to His Mother

Army of the Potomac
Flint Hill
Sept 6th 1861

My Dear Mother,

I wrote to John Harmon yesterday giving him all the news, Sam Means came yesterday evening, Andrew Moore‡ & Bill Woodruff§ came with him. Everything came right All our uniforms fit well and we are pleased. The only difficulty is that

---

* Probably Private William S. Bearden of Co. K who, according to Wyckoff, was admitted into the Petersburg General Hospital with measles on October 17.

† Foster is referring to the skirmish at Great Falls Maryland on September 4, 1861.

‡ Likely Andrew Charles Moore who was a classmate of L. P. Foster's at the S.C. College and graduated with distinguished honor. He studied law a the University of Virginia, graduating in 1860. Moore was killed in action at 2nd Manassas on August 30th, 1862. Landrum, *History of Spartanburg County*, 193.

§ Believed to be William A. Woodruff of Co. K, 3rd S.C.

we have too much. I fear more than we can carry, but we think of hiring another waggon. We can get one for 20 dollars per month which divided among the comp will not be much. We are very much obliged to you all. Father and I are especially obliged to you all for sending our things we would not change any of them if we could, dont send any more things soon. Father says he will not need anything else soon except two overshirts something like mine. Says he wont need another coat soon nor socks. He has had several pr wool socks given him, dont send the other things which I wrote for except my vest and undershirts & hat until I write. I will need my overcoat other suit and & shirts. And look if I remain here this winter so you may have them ready in 1 or 2 months, and I will be obliged & will write when I need them. I was glad to hear that our Hard Labor* friends were with you, I hope they will stay for a long time. Remember me most kindly to them all & tell them I would give any thing to be with them but there is too much live stock over the potomac for me to leave.

Tell Belle & Lizzie† to write to me. Belle owes me a letter. We are all well & have no needs. We have heard nothing of Mid. I suppose he is safe in Abrahams bosom long since. We will never meet again unless he becomes dissatisfied and comes back. They can never induce him to join their army, he can not stand the fire, we are getting along finely without him. Write to me soon. Remember me to all the family.

Yr affec Son L. P. Foster

L. P. Foster to His Sister, Probably Sallie

Army of the Potomac
Flint Hill Sept 10th 1861

My Dear Sister,

Father rec'd a letter from Mother last night, the first one have rec'd since Means came. Our letters still come very irregularly. Why it is I can not see. Mother said she had not had a letter from any of us in 13 days. How this comes I can not see for we have written almost every day. I have written to John, Sam, Tony and Mother in less than a wk. Col. Sims leaves us this morning for Columbia S.C. I will send some of my summer clothes by him also one my swords. I think I will send the one Toney sent, I have changed my notion greatly since I wrote to him to send them. I now see that it is very seldom that the sword is used in a battle by infantry and that it is best for one to carry as little as possible. I have no news to write you. We

---

* The Hard Labor Creek area is near the present-day town of Troy, S.C. Many of the Foster family relatives in the Chiles, Perrin, and Cothran families lived in this area.

† Belle is Anna Isabella Perrin. Lizzie is probably Elizabeth Perrin Cothran.

are just lying here on our oars leading rather an idle life. I am getting tired of this place but see no sign of moving or fighting here soon.

I suppose Aunty has left before this time.

I rec'd a letter from Nunie two days since her letters came pretty regularly.

Remember me to all and write soon

Ye affec brother L. P. Foster

L. P. Foster to His Mother

Army of the Potomac, Flint Hill
Sept 11th 1861

My Dear Mother,

Yours of the 4th Sept came last evening. It must have found a shorter route, as it came in 5 days after being mailed. You said you were sorry my letters of directions all came after Means left. You need not be for we have all we need for the present and would not change anything you sent. The only direction which I was much concerned about was my overcoat and I fear you have not got it as you did not mention it. In answer to the letter you wrote asking if I wanted an overcoat I wrote that I would like to have one after military style i.e. long frock with a cape & trimmed with Palmetto buttons if they could be got. If you recollect Tony Woffords overcoat then you have it. Lockwood can cut it from my uniform coat measure. I would like to be at home with our friends but there is no use of wishing. I have no news to write. Give my respects to Capt Kemper. Tell him I am expecting wonders of him. Tell Sallie and Lizzie to be good galls & be trying to win hearts now, tell them just wait awhile unless they know some way to keep from waiting. Ed stands the camp finely has gained several lbs since he came here. Father is well. We have had very warm weather until to day and today a regular South eastern gale makes it a little cool. Some of our sick are coming in from the hospital. Dr Robt Smith of our camp is at Richmond sick. We have not heard from him in some time when we heard he was better.

Tell Tony Sam & Jno H they owe me letters and to write. Remember me to the family & enquiring friends.

Yr affec son
L P Foster

CHAPTER 4

The Elephant Hides

In mid-September, Perrin Foster developed a severe cold that became complicated with jaundice and he was sent to a home in Charlottesville to recover. Traveling by railcars on the Orange and Alexandria Railroad to Gordonsville and then via the Lynchburg Railroad on to Charlottesville, he arrived at a private home on September 14th. His stay in Charlottesville until October 17th became a bright respite from camp life. The optimistic prosperity of the residents of western Virginia during this period and their solicitous care for the Confederate soldier is evident in Perrin's letters. He made contact with distant relatives, the Cloptons, while in Charlottesville. His recovery time was spent resting, on pleasant outings, and visiting with new-found friends and relatives. When the South Carolinians first arrived in Virginia, they were suspicious of the Virginian's commitment to the Confederacy. After a few weeks in Charlottesville, Perrin was enamored of Virginian life.

Meanwhile, Lieutenant Colonel Foster remained with the 3rd S.C. in northern Virginia. Following Bull Run, the Federals held defensive lines along the south bank of the Potomac River and enclosing Alexandria. The Confederate advanced forces held high grounds such as Arlington Heights and Munson's Hill overlooking the Potomac, Alexandria, and Washington. Advance units were frequently relieved and busied themselves in preparing defensive fortifications.

In the next letter we gain insight into Foster's thoughts on Mid, who had escaped. Foster mentioned seeking to hire a free person of color, and described being ordered by Beauregard to hang the white Virginian "yankie" who was helping people escape, if he could be apprehended. The letter illustrates how very dangerous it was during the war for both those seeking freedom and their abettors.

B. B. FOSTER TO HIS WIFE
──────────

1st Army corps of the Potomac
Flint Hill Sept 13th 1861

My Dear Wife

I received your letter one from Sallie to Perrin & one from Eunice to me today I wrote you yesterday Perrin has gone back to Charlottesville He had a severe cold which deranged his stomach and put him to spitting up what he eat. I determined at once contrary to his wishes to send him back to let him recruit and enjoy civilized society for awhile he left this evening I obtained for him a permit to go anywhere he choses to go in the state of Virginia a thing which is not common here you need not have any uneasiness about him. I was only fearful that he would not get along well with dropsy* seen in camp living as rough as we were compeled to do it is a great inconvenience to me to do without a boy yet I have never been permitted to saddle or feed my horses since Mid left John Nance Capt Hunt and others the soldiers have furnished me with a boy on all occaisions. Capt Kenedy invited us and would have us to eat with his mess. we boarded awhile but have give it up and have joined Kenedys mess. I have tried to hire a negro but have not succeeded yet. I would like to have one so as not to be dependent on others I will not bring another here. I shall write to Jim Williams† tonight to send me a free boy and I will pay him wages. If the confederate states maintain there independance I will be remunerated for the loss of Mid I feel very sure that few such governments as old Abes cannot subdue us nothing unusual in the army all quiet today not even a fight with the pickets we have arrested three men today suspicious persons coming into our camp they are here under guard we are drawing the strings on these yankies one of the yankie citizens here in a mile of our camp I think helped our negro Boriguard has ordered us to hang him if we can get proof of his being accessary to their escapes I have been watching him closely although satisfied he assisted them yet the proof is as yet not clear enough Eunice I think is rather the best soldier of the females of my family she writes like she was proud her father and brother is in the army her letters are very cheering to us. Tell Sallie to cheer up. give my love to Betsy & Lizzie oh how I would like to be there with you all tell Jennie I think of her very often remember me to John Harmon & Sam tell John to look to the hogs. I took at the Battle of Bull Run Abes brass horn tell John I will bring it to him. tell Majr L. he owes me a letter Rufus White‡ is down with the measles he is on the mend Johny Jimy and Elijah are all well one of Wm Smiths boys is in bad health not dangerous may the Lord preserve you all is my prayers

B B Foster

---

* Dropsy, a contraction for hydropsy, is a fluid buildup now known as edema.
† James Williams—apparently a neighbor from Spartanburg.
‡ Probably R. B. White of Company K, 3rd S.C.

B. B. Foster to His Wife

Advanced Forces Army of the Potomac
September 14th 1861

My Dear Wife,

In the morning at 8 o'clock our Regiment marches to munsons heights in front of Washington Citty to relieve some Regiments that have been stationed there for ten days we take with us four days provisions after which time we will return to our camp and others will be sent to relieve us. The boys are all anxious to move. I do not think that the yankees will leave their brest works to fight us and it seems to be the policy of our generals to act in the defensive we will be in sight of Washington Citty. I am anxious to see the place. Perrin has gone back into Virginia. I expect a letter from him tomorrow, but this march will destroy our mail arrangements for awhile. We are again placed in the lead for a few days Bacons Regt goes with us and one Regt from Longstreets Briggade besides the cavalry & artillery. I will write the first opportunity. I expect to find something interesting about munsons hill we can see the steam boats passing up the Potomac and Arlington is in full view. I am sorry to say to you that Dr Robert Smith is in Richmond and very sick Henry Barnett is still behind at Culpepper and I have no hope now of seeing Brother Barnett how I would like to see him. I told Perrin to stop and see him and try to get him a passport here I am delighted to see that Edwards* is Col.† in spite of old Wins‡ challange. I am glad that Edwards did not accept his challenge. I was down to see Berryman at Germantown about two miles from our camp, also in Jenkins Regiment I saw all the Spartanburg men I there learned in fact, I saw a note addressed to old Dr Win from an officer that will afford him a chance for a duel if he wishes one say nothing about this he made some remarks about the officer when he was here of a very insulting character, and he is called uppon to account Elijah Smith John Beard and Jimmy, Smiths boy are all well Wm boy not stout, we still have measles, Johny and John Dorch are well in fact those in our immediate neighborhood are well except Rufus White & the two Wm Beardens§ They have measles Rufus White is much better and seems like getting well soon, I saw Dr Hearst today our friends there are well. I want to be remembered to all my neighbors Hiram James and all of them what is Hiram doing is he married. give my love to Betsy and Lizzie and all the children tell Tony to write to me I have had no letter from Jno Norman tell

---

* Oliver E. Edwards organized the 13th S.C. Regiment, and was elected Colonel of that Regiment in the fall of 1861. He was a cousin to the Fosters.

† Landrum, *History of Spartanburg County*, 511.

‡ Dr. John Winsmith.

§ Lt. William Bearden and Private William S. Bearden.

him to write remember me to Sam may the Lord bless and preserve you all is my prayers B. B. F

(nothing of Mid yet)

Perrin Foster became sick with a severe cold accompanied by fever chills and a cough. His Father worried about his son's ability to tolerate duty on an advanced post and sent him to a home in Charlottesville to recuperate. Traveling by rail through Gordonsville, Foster arrived in Charlottesville on the 14th. *

L. P. FOSTER TO HIS MOTHER

Gordonsville Virg. Sept 14th 1861

My Dear Mother,

You will be surprised to see the post mark of this. I have but time to tell you how I came here. I have had a very bad cold and cough for a week or 10 days & Father became uneasy about me, feared I would get sick at an advanced post & advised me to come back to. So I left the camp Thursday evening for Charlottesville to which I will get this evening & write you. I am much better than when I left the camp for my cold being attended with sweats I became weak. Now I am stronger and think I will be at my self in a few days. I still have a bad cough but will get over it when I get in a house. I will remain in Charlottesville only few days, and return to the reg. Now don't think my case worse than it is for I have written just as it is & I have been in fine health until I took this cold.

Remember me to all.

yr affec son L. P. Foster

P.S. I would write more but the mail closes in a few minutes.

L. P. FOSTER TO HIS MOTHER

Charlottesville Virg. Sept 14th 1861

My Dear Mother,

I wrote to you from Gordonsville this morning to tell you about my trip here. First I will tell you I was not worsted by the trip. I met Drs. Laborde and Branch.[†] (The latter from Abbeville & seemed to know all the Perrins.) They were very kind when we got here. They got me a private house Mrs. Dunkums. Quite a nice place, so I am quite comfortably fixed, & will I think soon be able to return to my duty. Now I will tell you about my trip this morning and this place. I passed through some of the prettiest country I ever saw. The R.R. runs nearly all of the [way] just

---

* Lewis Perrin Foster, *Letter to Mrs. Barham Bobo Foster dated September 14, 1861* (South Caroliniana Library, James Rion McKissick Collection, P Box 1).

† Dr. Isaac Branch.

under a ridge of mountains on the right which I took to be the Blue ridge & much of the way seemed hedged in by mts on both sides. The valey between was beautiful, being in many places interspersed with tobacco fields, which looks very pretty, very much like our cotton when about knee high. At a distance So* the scenery was very fine, some of the country seemed old and worn out. The no† sides of the mountains gave them quite an old but nevertheless grand appearance, I passed a high hill upon which Jefferson was buried. What a change has passed over the county since his death & though he had been dead for a good many yrs yet he seemed to know the change would take place. This great seemed to overlook the condition of his whole country even as the tallest tree overlooks the forest. He saw there seed being sown which would germinate contending parties distracting elements thrown in the urn of state which must some day disrupt the whole and which a correctness which surprises us prophesied the scenes of strife which distracts our country adding that his only satisfaction was the he would not live to see the day. This place seemed to be situated in a cove formed by ledges of mountains which extend nearly all around I can see mts in every direction and the distance to them can not be more than 6 or 7 miles. Some nearer so the scenery is grand. I never have seen but two places present so much mt scenery and they are the two gaps in N.C.‡ neither being so completely surrounded as this place. So if I were a poet who could find muses in the mtains forest or cliff, I would write you a song of wonder grandeur & sublimity.

The virg university is about 150 yds from this house I have not been at it but from the campus & builders look fine. So you see I am in a nice place. Charlottesville is a neat little town about twice as large as Spartanburg. I am doing well and you may depend on it so let that be an end on it. I still have a cold a cough and have not entirely gained my strength but now I have a good bed and think I will soon return to our camp. I will write every day and if I get worse will let you know all about it. Father was quite well when I left the camp. Remember me to all. Write soon.

yr affec son, L. P. Foster

L. P. Foster to His Mother

Charlottesville, Sept 16th 1861

My Dear Mother,

I have been here now as you may know from my letters a part of three days and so far as my limited observation goes I must say this is a very pleasant place. The

---

* South.

† North.

‡ The "two gaps" reference is probably to Saluda Gap and Howard Gap, near Tryon, North Carolina, not far from Spartanburg.

people seem kind and willing to [do] whatever they can for the cause. I am better of my cough and think I am gaining strength. I am still a little yellow about the face and eyes but am getting my color. Dr. Branch came up to see me today said I was much better and would soon be well. I also saw Mrs. Branch and Mrs. Sosnoski who were with him. I sit in the parlor and talk to the ladies a goodeal of the time, which I of course enjoy. There is a Dr. here from Alabama named Debour attending a sick son who was in college with uncle Lewis. He is a very clever man and takes quite an interest in me. I am something like a mile from the gen'l hospital and have seen more of our men yet I think I will walk down tomorrow. I passed through Culpepper in the evening of the same day that Mr. Barnett left so did not get to see him. I write every day, hence can not find much which will interest you. In time of peace I would love to live here. It is a most delightful country.

Remember me to the family

yr affec son L. P. Foster

L. P. Foster to His Mother

Charlottesville Sept 18th 1861

My Dear Mother

I have written to you or sister every day since I came here hence can not have much to write. I am still improving—think I am nearly well of jaundice. My cough has also nearly abated. I will go to my Reg as soon as I gain strength. I have walked over a goodeal of Charlottesville this evening it is a much larger and more business place than I expected. I met several of my friends who are here sick in the S.C. Hospital. I have not heard a word from any of you since I came here. It has hardly been long enough though for a letter to come & it seems like it never will get long enough. I have now been here 5 days and seems to me about like a month—not that I have not had all I could wish but I am not satisfied here. I shall go to Jeffersons dwelling at Monticello in a few days. It is said to be a very romantic place. Some one goes there almost every day. You have to pay 25 cts to get in so you may know it is a subject of curiosity. It is situated on a curved wall* not three miles from here. I have no news have not heard any thing of interest from the camp since I came here. I saw some young men here this evening who left there Sunday nothing was stirring there. I can not see why Father has not written but know he has I suppose my letters are delayed at Manassas by carelessness of PM. The sick here are sure to be doing well. I wrote to you asking you if there were any Perrins left here when

---

* Thomas Jefferson designed the serpentine walls; the curved walls have the same strength as straight walls but use 25% fewer bricks, because the walls can be made one brick thick.

Grandfather* moved south. There are a crowd of Chiles in Louisa county but I can learn of no Perrins. I think I will have to remain here some time after this war to hunt up our kin. I know there is a "vast" of them here somewhere. The Lynchburgh R.R. passes in less than 100 yds of this town. There is an old preacher here named Ficklin. Miss Dunkums father quite an old and interesting man. These people know Mr Kennedy Mr. Broadus of the S.B.S. at Greenville was the former pastor of the B.C.† here. The people here think there never was such another man.

Remember me to all & write.

Directing to me University P.O.

Charlottesville Virg

Care of Miss Dunkums

yr affec son L. P. Foster

B. B. FOSTER TO HIS WIFE

Flint Hill
September 19th 1861

My Dear Wife,

I have just returned to camp from Munsons hill after being there five days we have been relieved by a Maryland regt. one from georgia and one from virginia we had no general engagement, we stayed five days in one mile and a half of Arlington heights in sight of Alexandria and the great citty of washington we had rare fun up there the first two days our pickets fought all day the first day and the second day until late I could see every fire The bullets fell thick and heavy but not one of our men was hit in the evening of the second day The enemys pickets threw up a white flag and sent a sergeant half across the field one of our men met him he wanted us to quit shooting at them and their men would not shoot at our pickets and the fighting stopped we think we killed several and I am sure many of them wounded. when we were relieved we left every thing quiet and no prospect of a fight. our mission was to hold the hill until we could fortify it and that is going on rapidly I really believe that Abes Army if left to them would disband in twelve hours. We took one prisoner he says they do not want to fight us the truth is our boys out shoot them and they are afraid of us. I am of opinion in a fair open field fight we can easily whip three

---

* L. P. Foster's grandfather was Samuel Perrin (1770–1828). In 1794, Samuel Perrin married Eunice Chiles and lived in the Hard Labor Creek area of Abbeville District. William Perrin, Samuel's father, had moved from Virginia to a land grant in South Carolina in 1773 with his wife, Mary Clopton Perrin.

† SBS is the Southern Baptist Seminary in Greenville, South Carolina. B.C. is the Baptist Church. John A. Broadus was one of the first faculty members of the Seminary.

to one. I am of opinion that arlington heights will not be attacked soon and when done it will be done by Johnsons command and our Briggade will not be there the Virginians will bear the brunt of that battle. we can take attacking without loss any time we want it we are throwing up fortifications below arlington to command the Potomac the fortifications will be complete in a few days planting heavy guns to blow up their steamboats and command the river I hope this war will soon be at an end the yankees destroy everything where they go burn houses and fencing, if you could see the destruction here you would say never let it come any nearer home I cannot form any opinion here as to when the war will end. This is sure I think that they never can conquer us. I believe that grand old capitol will be in ruins and that before a great while unless they make peace that is all the chance to save it. I am getting along very well without Mid we boarded awhile and then joined Kenedys mess we are living well enough The boys* are all good to me I am not allowed to do any drudgery hardly ever get to saddle my mare. in truth it has troubled me but little John Nance has two boys he makes one of them feed my horses black our boots and wait on us generally Lieut Harris† has two boys he came to my tent this evening and begged me to take one of his which I have agreed to do and shall not need another. Ed has written for me, if he comes we will mess to ourselves I have also written to James Williams to send me a free boy and I will pay the boy. I will not risk another here they are leaving constantly These yankees tamper with them in spite of all we can do more than half the men and women here are yankees you are right when you say we must have spies in the camp we know there is no doubt of it but we do not care much for that all we want is to get them to fight us and that soon if they would leave their fortifications we would soon end the war all the things came except one pair of boots I take it there must be some mistake about two pair one pair came for Perrin none for me, you must not send me any more cloths. I have a full supply one more camp shirt is all that I would have now. I do not need any boots or shoes. I have plenty of every thing after awhile when cold weather sets in I would like to have a pair of double more homespun pants and nothing more. order any thing you need from Coldwell Blakely & Company sugar salt molasses rice etc I am pleased with the camp shirt it is the best thing I have seen except the overshoes every body here likes the overshoes. I received a letter from Tony and by the by the most satisfactory letter I have had since I left home tell him I am truly obliged to him for it and hope he will write again very soon I will answer it as soon as I get a little leisure. I found two letters from Perrin, he has jaundice, he is at Charlottesville Dr Laborde and Dr Branch took him to a private house and have him in charge he is much better and all I fear is he will return to camp too soon. he was looking

* "Boys" refers to the enslaved when referencing people serving officers.
† Lt. N. S. Harris of Company I of the 3rd S.C.

better than I ever saw him until he was taken sick he had a cold, and I was afraid it might terminate in Typhoid fever, and I sent him back it proved to be jaundice, he did not want to leave camp. I know we were to go to munsons hill and was afraid he would be too much disposed I kept it a secret from him or he would not have gone back. he wrote today that I must be sure and let him know if there was any prospect of a fight he will not like it when he hears of our trip, Seaborn Lanford has had a new spell of Cow fever* he is better and I think will get well Dr Robert Smith is still in Richmond but entirely out of danger Wm Bearden and Wm Smiths sons are all better Henry Barnett is mending. I received a letter to day from Dr Craig in Richmond whom I wrote to look after all our sick in Richmond. Story† Wofford and Mc Arthur‡ are all mending. I hear from Henry Barnett by one of our men return-ing, you have no idea of the care I have on my hands. I know our friends all look to me to have their sons attended to and I do the best I can for them and after I have done that it is a pure chance. The truth is money would be no temptation to me go through what I am obliged to do here Love of Country is all that keeps me here Johny & Jimmy are both well and the fattest Beards I ever saw. They fatten like pigs Thom Zimmerman is in fine health perfectly sober and the finest looking Zimmer-man I ever saw. Littleton Bullmans§ son by his first wife is dead he belonged to the Spartan Rifles he died last week. Rufus White is almost well of the measles, I have not been able to hear from John West. he is in some Alabama Regt, but cannot find which one. Tell Jno Norman he must make his calculations to stay with us another year I shall depend on him to do so. I will write to him one of these days. The two Worford boys are doing well. I cannot account for you not getting letters Two days never pass without me or Perrin one writes and Ed writes every day we get letters from home regular the fault must be at Manassas such an amount of mail matter goes there that they do not get it off in time and the letters all suffered to lie over.

* Cow Fever is cowpox.

† Either George H. Storey or James S. Storey, both of Company K, 3rd S.C. Probably George Storey because he is recorded by Wyckoff as having died in Richmond two days after this letter was written.

‡ Either J. N. McArthur or Joseph M. McArthur of Company K of the 3rd S.C.

§ A Littleton Bulman from Roebuck, South Carolina, had a son named Alexander Bulman of Company K (Spartan Rifles) of the 5th S.C. Tedards identifies him as having died on September 29 from typhoid fever. This is confusing because in his letter of September 25, Foster refers to Bullman's son with a name beginning with an "E." I did not find E. Bull-man or Bulman in the Soldiers and Sailors Database managed by the National Park Service. "Descendants of George Bulman II, http://www.genealogy.com/ftm/i/b/e/Linda-J-Iben/ BOOK-0001/0006-0003.html (accessed September 29, 2016). Rosalind Todd Tedards, *A History of the Fifth South Carolina Volunteers* (Wilmington, N.C.: Broadfoot Publishing, 2013), 126.

give my respects to Mr Beard all the neighbors I desire to be remembered to the Montgomerys. All feel near to me oh how I would be pleased to see you all once more. I saw to day the church that George Washington worshiped at and held his membership. the yankees had been in it and scribbled all over the seats and walls what a shame can any people ever prosper that will do such things. I must say that Ed is mistaken about Col Williams drinking that is not so he is almost an infidel but not a drunkard so say no more about that, let it rest forever Col Williams treats me like a gentleman and is very kind to me he is unpopular but a clever man I think remember me to Sam and Mr Harmon and all the children, tell Jennie to learn her book and be a good girl you nor Sallie must not think of coming here it is no place for ladies may god bless and preserve you all is my prayers tell the negroes I have not forgotten them tell them all howdy for me

your affectionate husband
B B Foster

L. P. Foster to His Sister, Jennie

Charlottesville
Sept 20th 1861

Dear Jennie,

I have written to all of the family many times [since] I left home but you and have concluded to write you a few lines this evening. I will first tell you how I am. I am better than when I came here I am nearly well of my cough also of jaundice but still have dyspepsia.* Well now Jennie I suppose you are well as I never think any of you sick unless I have some grounds for thinking. I expect you enjoy yourself better than any of the rest. Do you love Sunday school now & do you go? Do you study any and recite your lessons to sister you ought to study every day and learn fast. You ought to be learning to write you see yr brother has been trying to learn to write for a long time and cannot write much yet. I want you to write to me and tell me what you do. Also what all the townfolks do and as many of the neighbors as you choose. Does Tony go to school yet and tell me how Capt Kemper is coming on. You must treat him well but be sure never to feed him out of the left hand as you will have him selling birds left handed. I suppose he is quite a smart young gentleman. I expect you had a fine time when Aunty was up. Write me something about them I hope to be able to leave here before very long & go back to the camp and watch uncle Abe and the first chance I get I will send you one of his little toe nails. i.e. If I can get it. I have now here nearly half of my time. When my time is out I shall come home to see you all. If the war does not end sooner. Remember me to

* Dyspepsia is indigestion or heartburn.

all the family also to Sam and Jno Harmon. Tell them all to write to me. If you were here you could see plenty of tents well I must close.

Yr affec Brother,

L P Foster

My Dear Mother,

You can learn from what I have written Jennie how I am. I saw a man today just from camp he saw Father. He was well and everything quiet, no present prospect of a fight. When you write direct to the care of Mrs Dunkum, Charlottesville Virg. I have not recv'd a letter from any of you since I came here.

Write Soon

Yr affec son

L P Foster

L. P. Foster to His Brother, Tony

Charlottesville

Sept 21st 1861

My Dear Brother,

I write to you all so much that I know my letters must very dull and uninteresting. I write every day whether I have anything to write or not. I have just returned from a walk to the university beside their chapel, lybrary, gymnasium grounds & c. There is much there to excite interest in the mind especially where it has had a liberal share of useful borrowing. There are many things here which will call to mind all he has borrowed and teach how little it is. The buildings are not so fine as I expected to see Their grounds are perfectly beautiful perfectly green with blue grass and clover. The view from the house is most splendid can see a great many miles from it. Though somewhat fatigued by the trip I felt paid. I feel better to day than any day since I came here feel well enough to go to camp if I only had a little more strength. My liver is not acting well yet and I will not get perfectly well until I get it right. Do not be uneasy about me you may rest assured of one thing, that is that if I ever get very low down here I will come home. I am dieting myself very strictly and think it will not be long before I shall return to camp. I want to ride out in the country 3 or 4 miles from this place and get me a boarding house out there. I will try to get a conveyance tomorrow and try it. I wrote the news from camp yesterday in Jennie's letter there is a Lieut from Alabama staying with me named Perry formerly from Edgefield.

The weather has turned much cooler & I fear we are going to have some rain as it is about time for equiniolial showers. Also for it to turn cold soon the people here say the winters are not severe until after Christmas. I have heard it hinted that some of the S.C. Regs camped among the rest were to be recalled during the winter for home protection. It is very doubtful whether it be so or not. Remember me to all and write soon.

Yr affec Lou—L P Foster

L. P. FOSTER TO HIS SISTER, SALLIE

Charlottesville Virg
Sept 23rd 1861

My Dear Sister,

I wrote to you yesterday but as I wish to send some things to you & Nunie and Jennie I will write again to you. I have been down in Charlottesville all the morning went to one of the many mineral springs of virg situated in one of the prettiest green lawns I ever saw. Weeping willows hang all around it making a green brown much [. . .] with the ground color and presenting retreat in which the most fastidious might have to dwell. I saw a squirrel skipping about the spring the second one which I have seen since I left S.C. As I came back back through the town I met up with Mr. Clopton* the colporteur† of the Albemarle association. He introduced me to his wife—they invited Lt. Perry and myself to go out in the country and spend some time at their house. They are Baptists and seem refined and clever. If we can get off we think of going. They live 15 miles from this place under the Blue ridge. These Virginians are kind people, but it realy seems to me that I meet friends every where, I have much to be gratefull for in this respect. I am still improving, go all about would go to camp but my medical friends think I had better wait little longer. I have no news to write you. I send you and Nunie 4 pieces of music you can divide them among yourselves. The words are pretty never heard the music—thought you might prize them as coming from virg. Only one is a martial piece viz the Alamo. I also send Jennie a little book *The Faithfull Dog* and the soldiers hymn book. She will prize them as coming from me. This is a great place for books. I see a great many here I would like to send home but the postage is heavy and mails are uncertain & I am afraid to risk your getting them. I [went] out to the Calibriel springs about 2 miles from here yesterday evening. It is also a lovely place situated in a shady hollow with a neat little pleasure house around it. We got some grapes & chinquapins on the road. These folks don't know what musquillad [. . .]‡ are—never saw any.

Remember me to all the family and all inquiring friends.

* L. P. Foster's great-grandmother was a Clopton before she married Samuel Perrin and settled in South Carolina.

† A colporteur is an itinerant seller of books, especially religious books.

‡ From the context, Perrin seems to be referring to muscadine grapes as being unknown in the Virginia mountain region.

Tell John and Josie to write to me. I have not rec'd a letter from any body since I came here yet I am not uneasy quesur lusit up troupe never anticipate evil the evil itself is hard enough to bear without the anticipation. Besides I look upon it as rather distrusting the goodness and mercy of god.

Write soon

yr affec Brother
L. P. Foster

L. P. Foster to His Mother

Charlottesville

Sept 24th 1861

My Dear Mother,

I wrote to Sallie yesterday telling her that I intended going out in the country to Mr. Clopton's for a few days. I am now in a store in Charlottesville writing to tell you that I will start in a few hrs. He lives 15 miles from her up in the mts Blue Ridge. It is said to be a delightfull place and my invitation was very pressing.

At first I thought I would not go but would return to camp in a few days but met Dr. Gunels of Laurens C.H. and he advised me not to return to camp yet as the duty was very hard and I not overly strong. I shall remain up there about a week then return and go to our camp. Lt. Perry & I have hired a hack, will enjoy a ride in the country. I am still improving have my appetite again for every thing but tobacco and don't think I ever will want it again. I am able to walk every where and will be at my self in a very [few] days. I rec'd a letter from camp yesterday evening. Two of our men had been wounded on picket guard & Dr. Toland was under arrest for meeting some of the enemy under a white flag and having a conversation will probably be sent to Manassas in disgrace. Father and Ed well. No other news.

Remember me to the family.

yr affec Son
L. P. Foster

B. B. Foster to His Wife

Army of the Potomac

Sept 24th 1861

My Dear Wife

I saw a letter from Sam to Perrin which is the latest from home I was glad to learn that you were all well I had a letter from Perrin last night he is improving all I fear is that he will come back too soon. I wrote to him this morning urging him not to come back too soon. Sebron Lanford is down with typhoid fever. he is low but thought to be better. Dick White is bad with the same both had measles and got well and took the flu Capt Kennedy has the Jaundice bad The other boys are tollerable well Jon & Jimmy Beard are in fine health so is Elijah Smith. The worford boys well The general health is improving in the camp I think we will have frost here in a few days

Nothing new in a military win. I think there will be no more at this place soon I think They are waiting on Floyd* Lee† and Wise Floyd has whiped Rosincranch‡ killed about six hundred of them without losing a man.§ This is believed here. yesterday a party of negroes attempted to cross the line of pickets to get to the yankees. They were fired uppon and the leader killed. I am fearful that it was Mid This occurred at Munsons Hill seven or eight miles from our camp he would be apt to be in the lead, the negro was buried and I had no means of finding out without taking him up and I have concluded to let the thing rest. It is a difficult matter to cross our line without being shot. The pickets are very vigilant. I am in fine health gaining flesh fast. I begin to feel like a man again Tell the children Dinah is as fat as a bear I have another very fine mare both in good file so is well remember me to my dear children tell them to write remember me to Sam and John Lancaster and all the neighbors

may the lord bless you all

your husband

B B Foster

B. B. FOSTER TO HIS SON, TONY

Army of the Potomac
Flint Hill Sept 25th, 1861

My Dear Son,

I received your truly welcome letter several days ago. Whilst on Munsons hill I was delighted to see that you had a good idea of the farm and things about home. I hope you will continue to take an interest in the farm and try to learn how to manage things to advantage. I am anxious about home and things there. I hope you will attend strictly to the hogs. Give them the slops from the kitchen tell Mr

---

* Brig. Gen. John B. Floyd.
† Gen. Robert E. Lee.
‡ Brig. Gen. William S. Rosecrans.
§ Apparently, a reference to the Battle of Carnifex Ferry in West Virginia on September 10, 1861. This engagement between Brig. Gen. John Floyd and Brig. Gen. William S. Rosecrans drove the Confederates from the Kanawha Valley, facilitating the establishment of West Virginia as a new Union state.

Harmon to save every shuck and all kinds of roughings wheat straw and every thing that will help to run to a cord and save the corn from the beginning. have every thing attended to tell Mr Harmon to gather up all the beef hides and swap them for leather and have the negroe shoes made begin in time we will not be able to buy shoes as they cannot be had. get leather at once have the gin house made secure and kept locked so that what cotton is made can be taken care of keep the corn crib secure you and Mr Harmon must exercise your judgement in saving wheat I want a large crop of wheat sowed the new ground cotton patch the one Gentry got his mule killed in must be sowed in wheat sow most of the May wheat the Brickyard field all of it in the Milgore wheat. tell John to gather that as soon as it will bear it pasture it down and sow it as early as he can. If he can I want him to pay particular attention to the oxens get them fat to help out the meat they are mycherious and I think we had better kill them. begin to sow in time is the right way. all things are going on here as usual nothing new the pickets keep shooting each other all have been returned from that position by the regiments and sent back to our old camp to secure it our pickets killed yesterday evening six yankees among them one captain a negro was killed there which I very much fear was Mid he is so headstrong they attempted to run across the line of pickets and the sentinel shot the front one dead. The others run back I would like to have you here with me but your mother must be cared for I want Mr Harmon to stay another year write me what he will do. I now think as I have done for some time that there will be no more fighting for a good while I think this demonstration in front of Washington citty is a military strategy uppon the part of our Generals to prevent Scot from sending his forces to other points until Wise and Lee can whip the Federal troops in western Virginia. Floyd has whipped Rosencranch badly killed 600 of his men without loosing any on our side.* I think Wise and Lee will sweep out the last Federal troops soon if so it must have a powerful effect. write soon I get a letter from Perrin every day. he is mending fast remember me to your mother & sisters Sam and John

your father B. B. Foster

I wrote that Lt Bullmans son E[. . .] was dead it is not so he is alive and better. Dick White is bad Seborn Lanford is better. I feel Nesbit[†] will die. Johny and Jimy well also Elijah.

---

* Another apparent reference to the Battle of Carnifex Ferry on September 10, 1861.

† Private W. A. Nesbitt of Co. K, 3rd S.C. died much later, on July 15, 1864 in Petersburg.

L. P. FOSTER TO HIS SISTER, PROBABLY SALLIE

Mr. Thompsons*
Charlottesville
Sept 25th 1861

My Dear Sister,

You will see from the above heading that our scheme for going in the country had been put in execution & succeeded admirably. Lt. Perry & I left Charlottesville he in a rockaway[†] with Mr. Clopton (who is Mr Thompsons son in law and lives here) and I in a waggon of one of the neighbors. It was not traveling in the finest style in the world yet I enjoyed it very much. We had a very rough mountainous country to travel over but yet one full of interest to a stranger—crossed several very pretty little streams—the dry creek and Ravanna River[‡] which are curiosities to me as I have been in a portion of Virginia where there are no creeks of any consequence. We got there after dark but not two late to get one of the very nicest kind of suppers. The family is composed of Mr Thomson Mr & Mrs Clopton and their little girl at least no others are here now. They are the kindest people you ever saw you could not take more pains to accommodate and please me than Mrs. Clopton. They are a refined yet plain old style Virginians. I never saw a place where every thing was kept nicer. We had one of the nicest dinners to day that I ever saw. A large ham splendid beans fine mountain Irish potatoes good sweet potatoes tomatoes nearly as large as a saucer cooked and raw fine mutton good chicken nice wheat and corn bread fine butter as yellow as gold cold milk honey as clean as expected & as nice peach preserves as you ever saw was some part of our bill of fare. Well you would like to be here. The family are very devoted Christians. Mr. Thompson a Methodist & Mr. & Mrs. Clopton Baptists Mr Thomps. who is 63 yrs of age yet an active & very cheerful man attends to his farm which is pretty large. The water here is very fine apples fine & some good peaches. Now I must try and tell you some setting of the situation. Well it is situated just under the blue ridge in much such a place as at Billy Mills was on the Howard Gap[§] except that the mts here are much more numerous and in plainer view. We can see them in almost every direction— the Blue Ridge and its knobs forming a semicircle around it and other mts visible

---

* From the description in a letter in *The McKissicks of South Carolina*, it appears that the Thompson plantation was on present day Fox Mountain, northwest of Charlottesville. Graydon, Graydon, and Davis, *McKissicks*, 193.

† A Rockaway was a type of carriage.

‡ Rivanna River, a tributary of the James River.

§ Howard Gap is located on present day I-26 between Tryon, North Carolina, and Saluda, North Carolina, where the interstate ascends the Blue Ridge Front into the Blue Ridge Mountains.

in the distance in the other half of the circle Some of the mts are or seem so high as Tryon* yet they seem grand and inviting. They are not near so steep as Tryon. It is 14 miles to the top of the B. Ridge but only 5 or 6 to the top of several wor[. . .] mts. Mr. Thomson is a pretty large tobacco farmer has the finest I ever saw with 1000 lbs per acre. He has a plantation upon the river 6 miles from here from which the view is very fine. I want to go up there soon. There are plenty of fox here and [. . .] fine hounds. If I was just right [well] I would have fine sport. I am gaining rapidly my cough nearly well and getting stronger. Mrs. Clopton gives me [. . .] for my cough. I will remain here about a week and return to my reg.

Remember me to all write soon.

yr affec Brother
L. P. Foster

Direct to Charlottesville

L. P. FOSTER TO HIS SISTER, PROBABLY SALLIE

Selma Albemarle Virg
Sept 27th 1861

My Dear Sister,

You will learn the name of this place from the above. I never found it out until yesterday Selma is surely the name of this residence. There is no p. office here. This mountainous country seems to be as thickly settled as ours and so far as I can see the people are all true citizens & feel a deep interest in the war. They will do any thing in their power for a soldier. They all seem to be good livers. Some of them sick. There are but few young men about here. All are in the army. The people here all know how to make their soldiers comfortable. Mrs. Clopton has the finest blankets I ever saw. All of her own make. Has a pr weighing 16 lbs each. All wool. They are fine as soft as wool can be made. I have spent my time here very pleasantly indeed. Mrs. Clopton & everyone else here are as kind to me as you could be. I would love to live here very much indeed yet I know it must be very cold in the winter. These people all seem prepared for it with good close houses. You see none of our large windows and doors here. No air holes—every thing tight. To day is a very wet day. I am compelled to stay in doors but as I have good comp I enjoy it very much. Mrs. Clopton is good company for any one. Miss Lucy Chapman also is here who is quite an interesting lady. Seems to be one of the best I ever saw. I have found no want of friends since I came to Virginia. Have been treated rather as a relation than a stranger. I do not now dread the winter so much as I did. I think we will stand it here as well or better than the Yankees we are more accustomed to

---

* Tryon Peak, at an elevation of 3234 feet, is located at Howard Gap on the Blue Ridge Front.

the open air. They have been in factories and stores all of their lives—besides this climate is not so changeable as ours. It will get very cold here about Christmas and remain so until the winter breaks. Which will render it easier to bear than if it were so changeable. Besides we will go into winter quarters some where. The war can not be carried on here with any vigor by either side during the winter. As the roads will be too muddy to allow the transportation of artillery waggons or any other kind of wagons. The mud in the part of virg where we are camped is very stiff having so much lime in it. Father was well when I last heard from the camp. No war news. If you don't get a letter every day now do not be uneasy as there is no p. office here. I am still improving will go to my Reg the 1st of next week.

Remember me to all

Write soon

L. P. Foster

L. P. Foster to His Father

Selma Albemarle Co Virg
Sept 27th 1861

My Dear Father,

I have now been at Mr. Thompsons three days & can say I never have seen a more pleasant place. The family are still as kind to me as any one could be. I am very much improved and think I will leave here for the reg next Monday but will not set any day yet. I went up to Mr Thompsons plantation on a Mt. 6 miles from here yesterday. It is on the top and sides of a pretty high mountain from which I had a splendid view of all the country round here on this side of the Mts. On the other side it was separated from the B Ridge by a narrow cove called Brown's Cove. The Blue Ridge is about a tall as Tryon as seems like one continuous mountain as far both ways as I can see. The view was the best I ever saw in my life. The land on the Mts is fine. Mr Thomps. sows corn and tobacco was very fine. I never saw better hill corn—yet the fields were so steep that you could not ride a horse up them—his hands were cutting tobacco and curing it hauling it & the air and water there was fine. We went to the house and got a bunch of corn bread, cool milk and butter. Our people at home know nothing of good milk and butter—I have never seen a family live better have better or nicer fare than Mr Thompson. All the people of this county—so far as I can see are loyal. The[y] seem very much interested in the War and willing to do any thing in their power for the Southern Cause. There are very few young men about here—all have gone to the seat of War. It is very rainy today and I am compelled to stay in the house—I have not rec'd a letter from you since I left the Camp and none from home—only our friend Ed. If any books come for me take care of them. I am some distance from any P.O. and hear very little of what is going on in the army.

Write to me direct to Charlottesville.
Tell Ed to write.

Yr. affec. Son

L. P. Foster

L. P. FOSTER TO HIS BROTHER, TONY

Selma Albemarle Co Virginia

Sept 28th 1861

My Dear Brother,

I think you must have a kind of aversion to writing letters at any rate it has been a long time since I have rec'd one from you. I think some 6 wks or two mos and perhaps longer. I have enjoyed my self very much here. The [people] of this settlement are very kind especially the ladies who seem to think the soldiers need and desire all of their time. Mrs Clopton is a pretty good Dr better than many a man whom the town has given a license to kill. at least such is my opinion. She had given me tar water* and wild cherry for my cough until she has near about cured it. She will nurse and dose you after her own way. This is a great country. The more I see of it the more I think I would like to live here. The people all seem to be good livers here we see houses and every thing which is good to eat. There are plenty of red foxes here and some grays plenty of wild cats and grown hogs and the finest hounds I ever saw in my life. Mr Thompsons overseer, Mr Coleman has some beautifull. They caught a red fox a few days since. They catch them almost every race. Mr Coleman offered to save me some puppies I shall tell him to save them and try to come by here when I go home and get them. They are very tall and slender very much like Lap. I would give a pritty if I could send some home to you now. I have no news to write you I am some distance from any regular PO hence can't get much news from the seat of war. Father was well when I last heard from the camp and everything quiet. I there is no chance of a fight in that part of Virg. but you will learn of fight in western virg every once and a while until one or the other army gains a decisive victory. I think they will rely more on the navy than their land army. They think to fight in a way that we can not meet them. But I don't think that their navy can amount to much. I am about well will return to the reg the first of next week

Tell John & Sam to write to me.

Remember me to the family and write soon.

Yr Affec Brother

L. P. Foster

---

* Tar water was a mixture of pine tar and water and was used as a tonic.

My Dear Mother,

I have just written to Sam all the news and shall enclose this in this letter. I write merely to answer what you wrote about our over coats. I would like very much to have one. Father thinks he will not need one. If Lockwood can cut me a long frock over coat, double breasted, with a long long cape coming below the small of the back I would like to have. I want one like John Wofford* had. I can have my measure taken here which I had better do. We are all well.

Write soon, I have tried to have my measure for my overcoat but failed. Lockwood can cut from my measure from uniform coat with the above directions. Make it heavy.

Yr affec son

L P Foster

B. B. Foster to His Daughter, Sallie

Army of the Potomac Flint Hill
Sept. 28th 1861

My Dear Sallie

We have just returned from an expedition which kept us out three days and nights without tents. It rained on us which made it disagreeable to have to be on the wet ground, we marched upon Lewinsville, a beautiful little village one mile and a half from the Chain Bridge which is immediately in front of Washington Citty. The object I think was to toll the Yankees out from their breast works but they would not come out. I went in half mile of their camp saw their tents and flag very plain. I cannot tell much about the prospect here but I am still of opinion that there is not much prospect of a fight soon. They are hemmed up and occupy but little space this side of the Potomac. I rec'd your letter yesterday, containing some strips of newspaper. I was surprised at your mothers complaint of not writing. I have written regularly. Perrin is still at Charlottesville or in that neighborhood, he speaks of returning in a few days, I have written to him and asked him to get a furlough and go home for a month. They say that he can get a furlough from that point. I think he is not likely to make the application as he seems anxious to remain in the army a furlough can't be had here. I am stouter and healthier than I have been in four months gaining flesh every day. The sickness in our camp is abating. Rufus White is still low but thought to be better and will likely get well. Sebron Lanford is mending and I think will get well. Our men are coming back from the hospital every day. Several came in last night, you must not think because a man is in the hospital that he is bad off. Our men are learning to go before they get bad and many

---

* Either John Henry Wofford or John Wesley Wofford of Co. K, 3rd S.C.

go that ought not to go. The ballance of Kenedys men are tolerable well. Kenedy has had the jaundice he is much better. Mr. Harmons letter came and I broke it and read it I was glad to hear from him tell him I approve of his plan of fattening the hogs early and on peas if he has enough tell him to save all the roughny he can and put the hogs up whenever he chooses to. We have fine fare here in camp have fine dinners, upon the whole we live well. Tell your mother not to be uneasy about our losing another boy we are doing very well. Ed Bobo is here well and hearty he has had affection of the bowels slightly but is now entirely well and seems satisfied as well one could expect him to be. Remember me to your dear Mother, Tony, Jennie Sam and Mr Harmon and all the neighbors. Write often. May the lord bless and preserve you all is my prayer.

Yr. affectionate Father
B. B. Foster

B. B. Foster to His Wife

Advanced Forces Army of the Potomac
Sept 29th 1861

My Dear Wife,

Woodward Allin* is here and although I wrote to Sallie yesterday I have concluded to write today. We are all back from our trip and in camp. We had a trip of three days to Lewinsville near chain bridge in a mile and a half of the place. They would not leave their entrenchments to fight us we did not attack their fortifications, so we returned from camp. I look for Perrin back to camp in a day or two. I wrote to him to take a furlough and go home. He can get one there at Chancellorsville but not here. He is so fraid that we will get in a fight and he will not be in it that I think he will not go home. A letter came to him from Mary Perrin and a postscript from Luis.† They are well and have moved to Cynthiana. Things were so warm where he was he did not consider it safe to remain. the letter came by hand some young men came on and joined the army from Luis's county. He says all the young men nearly are with us and will fight for us. The sick are all better and the sickness abating. Rufus White is better & Lanford is improving. Johny Jimy and

---

* Woodward Allin is likely Woodard Allen from Cedar Spring, South Carolina. Landrum, *History of Spartanburg County*, 568.

† Probably Perrin's cousin, Mary Eunice Perrin, the daughter of Lewis Perrin and Elizabeth Hinde. Mary Eunice Perrin married an Achilles Perrin. An Achilles Perrin was an early editor of the Cynthiana Democrat newspaper in Cynthiana, Kentucky. The connection is plausible but not confirmed.

Glynn all the boys very well. I have gained flesh fast and never felt better oh how anxious I am about you all at home remember me to the children Sam Harmon and all the neighbors what has become of Hiram James may the Lord preserve you is my prayer

Your affectionate husband
B. B. Foster

B. B. Foster to His Wife

Army of the Potomac
Flint Hill Sept 30th 1861

My Dear Wife

I have no news to write nothing new has occurred here since I wrote last. I must confess that I cannot see through Beaureguards movements We have glorious news from Mosouri our forces there have whipped them badly and took prisoners & arms any amount over 1/4 of a million specie.* The northern papers acknowledge it. I think you will hear in a few days from western Virginia we sent reinforcements to Wise from Richmond They have had time to get there I think the next big fighting will come from that quarter. Perrin has not returned Dr James saw him Sunday he was mending fast and said he thought he would come back today. I have urged him to stay and go home he is so anxious about the army that he will I suppose come back. I am sorry to say that Rufus White is very bad and I would not be surprised if he dies all the ballance of the boys are doing well Ed Bobo is getting fat Joe Walker† and Alfred Foster‡ are here. I have a bad pen and nothing to write remember me to the children and all the neighbors tell Jennie to be a good girl and I will bring her something

May the Lord bless and prosper you all
is my prayer who goes to the Association

your affectionate husband B B Foster

---

* This refers to Col. James Mulligan's surrender of the Federal outpost at Lexington, Missouri, on September 29, 1861 to General Sterling Price's much larger forces.

† Joe Walker is likely Capt. Joseph Walker of Co. K (Spartan Rifles), 5th S.C.

‡ Capt. Alfred Harrison Foster of the Morgan Light Infantry (Company F) of Micah Jenkins's 5th S.C. Regiment.

B. B. Foster to His Wife

Flint Hill
Army of the Potomac
Sept 1861

My Dear Wife,

I see from the newspapers that you are all stirred up about us here. I see that Williams fifth Regt. instead of the Third has been engaged and cut to pieces. it is all false our regiment had had no general fight only our pickets or in other words our advanced guard did engage the enemys advance guard but not one of our men was hurt or touched by a ball. That was at Munsons hill. I wrote you from that place and after we returned to camp at this place I wrote a long letter and am utterly supprised at the newspaper reports I think you ought not to depend uppon them they seldom report the truth, and now say that the telegraph wires have been extended to within a mile and a half of our camp and if any thing like a battle takes place you will see a telegraph from me in the guardian* or some of the Columbia papers. if there is any thing like taking arlington or washington on hand I am not aware of it. I think it ought to be done and fully believe we can take it but still I think it will be the last resort. I received a letter from Perrin last night he is much better he has had Jaundice and we have at least twenty cases of it in our camp now. The health of our camp is improving The sick ones are returning every day our regt is much stronger than it has been In a few more days I think we will have frost. it is very cool now all of our sick as far as I am able to hear is improving and doing much better than I expected few deaths considering the number of cases. I cannot account for the mails why it is you do not receive our letters it is not our fault. we write often at least every other day and most of the time every day dont trouble yourself about a boy for me I do not want one sent. I cannot trust them. I will make some shift. I am now doing very well have no drudgery to do. Our men are all in fine spirits and anxious for a fight. I must confess that I am anxious to have the war to a close and as nothing but fight will do it I am willing to try my hand and take the chances. no one knows how anxious I am about you all. I feel like I must see you all before long, money would be no inducement for me to stay here, love of country is all that keeps me oh how I would rejoice to lay my eyes upon my dear wife and children once more tell all the negros haody for me, I am anxious to see them, My dear wife you must not think of such a thing as coming here it is no place for a lady, if it was I would send for you all. remember me to my dear children Mr Harmon and Sam and all the neighbors may the Lord bless and preserve you all is my prayer your husband
B. B. Foster

* *The Daily Southern Guardian*, a Columbia, South Carolina, newspaper.

B. B. Foster to His Wife

Army of the Potomac Flint Hill
Oct 1st 1861

My Dear Wife

I have nothing to write about we have had but little excitement here for several days. a considerable moving of troops but no fighting. The health of our camp is improving hardly any new cases. we sent of the last one of our sick to the hospital day before yesterday Rufus White was very bad and shall be surprised if he gets well. our Regt is recruiting fast. we are getting stronger every day. We had the pleasure of seeing Jeff Davis at our camp today he is at Fair Fax C.H. a noble looking old fellow he is The boys cheered him he raised his hat and complimented them. Perrin has got well and will be in camp in a day or two I sent you his letter. The boys Johny Jimy Elijah are well Benjamin Smith is puny not very stout at no time sick is better and will start home discharged in a day or two The worfords are well. I learned that James Williams has started me a free negro and that he will be here in a few days Cunninghams* wife writes that negro would start last Thursday. I think Ed will be at home in ten days. He is home sick and wants to see his wife. I tell you the sight of a woman here is good for the sore eyes. When our Regt went to chain bridge or Lewinsville we were camped in three miles of where Miss Martha Swink lives. as soon as she found we were there she sent her sister and a negro boy in a carryall with a jug of firm buttermilk a jug of wine home made two firm cakes of butter three baked chickens a fine pone of light bread and about a peck of nice biscuits all for me and Perrin Miss Martha was sick herself and could not come her Father had gone south with his negros I would have gone to see Miss Martha but could not leave the Regiment. This was a great piece of kindness. If I had not got it I would have suffered. We had no time to prepare rations we had only half an hours notice before we had to start to stay three days and nights. When we go into winter quarters, I will I think get to go home and not before we had a fine frost this morning remember me to the children Sam and John all the neighbors tell Majr Lancaster to write me I would like to hear from him may the lord preserve and save you is my prayer

Your affectionate husband
B B Foster

In the next letter the Garnett Affair refers to the engagement at Rich Mountain in Western Virginia on July 11, 1861, in which Confederates under general command of Brig. Gen. Robert Seldon Garnett and directly commanded by Col. John Pegram were outflanked by Federals under command of Gen. Rosecrans. The Confederates

---

* Probably the wife of Henry M. Cunningham of the 3rd S.C.

surrendered 555 soldiers to Federal troops. Gen. George McClellan was given credit for the victory, significantly enhancing his public image.

L. P. Foster to His Mother

Selma Albemarle Co. Virg
Oct 1st 1861

My Dear Mother,

I rec'd your long and interesting letter last the first which I have rec'd from home since I left the camp. I also rec'd one from Nunie & one from Ed Bobo. I will I assure take care of my self and not return to camp too soon—yet I will return in a day or two & don't think I will be returning too soon. I'm very much improved—our reg was not engaged regularly at the time you spoke, on Munsons Hill. They had some skirmishing but no one touched. Father and Ed were well—you asked If Ed had been with me. He has not. I meant by we some other sick soldiers at Mrs. Dunkums. Kershaw's reg had engaged the enemy at Lewinsville and driven them off. With considerable loss to him and three of ours of the Butler guards killed and another wounded. A Lieut. In our reg was ordered to sustain him but I don't think they got a fight, as Ed said in his letter. The enemy were quick and it was not probable that they would have a fight.* I saw the piece Father wrote for the Spartan, and did not think it severe. It was not intended for a rasping. I think our Batallion has done much perhaps enough for the present yet I contend that they have no right to cease to give so long as they are able and there is a necessity. I fully appreciate all they wrote about it and acknowledge its justness. I suppose I will get the things you sent by Allin as our reg remained on Munsons Hill only five days and he must have remained longer than that but I doubt whether he will get farther than Richmond. The Chiles here spell their name as you say—and there are plenty of them in this state. Mrs. Clopton says that if you are a relation of Abner Clopton you are related to her husband—says all the Cloptons in America are spring from one who is buried at St. Peters Church in Kent Co Virginia. One of Judy Cloptons sisters has laid out the geneology of the family. She says there are plenty of Cloptons and Crumps in Kent Co. I have met no Lees nor Whites as yet but there are plenty of Sullivans living in Gordonsville. Also Quarles. I suppose the recent victories of our troops will revise the map. The news is indeed cheering—why should any one feel a doubt we have whipped them in every fight—yet save that little Garnett affair. I hope yr apprehension as to a swift union association is unfounded. I can not believe that such view would ever assume such form. I intended to have gone back to camp yesterday but have been persuaded by my friends here and yr letter to defer it for

---

* This probably refers to the engagement at the Vanderburgh's House near Alexandria on September 28th and 29th.

a day or two. The people here are still very kind & seem unwilling to give me up. Miss Lucy Chapman is still here. She is a great girl. One of the kind who can turn her hand to any thing she wishes to. Is there any talk of our congressional election. Will Farrow* be elected. If no one but he and Rudsuns I hope he may be elected. I was glad to hear that our coast defenses were becoming so strong. I don't think S.C. will ever be attacked, yet it is well to be ready for any emergency. If I should get worse I will be sure to write to you of it—but I do not apprehend any such thing.

Remember me to the family & all enquiring friends.

Tell Sam & John they both owe me letters.

Write Soon

yr affec son,
L. P. Foster

L. P. FOSTER TO HIS MOTHER

Selma Albemarle Co. Virg
Oct 2nd 1861

My Dear Mother,

Every day brings with it the duty of writing home whether I have any thing to write or not. I have seen no papers since yesterday and can give you [no] news. I am still improving, but concluded to take yr advice and remain a day or so longer. I rec'd a letter from Ed saying that he had heard that all of his children were very unwell, and if they did not get better soon he should go home. To day has been a rainy day and I have been in the house all day. Mrs. Clopton is a right good Dr. and a better nurse and will make me do as she thinks best. I have such a good appetite that she can not do much with me at the table. Ed said the sickness of croup was abating and our sick men coming back rapidly. Of this I was glad to hear for nothing is so dispiriting to soldiers as to see their comrades sick and unable to help. God grant that the day may soon come when our army shall be free from sickness and all able to do duty. Then I think proud Washington would like Troy fall in her own ashes. Mass of rottenness. Miss Lucy Chapman is here. She is as kind as a sister and wants to do all she can to make me spend my time pleasantly, I am afraid she keeps me in the house talking to her too much so that I can't take exercise enough.

Remember me to all.

Tell them to write to me. Yr affec son

L. P. Foster

* This may refer to James Hamilton Farrow who represented Spartanburg to the S.C. state legislature from 1860–1862. He served in the First and Second Confederate Congresses from 1862 to 1865.

B. B. Foster to His Daughter Sallie

Army of the Potomac Flint Hill
Oct 3rd 1861

My Dear Sallie

I have recently been writing mostly to your mother. I rec'd your letter some time since and have not answered it. I have nothing of interest to write every thing quiet here and has been for some time. I cannot find out any thing about the course to be pursued in this war. What will be the next move, I am not able to see. I am tired of inactivity much prefer to be moving. We are hard up for something to eat. We have eat out this country we have beef and flour plenty no bacon no lard sometimes coffee and no sugar we cant buy any butter eggs or chickens and what these people that live here will do I cant say. They are bound to suffer. I hope we will be sent south to winter, our boys seem to enjoy themselves very well and are anxious to press forward. I am looking for Perrin back tomorrow our sick is all getting better that have not died. John Roebuck* of Kenedys company is dead. Rufus White has been sent back and I have not heard from him since he left. Remember me to your mother and Tony and Jenny Sam and Harmon Majr Lancaster and all the neighbors write soon let me know what has become of Mr. James Tell him to write to me. God bless and preserve you

your father
B. B. Foster

B. B. Foster to His Daughter, Probably Eunice

Army of the Potomac
Flint Hill Oct 4th 1861

My Dear Daughter

I received your letter tonight and although I wrote you yesterday I will answer. I was rejoiced to hear that you and your mother had spent the day with Mrs Enuch Smith, I now think the war will surly end after that visit. Did it rain before you got home. I hope this will not be the last visit you will pay to the neighbors. I think if you and your mother could get in the way of it and not stay at home so much you would enjoy yourselves better. I would be delighted to hear of your visiting more. I am compelled to stay in camp most all of my time, it is a great relief to me when

---

* John Roebuck of Co. K, 3rd S.C. Wycoff states that it was Jesse Jefferson Roebuck who died of measles in the Lynchburg Hospital on September 27, 1861, and that John Roebuck was captured on 6/30/64 and presumably survived the war. Landrum agrees that Jesse J. Roebuck died of disease at Lynchburg. Apparently, Foster had received erroneous information. Landrum, *History of Spartanburg County,* 671.

I am sent out to take charge of the picketts. I get to see the country and the air seems more pleasant and besides I see now and then a Lady, which reminds me of Carolina. The duties of the camp are familiar to me and drilling the Regiment is not an easy task. I do not have to studdy and about the greatest trouble to me is writing letters without a table no conveniences for writing. I am truly glad that you are about to get up an association for the benefit of the Third Regiment. I hope you will first make Capt Kenedys company comfortable first and after that then if any thing to spare let it be for the Regt. I think if you provide for that company you will have done a good part without any more. You are mistaken about the soldiers suffering They all have plenty of clothing as much as they can carry or take care of and will need no more clothes until the last of november or the first of December, and then nothing fine coarse strong clothes is the thing for the army coarse shirts pants [. . .] socks &c all coarse and strong. There is no use in sending light and flimsy things here. I would like to have one more flannel shirt and one camp shirt tell your mother that the camp shirt she made me was too long in the sleeves and I would prefer risband and buttons just like any other shirt in all other respects it is just right another like it and then I shall need no more clothes for my term of service. I have a plenty tell her the boots did not come and I don't want them if they will do for Tony let him have them tell Tony to practice shooting with a rifle off hand shooting make himself a marksman and if he has time study his tactics. If the war continues long we may have use for it, oh how anxious I am to be with you all nothing but my duty keeps me away our all is at stake and my country needs my services and hard as it seems to be it must be so for awhile. May our heavenly father reconcile us to our fate preserve us all and at last take us to himself is my prayer do remember me kindly to your mother Tony and Jennie Sam and Norman

Your father B. B. Foster

Rufus White is better. Benj Smith is improving balance of the boys well. Dr. Robert Smith is mending fast. Jonny and Jimy fat and Elijah.

Henry Barnett has since come back. Perrin will return tomorrow or next day he is well riding about in the mountains he stays with an old man at the foot of the mountains.

L. P. FOSTER TO HIS SISTER SALLIE
_____

Selma Albemarle Virg.
Oct 8th 1861

My Dear Sister,

Yours of the 27th came Saturday. I would not be willing to see you here in the capacity of nurse or in any other capacity. Could you be here as nurse of only a few say a dozen all the time it might do, but for you to be placed a hospital with 6 or 7 hundred sick of all classes and with various diseases. These not all in same but different houses would be too much for you to stand too much for any but stout men or very masculine women. They have several lady nurses in the S.C. hospital. And every thing is kept neat and the sick well cared for, but it is not a gen'l hospital not more than 100 in it. Now you may think these numbers very great, they are, but not so much so as you might suppose. These hospitals i.e. the various hospitals in virg—are filled from an army of over 200000 men perhaps three hundred thousand. I doubt whether they are as great as the proportion of the sick in many parts of our state. Yet it is much greater than it ought to be. There is not that can be paid to [. . .] that there ought to be. Col. Williams is very particular and if we had had as easy a time as many other regiments, I imagine our sickness would have been light. I wrote to Tony yesterday telling him of my conclusion to remain here and recruit another week. I am better than I have been but when I went to Charlottesville Dr. Rhunbert advised me to come back here and remain a week longer, so I hired a horse and buggy and came here yesterday morning. All seemed glad to see me. Lieut Perry still here with me, will I suppose have a pleasant wk. Have wet weather. Saw Dr. Gunnels at Charlottesville just from camp. No sign of a fight. All well. No news to write. Remember me to all and write soon.

Yr affec Brother
L. P. Foster

When nations come under stress, money begins to flow and profiteers have their day. These letters contain many accounts of price gouging and profiteering during the Civil War.

Letter L. P. Foster to His Mother

Selma Albemarle Co. Virg.
Oct 9th 1861

My Dear Mother,

I love just helping Wm Thompson gather cucumbers gathered two half bushels growed since Saturday. Fine vegetables coming on I have not much to write about. Have been pretty weather A man came through this settlement yesterday purchasing teams and wagons to haul provisions from Staunton to the army in western virg. Purchased a driver, waggon and whole team from Wm Thompson. I am glad this war has not broken out in S.C. You have no idea how heavily if bears on some of the Virginians who live near the scene of war and who are loyal citizens. The yankee Virginians all manage to make it a matter of speculation. Their motto is to make money while their lives are spared, which if I had control of things would be no great while. They are all fit subjects of the gallows. And if this war lasts much longer, soldiers will take the thing in hand and rid the country of their traitorous defrauders. They will prolong this war many a month if allowed to remain here and who will suffer more from them than the soldiers yet have been compelled to let them alone tho we are here for the avowed purpose of driving our enemies from our soil. Things should not and can not remain thus. No news to write. I am getting quite stout. Remember me to all. Write soon

Yr affectionate son L. P. Foster

CHAPTER 5

Winter Quarters

Perrin Foster returned to his company from Charlottesville on October 15 to find significant troop movement in progress. Beauregard and Joseph Johnston had concentrated their forces around Fairfax Court House in preparation for a proposed invasion across the Potomac and an attack on Washington.[*] No such attack was authorized and on the 15th, after some indecisive marching, the Confederates withdrew from Fairfax back to the Centreville area, camping on the grisly Bull Run battlefields.

Winter campaigns involving large forces were nearly impossible because roads turned into deep mire, preventing effective troop movements as mentioned by Perrin Foster in his letter to his sister on September 27. However, Confederate leadership seems to have been unsure whether McClellan planned a late autumn offensive. By October 25th, the brigade had returned to Centreville where the soldiers expected to go into winter quarters. Centreville was chosen over Fairfax Court House because of the good supply of wood needed to build cabins and for fuel and because of the good water supply available.[†] Instead of ordering the soldiers to begin preparing snug winter quarters, though, the Confederates were set to preparing fortifications. By the time the soldiers were finally ordered into winter quarters in the closing days of 1861, many soldiers had already built cabins or attached fireplaces to their tents to better fend off the winter cold. With extra time on their hands, letters grew longer and more frequent, and a detailed picture of the soldiers' camp life emerged.

L. P. FOSTER TO HIS MOTHER
———————

Blackburns Ford Near Manassas
Oct 18th 1861

My Dear Mother,

I am again with the regiment came to Fairfax Station on the cars Tuesday night found everything in confusion preparing to fall back on Bull Run so I set out fast

---

[*] Dickert, *History of Kershaw's Brigade*, 77–78.
[†] Dickert, *History of Kershaw's Brigade*, 82.

back for our regiment 5 miles not knowing whether I would find them or Yankees in possession of Flint Hill. I found them preparing to march. They left about 3 oclock that night marched two miles when Col Williams gave the command right about march. We went back to our camp remained there in line of battle all day. A little after dark again took up line of march. Marched here 10 or 12 miles where we now with any am't of troops all around us. What it all means no one seems to know. No one seems to apprehend a fight. All seem to think our generals are trying to draw the Yankees out—show no idea that they will follow us & hence think there will be no fight. They have not advanced this side of Falls Church. We did not fall back because we could not hold our positions but they would have greatly the advantage fighting there so near their fortifications—as they could retreat behind them so soon as worsted. We have rough times in every respect quite a contrast to what I have had lately. I have stood all finely—feel well as ever. Father looks better than I have seen him since we joined the army. I think equally as fleshy as before—and in very fine spirits. Our reg has increased in numbers a great deal. Most of our sick back. James Story is in very bad health does not complain much but looks very bad. We are getting a furlough for him to go home and recruit. I stopped at Culpepper a very few minutes inquired of Henry Barnett there about Dick White. He is much better getting well fast. Henry Barnett came on with me looks tolerably well as well as he has since he joined the army. Health of regiment good no more of interest. Write soon to

yr affec son

L. P. Foster

I met Dr. Lucken at Charlottesville—Lieut [. . .] Allen. Came to Culpepper with him where Allen is. He got off there—intended coming here but I don't suppose they would let him pass Manassas & we can not go there for him now. Allen getting well. I am much obliged for things by Mr. Allen. One of our mess prepped a turkey today we will have a fine time over it.

LPF

Father got two letters from you this evening.

L. P. Foster to His Sister, Probably Sallie

Blackburns Ford
Oct 20th 1861

My Dear Sister

Two days have passed since I wrote to mother & no sign of Yankees advancing. I still have not much hopes of coming on us. If they would come I think we could put a stop to the war in Virginia for this winter. I however don't think there will be more regular fighting unless it comes off in a very few days They may be cavalry fighting but armies will have to go into winter quarters at least by Christmas. We

have had no cold weather here yet last night coldest night we have had lately and our blanket enough cover. I think our troops will stand the winter here better than they have the summer. Our troops are returning from the hospital every day. I am standing it finely. Father is on picket. Will come in today. I am with the baggage detail at camp. I rec'd several letters from you just before I came back but had no way to carry them, had to tear them up. If there were any questions in them I do not recollect them, we are now camped on the battle ground on which the 5th S. C. Reg was engaged on Sunday evening. [. . .] some 4 or 5 miles below the [main] battle ground and only a short distance from the battle ground of [Thurs]day.* There are plenty of dead yankees on the battle field yet. They were buried so shallow that they have either washed up or curious persons pulled them up. Many of their heads have been taken off. This would be a bad camping place for the superstitious. It is strange how little men are moved by such spectacles. They seem to regard them only as so many dead hogs. I can not feel towards as towards lowest men. The remembrances of the past comes to vividly to mind. When I think of them how in cold blood they murdered our men and fell victims to their own folly. It is sunday and chaplain still absent. Things too unsettled to have any preaching. Tell Toney to send me a good gold [. . .] and staff if he hears of any one coming here. Remember me to all
    Write soon.

Yr affec Brother

L. P. Foster

The fight at Leesburg on October 20, 1861, described in the following letter, is known as the Battle of Ball's Bluff. What began as a Federal surprise attack lead by Gen. Charles P. Stone on a small Confederate camp commanded by Col. Nathan George Evans, resulted in the Union forces being trapped against the Potomac without transportation across the river. Of the approximately seventeen hundred attacking Union forces, about nine hundred were killed, wounded, captured, or missing. Confederate losses were light. The Federal attack was viewed as a huge blunder and, following the debacle at Bull's Run, was the last straw for the Republican leadership. General Winfield Scott was forced into retirement on November 1, and was replaced by George B. McClellan as the new general-in-chief, with a mandate to take action against the Confederates across the Potomac.†

* The 5th S.C. was engaged at Blackburn's Ford late in the afternoon of Sunday, July 21, 1861 at First Manassas. This unit had participated in the Battle of Blackburn's Ford a few days earlier on Thursday, July 18, 1861.

† DeWitte Boyd Stone, Jr., *Wandering to Glory, Confederate Veterans Remember Evans' Brigade* (Columbia: University of South Carolina Press, 2002), 7–8.

L. P. Foster to His Sister, Probably Sallie

Blackburns Ford
Oct 22nd 1861

My Dear Sister

Your letter directed to Charlottesville came day before yesterday. I have nothing of importance to write. There was a considerable fight at Leesburg day before yesterday.* Our men under command of Gen'l Evans† gained a decisive victory— drove them back and took several cannons. This is all that we have heard relative to it. This much came from gen'l Bonham & I suppose is true. We have wet bad weather—but it is not very cold. Our position seems to be very unsettled and probably will be for some 3 wks. We will be moving about trying to decoy the yankees from their dens. This is my opinion now, after that time I think we'll go into winter quarters somewhere but it is just impossible to tell anything about our future movements. Some think some of our troops will be sent to Kentucky, others to the coasts. I think that all will remain here, which I think most probable. There no signs of approaching yankees yet & I don't think our genl's can get them here. I have no idea that McClellan will risk a general engagement. He would have to bring his entire army were he to attack our present army here—some of this country looks like a boundless citty of camps.

Have you seen Ed‡ since he came back. How is his family. I did not get to see him at all. Did Wm. Hatchell & Miss Lizzie have a wedding. I have nothing that could possibly interest you. Dr. Hearst Tom Q. Wade C. & Tom C. are all in fine health. Write soon yr

affec Brother L. P. Foster

L. P. Foster to His Mother

Blackburns Ford Oct 23rd 1861

My Dear Mother,

Not much news—but what I have is glorious. The report of a victory at Leesburg true—52 prisoners were sent to Manassas this morning. It is estimated that 300 drowned in the river. Their retreat from the battle field was attended with so much panic that when the reached the river so many crowded on the boat that they sank it. Other casualties on other side not known. Our men captured 6 pieces

---

* The reference is to the Battle of Ball's Bluff near Leesburg on October 20, 1861.

† Gen. Nathan George "Shanks" Evans commanded the 7th Brigade in Beauregard's First Corps at the time. He later commanded the 18th S.C.

‡ Edwin Henry Bobo.

of artillery. Does this not look like invasion and the subjugation of a brave people. The[y] make a better effort at return to their side of the Potomac than at any thing else that I know of. They can't stand fire at all. They profess to be our masters to be about whipping us into subjection yet stand crouching before us and when we advance upon them then panic seizes them. They want to see the other side of London. There are no signs of a fight here. The appearance of the camps here is grand—especially from Centerville—where there seems to be a boundless city of camps. We had a great deal of rainy weather, but it looks like clearing this morning. Dr. Lucken in camp—leaves tomorrow. Sam Means left day before yesterday. I have no news to write. When or where we will take winter quarters I can not yet tell. Some times I think the winter campaign will be on active one. They have been carried in colder climates even in Russia.

Remember me to all and write soon. yr affec Son

L. P. Foster

P.S. The victory at Leesburg was better then first reports—732 prisoners have been sent to Manassas. 1200 stands of arms taken 400 yankees killed and wounded—300 drowned in crossing the river in their retreat—Gen'l Evans had only 4 Regs—the enemy 10,000 god is with us—we have nothing to fear. L. P. F.

L. P. FOSTER TO HIS SISTER

Centerville Oct 26th 1861

My Dear Sister

Father rec'd a letter from Mother yesterday evening asking about what kind of gloves best for soldiers. I don't think they will be of much service without fingers as a soldier has to use his fingers when ever his guns [..]. No sign of Yankees yet and I have no idea that they will come here at all. I would not be surprised if we are now in the camp where we will take up winter quarters. I think it probable that we will be moving about for some time yet and it may be most of the winter. I sent you a little relic from the battle field also one for Jennie. They are made from the splinters of tree struck by a canon ball shot at Col. Jenkins regiment. I could not get good pieces as a great many had been taken. I will need some more union shirts and some over shirt before the winter is out. It will be pretty cold here. I will wear 2 or three under shirts in real cold weather. If you can buy me 3 or 4 knit shirts like those you sent also 2 pr drawers at a reasonable price or can make them of flannel & can make me two more camp shirts, I will be much obliged. I will write where to send them. I plan to keep you all all of yr time sewing for me, but I can get nothing sewn at any price. If you can buy the heavy knit shirt and drawers I will like them as well and they would be less trouble to you. I have no news to write.

Yr affec Brother L. P. Foster

SALLIE FOSTER TO HER SISTER, EUNICE

Home
October 31 [1861]

My Dear Sister,

The time for writing to you has arrived and really not one thing of importance to write.

We are all getting along very quietly at home, go through the same routine every day of which will give you a portion of the routine, work for the soldiers, write letters, send to the office, and read the papers. Elias goes to the office every day but as yesterday was so cold Mother concluded not to send him. After supper was over she stood it as long as she could, and sent Sandy post haste to the office. We did not get any letters, only the Guardian and very little of interest in that. We received a letter from Brother this week dated the 22nd which is the last we have had from him. When he wrote, he was at Blackburns ford on Bull Run. I expect you have seen from the papers that our forces have fallen back to Bull Run and Manassas. Brother wrote that there was tell any amount of dead Yankees all around their camp. It is perfectly horrifying for me to think of it. Tony received a letter from Elijah Smith. He said his pillow was a tomb stone and that they were having a rather ruff time of it now.

Cousin Edwin came down to see us Monday. He looks better than I have ever seen him, is real fat. He says Father looks better than he ever saw. He gave us a full history of camp life which was very interesting and entertaining. He does not expect to go to Virginia any more but speaks of going into service in his own state.

Sallie and Ellen Beard left here this morning. Jennie has gone home with Shem to spend the day. They only spent last night with me. Sallie is considerably taller than I am. She is taking music lessons from [. . .] Peake. Ellen is very interesting and I think has improved.

I have knit Father a scarf this week and one for the Society* and have three others to knit for the Society. We expect to send Father and Brother this week a box of clothes and something to eat, but I can tell you it is hard times about something to eat here. We have beef all the time nearly and we are now using confederate coffee. If you don't know what that is, I will tell you, it is Rye. Jennie is knitting a pair of suspenders for the Society. She says she don't see any use in her playing all the time when her poor soldiers are fighting for her. She made us quite a patriotic speech about it the other day, it is true patriotism in her, not work for the soldiers for she don't love to work. Mother and I spent Tuesday evening with Mrs. Lancaster,

---

* Ladies' Aid Societies sprang up throughout the Confederacy to provide clothes, blankets, flags, and foodstuffs to soldiers, usually units associated with their home communities.

found Mrs. Barnett* and Sutt there. Mrs. Barnett can certainly talk more than any one I ever saw.

Mr. Harmon is busily gathering in the corn.

I hope Carries mother will give her consent for Carrie to come home with.

I must close this scrawl. Write soon. Give my best love to Anna Belle and Nonie.

Your Devoted Sister

Although Oliver E. Edwards was somewhat older than the Foster brothers and sisters, he had long, close associations with those cousins. He had lived with the Fosters as a young man while studying at the Spartanburg Male Academy and later brought Perrin Foster into his law firm while Foster studied for the bar exam. Edwards was a law partner with Simpson Bobo in the firm Bobo & Edwards, one of the most prominent law practices in the Spartanburg District.† He was a representative from Spartanburg district to the S. C. House of Representatives in 1856, 1858, and 1860. When war broke out, Edwards volunteered into Col. Micah Jenkins's 5th S.C. In the fall of 1861, he returned to South Carolina and organized five companies of troops from the Spartanburg District and brought them to Camp Johnson at Lightwood Knot Springs near Columbia, South Carolina. These companies formed the core of the 13th S. C. Volunteers.

By late December, the 13th S.C. was stationed at Pocotaligo, then soon moved to nearby Green Pond along the Charleston and Savannah Railroad Line. The 13th and other regiments defended South Carolina from Federal units that had occupied Hilton Head in November 1861. Tony Foster enlisted and joined Edwards's 13th S.C. in March 1862. Edwards led the 13th in the Seven Days Battle, Second Manassas, Antietam, and Fredericksburg before receiving a mortal wound at Chancellorsville in 1863.‡

Col. Oliver E. Edwards to His Cousin Sallie Foster

Camp Johnson
Oct 31st 1861

Dear Cousin Sallie

If I am not mistaken you once asked me for my ugly face. I have recently had some taken & have concluded to risk sending one to you. They are not as good as I desired, but the artist says to take the whole person on a scale so small, he can do no better. I know you will be surprised to get this letter, but I hope it will only assure you that whilst my perplexities are very great, I have not forgotten my good

---

* Mrs. Barnett was probably the mother of William Henry Barnett.

† Eelman, *Enterpreneurs*, 18.

‡ Landrum, *History of Spartanburg County*, 508–513.

cousin. I was sorry to hear of your father's loss, but a great deal more interested for the health of Perrin whose health I learned is precarious, or was so. I hope he is quite well by this. I presume you are all tired of living without father, husband and brother. This nefarious war will not only separate many of us temporarily, but forever in this life. It is meet and holy to reflect upon the inroads which are being made into the domestic circle,—but duty before every thing. I am now at the head of a considerable family—some complaints, but I am pleased to say the most of them have grown out of my refusal to furlough. More complaints by outsiders than in the Regt. The health of my men has been bad—getting much better—one wing of my Reg't leaves next Monday—the other Wednesday. I shall not go for a few days as Gen Ripley* has given me permission to attend the Legislature. We go to Ridgeville a mile above Summerville on S.C. Railroad. Your cousin Jane† is at her mothers— will go home Saturday. Can't you go & see her while she is there?—she will follow me when I get settled. Where is Eunice? What is Toney doing? Who looks after your fathers businesses? How is his crop? Write me a long letter to Columbia next week & tell me all the news. Give my love to your Ma, Eunice, Toney & Jennie. Accept a great deal to yourself from your

Cousin Oliver

Medora Snipes left for Fla. yesterday.

In October, Lieutenant Colonel Foster was sick and given leave to go home on furlough. He did not return to his regiment until December 14th.

L. P. FOSTER TO HIS FATHER

Oct 31st 1861

My Dear Father

[. . .] you will want to hear [. . .] our regiment [. . .] you return to [. . .] nothing of interest has occurred this evening since of any importance. Our brigade was out this evening the old field where we spent our first night after leaving Flint Hill for drill on the exhibition of a <u>battle</u> flag to be our guide in future actions. I will say nothing as to the design as I think it is imprudent to commit it to paper. It is very [. . .] pretty and appropriate. One will be given to each regiment. Some seem to expect [. . .] but I can see nothing to indicate a fight. The health of our reg fine a few cases of jaundice & diarrhea are about all. We now have our men nearly all returned from the hospital. I paid off our acc't with the commissary [. . .] Some

---

* Brigadier General Roswell Sabine Ripley, Commander of the Department of South Carolina.

† Cousin Jane was Edwards's wife, Jane Gary Edwards.

one say they saw you at Gordonsville. Fannie's leg doing well. Col. Williams better. Yr friends inquire after you often. All in fine spirits. The package which John Coats sent you a fine bottle of whiskey marked to be taken in small doses three times a day as a detersion to rogues but I soon smelt a rat and tasted the medicine which proved to be whisky. Remember me to all & write soon. as we are anxious to hear from you.

Yr affec son

L. P. Foster

L. P. FOSTER TO HIS FATHER

Camp Near Centerville
Nov 7th 1861

My Dear Father,

I suppose you are at home before this time as I have heard nothing from you since you left Richmond. Our reg was paid off day before yesterday to the 31st Aug. There is a man here named Whipple Hill a merchant from N.C. but originally from S.C. trying to get permission to furnish supplies to this reg but Col. Williams seems not to be in favor of having any such thing connected with the regiment. Canada Scott our boy wishes to go home by the 15th of Dec, says that he is compelled to move his family and get a place for them to live at next year. The papers and camp are rife with rumours with regard to the yanky government such as that Scott has resigned that Cameron[*] and Seward[†] have quit the cabinet that Fremont[‡] has refused to submit to the administration and says he will prosecute the war on his own responsibility. That McClellan threatens to resign if they force him to make the advance before spring. There is no doubt I suppose but that there has been another fuss in the cabinet and that negotiations of some character are going on between the two governments. Some say concerning peace. A courier from Lincoln went to Davis day before yesterday with dispatches there an also various reports about the intervention of foreign powers. What it all amt's to it is impossible to tell. Lieut Weir[§] of the Quitman Rifles died day before yesterday was sick but a short time. Tell Mother please to knit me a thick pair of wool gloves with long arms coming to the elbows so as to go up under the coat. Gamaliel James[¶] folks sent him a pr that were

[*] Simon Cameron, Lincoln's Secretary of War.
[†] William H. Seward, Lincoln's Secretary of State.
[‡] Gen. John C. Fremont.
[§] Robert Long Weir of Co. E, 3rd S.C. died of typhoid pneumonia on November 5, 1861.
[¶] Private Gamaliel W. James of Co. K, 3rd S.C.

just the thing let all the fingers be closed. Col. Williams better. No war news. Every body gives out the idea of a fight. Remember me to all and write soon.

Yr affec son L. P. Foster

On November 7 and 8, 1861, Commodore Samuel Francis DuPont attacked and occupied Port Royal Sound and occupied Phillips and Hilton Head Islands. The cannons on the Federal gunboats devastated the Confederate artillery at Fort Walker on Hilton Head Island and sent the defenders running for safety. DuPont sent a boat ashore, found the fort empty, and raised the United States flag there.

In the letter below, Foster reported the superior skill of the Union gunboat artillery crews at Port Royal. In subsequent letters, he repeatedly reflected Confederate respect for the firepower of the Federal gunboats. Nine months later he similarly commented on the superior Union artillery performance at the Battle of Malvern Hill.

L. P. FOSTER TO HIS FATHER

Camp Near Centerville
Nov. 9th 1861

My Dear Father

I have not heard from you since I left Richmond nor have I heard from home in several days. I however hope you are at home by this time. I have not yet taken up the note you mentioned. I have had two rides in search of it. Maj. Fisher knew nothing of it but when I told him where it was given he said Maj. Barber had it. He is at Centerville. I will take it up today. We are all anxious to hear from Port Royal. I stayed at Manassas last evening until the cars came to get the latest news, but got nothing encouraging. Several of our guns had been dismounted & 7 vessels had passed our batteries. The enemies gunners shooting with accuracy and ours at random. They were expected to land that night. That is the 7th. I wish they would send us there. We know those Yankees and know they are not to be feared. We know that when the bayonet is drawn down on them they will run like craven cowards. I hear the S.C. army is greatly demoralized. Write soon about it. Gen'l Jacksons Brig. Was sent to Winchester last night. They are expecting a fight there. No signs of fight here. Every thing quiet. I hear that Bonham is going to have winter quarters put up here, has already sent for [. . .] boards we have made requisitions for new tents.

Remember me to all & write soon.

Yr affec son L. P. Foster

P.S. Bob Weir 2 Lt of Quitman Rifles died a few days since. He made a profession of religion and joined the Methodist Church. His death bad.

L. P. F.

L. P. Foster to His Father

Camp Near Centerville
Nov 10th 1861

My Dear Father,

I heard last night through a letter from Cap't Cates that you had arrived at home and was quite sick unable to be out. I have not heard from home in near a week. & am very anxious to hear from you. I have no war news in virg except that there was a fight going on yesterday at Winchester*—casualties not known—accounts from S.C. are very gloomy. Indignation is the prevailing feeling our camp this morning. We heard last night through gen'l Bonham that the Yanks had driven our forces back at Pt. Royal and effected a landing that now two union flags are floating over our soil—that our forces retired with a loss of ten men killed. If this is so it is disgracefull in the extreme. Not a comp in this regiment would run with less than three times that loss if then. I have heard that the army in S. Carolina was sadly demoralized & now I am disposed to believe. I feel much more than I will say, but this much. I feel certain that if the S.C. Troops in virg had been there things would have been different. We are all anxious to hear the result. I heard from good authority last night that gen'l Bonham had made application for his brigade to be sent to S.C. but was refused, so we must remain here and await the result. I trust in god and the justice of our cause—from accounts we have not much to hope from our army. No news here. Fanny's foot is nearly well. She has [. . .] slightly. This winter will be very hard on horses. Dina looks well but if I had a good chance I should send her to you.

Remember me to all and write soon.

Your affec son L. P. Foster

L. P. Foster to His Sister, Probably Sallie

Camp Near Centerville
Nov 11th 1861

My Dear Sister,

Your letter came last night informing me that Father had arrived at home and was better. I had nothing from him before since he left Richmond and felt a little uneasy about him, but now hope that he will soon be well. If I were in his place I should remain at home until I got well yet thoroughly well. I have heard nothing

---

* Maybe the news concerned the engagement at Cockpit Point on November 9 involving Confederate artillery commanding the Potomac River. Cockpit point is nowhere near Winchester.

forth from Winchester, don't suppose there has been much of a fight there or I would have heard. No sign of fighting here yet. From the amount of frost & ice we have here almost every morning one would suppose it cold, but I have scarcely felt it yet. I suppose I have been exposed so much that cold can have little effect on me. I have not had my overcoat on since I went on picket. I have ceased to dread the winter. I am in fine health weigh 147 lbs which is within one lb of what I weighed when I joined the army. Our regiment increases in size daily. It seems quite large & is in good fix for fighting. Wade & Tom are well and looking hearty. The news from S.C. is any thing but flattering. I can not see what those fellows have been doing. Port Royal seems not to have been well fortified and to have been untenable. Some here are down on Pickins,* think he has neglected his duty, but Gen'l Boreguard said it would take 20 yrs & 50,000,000 of dollars to fortify it. We are anxious to hear from them. I am not down on the soldiers there so much as some of our men are. Think their retreat may have been a matter of policy not of cowardice.

Remember me to all & write soon. yr affec Brother

L. P. Foster

L. P. FOSTER TO HIS FATHER

Camp Near Centerville
Nov 12, 1861

My Dear Father,

I have nothing of interest to write you. We are still here doing as when you left us. Most of the troops below us, that is towards the McLanes ford & Bull Run have been moved, some to Centerville, some I know not where. Our genls are still going on with their fortifications at Centerville. I think it now much better fortified than Manassas. I was there to day and never have seen such a display of tents in my life. They are crowded thick all around Centerville. I can not see their object in concentrating so many troops in so small a space unless they intend to let them surround them and fight from all sides. They are also having most of our camps fortified. It would seem that our genls expect an attack from the enemy but I can see no more signs of it than when you left & have no idea that they will come here unless they can get us to weaken our strength here by sending troops to other points. Every thing seems to indicate that our winter quarters will be built here. Lanes Brigade† was moved to Centerville to day. the 3rd division has been temporarily disolved

---

* Francis W. Pickins, Governor of South Carolina from 1860–1862.

† Gen. James H. Lane commanded a brigade consisting of the 7th, 18th, 28th, 33rd, and 37th Regiments of North Carolina troops.

Lanes Brig reports to genl Longstreet and ours to Genl Vandorn.* Our Reg in good health and fine spirits. Col Williams seems well again. When he and old potomac are out of fix every thing turns out wrong, but when they are on then feel all goes right. I went to see Maj Barber about your notice but he is off sick and I could not get the note as soon as he comes back I will attend to it. Maj Baxter asked me to tell you please to send the money but you have when I wrote off to his wife by hand on letters that he would suffer the loss if it did not reach him. I offered to pay it to him he said he did not need it at all and only asked as it would be more convenient than sending it home from here. Said he hopes you would not consider it a [demand?] His wifes name is Fannie N. Baxter. If Mr Shands should ask you about his son Anthony† tell him he is here well. Tom begs to be remembered to you. I am asked about [you] very often every day. We are all anxious to hear from S.C. I hear that a great many troops have gone there from Georgia, N.C. Tenn & Alabama and hope it is so. as we can not go I hope they by teach yankees that death is the only price which will pay the penalty of invading So. Carolina. I don't think they should allow one to escape if it is possible to prevent Neither ask nor show any quarter our troops are all in dig outs and if they were there would make it a bloody affair. you know they are not much in favor of taking prisoners away. Remember me to all and write soon.

yr affec son
L P Foster

L. P. FOSTER TO HIS SISTER, PROBABLY SALLIE

Camp Near Centerville
Nov 13th 1861

My Dear Sister,

I rec'd your letter two days telling me of Father's arrival at home which is the last I have had. I wrote to Father yesterday giving him all I had of interest. I write now merely because I go on picket tomorrow and may not have the chance to write again in three or four days as we will be out that length of time. We are out three days in every twelve, which will if we remain here until our time is out give us about 11 more trips. It is the only duty that I dread. The weather is quite cool. I think last night was rather the coldest that we have had. We have no news from So. Ca. yet. I am extremely anxious to hear from there. I know the whole state must be in commotion. I think those Yankees should be run from our soil if it requires every man

---

* Maj. Gen. Earl Van Dorn commanded the 1st Division, Potomac District, Army of Northern Virginia.

† Anthony Shands of Company D, 3rd S.C.

in the state who is able to bear arms to do it. No war news here, every thing quiet. I rec'd a letter from Belle Perrin the other day she seems very much pleased with Limestone. She writes a tolerably good letter for one of her age. Wade and Thom are well. I have not heard from Dr. Hearst since he left for Salem 20 miles below Manassas. I was not surprised to hear that Jim Moore had treated Father so kindly. His treatment of me whilst at Charlottesville was of the same nature. He is certainly a gentleman and one of many noble hearts. I wish I had some thing to write which would interest you. When you write, mention the Montgomerys and Martha Barnett. I sometimes think of writing to them, but conclude they would not answer my letters. Where is Vic Peak. I remember all my old associates very often, perhaps oftener here in the busy times of camp they think of me.

Remember me kindly to all the family. Also John Harmon, tell him to answer my letter. Write soon and often.

yr affec Brother

L. P. Foster

L. P. FOSTER TO HIS FATHER

Camp Near Centerville
Nov 18th 1861

My Dear Father

Yours of the 11th came to hand last night. I was glad to hear that you were still improving. You said in your letter that you had sent me the dispatches I have not rec'd them. I have but little news to write. Our cavalry captured 32 yankees, 38 horses, and 4 waggons night before last between Fairfax and Falls Church.* Our genls still fortifying and preparing for a fight. Holms of Bonhams staff said this morning that genl Beauregard was expecting an attack between Union Mills† & Evansport,‡ but all seems quiet and I can see no sign of it. Van Dorn has ordered that our drills be assumed. Regt drill every evening and Brigade drill twice a week. He has made several changes in our order of things. We are now to have troup every morning at 8 o'clock when the Regts turn out in full strength. Afterwards the guards of the Brig pass in review of the field officer of the day under command of Holms a. as§ genl All the music of the Brig turns out which rends the ceremony imposing. Capt Kennedy read a letter from Capt Glenn last night written from Columbia

---

* This refers to the engagement at Doolan's Farm, where a Union foraging party was captured by the Confederates on November 16, 1861.

† Union Mills, Virginia, was an important defensive position protecting the Manassas Junction railroads.

‡ The Confederates had batteries on the Potomac River at Evansport, Virginia.

§ a. as—acting as.

he will come no farther. He boxed up the things went to our camp and sent them by R.R. to Capt Kennedy. Its doubtful whether they ever reach us. My Overcoat is with him. They are due at Manassas tomorrow. I am on guard to day. Dr Hearst has returned. I saw him yesterday. He told me to remember him to you and family. Also Thom Quarles and Wade. Thom Moorman* sends best regards to Aunt Nancy but has never come to hand. Thom Zimmerman left for a hospital in rear a few days since. has rheumatism. Remember me to all and write soon

y. Affec Son

L. P. Foster

L. P. Foster to His Mother

Camp Near Centerville
Nov 19th 1861

My Dear Mother

I rec'd Fathers' letter of the 13th this evening and glad to hear that he was still improving. I was not surprised to hear that our state was in very great excitement about the yanky fleet at port Royal. The state has furnished Pickins with troops enough to have rendered her coasts impregnable had he put them to work and made them fortify the ports of entry instead of keep them about Columbia and Aiken to frolic and drink whiskey.† He justly merits the condemnation of a brave people. His camps of instruction have been camps of distruction and now the enemy have come on him [. . .] with his ports unfortified but with an undisciplined army. I think Father's notions about sending Tony to Uncle James comp very good for I had rather join the regulars than to a militia, especially when it has such illustrious soldiers at its head as the 45th Regt‡ now has. I suppose though the order calling out the militia has been revoked as I see acct's to that effect. Tell him that I agree with him in his notion as our all being away from home at the same time. It will not do. Though I do not apprehend such a state of things. On such a case he may decide himself as to whether he or I shall leave the army. His horses are doing very well. I find it very hard to get hay for them. Fannies foot is about well. I have nothing to interest to write you. No war news. Our cavalry brought in 24 prisoners last night taken between Fairfax C.H. & Falls Church.§ We are entrenching our camps and making our defense here in case the Yankees do come. The working and

---

* Thomas Samuel Moorman of Co. E, 3rd S.C.

† Aiken, South Carolina, has been a place for sport and entertainment for a very long time.

‡ The 45th S.C. Militia Regiment was also known as the 5th S.C. Militia Regiment.

§ On November 18, 1861, there was a skirmish on Falls Church Road near Fairfax Court House.

guard details from our Reg't are much heavier than they have been for some time past. I would love to be at home with you all. With 7 ms have past—4 more will soon pass and then I will be apt to see home if I am alive.

Remember me to all and write soon.

yr affec Son.

L. P. Foster

L. P. Foster to His Father

Camp Near Centerville
Nov 21st 1861

My Dear Father,

I wrote to mother yesterday and have nothing of interest to write today. Sebe Lanford and Bill Woodruff came back yesterday. Dick Gist left last night & Tom and Bill Nance left with him. They go to Charleston at gov Pickens order. Our independents have nearly every one left us. I had no idea that any of them would stay here during this winter. Our tents were partially arranged yesterday. The front is as it was but each camp has put its tents all on same line to have more room. Col. Williams seems to discourage improvement, seems to think that we will not remain here long. Some construe it in to being ordered home, and are certain of going. I think it means no more than that for some time our position will be doubtfull. The health of the regt very good. Your horses look very well considering how seldom I get any hay for them. We get no hay now except what we haul from Loudon Co. and not much from there. Write me whether you want Dinah sent home or not.

No war news—every thing quiet.

Remember me to all and write soon.

yr affec Son, L. P. Foster

L. P. Foster to His Sister

Camp Near Centerville Nov 22nd 1861

My Dear Sister,

You have not answered the last letter I wrote you yet. I will write you another this morning as I am getting anxious to know what all the folks are doing. I have nothing of interest to write you. We just stay at our camp and do as we have been doing. Some of our men are busy building cabbins to spend the winter others are building chimneys to their tents and preparing to keep warm. This you would think a strange sight a chimney to a tent, but there are more than 20 in our camp. If you were here you would hear more large guns than you could ever think of our artillery are practicing and we can hear them firing every day. Some of the guns are very large louder by far than any you ever heard. The sound would jar you so that you could not stand up if you were very near them when they fired. We have no news for our yanky friends and fear they will not give us a call this winter as bad as we want to see them, they are not very accomodating neighbors. Tell mother that my overcoat has not come to hand yet. I have sent to Manassas twice for it. I reckon you are having a fine time as all of you are at home, write me all about every body. Remember me to all the family.

Yr affec Brother L P Foster

L. P. FOSTER TO HIS MOTHER

Camp Near Centerville
Nov. 24th 1861

My Dear Mother

It is Sunday morning, cold and cloudy. I suppose we will have no preaching, as a grand review of this army will be made to day by gen'l Boreguard. All the troops except those on picket will turn out, Artillery, cavalry, and infantry. It will be a grand display, and will consume much of the day. You will doubtless think it strange that the Sabbath should be chosen as the day for such a display, but to me it does not seem strange, knowing as I do that all of gen'l Boreguards time is taken up. A. T. Shurbutt* is much better. I have not rec'd a letter from any of you in near a week, and am very anxious to hear from you. We are all anxious to hear from Pensacola.† Latest acct's report four hours fighting. The yanks seem bent on doing something with their fleet. They prefer to fight where they can not be followed when running time comes.

Please send me a pr of pants by Father if you have time to make them. If my [. . .] are done they are the very ones. All our comp or mostly all of them will soon need new pants.

Remember me to all & write soon.

yr affec Son L. P. Foster

In the following letter, Foster refers to the event that became known as the Mason and Slidell Incident. On November 8, 1861, the U.S. warship Jan Jacinto intercepted the British ship, Trent, and apprehended Confederate agents James Mason and John Slidell. This touched off an international incident between the United States and Great Britain, lending support to Southern hopes of increasing engagement by Great Britain on the Confederacy's behalf.

* A. Thomas Shurbutt of Co. K, 3rd S.C. died just two days later of pneumonia.

† Refers to the fierce artillery bombardment between Fort McRee (Confederate) and Fort Pickens (Union) on November 22, 1861.

L. P. Foster to His Sister, Eunice

Camp Near Centerville
Nov 28th 1861

My Dear Sister

Yours of the 21st and Father's of the 23rd came this evening and though I have been on picket duty for three days marched 4 miles this morning and was drilled on hour in brigade drill. this evening I will try to answer them tonight. It has been several days since I heard from you before. I get letters about every five days from some of you & don't think I miss writing more than one day in the week. I will enjoy being at home with you all & our visiting relations very much indeed. Yet I must enjoy the anticipation of that for some time before I can realize it. Yet I have [to] stay here exposed myself and worked hard until I don't mind it much. I think of home as much as ever, but am content and shall serve my time out right cheerfully and I will be ready to serve my country as long as my services are needed. I hear through a letter to Bill Woodruff that Ed has failed to raise his company. If it be so I am sorry for it. I wish they could raise a comp. I suppose Bill Roebuck and Andy Woodruff* are helping him. Roebuck fought gallantly on the 21st† & was shot after fighting three or four hours. Col. Ballengers comp I suppose will fail. This easy to see what is the matter. Every body wants office and everybody cant get one. There must be some privates. If the number of officers in the C.S.A. and their pay was reduced it would be better. They might then raise the pay of the privates. I do not mean by this that money makes office seekers in the army. It is rather the fear of hard labor and exposure which is fear based upon ignorance on the hope of shirking out of duty for if an officer does his duty his share of exposure and labor falls little short of the privates. I fear it will be a long time before our soldiers in So. Ca. can "land the Yankees on the other side of the Jordan." I am glad to hear that Father is still improving. I would like very much to be at home to eat some of Toney's suckers and opossum. Tell Miss Sallie that if I were a believer in spirit mappings I should certainly think her a medium. The conversation to which she allowed took place at Charlottesville in Jim Moores room have but he & I present. Toney had written to me that there was to be a wedding in the settlement which I told Jim. He guessed Miss Sallie would be one of the party saying he had heard that she was to be married soon but how she heard of it is the mystery as I don't recollect to have said any thing to any one on the subject. It seems that we can scarcely think a thought here that does not by some means make it home. Our words at least seem homeward bound. Give her my very best respects and ask her if she means to [deny] her absent

* This could be Andrew B. Woodruff of Holcomb's Legion but this is not certain.

† This might refer to the action at Balls Bluff on October 21, 1861, although no South Carolina units are listed as being engaged in that action.

friends the pleasure of mentioning her name in their conversations. We returned from out post on picket this morning. When we left here the ground was white with snow but it was not deep and soon melted off. We had three very pleasant days for picketing. It was quite cold, but we do not mind that. It was the first time that we have been out without rain in a long time. All enjoy picketing in clear weather. We have another division review tomorrow at 12 oclock when our Battle Flag will be presented. Reviews seem to be getting very frequent. Our gen'ls are still expecting a fight on this line and say now it will come off before next Wednesday. What the indications are I can not see. Every thing seems quiet and I still think there will be no fight here and this is not because I don't want one for I wish they could come and get their whipping and let us go into winter quarters, say in Washington! It is rainy now and seem that we are going to have another wet spell. A. T. Sherbutt of our comp died last Monday night of pneumonia. His sickness was short but violent. He was one of the stoutest men we had and a very good soldier. He was buried at Manassas. Capt* applied for a furlough for his brother† to take him home but gen'l Boureguard refused to grant it. Father asked me if we had housed our horses. we have not yet I shall make a stable as soon as I can get time. No news from my overcoat yet. I hope it may come but doubt it. Tom Zimmerman is at Richmond in the hospital. Seargt William Brandon has gone to the hospital at Charlottesville. Mansel Garvin also there. They have all been sick but I think they are now better. We are faring betting than we have been. We have ham, molasses, and good butter also Irish potatoes. I miss milk and potatoes more than anything else. What will be the action of the English government with regard to the capture of Messrs Mason & Slidell is still a matter of discussion here. The news papers would lead us to believe that England will demand them of the N.S.‡ as well as a declaration that they were not captured by their wish. I am not diplomatist enough to even guess at the end. I have written you all the news. Remember me to all the family and inquiring friends.

Your affectionate Brother
L. P. Foster

L. P. Foster to His Father

Camp Near Centerville
Dec 2nd 1861

My Dear Father

I have nothing of interest to write you & merely write to let you know how we are getting along. My mumps have not hurt me much and I don't think they will.

---

* Benjamin Kennedy, Co. K, 3rd S.C.

† S. Z. Sherbutt, Co. K, 3rd S.C.

‡ Northern States.

I am doing nothing for them but sit in the tent by the fire. I suppose they have to run their course. Yesterday morning we expected to have to leave this camp all our conveniences of cabbins, fire places & beds, but I hear the order has been countermanded and suppose we will still remain here. We expected to be moved back nearer the Run near where the Louisiana camp was when you left. Cap't Kennedy has applied for a discharge for Elihu West.* He has done no duty in a long time. I suppose he will get it. I expect my overcoat is at Manassas as I hear there is a box there for Cap't Kennedy. He is going to see after it today. We have some right cold weather, but not so much wet weather as we had some time since. Every thing quiet so far as I can see. A great many court martial sentences were read out a few evenings since against troops from Louisiana. None against S. Carolinians. The Regulations are more strictly enforced now than when you left. Papers have to be signed by the gen'l and if to stay out of quarters during the night by a Maj gen'l. Remember me to all and write soon.

your affec Son L. P. Foster

L. P. Foster to His Mother

Camp Near Centerville
Dec 5th 1861

My Dear Mother

I did not write to you this morning from the fact that I had nothing to write and I have but little news to write now. I am having rather a dull time since I have had the mumps. I have stayed in my tent very closely, not because they made me sick from fear that they would. They never have hurt me any of any consequence and I think I shall be well in a few days. My jaws are swolen a little yet. Our gen'ls are still expecting a fight here and seem to be preparing for it. They seem to think it will come off between this time and Christmas. I can not yet think that the Yankees will come here. They may and if they do then the great battle of this war will be fought. I do not think they will fight any better than at Bull Run but there will be ten of them killed to where there was one there. Have more troops and they are more experienced may not fight braver than they did at Bull Run but will to more effect. More deliberation will be exercised. Our position is now much stronger than the one our army then occupied and we [have] more artillery besides. The same God who fought for our little army then will be with us again at least such is my belief. Were it not I would soon leave the army. I have just rec'd Fathers letter of the 28th and am sure he is coming here too soon. If he has not left when you receive this tell him to stay at home until he gets well. He asks if we are preparing for winter from which question I fear you do not get all of my letters I write almost every day.

---

* Elihu M. West of Co. K, 3rd S.C. was discharged on Dec. 2, 1861 for chronic diarrhea.

Do you get my letters regularly? We have made a goodeal of preparation lately for winter, but it has been to some degree suspended now by an order advising its discontinuance for the present. I suppose in anticipation of a fight. Many of the men have good cabins and others good chimneys to their tents of which I have written before. Elihu West and Glenn Bearden* have been discharged from camp. Elihu left for home this morning and Glenn leaves in the morning. Both of them have been sick for some time. I hear a goodeal of talk about Roebucks and Tuckers companies. Will either of them get the requisite numbers of men. I hear they have each about 50 men. Why don't they amalgamate the two and get a good company. I hear to day that there was a considerable picket fight near Fairfax C.H. last night.† Our sentinels heard the firing. I have not yet heard the result of it. Skirmishing about Fairfax C. H. is getting to be a very common thing. Our cavalry bring in some prisoners almost every day. That is the way the skirmishes end viz in the Yankees throwing their guns down and crying for mercy which they don't merit but always get but if they meet us in battle again they will not find in the Southern Soldier quite so much of the polite gentleman. Our patience tires of this kind of work and want to give them a decisive blow when ever we meet. I rec'd a letter from a lady friend a few days since telling to take prisoners but kill them all. She is as good a Methodist as you ever see of her age, but her judgement was at fault. Like her I believe they do not merit any mercy from us, but then they have some of our bravest men as prisoners of war and when ever we proclaim that we show no quarters their fate is sealed. They will of course [be] shot. We owe them more respect. At the presentation of the Battle flag to the Regt's of this division gen'l Boureguards chaplain (a catholic priest) officiated. You know that gen'l Boureguard is a strong Catholic. It is said that he held prayers before going on the battle field on the morning of the 21st July. My overcoat has not reached me yet. Tom Glenn told Capt Kennedy in a letter that he sent it by Southern express. It may still be in the express office in Columbia. It might be well for Father to inform the agent that it has not come since I can not recover the worth of it unless he be informed written sixty days after the goods were delivered to him. It is in a hat box marked to Cap't Kennedy. I am inclined to think that the express company are making the contents of a many a soldiers box cleared of expenses. I may judge them wrongly but they look too many. Tom Zimmerman and Bill Bearden are still off at the hospital. The former at Richmond and the latter at Charlottesville. Mr. Cunningham, the Glenn Springs teacher went to the hospital at Charlottesville yesterday. He has been unwell for some time. I saw Tom Quarles the other day in ranks. He was looking very well. I have not seen Wade & Dr. Hearst in some time. When I saw them they were well. Theirs is not ¼ of a mile from ours.

---

* Glenn Bearden of Co. K, 3rd S.C. was discharged on December 5 with tuberculosis.

† There was a skirmish on Dec. 4 at Burke's Station about 3 miles east of Fairfax Station on the Orange and Alexandria Railroad line.

We have very cold weather but I am very comfortable in my tent. Cold weather does not seem to have much effect on me. I think I am pretty well hardened. Our Reg't goes on picket next Saturday morning. As I have had the mumps I shall not go with it, but remain in camp. What kind of a time do the galls in our settlement have. No boys to worry them or please them either. I reckon they have some sort of a fine time. Well tell them we will be at home some of these times. So they must not cry & spoil their pretty eyes and faces.

Nothing of interest to finish on.

My love to all & the galls to boot.

> Write very soon. yr affec Son
>
> L. P. Foster

P.S. Dec 6th nothing or interest.

There seems to be an ingrained division between the lowcountry aristocracy and the farmers of the upcountry in South Carolina. The wealthy coastal plantation owner enjoyed the bright culture of antebellum Charleston and thought well of their long, colonial ancestry. The marshes and coastal islands yielded relatively easy wealth (with adequate slave labor) from crops of rice, indigo, and cotton. The upcountry planter family had immigrated more recently down the Great Road of the Shenandoah Valley, and extracted a difficult living from the red clay hills. The abandonment of South Carolina's coastal islands to Federal occupation provided an opportunity for these feelings to become manifest.

L. P. FOSTER TO HIS SISTER, PROBABLY SALLIE

Camp Near Centerville Dec 8th 1861

My Dear Sister

Yours of the first of Dec came a few minutes ago. I will answer immediately. To day has been rather a dull Sabbath. We have had no preaching our Regt being on picket. I suppose our chaplain thought the few sick and convalescents left behind were too small fry for <u>him</u>. I went over to Col. Bacons reg't this morning to see Wade, Tom, and Dr. Hearst. I saw them all and took dinner with them. They are all looking well and enjoying fine health. Tom is looking better than I ever saw him. He came over to our camp with me, spent the evening, took supper and has just returned to his camp. He begged to be remembered to all of you. Tom Moorman rec'd some things from home today. Among others thing a worsted cap for Father and a Norwegian cap for me sent by Mrs Reuben Cheek. I think it quite kind in her. I never saw her in my life. I also rec'd some beautifull palmetto trees a few days since from a lady in Columbia you see I am popular with the ladies not at all to my discomfort. I always did like em mighty well & don't think by any means a bad institution.

Our Reg't was released from picket duty this evening & has returned to camp. I was out only two days. It seems that another Brig is to share our picket post with us in the future and only one battallion instead of a whole reg't will go out every time which reduces our picket duty very much from one in 12 days to one in 48 days and will I think save the life of many a soldier in our brigade. The exposure of picket duty is the worst thing that we have to contend with—fighting yankees not excepted. All of our genl's seem to be expecting a fight some where on this line daily. When or where it will take place I can not tell. The gen'l supposition seems to be that it will be on our extreme left near Evansport* but I think that if that point be attacked others will at the same time as they will try to prevent a concentration of our troops at any one point. It is said by men from that point that it is as well forti- fied as this. However that will make but little difference as you can never get Yan- kees to face a breast work. They will cut roads and go around our flanks and thus make it an open field fight which is all we ask of them. I still doubt their coming at all. It is certainly not McClellans policy to advance but Congress may force him to do something. If they come I have no fear as to our success & think their rout will be worse than that at Bull Run. Our camp is in a very unsettled condition. All our preparations for winter have been suspended and we are listening every day for orders for moving somewhere. It is a pitty for us to have to leave this camp, having done so much work here in the way of making ourselves comfortable. Many of the men have built snug cabins and many others chimneys to their tents so that every thing presents an air of comfort. You seem anxious to hear of our going in winter quarters soon as if you thought we were all freezing. We have had [no] weather here yet that was cold enough to make me feel it much. It is true the ground has been frozen a good many days yet you must recollect that we are accustomed to the air. If we have no colder weather than we have had I would not walk 50 yds to exchange my tent for a good house. This may seem strange to you but I have learned that men can get used to almost anything. I don't dread the winter here. I think I will stand it better than I have the summers at any rate it is agreeing with me finely just now. I have had mumps for 8 or 9 days and weigh 147 lbs. The mumps have not hurt me much. I am about well of them. Jimmy Beard has them now. There are a good many cases in the reg't. I expect you all are having a hard time in getting wool. From the am't of woolen clothes which has been sent here I judge it must be getting scarce. I am glad to hear that southern planters are applying the torch to their farms. Had not the resids of Beaufort who have always claimed to be the chivalry of our State been scared out of their witts and let all behind the yankees could have boasted of nothing. But they, like all people who rely upon their tongues relied also on their

* The Evansport Battery, along with Confederate batteries at Cockpit Point and Freestone Point, blockaded the Potomac downriver from Washington. Foster's reference to Evansport being on "our extreme left" is unclear.

legs and in stead of destroying their property left for our enemies. An inglorious stampede of mud fish aristocracy. Well I reckon they will distrust money & birth more in the future having found legs quite usefull. I can not see the sense of any leaving except those living in front of our out posts and those who did have should have burned every thing except livestock and carried it with them. Your information that the enemy are at Fairfax is false. Unless they have got there tonight which is improbable. I was sorry but not surprised to hear of Billy Lancasters accident, but it may not prove serious. I am afraid that Eds and Roebucks comp has withered out. As I hear they had quite a time of it in electing officers and several withdrew at the time. What good will such men do in our army. Better keep them at home in disgrace. Can't you pass them off as old women & put them to weaving soldiers clothes or knitting or may[be] crying chick chick will suit them better. Will Dr. Lucken raise his company—He boasts on his basics says it is of the right material. I look for Father day after tomorrow.

Remember me to all and write soon

Yr affec Brother

L. P. foster

P.S. Monday morning—nothing of interest, all quiet.

B. B. Foster to His Wife

Richmond Friday the 13th 1861
[December 13, 1861]

My Dear Wife

I am here well and hearty after being nine days on the road. I think it will be the last time I will ever try to carry goods to our boys. I have no idea when I will get away from here it will be a day or two I suppose. I have so managed that I have not been exposed I have trouble altogether in daytime I met here several men from camp all is quiet there no chance for a fight. The yankees are just where they were when I left. There is no use in our staying and I think we will surely be sent to the coast. I learn from reliable authority that fifty thousand of McClelans men are sick and the ballance demoralized and he cant advance. Sam Simmons* is here he says that Perrin is well. I want you to make an effort to get cotton cords. I have two here and cant get them under four dollars a pair wool has gone to $1.00 a pound and coffee the same price. Salt $22.00 a sack send over to David Smith† and ask him if he will pay that sack of salt. if does not do it you had better send the money to Spartanburg and buy a sack for Lancaster. I am of opinion that bacon will be worth forty cents per #. I want you to make the meat go as far as possible

---

* Sam Simmons was Samuel P. Simmons, Co. A, 3rd S.C.

† David Smith was apparently a neighbor of the Fosters in Spartanburg.

and tell Anthony and Mr Norman to keep the cribbs locked and count the corn to the horses. and give the slop from the kitchen to the pigs. remember me to the children and all of my neighbors tell David Smith I done his business for him in Richmond

your affectionate husband

B B Foster

L. P. FOSTER TO HIS MOTHER

Camp near Centreville Dec. 15th 1861

My Dear Mother,

The last few days have been days of sadness. In those days I have witnessed so much suffering. Wm. Woodruff* of our Comp was taken thursday morning with a chill at 4 'clock. He had another chill before breakfast. It was the beginning of a spell of pneumonia which ended in his death at 10 ½ oclock last. This attack was very violent from the start and he suffered a great deal, but was most of the time sensible. The doctors told him Friday night that he would have to die. He was calm and resigned. Mr. Mayfield sit up with him most of the night and talked a goodeal with him. He told him that whether he was lost or saved he felt that god would be glorified, but that he had a hope that his sins were pardoned but had doubts. Mr. Mayfield prayed with him twice, he then said he had a bright hope and had but one thing to regret which was that he had not joined the church when he was under serious impressions, that he then suffered the frowns of the world to deter him. He warned some of his friends as a dying friend to embrace religion and join the church, told them that if they did not they never would appreciate it until a dying hour. Although we are sorry to part with him yet the manner in which he died is cheering and joyfull. I trust good will result from his death and living. I was very intimate with him and it was hard for me to give him up. Hamby† of our camp died last week at the hospital at Warrington. We have now three cases of pneumonia, Gamaliel James, Nathan Pettit,‡ and James Riddle, but all of them are much better and will I think soon get well. It is strange that our comp should have had so much pneumonia. There is not a case in any other comp in our reg't. I can not acc't for it. Our men are fixed more comfortably than most of the comps. We have lost 4 men from it in three weeks. I hope now that the worst is over. I think your fears as to the effects of this climate on us are unnecessary. I know the winter will be severe,

---

* William A. Woodruff of Co. K. died December 14, 1861 of pneumonia in Centreville, Virginia.

† James H. Hamby of Co. K, 3rd S.C. died of typhoid fever on December 11, 1861, at Warrenville Hospital.

‡ Nathan H. Pettit of Co. K, 3rd S.C.

but think the troops will stand it better than they have the summer. Father came last night. All seemed delighted to see him looking so well. His tent is crowded all the time. He will get his baggage to night and Tuesday. He found great difficulty in getting it transported. He is looking very well, much better that I expected to see him. The body of Wm. Woodruff will be sent home tomorrow. I have no news. Every thing quiet.

Remember me to all and write soon.

your affec Son
L. P. Foster

B. B. Foster to His Wife

Army of the Potomac Dec 19th 1861

My Dear Wife,

I am here sitting by a snug fire and must say that I had no idea that a tent could be made so comfortable. The yankees are still where they were when I left for home all this talk of fight and advancing is all stuff. They have not advanced an inch in five months and I firmly believe that they will not this winter. A large amount of work had been done in our fortifications since I left and all are now nearly complete. Then this army will go into winter quarters behind the fortifications houses will be built since I left the camp we have lost several men when I returned one of Garlingtons men was dead and woodroof died that night. Gamaliel James is very low and has been for some time. I think he is better and will get well, yet it is very doubtful Jim Riddle is also very low Nathan Pettit is also very low The ballance of Kenedys are well. I mean all that are in camp I saw Dick White on my way here he is looking as well as I ever saw him. yet he says he is not sound. Perrin stands it exceedingly well it is our stoutest men that suffer most as to myself I feel very well and would conclude that I was as well as ever was if it was not for the swelling of my feet and legs and that is just as it was when I left home I dont like it and have concluded if it continues to quit the service and come home. I hope it will pass of[f] I do not intend to mislead you and you must not expect me but I have determined to try it awhile until about the tenth or fifteenth of Jany and if it does not disappear I will certainly quit the service and come home. I hope I shall not be compelled to leave we are more comfortably situated now than we ever have been since we entered the service and we now have to go on picket only once in twenty four days. This is a decided change for the better Perrin cant get a furlough to come home he has no excuse to offer so you must not look for him. I would like for him to go home but he thinks he will not be able to get a furlough unless he was sick tell Tony to look well to everything about home save all the corn he can. He must not leave the cribs open at night and dont feed extravagant now is the time to sow dont sell the wheat too close and get the mony when you do sell remember me to all the children Normon and the neighbors may the Lord preserve you all is my prayer

your husband

B B Foster

The next two letters refer to an engagement on December 20, 1861, near Dranesville, Virginia, where J. E. B. Stuart led a combined force cavalry, infantry, and artillery to protect a foraging expedition. In Perrin Foster's December 23, 1861 letter, he says that, contrary to history, Stuart was moving "under a pretence of foraging but merely to bring on a fight." When Stuart encountered Brig. Gen. E. O. C. Ord, a firefight began. Stuart held his position until the foraging units made it safely to rear areas and then withdrew his forces. This battle was seen as the first Union victory in Virginia and was widely celebrated in the Northern press.

B. B. FOSTER TO HIS WIFE
___

Camp near Centerville Dec 22nd 1861

My Dear Wife,

Your letter to Perrin came to hand yesterday, all is quiet here and we will soon go into winter quarters The sick are getting better I weigh one hundred and seventy and feel well as usual Still I have some swelling about the legs just as it was when I was at home. I dont know what to say about Tony, I think there will hardly be a draft from his beat it has already furnished its quota If the draft should come tell him not to stand but choose his company among the twelve months men and go to it equip him as well as you can and furnish him with money if he can stay until I can come I will be truly glad I mentioned the twelve months men but just let him go where it suits him best old Pickens is a great fool and is badly scared. Our troops had yesterday a skirmish seventeen miles above here at Drainsville our men drove them our Regiment was not there. I am hurried the post boy is waiting Perrin is very stout and seems very well indeed remember me to all the children and neighbors

    may the Lord bless you all

    is my prayers

B B Foster

On December 11, 1861, large sections of Charleston burned from a fire that started in a sash factory and burned from the Cooper River across the city to the Ashley River. *

---

* Francis Butler Simkins and Robert Hilliard Woody, *South Carolina during Reconstruction* (Chapel Hill: University of North Carolina Press, 1932), 5. "The Charleston Fire," http://www.sonofthesouth.net/leefoundation/civil-war/1861/december/charleston-fire.htm (accessed May 10, 2005).

The fire, Federal bombardment, and economic impoverishment reduced Charleston to ruins by the end of the war.

Benjamin Finch of Spartanburg believed that Dr. Gideon H. King had circulated a broadside accusing unnamed persons of treason and was responsible for the rumor that he (Finch) was preventing his son from enlisting. At about 8:00 AM on December 17, 1861, Finch, carrying a shotgun, confronted King on a road. Dr. King drew a pistol while dismounting his horse, and was shot by Finch. The murder trial was delayed until after the war. Finch was tried and acquitted of murder in April 1866.* Dr. King had a practice in Walnut Grove, South Carolina.†

L. P. Foster to His Sister, Probably Sallie

Camp near Centreville Dec 23rd /61

My Dear Sister

Yours of the 16th came to hand this evening. I have heard several days since of the burning in Charleston and feel very much for those who have remained there all the while and shared the fate of the city, but for those who deserted their homes as soon as a yanky foot had pressed our soil, I feel but little sympathy. I almost believe it was a punishment sent on them for their want of faith in god. A subscription has been taken up in this regiment for the sufferers of Charleston. I think about $800.00 were raised. I think every reg't in this brigade will give that much which will help them some. I wish I could be at home to fly around the ladies but then I would not be contented to rest long while my friends are fighting Yankees. Our officers have commenced giving furloughs. They are furloughing 2 capt's 5 lieuts' and 10 privates at the time, but as they are giving married men the preference and I am stouter than I have been since I joined the army and therefore can not plead sick, I can not get a furlough for some time yet, may be not at all. Well if I ever go into any more wars I reckon I will have one of those articles called wives. At any rate, I mean to commence looking for one mighty soon after this war ends. I think the fire in Charleston entirely accidental and not the work of an incendiary as seems to be supposed. People are always wont to shift the effects of their own carelessness upon other mens sholders. We have just heard this evening through some letters to some of our men of the murder of Dr. King. As you may imagine we are all indignant, but I for one am not much surprised to hear of it. I have never had any confidence in Ben Finch or any of the name except James. I think the case should come before the vigilance committees of the districts and not await the slow and at this time doubtfull proofs of the law. Such cases should be met with the greatest possible promptness. Had I been at home he would have been just as apt to have

* Racine, *Living a Big War*, 85–86.
† Landrum, *History of Spartanburg County*, 281.

tried me as King. I suppose a draft has been ordered. A thing I hoped might never be in S. Carolina, yet I am glad it has been ordered and think those men who will not volunteer may now be reached. You will have heard of the fight at Drainsville* before this reaches you. Gen'l Stuart took 274 waggons, about 1800 men, and 6 pieces of cannon under pretence of foraging but merely to bring on a fight. He was met by about 15000 troops. Our men fought desperately but were compelled to retreat. Their loss was very great but estimated at one tenth of the enemies loss. Col. Wirden† lost a good many men near a hundred killed and wounded. Our men were reinforced the next day and took the field and recovered our dead and wounded. The enemy retreated as soon as our men on the first day, but came back and rifled the packets of our dead men also cut the straps and buttons from their coats. They treated our wounded men very kindly. It may be considered a sort of draw game yet from accounts the enemy must have lost many more men than we did. It seems to be a rash attack and some censure gen'l Stuart but he is a brave man and has been one of our most active men & I am not disposed to blame him until I know more of the case. We have some fortifications to finish and will then go into winter quarters 8 miles below here Davis ford on Bull Run. I can not tell how long it will be before we leave here. Gen'l Bonham has gone to Richmond. Col. Kershaw who is Senior Col. In our Brigade has gone home and Col Williams, who is the 2nd ranking Colonel is acting Brigadier gen'l, which gives Father the command of our reg't. Gen'l Bonham will be back in a few days.

Our sick are all improving. We have but three cases that are much sick. I think they will soon be well but will have to be discharged as they can not stand the winters. Well Christmas will be here in two more days. Merry Christmas to you all. I wish I could be with you. I bought three turkeys a few days since and with them and the potatoes you sent; also 7 lbs butter for which I gave $3.50. I expect to have some Christmas. I gave $5.50 dollars for my three turkeys. Give my thanks to Mrs. Lancaster for the jug of wine. Cap't Kennedy will soon acknowledge the receipt of the goods sent by your society—they [. . .] such an were mostly received by the men I will give you a list of what the company needs very soon it if needs any thing. I think it has enough at present. Tell Mother that I thought she had already had cloth to make my coat a piece like my pants but if she has not got it not to put herself to much trouble about it as I can make out very well with what I have. If she makes it she can sent it by J. H. Cunningham, one our mess who will I think go home soon on furlough. It has been snowing and raining all day, but is now nearly clear, and the wind blowing very cold. I do not feel cold much here.

* The Battle of Dranesville, Virginia, on December 20, 1861.

† The writing is difficult to read but Colonel Wirden is a possible reading of this name. There was no colonel whose name started with a "W" at the Battle of Dranesville. Lieutenant Colonel Secrest led the 6th S.C.

Remember me to all. Tell them I am quite stout weigh with a light coat 150 lbs. Write soon.

Yr affec Brother

L. P. Foster

Col. Edwards's letter shows the same upcountry disdain for the lowcountry aristocracy that Perrin Foster expressed in an earlier letter. In the earlier letter Foster castigated the Coastal first families for abandoning South Carolina land to the Federals; in this letter, Edwards expressed resentment at having to defend those who once boasted their manners and chivalry over the so-called uncultured, upcountry Piedmont planters.

Green Pond was a small station on the Charleston and Savannah Railroad about half way between those two cities. Edwards's regiment was protecting the lowcountry and the railroad from Federals who had occupied Port Royal.

Edwards's wife, Jane, followed him on his assignments, living as near to him as possible throughout his Confederate service.

COL. OLIVER E. EDWARDS TO HIS COUSIN SALLIE FOSTER

Green pond Station

C & S R.R.

Dec'r 24th 1861

My dear Cousin Sallie

Your long & interesting letter came to me some days since. I think it likely you will be surprised to hear from me so soon. This is Christmas eve. I shall be unable to give my friends any other present than a poor letter from a poor soldier. I am to spend this Christmas as I never spent one before & as I hope never to spend one again. Since I left Charleston my Reg't has been moved four times Commanded by Gen'l Ripley, Lee[*] Pemberton[†] & now Maxy Gregg. We are now 40 miles from Charleston between Ashapoo & Combahee Rivers where we will go next I cant begin to tell. I cant hope to be stationary long at present. I'm sorry to say I am in country of illiterately Here we are from the up country to defend the people of the low always boasting of Chivalry and yet in this neighborhood some of my staff were washing where there were plenty of negros willing to do it. We pay the highest prices for every thing we get & get no variety. As a general rule the people are gone. The troops are from abroad excepting a few. If a fence or rail is burned or a turnip taken great complaints are rendered to the Col. Whilst my position is an honorable

---

[*] Robert E. Lee commanded the Coastal defenses in the early months of the war.

[†] Gen. John Clifford Pemberton was assigned to the S.C. Coastal defenses in December 1861 and in March 1862 he assumed R. E. Lee's Coastal defense duties. Pemberton is best remembered as the defender of Vicksburg.

one, it is perplexing and responsible. I have to deal with so many characters it is impossible to please I therefore try to do right. You are about as well posted in reference to yankee movements as I can post you. I do not believe we shall have fighting here. I think the enemy is satisfied with present achievements. They land sometimes but leave very soon again. We cant get to them on the island. In this country we are getting a pretty good force though nothing like what we ought to have if the enemy were bold. My Camp is now in the woods at the summer residence of some of the Nabobs of the country. The plantations are very fine & beautiful. All the streams are navigable. The Combahee where we are now is deep enough for any vessel to come up. I never knew the geography of the country before & can't easily learn it now. When we were on the Coosawahatchee I brought my better half to Gibsonville and fewer miles of me. When we went to Pocataglio she was low minded Now she is 25 miles and the gen'l rather particular about my leaving Camp. There is no white lady about here, consequently cant bring Jane. She had almost as well be absent in a safer place. I live pretty well. If we could get butter. I get along very well. There is every [. . .] of the article in the country. I was sorry to hear of the death of Dr. King, although he was always my enemy. I have not heard particulars. Write to me often. I should like to hear from Eunice. I will write as often as my duties will allow. Your uncle James Perrin is somewhere this side of Charleston. My best love to your Ma, Eunice, & Tony. Regards to friends, the Misses Montgomery & others. Accept the love of your cousin.

Oliver

B. B. FOSTER TO HIS WIFE

Army of the Potomac Camp near Centerville
December 26th 1861

My Dear Wife

Your letter was received last night I was truly sorry to hear of the murder of Dr King. I have no idea that there will be any danger of the ballance of the Union crowd Finch was the only one that would shoot Gentry is to shrewd a man to shoot any one. I am sorry for Ben Finch. I am afraid that he had intended to kill King there was no good reason for his carrying his gun wherever he went. I suppose justice will take place. I see by the order issued by the Governor or adjutant general that an overseer is exempt from draft. I was in hopes that Anthony would have taken that chance and have stayed at home until I could get there. I wrote you that I thought I would be at home by the fifteenth of January. I have determined to come home, as soon as Dr Ewart* comes back I shall make application for discharge. I prefer discharge to resignation the application will have to go before the secretary of war

---

* David Edwards Ewart, surgeon for the 3rd S.C.

and it will take some time to get to Richmond and back. Ewart has gone back sick I learn he will return tomorrow. I still have symptoms of dropsy. Just as it was at home our surgeons advise me to quit the army and I shall do so. If Anthony does go fix him as well as you can for the trip. I suppose Harmon will go too If so get Schon Hewit to come from home and see to the negroes until I come he will do some good. I must say in all candor that Perrin is stouter and looks better than I have ever seen him before he stands the service well no one is suffering here for anything The soldiers is clothed well and a few more comforts would answer them for some time to come George Simmons* of Kenedys company needs a pair of wollen pants. Gamaliel James is mending and I think will soon be up also James Riddle Johny and Jimy Henry Barnett Elijah Smith in fact all our neighborhood boys are in fine health all is quiet here not anticipating a fight we all have comfortable tents with chimnys they are as warm as a house our Regiment has given to the sufferrers in Charleston one thousand and thirty dollars. and I believe that this army will give at least sixty thousand dollars. I gave twenty five dollars myself. so you see if we are in an army that we have not forgotten to be charitable to those in distress. I hope you will all get along smooth and do the best you can. I hope soon to be with you remember me kindly to the children and all the neighbors I regrett exceedingly that I am compelled to quit the army I hope however to recover by the opening of spring and then I will be able to take the field again and serve my country may the Lord bless and preserve you all is my prayer

your husband B B Foster

L. P. Foster to His Mother

Camp near Centreville
Dec 30th 1861

My Dear Mother,

As our battalion goes on picket tomorrow and will not have an opportunity to write again in three days, I will write this morning. I have nothing of interest to write you unless it be that we have at last been ordered to get into winter quarters as soon as we can build them, which I hope will not take a great while. The weather is still cold and dry. It has been some time since we have had any wet weather. We have but little talk of a fight here now. All think the winter campaign ended though the enemy are still in their tents. We are constantly expecting to hear of a fight in the South Carolina and are anxious to share the warfare of our own state, but hear nothing of our being sent back, nor do I think it probable that we will for there are troops here who can present stronger claims to be sent home than we can who are

---

* George Simmons of Co. K, 3rd. S.C., later killed at Cold Harbor.

not allowed to go. I mean the Kentucky troops. Cap't Kennedy has written to the editors of the Spartanburg papers acknowledging the box sent by your Society as well as every thing sent by any lady. I was invited yesterday to Cap't Bradley's* tent to a turkey dinner but did not go. Father went. Wade, Dr. Hearst and Tom Quarles well and hearty. Our sick men all better. Father met the other day Robt Perrin Cap't of cavalry comp from Miss—called the "Jeff Davis Legion"† with two or three of his brothers, sons of cousin big Abner Perrin.‡ Also John Rainy.§ Father says he is a fine looking man and had a fine comp finely mounted and armed and well drilled—can take a whip from the ground without dismounting. We have a great many relations in the service. Col Bacon¶ of the 7th S.C. Reg't is quite [ill] at the hospital at Charlottesville, not expected to live.

I hear but little talk of revolunteering here and think our brigade will go home unless circumstances over which I have a most urgent necessity for us here. Every one seems very anxious to serve in S.C. I am sure the remainder of the service will be easier here than in S. Carolina yet I prefer to go there and expect to do so. We have had a quiet Christmas and I can scarcely realize that it has passed.

I rec'd a letter from Belle Perrin a few days since. She has had a severe spate of broke bone fever** but has got better and is now staying with her grand mother. She expects to go back to Limestone next yr if her Father can get money to send her. The children were well. I have no more to write.

Remember me kindly to all the family and enquiring friends. Write soon.

your affec Son L. P. Foster

---

* Captain P. H. Bradley of Co. C, 7th S.C.

† The Jeff Davis Legion was the 2nd Battalion, Mississippi Cavalry led by Col. William T. Martin. Capt. R. O. Perrin commanded Company C, the Kemper County company.

‡ Abner Perrin rose to rank of Colonel of McGowan's 14th S.C. Volunteers and was later promoted to brigadier general for gallantry at Gettysburg. Gen. Perrin was given command of Wilcox's Alabama brigade and was killed at Spotsylvania. As he led his troops into that battle he remarked, "I shall come out of this a dead brigadier general or a live major general."

§ Possibly John Reaney of Co. B, 8th Louisiana Infantry which was in northern Virginia at the time.

¶ Col. Thomas Glasscock Bacon of the 7th S.C. He did survive this illness, but failing health later forced him to resign and return to his home in Edgefield, South Carolina, where he led the Seventh Regiment State Troops. Dickert, *History of Kershaw's Brigade*, 101.

** Dengue fever is also called broken bone fever because of the severe joint pain that results from this disease. It makes you feel as if your bones are being broken.

SALLIE FOSTER TO HER COUSIN, ELIZABETH COTHRAN

Glenn Springs
Dec. 31st [1861]

Another year is near closing and my last act with this final scene is writing to my dear Lizzie. It is quite late, the rest of the family have gone to bed, left me alone, and thinking of you concluded not to neglect you any longer.

Christmas passed very quietly indeed, and had it not been for the negroes to remind us by their "Christmas Gift, Missus" and [. . .] it would scarcely have been noticed. As for my part, I thought too much of how our poor soldiers would have to spend it to enjoy it. I received a letter from Brother last night—he said they would soon go into winter quarters about 8 miles from their present camp. Father was not very well, I am very much afraid he will get sick again. He returned too soon to camp, consequently, fear he cannot stand the winter. Brother wrote* that their officers were furloughing two captains, five Lieuts, and ten privates at a time, and as they give married men the preference, hope sincerely Cousin Wade can come home soon. I was sorry to hear that he was refused a furlough. Guess some of the young men wish most heartily that they were married.

Well, Liz, how to interest you with news from these lonely parts is impossible for me to tell. Glenn Springs is filled with refugees from Beaufort and other islands on the coast. I went over the other day and called on some friends and upon the rest of the ladies on [. . .] a thing quite uncommon for me. Do tell me what has become of Phoebe Townsend. I feel anxious to hear if she has left home.

I have a homespun dress, dyed and all ready for the loom, so you see I am beginning to practice economy in earnest. It is hard to get anything but homespun these days. There has been a good deal of excitement here owing to Pickens' call for more troops. Several companies have been raised and gone, and the excitement has very nearly ceased. Cousin Edwin Bobo has gone again, as a Lieut in Capt. Roebuck's company. I think he will "stick" this time. Our Society gets along very well, but slowly. We are busy making comforts—we cant get blankets, consequently have to resort to making comforts.

I would be delighted dear Liz to pay you a visit this winter, but hardly know how I am to get down to Millway, for Tony has charge of everything here, as Father did not get an overseer and so far I hardly know whether he can leave. But I will come if possible, will promise that much but cant tell now when. Nothing would do me more good than to be with you once again. It is indeed something very uncommon for Sallie Perrin† to stay so long from home. Sister Eunice I don't think will return to Limestone next year—the times too hard and money scarce.

---

* See Perrin Foster's letter of December 23, 1861.
† Possibly Sarah Eliza Perrin.

The weather is quite cold and disagreeable, and it has been so for some time. The 22nd of this month we had sleet.

I received a letter from Cousin Oliver Edwards, who commands the 13th Regiment, now on the coast, the other day.* He does not think there will be any more fighting—that the Yanks are satisfied with present achievements. I wish most heartily that our men could get to them on the islands and drive them Bull Run speed from our soil. Oh! That this unjust war would end. I am heartily sick of it. I do hope most sincerely that England will interfere, but how in the world can the North get out of the Mason and Slidell affair after approving the course of Capt. Wilkes,† passing compliments on his actions in Congress etc. etc. I don't know how they could manage it unless in their <u>usual</u> way, that is lying out of it. Mr. Harmon leaves next week for the coast—he has volunteered in Duncan's company.‡

Mother says she would like very well indeed to pay you all a visit this winter but doesn't think she can leave home, and I intend to try my best to get down to see you.

We are all well—a good many of the negroes have had diphtheria, but are now nearly over it.

Mother joins me in sending best love to you and Auntie. Write soon—excuse all mistakes—I shall expect to hear from you very soon.

As ever, your devoted
Cousin Sallie

B. B. Foster to His Wife

Army of the Potomac Camp near Centerville
Jany 1st 1862

My Dear Wife

Your letter was received this evening as also one from Eunice to Perrin. I was truly glad to hear that you were all in health and up to your eyes in backbones and sausages you need not think we are altogether behind you we have some too. it is brought in from the country and sold to pork at 15 cts per lb sausages at 85 cts we all now living better than we ever have done we are more comfortable our tents all have chimneys and really nice are just snug enough. we now have orders to fall back on Bull Run and build houses for the winter we will go at it as soon as our men return from picket. I may go out in day time and return to my den at night.

---

* Sallie Foster is referring to the December 24th letter from Colonel Edwards.

† Capt. Charles Wilkes commanded the U.S.S. *San Jacinto*, the warship that intercepted the British *Trent* and apprehended James Mason and John Slidell, Confederate envoys. Bruce Catton, *Terrible Swift Sword* (Garden City, N.Y.: Doubleday, 1963), 108.

‡ Probably refers to Capt. David R. Duncan's Company C of the 13th SCV. The 13th was on the Coastal defense at the time.

Perrin is out we have huts put up at the outposts for the pickets to stay in and there is not half the exposure on picket that there has been. Perrin is stouter than he has been since he came into the army I think he looks better than I ever have seen him before. I mean what I say. The health of our Regiment is much better than it has been at any time our boys Johny, Jimmy Beard Elijah and Ben Smith Dr Bob Henry Barnett are all well. I was truly sorry to hear of the murder of Dr King. I suppose that justice will take place. If a Dr is needed in our family I would send for Boyd.*
I suppose you all have the satisfaction to know that Hiram has a woman. I think he is old enough to be his own judge. if he is pleased no one ought to complain I hope they will do well live long and raise soldiers for the next war old Johns boys wont volunteer perhaps the James crop will improve the breed Gamaliel James has been sent back to the hospital he was out of danger when sent back. Eunice said to Perrin you thought you had lost some money. I left one hundred and sixty dollars in paper and twenty in silver making in all $180. I wrote you some time ago that I would be at home about the fifteenth of this month I still think I shall leave about that time perhaps not before three weeks and get home about the 26th. I want to see the Regt in good winter quarters and then I shall leave. I still have swelling in my feet and legs about as it was when you saw me and I am afraid to stay here longer. I want Tony to see particularly to the hogs horses and cattle and try to save all the corn he can save the slops from the kitchen and make everything go as far as he can keep leaves in the lot and stables plenty of them. remember me to all the family and neighbors may the Lord keep and save you is my prayer

Your husband B B Foster

L. P. Foster to His Sister, Probably Sallie

Camp near Centreville Jan 2nd 1862

My Dear Sister

As I got slightly wounded yesterday out on picket and am off duty I will give you a few lines. We went out day before yesterday and our comp was placed out on post that day. We were relieved next morning and after we returned to our reserve Capt Kennedy, David Bray and myself concluded to build us a hut to shelter us while on picket. So we went to work and after we had cut nearly all of the logs I cut my big toe with the axe. This cut just on the outside of the nail. It is not a bad cut—did not cut the bone I think and does not hurt much except when I walk on it which keeps me in my tent this pretty weather much to my dislike. It also made a considerable hole in my fine boot which I assure you I did not much fancy and two of my socks being between said boot and said toe got both cut and bled on. The toe I think will

* Probably Dr. J. J. Boyd of Spartanburg. He later married Jane Gary Edwards after the death of her husband, Col. Oliver E. Edwards. Landrum, *History of Spartanburg County*, 512.

be well in a short time but my boot I am sorry to say is still no better. We had a new post this time on picket and a better one than we have had before. One of our post was very near an old ladies house and the pickets on post before us said she had a pretty young lady staying with her so I thought I should have a nice time, but she seemed to be a married woman and ugly to boot.

Our battalion will return from picket tomorrow—will not have to go out again until the 23rd of Jan. I have nothing of interest to write. I rec'd nunies letter announcing that Hiram had taken on Lony Ann Ganoble to wife. I[t] did not surprise me knowing how badly both parties wanted to marry. I think John West and Patsy* are kicking up a dust for nothing. I expect Lony Ann is about as good as they are and if I was in his place I would have my house I think he has strewn his future path with more thorns than roses. This is too much of a utilitarian age for the fancy of <u>youthfull</u> <u>beauty</u> to inebriate the brain of an old man at the time. We are having rath[er] a dull time now. We have but little to do and I find it hard to employ my time. I have nothing or almost nothing to read. We get newspapers every day but they contain but little that is reliable.

Remember me to all the family, also enquiring friends. Write soon. your affec Brother

L. P. Foster

P.S. Jan 3rd nothing of interest.

L. P. Foster to His Sister, Probably Jennie

Camp near Centerville Jan 4th/62

My Dear Sister

You have not answered my last letter you ought to have written and told me all about Mr. James and Sarah Ann Ganobles wedding. I know you could have told me all about it. Then you could have told me about Christmas and the girls. I am very anxious to hear all about them. I suppose they are all engaged. I did not think that Miss Sallie Montgomery was engaged but from what I have lately heard I expect she is mortgaged to a volunteer in the army of the Potomac our sector with whom I used to be acquainted but don't you tease her too much about it. Well every thing here looks pretty and white it snowed and sleeted here last night the snow is very light scarcily covers the ground but it is quite cold we do not mind it and if it does not get worse than it has been yet we could stand the winter finely in tents. our men are now building little cabbins at McClanes ford on Bull Run to spend the winter

* Likely John West of Spartanburg, who was married to a Patsey (Patsy) Wofford, daughter of Isaac Wofford was married to a John West in Spartanburg about this time. "Descendants of Unknown Wofford," http://www.genealogy.com/ftm/w/o/f/Melinda-M-Wofford/GENE5-0008.html (accessed August 10, 2016).

in. We are all quite lively make Henry Barnett and Jolly Bobo play the fiddle for us. We don't have anything like as bad a time here as you all think and as some of the fellows who ought to have petticoats on write home about. It is true we don't have any cake nor honey nor milk nor cornbread with cracklins in it. ran out of it. nor such like stuff preserves & c but then we have biscuits and wheat bread with marks across it and wheat bread without marks across it and stake and fried beef and boiled beef and baked beef and stewed cow and beef hash and gravy and sugar and some bacon occasionally. Plenty of rice and now and then butter and pretty generally molasses at 1.75 per gal and every now then coffee with out rye and then sometimes coffee made out of sassaphras root and sometimes we can buy turkeys and pork and sausages and well don't believe that is any more and to it. So you see we get plenty to eat and have a good bed to sleep on and plenty of cover on a tent as warm as a mothers room and if no one would get sick we could do finely but this is a bad place for a sick man. We have sent our sick men to the hospital and sent two home yesterday. Samuel Stripling* discharged on account of pulmonary consumption and Theodore West† furloughed on account of general dibility. They will be at home before this reaches you. Cousin Tom Quarles was over here last night. He is very well and am to remember him to all of you. Tell Meenie she had better quit getting tight. Well it is about three months until our time will be out then maybe I will come home and see you all a while before visiting Abes men any more. I don't think there will be any more fighting here soon but next spring there will be a sight of it somewhere about here if I mistake not Are you studying and learning to write? You ought to be at it every day.

You must write to me soon.

Remember me to all the family and enquiring friends.

Yr affec Brother L P Foster

Jan 5th nothing of interest

L. P. FOSTER TO HIS BROTHER, TONY

Camp near Centreville Jan 6th 1862

My Dear Brother

I have not rec'd a letter from you in a long time. I suppose you have been very busy at hunting during the past two wks as that is generally our employment during Christmas. Have you had any snow lately—if not and you need any you can get some here very cheap. You could get a handful anywhere here this morning. The fellows have been snowballing each other and rabbit hunting all the morning. I saw them catch a rabbit in a few steps of my tent a short time since. This shows how

---

* Samuel Stripling of Co. K, 3rd S.C.

† Theodore J. West of Co. K, 3rd S.C. Subsequently, West reenlisted and was killed at Second Manassas.

little they care for cold weather and snow. It snowed last night and night before but the snow is not deep about 2 inches. It is no rarity here of late days. We have had no rain in a long time. I believe it is too cold here to rain. Our men all in fine spirits. Some companies in our Brigade are reenlisting. Three in Kershaws reg't* and some in Bacons† have already reenlisted. None of our companies have yet acted. I think some of them will act and some will not. 40 is the number required for a basis. Some companies have not very many more now than the basis. Our comp has suffered from death and discharge until we have now not more than 65 men on ours and I doubt whether enough of them will volunteer to make the basis required. I have not yet made up my mind on the subject. None seem anxious to quit the service all seem willing to serve but anxious to serve in S. Ca. The aspect which affairs assume in S. C. If the prospect for fighting there is good many of the troops here will go there. If the 12 Ms‡ volunteers do not volunteer I can't see what the government will do for troops with which to defend this line. It is said there are 42,000 in this line which is more than half of this army. The service here will be less severe hereafter than in S. Carolina even if there should be no fighting there since this is a much healthier climate than that of the coasts of S. Carolina. My game toe is nearly well.

Bill Wofford is in my tent telling yarns and mimicking every body. The wars have not changed him at all. He can get a crowd around him any time.

I suppose Hiram and Sarah Ann are enjoying themselves finely. Have they got a house yet? I hope they have.

Remember me to all the family & enquiring friends.

David Bray begs to be remembered to you.

Yr affec Brother

L. P. Foster

P.S. Jan 7th I rec'd a letter from Mrs. Clopton last night she has sent me a box of provisions which will be at Manassas tonight. It was sent by Miss Lucy Chapman and herself. They are very kind to me. Miss Lucy sent me a picket cap.

L. P. Foster

Col. Oliver Edwards to His Cousin Sallie Foster

Green Pond Station

Jany 7 1862

My Dear Cousin Sallie

I know you will be surprised to hear from me now just after so much excitement in this part of the world no one could expect me to engage in so small a

---

* Kershaw's Regiment was the 2nd S.C.

† Col. T. G. Bacon's Regiment was the 7th S.C.

‡ Months.

thing as letter writing. But you know I am a good sort of fellow & often act different from many others. I do not remember whether I ever answered your interesting letter rec'd a long time ago at Coosakehatchee. If I did you have not done your
duty & I am doing good for evil. If I did not I ought & could not write at a better
time. During this new year I have had real Virginia living—on New Years day—I
had prepared to go & see my wife. Before I started I heard a heavy cannon some
ten miles off.* I decided to stay & well I did. The firing increased & became decidedly interesting. In the evening I was ordered to move with five companies in the
direction of the fight to Combahee ferry 4 miles. We got there in the night with
40 rounds ammunition and no tents. In the night I was ordered to send 2 companies back this (East) side the river. Then I had 4 left. One had been stationed at the
ferry before I went with five. The next morning the firing began at 10 oclock & we
were certain we would have a chance but were never ordered & heard at night that
it was the cowardly Yankees firing shell all about for fear we were in ambush. Our
forces had retired the night before hoping to draw them from under cover of their
gun boats. The feint did not succeed. They remained near the river where our men
could not get at them without exposure. On Wednesday they (the enemy) fired till
sundown. Those who came out on land—many thousands some say, were met by
Jones[†] & Dunovant[‡] and repulsed. the enemy bolted it is said like wild colts. My
men remained from then till to day without tents or any regular arrangements for
food doing a heavy piquette-all the while under excitement from [. . .]. Today I
was ordered back to my Camp 5 miles from the Railroad. I now have 3 companies
here Col. Calhoun[§] 4 at the Combahee Ferry—Maj Farrow[¶] two at another place &
one at another. Now with all this to perplex, how do you suppose I get along badly. I
can assure you my men are obliged to suffer—and then to think we are in one of the
finest country for rice potatoes, bread, turnips. He said the people so illiberal in a
general way they will not let the soldiers who are here suffering so many privations
for them have any thing without complaint. The citizens are scampering from the
country carrying some & leaving a great deal—scared to death many of them able
if willing to fight a good fight. We from the Anderson District have it all to do or it
is not done. We have very little idea where the enemy will turn up next. I assume
my time will come soon. I am & have been all the while in an exposed section. I
am not afraid of the result when we have a fair chance. I have a great deal of sickness. Two men died yesterday & two will die to night. The Drs. say my own health
is very good. I think we are now pretty well prepared to defend the state. At one

---

* Edwards is describing the Battle of Port Royal Ferry on January 1, 1862.
† Col. James Jones led the 14th S.C. at Port Royal Ferry.
‡ Col. R. G. Mills Dunovant led the 12th S.C. at Port Royal Ferry.
§ Lt. Col. P. L. Calhoun of the 13th S.C.
¶ Major T. Stobo Farrow, 13th S.C.

time a bold enemy might have taken the whole country, Charleston, & Savannah. The country is a fine one for us. A few men can whip a great many. I never had an idea there was a country such as this so near me when at home—filled with navigable rivers and the finest plantations I ever saw. The waters full of fish & fowl. The land covered with game of many kinds. The people are all rich. There are no poor people here. The big fish have eaten up the littles.

My wife is 20 miles off & not much prospect of getting nearer. I have not seen her in two weeks. She says she will not go home however.

I hope you have spent a more pleasant Christmas & New Year than I. But I guess there will be but little enjoyment till this war ends. And not very much prospect for that. I hope you will write to me very soon & give me all the news. I was sorry to hear of the murder of Dr. King, although I am bound to believe he was a mean man. The man who killed him no better. Where is Eunice? Give her & your Ma my love. My regards to Toney the Miss and Montgomery, Maj Lancaster & wife an all my friends. Accept a great deal of love & believe me your devoted old

Cousin Oliver

L. P. Foster to His Mother

Camp near Centreville
Jan 12th 1862

My Dear Mother

I rec'd Tonys letter a few days since. I expect you are all having a pretty lonely time of it since Mr. Harmon left you, but hope that you may all be able to exercise patience to the end. The necessities of a war in which is involved the very existence of a nation know no law hence all the tenderer ties of nature must for a time yield to their demands if we should have national existence and independence. Our prospects seem to me brighter than ever before. The rapidity with which the Confederacy has gained character in the last few months among other nations is truly flattering as well as the rapidity with which our enemy the north is loosing character. I don't think history presents a parallel, besides I think the S.C. better able now with means and money to defend itself than it ever has been. Our army is large, composed of the best material and well disciplined, confident—bonds are taken at par while the north is hard pressed to get money at all and congress legislating the propriety of levying a very heavy tax. I have no war news except what you see in the papers. Everything here seems quiet and from present indications I think no one is anticipating a fight. We will move to our winter quarters in a few days. The health of our reg't is very good. I went to Manassas yesterday after a box sent me by Mrs. Clopton and Miss Lucie Chapman, but did not find it. I suppose some one of the many rogues on the R.R. and about Manassas has appropriated it to his own use. I regret not getting it as I know the things were nice. I never saw anything at Mrs.

Cloptons table that was not nice whilst at Manassas I saw a sight which I hope I may never see again and which I never saw before. I saw five soldiers in stocks with balls and chains to their feet, quite a debasing and by no means mild punishment. They all seemed to be Irishmen and not to mind it very much. I do not know the offence for which they were thus punished. It must have been of a very aggravated nature. Military law is necessarily very rigorous as in that way alone can good discipline without which an army is a curse to any country, be insured.

This is now the muddiest country I have ever seen in my life. It has turned very warm and the thaw makes it very muddy. We have had no preaching to day in consequence of the absence of our chaplain. I long for him to return you can have no idea of what a difference in the morals of a regiment divine service makes whilst it is a great comfort and pleasure to Christians. It seems to awe the sinner and prevent many an out burst of sin. If Christians would do their duty and let their lights shine around then many sinning soldiers might be made to bow to Jesus. Oh that every soldier in our army was a Christian with the promise' "God is our refuge and our strength a very present help in time of need"* written on the tablet of his heart. What could we not accomplish then. I hear that in Augusta Georgia every day at one Oclock the city bell rings reminding its people of the hour of prayer for our country. Would it not be well for <u>every</u> <u>town</u> and <u>village</u> in our whole country to swell the notes of prayer thus uttered. Can a more sublime thought be conceived than that in which we see a whole nation throbbing in prayer to god at the same time. If there ever was need of earnest and grateful prayer it is certainly [now]. War is a calamity dire indeed even to the victorious and what can be so effectual in averting as prayer. "The righteous cry and the son heareth and delivereth them out of all their troubles."† Drunkenness is the curse of this army. I think troops should have spirits but at the same time think that it should be given with prudence, else all the good is lost and harm done. Maj. Genl Earl Van Dorn who has been commanding this division of the army of the Potomac has recently been assigned to the department of Missouri and gen'l Bonham being Senior Brig gen'l of the division is now acting Maj gen'l protem and in absence of Col. Kershaw, Col Williams takes command of this Brigade and Father of our Reg't. Father is still on court marshall. The proposition for reenlisting has not yet been put to our reg't. Rob't Wilkins an old scholar of mine died last wk at Culpeper C.H. I don't know whether his remains were sent home or not but hope they were. I see that gen'l Samuel McGowan‡ has given himself considerable newspaper notoriety by going in 100 yds of the enemy's lines after our wounded. A statement I am not inclined to believe if it be so they have the poorest marksmen to contend against that I have ever seen. A man in our

* Psalm 46:1.
† An adaptation of Psalm 34:17.
‡ Col. Samuel McGowan, 14th S.C.

reg't not long since killed a cow near 400 yards with his rifle off hand and had to pay for it to boot. A man would stand a bad chance being shot at by this reg't 100 yds his hyde would not hold shucks. Our friends were well at last acct's. Tom Zimmerman has got a discharge and expect has gone home before now. Our comp has suffered very much from discharge and death. It is so warm that I am perspiring freely. Has the convention of S.C. done anything. Every one here thinks they met to attend to gov Pickens case. And all seem to hope that the time of their adjournment may find the said governor junitus officio. I think here certainly merits the indignation of the people. This last act viz reviewing 12,000 volunteers at such a time as this was on a par with all of his others and bears the impress of a weak or besotted man. But I must close. Remember me to all.

yr affec Son
L. P. Foster

B. B. Foster to His Wife

Army of the Potomac
Camp near Centerville
Jany 15th 1862

My wife

Your letter finished by Eunice was received this evening. I expected to have been at home by this day. it is hard for me to give up the army. I am now better off than I have been since I left home although I am not free from the swelling of my limbs, the proposition will be made in a few days to the South Carolina volunteers to reinlist for two years. I have no idea that they will do it I am sure our Regt will not. I will not. I cannot now determine what I will do in April. my notion now is as soon as I get the boys into their winter quarters to leave the army and go home. The ground here is several inches deep in snow and it is still falling. I would not be surprised if it should be one of those old fashioned deep ones this time and just to think that we are in a cloth tent we however have a good fire place and plenty of blankets. I have not suffered a moment from cold day nor night. I am still on that court martial and it will last at least this month out. Perrin is well his toe is not injured he is in favor of volunteering but will be governed by me I will not leave him until that thing is settled and all firm. I think it is unreasonable to expect our men to reinlist before going home and I will not ask them to do it. I think Betty ought to let uncle Hiram* rest. I am sorry for him he has however made his own choice and no one has a right to say anything. our boys are all up Johnny and Jimmy Beard Benjamin and Elijah Smith or Robert. Henry Barnet is the stoutest man of all his kin he is very fat and seems to enjoy himself very well tell Tony he must have rails split to

* Hiram Bobo.

repair the fencing wherever it needs it and have the logs cut and split for firewood he must also have coal wood got and burn coal The coal ought to be burnt as soon as possible so as to be ready to break up stubble land as soon as the ground will bear it tell Jenny she must learn that book of hers and learn to write. remember me to the children and Major Lancaster and family and all the neighbors may the Lord keep and preserve you all is my prayer your affectionate

husband B. B. Foster

no prospect of a fight here all is quiet on this line

L. P. Foster to His Sister, Probably Sallie

Camp near Centreville Jan 16th 1862

My Dear Sister

Although I am not sad this evening yet I can not say with Longfellow

> "O precious evenings! All to swiftly sped!
> Leaving us heirs to amplest heritages
> Of all the best thoughts of the greatest sages.
> And giving tongues unto the silent dead."

Having no Mrs. Kemble to render them enchanting by "interpreting by tones the wondrous pages"* of Shakespeare or even a Shakespeare to read myself or anything else to prevent me from contrasting the scenes of this cold day. "When winter winds are piercing chill, and through the hawthorn blows the gale"† with the many winter evenings which I have so pleasantly spent at home when the hearthstove was warm with the glowing fire and we around it happily talked and each enjoyed the others life. Memory will give rise to such contrasts yet we have many pleasant hours here. Pleasures to the stout hearted soldier whom trifles can not shake. I love to be with such men. Men whose hearts quail not but stand firm alike amid the fierce shock of battle. The [various] hardships and trials of camp with, yes even steady upon the good they would reach, the zenith star of their country liberty—a zenith from which it will never wane, one which will steadily rise as the circle of its power and enlightenment extends. I dread very much to see this reg't brake up for I don't think there ever was one composed of better material. I do not believe that it will reenlist here as a reg'mt and doubt whether it ought to or not. I believe all are determined to try their countrys warfare to the end, but we are getting anxious to see our homes for at least a short time and many companies have not enough to reorganize and

---

* The excerpt above and this quotation are from "Sonnet on Mrs. Kemble's Reading from Shakespeare" by Henry Wadsworth Longfellow.

† From "Woods in Winter" by Longfellow.

fear they can not raise enough at home to fill out the number requisite, hence are afraid to reenlist, lest they should be thrown as remnants with other companies and thus loose their choice of officers. I think we will leave here by the 24th of March. We have clear cold weather-much of the snow having melted but the ground is still white. Some of our reg't have moved in their winter quarters and I hope the remains will soon move if the weather continues good. Col. Williams expects to move tomorrow or the next day. I don't think Father will move so soon as we want to get a chimney done before we move. Rev Brant Brown and Capt's Real B. Seay* Jacob Carpenter† and Mr. Foster‡ visited us yesterday. Father was off on court marshall and did not return until evening. I had to entertain them myself. Bill Foster is as full of live as ever. I got a fiddle and made him play and sing at which Bill Wofford§ says Mr. Brown hung down one corner of his mouth indicative of displeasure. I did not notice him so closely. Mr. Roebuck has been with us a few days. He came on to see his son John who has been sick and furloughed for 40 days and take the remains of J. H. Hamby home with him. Our reg't is still enjoying good health notwithstanding they have lately been exposed a greatdeal in building winter quarters. Your letter (to Father) from the village came yesterday evening and Mothers of the 10th (to me) this evening. I was glad to hear that you were at the village. I think you should all visit more than you do. Time would pass much more pleasantly if you would seek the company of your friends more and prophesy less. At least such is my notion of things. I am not surprised to hear of the illiberality of the low country soap soiled mud fish for men who are too cowardly to protect their homes, are generally supplied with any and all other mean traits of character and especially selfishness. If I was there I would love to worry them by burning their rails—eating their fowls, hogs &c. They deserve to have their property confiscated and be sent across the Potomac in to the land of their kind. Father is about as he has been. He suffers no pain from his legs yet they swell some every evening. He now says he thinks he will quit these parts as soon as we get well settled in winter quarters. He seems anxious to see us fixed up before he leaves. I have heard nothing of his having been warned and he denies it so the report must be false. I see no excuse for your merchants not keeping paper as there are paper mills in the confederacy. We can get plenty here at 50cts per gum. I could send you some from here if any one was going home. You have seen from the papers that our troops have achieved a

---

* Capt. Real (Rial) B. Seay of Co. K, 5th S.C. died of apoplexy in Virginia. Landrum, *History of Spartanburg County*, 675.

† Capt. Jacob Quickle Carpenter of Co. G. 5th S.C. Landrum, *History of Spartanburg County*, 581.

‡ Probably Maj. William M. Foster of the 5th S.C.

§ Probably William B. Wofford of Co. K, 3rd S.C.

brilliant victory in Kentucky.* One is also reported in western Virginia or rather in the department of the upper Potomac near Winchester.† I do not know the particulars. But I must close this letter. "Cuius velut aegri sommia vanae fingentur species ut nec pes nec caput uni reddatur formae."‡

My love to all the family. Write soon.

Your affec Brother L. P. Foster

Ps. Jan 17th nothing new.

The change in address heading indicates that the long-awaited move into winter quarters finally occurred. Winter Quarters were established on the south bank of Bull Run near Blackburn's Ford, scene of fighting during the Battle of Bull Run. The camp was named after James Lawrence Orr, a prominent South Carolinian politician who had served in the House of Representatives. He was a signer of the Ordinance of Secession, represented the CSA to the Federal government in negotiations over Federal forts in the Charleston harbor, and led a regiment named Orr's Rifles in the first year of the war. After the war, he was elected Governor in 1866 as a Republican.

Foster laments the Confederate defeat at the Battle of Mill Springs, also known as Logan's Crossroads, near Somerset, Kentucky on January 19, 1862. Although a small engagement by Civil War standards, the Confederates lost control of the Cumberland Gap and a presence in Kentucky, helping to solidify Kentucky as a Union state. Foster thinks little of political military appointees in general and appears to consider Confederate General Felix Zollicoffer, a former congressman, a case in point. Zollicoffer was appointed as brigadier general in the early days of the Confederacy; although lacking a military background he was considered a competent military leader. He also lacked good eyesight. At Mill Springs, this defect combined with smoky conditions, caused him to mistakenly approach the Federal forces. Colonel Speed S. Fry of the 4th Kentucky was credited with firing the shot that killed Zollicoffer.

L. P. Foster to His Mother

Campground James L. Orr Jan 26th 1862

My Dear Mother

This is a bright sunny Sabbath. The snow is nearly all melted away and if it was not for the cold wind we would have a very pleasant day—a novelty to us of late

---

* Probably refers to an engagement between Gen. James A. Garfield and Gen. Humphrey Marshall on January 10 at Middle Creek near Prestonsburg in eastern Kentucky. Both sides claimed victory, but the Confederates withdrew during the night.

† This may refer to action near Romney, in western Virginia (now West Virginia) on January 7, which resulted in the Confederates evacuating Romney on January 10.

‡ "Like the dreams of someone who is mentally ill, so that neither the foot nor the head can be attributed to a single form"—Horace, from "Ars Poetica."

Confederate Winter Quarters, Centreville, Virginia 1861–1862. Brady-Handy Collection. *"Centreville, Va. Confederate Winter Quarters."* Courtesy of the Library of Congress, Prints and Photographs Division, Washington, D.C. Reproduction number LC-DIG-ppmsca-32991. January 24, 2017.

days. There is a considerable thaw and it is a little muddy under foot. The mts are in plain view and we can see the snow on them very distinctly. The papers of yesterday and day before contain acct's of our disaster at Somerset Kentucky. We are very sorry to hear of it and I fear it will protract the war. I can see nothing in it except the rashness of our gen'l there. When we have experienced a few more disasters our war department may learn that good politicians and learned men do not always make good gen'ls. The report says the yankee loss was much greater than ours, but I think that very doubtfull and if it were true, it only makes matters worse. That army has lost all of its baggages and will be unfit for service for some time to come, and I fear the Yankees will get possession of Cumberland gap and thus cut off our connection with the Miss valley. I trust god for the end. All our destinies are in his hands and He not Lincoln will wield them. The health of our camp is generally good. Every thing quiet on this line. The yankys fired their cannon two days on the strength of news from Sommerset Ky. We heard their guns very distinctly. Father

Confederate Winter Quarters, Centreville, Virginia, South View 1861–1862. George
N. Barnard, photographer. *"Centreville, Va. Confederate Winter Quarters South
View."* Courtesy of the Library of Congress, Prints and Photographs Division,
Washington, D.C., Reproduction number LC-B817–7212. January 24, 2017.

is about as he has been. He talks of resigning but seems anxious to see me settled
in winter quarters before he leaves.

I have nothing more of interest to write. Remember me to all and write soon.

yr affec son
L. P. Foster

B. B. Foster to His Wife

*Camp James Orr South
Side of Bull Run Jany22nd 1862*

My Dear Wife

I received your letter this evening I was supprised to hear that you had heard
nothing from me since the first of Jany and that you were looking for me at home
every day. This is not my fault I have written regularly at one time I said I thought
I would come home by the 15th last the next day I wrote again and said to you not
to look for me since then I written frequently. I cannot see how so many rumors
reachs home I have not been wounded in any way. Perrin had his toe cut and it has
got well long since. I am not entirely well still have symptoms of Dropsy. my legs

swell about as they did when at home, I have had dysentary for several days. but have not been confined or prevented from attending to my duties. yet in truth I am fearfull that if I stay here this winter it will perhaps injure me to some extent and I think after awhile if I do not improve I will leave for home, I am watching myself and shall whenever I discover that I am growing worse leave here as to marching orders we have received none, and I tell you now that unless old Abe invents some plan by which he can transfer troops through mud from one to three feet deep he cant get here we will be truly supprised if a fight takes place here now. There is really no prospect of fighting any thing new but mud and bad weather it is now snowing there will not be much this time it is too warm. I shall go to putting up a house in the morning we have here a chimney to our tent we have not had time to put up a house. I shall put a good one so that if I leave I shall leave a good place for Perrin I am anxious to stay my time out if I can with safety Perrin is well he is nearer than he ever was one Battallion of our Regiment is out on picket. I am on a court martial which relieves one from all other duty and I get $1.25 per day beside my regular pay. Perrin did not go, I suppose Dr Toland thinks he will get Kings practice never do you send for him or sell him anything tell Tony not to have anything to do with him* I suppose Murphy may do I cannot tell but if need a Doctor send for him but be sure you need one before you send for him or any one else, it does me good to hear that Tony is attentive to business and that you are making all stand about as Nina says may you all do well is my constant prayer remember me to the children and neighbors. I hope Lancaster is Major.

your affectionate husband
B B Foster

Between January 22nd and February 3rd, Lt. Col. Foster, under orders of the surgeon, resigned his commission due to his deteriorating health. He wrote of having a significant level of edema (dropsy) in his legs; this may typically be caused by circulatory, kidney, liver disease, or malnutrition. In her letter of May 9, 1862, Sallie Foster describes her father's continued weakness. After Foster's death in 1897, his daughter Eunice wrote that he returned from the war a "constitutional wreck,"[†] so his condition must have been significantly worse than he described in his letters. Augustus Dickert, a fellow soldier, confirmed that his health had completely given way and that he required long nursing to return to health.[‡]

* On September 24, 1861, Perrin Foster wrote that Toland was arrested and disgraced for having met with the enemy under a white flag.

† Landrum, *History of Spartanburg County*, 432.

‡ Dickert, *History of Kershaw's Brigade*, 100.

L. P. FOSTER TO HIS SISTER, PROBABLY JENNIE

Camp James L. Orr
Feb 3rd 1862

My Dear Sister

I received your letter yesterday evening. I was very glad to hear from you again. I expect you do not try hard enough to learn to write. You ought to learn to write with your right hand. If you will write me a letter before I come home I will give you a nice gold pen when I get there. You ought not to let anything keep you from studying your lessons. If you will study four hours every day you will soon get to love your books so much that it will not be hard for you to learn. I am in hopes that you will have the oxen killed and ate up before I get home as I am very tired of beef of any sort. I suppose Miss Hannah and her sweetheart are having a fine time. Next time that you see her ask her if her rose cuttings are living and doing well. I was sorry to hear that Billys arm was stiff and I suppose you are too. Our boxes have not come yet. We are looking for them soon. I expect the cap made by Sallie for Toney is a pretty one. When I get home I expect I will have to get her to make me one "a la militaire." I wrote to Sister Sallie yesterday. The snow had then nearly all melted away and it was clear and sunny, but when I got up this morning it was snowing very fast and very prettily. The ground was white. Now the snow is four or five inches deep and every thing looks very pretty and white. It has quit snowing, but is still very cloudy. The snow clouds here are very bright and pretty. I went today to see cousins Tom and Wade both of them were a little unwell with camp diarhea. I hope they will be soon well. Tell sister she need not caution me to say nothing of Uncle Samuel's being about to marry.* I have known it for two or three months. All the kin here know it. They went to Edgefield not long since to buy their wedding duds and a milaner [milliner] in Edgefield is now making a wedding dress for her (his intended bride). I hear they are to have no wedding, tell Father when he gets home that his resignation has been accepted. that I have the order under which it was rece'd and for him to write me whether I must send it to him by letter. I have nothing more of interest to write. We are all getting along after the same old style.

Feb 4th. It was clear for a short time this morning. Nothing more of interest. Write soon. Remember me to all and remember the gold pen.

Yr affec Brother.

L P Foster

---

* Samuel Perrin's first wife, Emma Blocker, died June 7, 1860; they had 4 children. On February 25, 1862, Perrin married Julia Quarles; she died May 1, 1874 after giving him two more children. Samuel Perrin married his third wife, Fannie Quarles, on November 4, 1875.

L. P. Foster to His Sister, Probably Sallie

Camp James L. Orr
Feb 7th 1862

My Dear Sister,

Yours of the 31st Jan came last night and Nunies of the 29th Sunday evening. I was very glad to hear that cousins Lou and Anna* were with you. It looks some like sociability—most of which if I mistake not-has been driven out of our state by the war. I think in this respect the Virginians far excel our people. We have a very cold but clear pretty morning. Nearly all the snow has gone and I hope we may have more pleasant weather. You ask about our cabins. They are common pine pole cabins 11ft by 13ft from 11 ft from 7 to 11 logs high as high as Janes house and most of them as comfortable. We have beds of pine poles generally from 4 to 6 men in a cabin. I have never left my tent yet not because I could not go in a cabin but find the tent comfortable enough. I can go in a cabin any day that I wish. I think good wall tents more healthy than cabins and they are equally as warm. We have plenty of camp stoves and don't sit on the ground. Mrs. Hunt† is sharing her husbands tent as well as some other S.C. ladies with whom you are not acquainted. I suppose the old ladies begin to think your time of marrying has near about past, you said that if I intended to marry in april, it was time that I was letting you know it. I will let you know 3 days before hand, time enough to wash your homespun frock and dry it. I have no news. The question of volunteering again before us urged by a circular from gen'l Johnson‡ in a very strong light. Maj Baxter has risen to Lt. Col. And Capt Garlington to Maj.

Remember me to all

Write soon. yr affec
Brother L. P. Foster

L. P. Foster to His Mother

Camp Orr Feb 11th 1862

My Dear Mother

I wrote to Nunie this morning but was so hurried by our mail boy that I could write only a few lines. I rec'd a letter this evening from Nunie to Father—was glad to hear that you were all well. Jimmie Beard is very sick of pneumonia in both sides. He can not live unless there is a change for the better in a very short time.

---

* Likely Anna Isabella Perrin and Louis H. Perrin, the daughter and son of Samuel and Emma Perrin.
† The wife of Capt. James Hamilton Hunt—3rd S.C. Commissary.
‡ General Joseph E. Johnston.

He has now been sick seven days. The surgeons think he may get well and I hope he may, but regarding him in a critical condition. I telegraphed to Mr. Beard this evening—he has not been very ill until last night. I have not heard from Father since he left Petersburg. We have heard of the capture of Roanoke Island by the federals but have not heard the particulars in a reliable way. It is said that our forces killed 1700 hundred of them. There is no doubt but that our men fought desperately. Our force 3000 theirs 12000.* We also hear that gen'l Pryce has whipped them in Missouri† which I hope is true, yet I am not despairing. I look upon this war as a very great affliction sent upon us by an all wise and just god for some wise and good end and have as much faith in the justice and final success of our cause as I ever have had. The time is known to god. I believe now as I ever have that we have much to endure before this war ends. We have not seen and felt as yet what our ancestors saw and felt in their struggle for national existence and unless we be willing to fight and live as they then I fear we are unworthy of the prize for which we are contending. We have had more snow this evening, but not enough to cover the ground. We have very cold weather. I went to the camp of the 20th Georgia Reg't yesterday to see an old college friend. Lieut. Mitchell of Columbus Georgia‡§ He lives next door to Cousin Charlie Harrison.⁵ I have a great many acquaintances & friends in this army—and would spend the time very pleasantly if it were not for the bad weather and inactivity of camp life.

P.S. Feb 13th—I forgot to send this letter to the office yesterday. Yrs of the 5th came yesterday—you ask me I if intend volunteering here. I do not think I shall. I wish to serve in this army, but can not raise our comp. I think I will come home before I enter the service again. Jimmie Beard is much better and I think will get well. Remember me to all and write soon.

Yr affec son

L. P. Foster

P.S. Feb 15th. I went to get [. . .]. I am well Jimmie Beard slowly improves. [. . .]

---

* On Feb. 7–8, 1862. Ambrose Burnside with a superior naval assault force took Roanoke Island, an important strategic point because of its commanding position on both the Albemarle and Pamlico Sounds.

† The text is difficult to read; it could be Pryce, Pryor, or Payne. I believe that the reference is to an engagement on February 10, 1862 in which Union General Samuel Ryan Curtis surprised Confederate General Sterling Price. A series of skirmishes between the two armies followed, leading to the Battle of Pea Ridge on March 7–8, 1862.

‡ Probably Henry Carleton Mitchell who graduated from the South Carolina College in 1857. He is identified as being from Georgia.

§ Andrew Charles Moore, *Roll of Students of South Carolina College 1805–1905* (Columbia, S.C.: no publisher listed, 1905), 27.

⁵ Probably a relative of Francis Eugene Harrison, the husband of Mary Eunice Perrin (L. P. Foster's cousin). Mary Eunice was the daughter of Thomas Chiles Perrin.

Foster had good reason to feel anxious about Fort Donelson on the Tennessee River. Ulysses S. Grant took Fort Henry on Feb. 6 and positioned his troops around Fort Donelson. On the 14th a duel between Union gunboats and the Fort resulted in the withdrawal of the gunboats. A breakout attempt by the Confederates on the 15th was attempted and ended with the Confederates returning to their positions inside the Fort. Foster's statement that "our men had whipped them" may refer to either the Fort-gunboat duel or the breakout attempt. On the 16th, the Confederate defenders surrendered unconditionally to Grant. As a result, southern Kentucky and much of middle and western Tennessee fell under Federal control. This gave the Federals an excellent network of rail and river supply routes, isolated the western states of Missouri and Arkansas, and finished off any hopes of gaining Kentucky as a Confederate state.

L. P. FOSTER TO HIS FATHER

Camp Orr Feb 18th 1862

My Dear Father

I have rec'd two letters from home since you arrived on this evening from Nunie and was glad to hear that you were no worse. I feard your trip home would make you sick and was very uneasy about you until I heard you were at hope [home]. I sent you a proscription for yr disease sent one by Mrs. Clopton which seemed to me very simple and was [. . .] write whether you get it. I showed it to a physician and he said he knew it to be a good thing. I have no news to write you. The reg't has been very quiet since you left. Dr. Ewart is here. Col Williams has not returned yet. Col. Templeton* has been discharged. Early's Brig† now share our picket post with our Brig and it will be some time before we will have to go out again. The 13th Tennessee reg't has been sent to Ft. Donelson and I hear this evening that the 5th N.C. Reg't has been ordered to Roanoke Island. There are all the changes since you left. No Reg't in our Brig have [. . .] except ours. Their [teams are] too badly broken down to haul timber. They have chimneys to their tents and seem to get along about as well as we do. Capt Hunt is very sick with typhoid fever. His wife is with him. Lieut Nance‡ is still at home. He now has measles. Capt Nance§ has not returned

---

* The text seems to clearly say "Col. Templeton," but I cannot identify him. There was a David C. Templeton who was in Co. I of the 3rd S.C. and was discharged February 13, 1862. Wyckoff reports that this Templeton was discharged for being overage (50) and for debility. It may be the same person; it is possible that Templeton had a militia rank of colonel at some point.

† Gen. Jubal Early was commanding Van Dorn's Brigade at the time, in D. H. Hill's Division.

‡ Lt. Jonathan King Griffin Nance of Co. E, 3rd S.C.

§ Captain, later Col. James Drayton Nance of the 3rd S.C.

and is said to be quite unwell yet. I have drawn your court marshall money. Jimmie Beard is still improving and without some great change for the worse will get well. We have not heard from Davis in a day or two at last acc't he was better. The cars are now running across Bull Run and will reach Centreville by Sunday night. A new battery of [...] small caliber was sent to Centreville a few days since from Richmond. Considerable anxiety exist here with regard to the fight at Ft. Donelson at last acc'ts our men had whipped them but they were reinforced and expected to renew the attack. I went this evening to hear the camps of the Jeff Davis Legion to see Cap't Perrin and brothers but could not find it. I saw Tom Quarles—he and Wade are well. Capt Brady is trying to raise his comp for the war. The Brooks Guards* of 2nd Reg't have all volunteered except 2 or 3 men and have gone home.

Remember me to all and write soon. yr affec Son

L. P. Foster

P.S. [...] no news. Jimmie Beard is still better.

L. P. F.

L. P. Foster to His Sister, Probably Sallie

Camp Orr Feb. 18th 1862

My Dear Sister,

Your letter of the 10th inst. has been rec'd. I was very glad to hear that father had got home and was able to be up. I hope he will still improve. Did he get a letter from me containing a proscription for dropsy. Mrs. Clopton sent it to me and I tore it out and sent it to him. I have stayed in my tent this long from preference. I find it very comfortable. I can go in a house any day I chose. A tent is very comfortable except in windy weather. We have very bad weather sleeted nearly all day yesterday ground nearly covered with snow now. You ask about my reenlisting. I have written my notions about it in a letter which has reached you before now. You also ask about my marrying. Well! Well! Well! I have nothing of interest to write. Jimmie Beard is getting better. No war news on this line. Remember me to all. Write soon.

yr affec Brother

L. P. Foster

L. P. Foster to His Mother

Camp Orr Feb 20th, 1862

My Dear Mother,

I rec'd a letter yesterday from Nunie, and was glad to hear from you. I have been very busy this evening covering my cabbin. I will finish it in the morning. It

---

* The Brooks Guards were Company K of the 2nd S.C. Volunteer Infantry.

will be very comfortable. I saw Wade Cothran and Tom Quarles today. They were quite well and trying to get their comp to reenlist. Wade said his boy was very hearted and talked about volunteering but that he asked him to oversee. They said uncle Samuel was married a few days ago. I suppose they had no wedding owing to the death of Aunt Julia's* step father. He said he went to Augusta to get a clean shirt, new pants, and a new cravat, that his cravat was a good one only the knot had become worn by his allowing it to slip around under his ear to much. They are a lively set. Jimmie Beard is still improving and will go home so soon as he is able. Which I hope will not be a great while yet it will be I think some ten days. Adolphus Davis[†] of our comp died at the Moore hospital at Manassas on the 17th last of typhoid fever. We did not hear of it until yesterday evening. We have heard various rumours as to the fall of Ft Donaldson and the defeat of our troops there but all up to this time have been very vague and unsatisfactory and most of these absurd and unreasonable. The most reliable dispatch places our entire loss at 1500 hundred men & that of the enemy much greater between 7 & 9 thousand. It seems certain that our forces have left the place and fallen back to Nashville where they intend to make a determined stand. The report of Nashville having surrendered is false. It seems that our reverses come quite frequent. They do not shake my faith in our cause at all. So long as there is an armed body of men in the Confederacy to resist their oppression I expect to fight them god being willing. I have nothing but newspaper news which I do not credit & which you will see. So will close. Tell Annie to write me who the "Beauty of Glenn Springs" is also the compliments passed on me by said "Beauty."

My Love to all the family. write soon, Yr affec son.

L P Foster

P.S. Feb 22nd I forgot to mail this yesterday. nothing new I am well LPF

L. P. FOSTER TO HIS FATHER

Camp Orr Feb 26th 1862

My Dear Father,

I received a letter from Nunie this evening, and was very glad to hear you were no worse. I wrote you a P.S. this morning giving a brief and unsatisfactory account of our movements here. I never have been so at a loss to understand the movement of our army before. We were yesterday moved to send all heavy baggage back. I went to Col. Baxter for an explanation but he seemed to know but little more than I did. He said he thought it quite probable that we would move some where and seemed to express the belief that we would have to give up this line yet

---

* Julia Quarles, second wife of Samuel Perrin.

† Adolphus T. Davis of Co. K 3rd S.C. died February 17, 1862 of typhoid fever as described by Foster.

a thousand men or more are now at work on the fortifications at Manassas which does not look like giving, up the line. There seems to be no report of an advance of the army in front, but some rumours of a fight at Winchester & a column of the Enemy pushing down the vally in our rear towards Culpepper C.H. but citizens from that country to day contradict the report so that the idea that we are to fall back to the Rhappahannoc River to meet that column seems absurd. Some think that our whole Division is to be ordered somewhere else, perhaps to Weldon[*] but none of [us] know anything about it and all we hear of vague speculation. The idea that we must give up this line because we can not hold it is absurd and would be met by any [. . .] by every soldier in this army. What the actions of the Enemy in other parts of the C.S. and the necessities of the C.S. may compel this army to do we can not tell. I shall send my trunk back in the morning. Our sick all went back to day Jimmy Beard went back. I hope he is strong enough to stand it, yet I fear he will have a rough time. Elija Davis came on 2 or 3 days since to see his son whom he had heard was sick and found him dead.[†] He left today. I found your commission in my trunk today. I send it enclosed as I will not have a place for it.[‡] I have nothing more of interest to write.

   Remember me to all. Write soon. I will keep you advised of our movements.

yr affec Son L. P. Foster

P.S. Feb 27th Nothing. Supplies were being shipped from Manassas back yesterday

L. P. Foster

L. P. FOSTER TO HIS MOTHER

Camp Orr Feb 27th 1862

My Dear Mother,

   I wrote to Father last night giving him all the news, but know that that letter will make you anxious to hear again from our line. I have nothing new to write. We have many vague rumours but nothing reliable whatever. Nothing as to our future movements seems certain. I am satisfied that momentous movements are on the topics of consideration but what will be the result I could not tell or have much idea. I sent my trunk back this morning whether I will ever see it again or not is very difficult to determine. I fear there is a rough time ahead of us either marching or fighting and perhaps both but I do not murmur I am willing to endure anything for my country. I see no chance for our getting home soon now. I can see but little

---

   [*] The Weldon Railroad connected Weldon, North Carolina, to Petersburg, Virginia, and was an important supply route. This might be Foster's reference.

   [†] Elija Davis's son, Adolphus T. Davis, died of typhoid fever on February 17, 1862.

   [‡] This commission, signed by S.C. Governor F. W. Pickens and Gen. States Rights Gist, survived the trip home and is still in possession of the editor's family.

rest time ahead nor would I see the rest of a slave or coward am willing to sacrifice all for independence. Our enemy are bearing down heavily upon us but I look up our adversities as afflictions sent by God to chasten us and try our faith.

Remember me to all and write soon. Your Affec Son

L P Foster

P.S. 8th Nothing New

L. P. FOSTER TO HIS SISTER, PROBABLY SALLIE

Camp Orr March 2nd /62

My Dear Sister,

I have not rec'd a letter from home in several days. Nothing has transpired which brings to light our movements here. We are still in our cabins and I am getting to thin[k] will remain in them for some time yet. I think much of our present movement may be strategy. I saw Tom Quarles this morning he is well. I heard from Jimmie Beard since he left. He is at the University hospital at Charlottesville and doing quite well. This is Sunday. Mr. Mayfield I suppose will preach. The weather is rather mild now. We have had clear weather for several days and any amount of wind. The ground has dried off very much and the roads are getting very good. If McClellan intends to come here he can now have a chance. I for one look for him to attack but not in front. I think he will come on our flanks and fear if we have a fight here it will be desperate. We all know that it will not do for this army to [be] whipped. We hear that Col Williams has rheumatism and don't know when he will return to camp. I am getting anxious to see him. I have but little confidence in Lieut Col Baxter as an officer. It is reported here that gen'l Jackson whipped the enemy at Winchester yesterday morning.* I thin[k] our movements will depend very much on his. Remember me to all. Write soon.

yr affec Brother

L. P. Foster

L. P. FOSTER TO HIS MOTHER

Camp Orr March 3rd /62

My Dear Mother,

Yours of the 23rd came this evening. I was very glad to hear that Father was improving so rapidly. You say truly that our country presents a dark picture. Our reverses have come fast and heavily, yet I see nothing in them beyond what we might expect. The government has refused to act on the aggressive for want of

* I find no record of any significant action near Winchester, Virginia, in the days preceding this letter.

strength yet by dividing the armies in mere skeletons has tried to defend all of its boundary. Our armies will have to be concentrated and made stronger. More marching and less dirt digging will have to work our movements. Our people will have to waken up from their present state of care and do more fighting and less talking, will have come to sacrifice all to the torch applied by their own hand in the face of an invading army. If we are subdued it will not be from want of strength but because we are not brave enough to make the sacrifice and exertions necessary to attain the glorious goal in [. . .]. God even yet rewarded the inaction of the sluggard. I do not feel discouraged by our reverses and am determined never to give up the struggle which an armed patriot will raise his arm in defense of liberty. God being willing I would rather have my country a mouldering heap of ashes dotted all over with the graves of those who have dared nobly to die for just rights than have it in wealth and luxury yet swayed by a tyrants will. Rather let me die in the struggle of liberty than live to see our country a subdued province. What brave man would not shoot the first federal that gathered on property confiscated who dares to enter his house. No let us show to the world that the rights of a brave people can only be snatched from them with their lives. Let the last drop of blood trickle from the last patriotts heart upon our beautifull battle flag ere it be carried to a federal capital as a proud trophy of arms. If it be a trophy let it remind them of a noble but perished people. These are my feelings.

Things here remain "cie status quo." Every thing in readiness for something we know not what. We had it pretty snow yesterday of about 2½ in. Every thing sloppy. I rec'd my coat and cape but sent them off in my trunk. I could not carry them. Some of the boys told me I had better keep them to wear to Washington in case I would be taken prisoner but I shall never prepare for such a thing. March 4th we have a clear but very cold morning. Bull Run is partially frozen over. There has not been very many days here since Christmas in which would not have frozen.

Remember me to all write soon

yr affec son
L. P. Foster

L. P. FOSTER TO HIS FATHER

Camp Orr March 5th 1862

My Dear Father,

Yours of the 26th was rec'd yesterday. I was glad to hear that you were still improving and hope you may soon entirely recover. I have nothing of interest to write. There was a picket skirmish at Germantown yesterday in which our men captured 28 prisoners. There was also a skirmish on the Occoquan. One of the Hamptons Legion was killed and another wounded. I know of no new movements of the

Enemy—we are still here ready for anything. What is to follow we can not tell. Col. Williams has not yet returned. We are anxious to see him. Capt Rutherford has gone home to get married.* I don't know when he will return. Dr. Dorrah† is still at home.

Remember me to all and write soon.

L. P. Foster

March 6th Nothing new

---

* William Drayton Rutherford married Sallie H. Fair. He was ultimately promoted to Major in the 3rd S.C.

† Dr. Jonathan Francis Dorroh was a surgeon in the 3rd S.C. Dickert spells the surgeon's name "Dorroah."

CHAPTER 6

The Peninsula

The Elephant Returns

In November, Gen. George McClellan had promised quick action in Virginia. He planned to land a large force in Urbanna, Virginia, on the peninsula between the Rappahannock River and the York River, for a march on Richmond. A large Federal army landed at Urbanna could have easily taken Richmond and dispensed with Gen. Joseph E. Johnston's much smaller force to the north at Centreville. Concerns that Johnston might march on Washington caused a significant delay while plans were made to ensure that a substantial force remained along the Potomac to protect the capital.

McClellan contracted a mild case of typhoid fever, which delayed any action against the Confederates. As January 1862 ended, no significant movement against the Confederacy in Virginia was evident. With McClellan's return to work in late January, planning for the Urbanna landing continued. First, however, McClellan wanted to secure Harpers Ferry, to protect the Baltimore and Ohio railway, and to replace the lost bridges there with pontoon bridges built upon canal boats floated up the canal from Washington.

Harpers Ferry was adequately protected and controlled; however, the pontoon bridge plan was a bust. Despite all the engineering preparations, the canal boats were a few inches too large to fit through the locks and could not be brought to Harpers Ferry. While this embarrassing production ran its course, time was passing.

Since the middle of February, General Joseph Johnston had been preparing to evacuate Centreville and position his army where it could better counter the expected move by the Federals against Richmond. Despite having fortified Centreville with breastworks and cut logs disguised as cannons, Johnston's 40,000 Confederates were at a great disadvantage against McClellan's army of 120,000. Further, Johnston did not intend to allow McClellan an opportunity to move his army between Confederate forces at Centreville and Richmond. On Sunday, March 9, Johnston put his army on the march south.

As the army passed through Manassas, the huge stores of food, clothing, ammunition, railroad equipment, and manufacturing facilities were burned; stores the

Confederate Defensive Works at Centreville, occupied by Federals and
showing cut logs disguised as cannons, also known as Quaker guns. George
N. Barnard, photographer. *"Centreville, Va. Fort on the heights, with Quaker
guns."* Courtesy of the Library of Congress, Prints and Photographs Division,
Washington, D.C., Reproduction number LC-B811–334A. January 24, 2017

army could not carry would not be left for the Federals.* Many soldiers lost their
few personal possessions in the fires. The Confederates marched along the Orange
and Alexandria Railroad line, arriving at Rappahannock Station across the river
on Tuesday, March 11th, having spent Sunday night at Bristoe Station and Monday
night at Warrenton Station. On March 19th, they marched to Rapidan Station and
remained there until the 28th when they marched to Orange Court House.

The Federals advanced and occupied the abandoned Confederate defenses at
Centreville, but the plan to launch a campaign against Richmond from Urbanna
was finished. Johnston had relocated to a place where he could better move to
defend Richmond and reduce the exposure of his army. Having lost a key advantage in the Urbanna landing, McClellan abandoned those plans.

* Dickert, *History of Kershaw's Brigade*, 91–92.

Wreckage of Orange and Alexandria Railroad at Manassas Junction by
Withdrawing Confederates. George N. Barnard, photographer. *"Manassas,
Va. Orange and Alexandria Rail Road wrecked by retreating Confederates."*
Courtesy of the Library of Congress, Prints and Photographs Division,
Washington, D.C., Reproduction number LC-B817–7197. June 10, 2008

New planning began for a landing on the next peninsula to the south, formed
by the York and James rivers. An overwhelming Union force landed at the Federal
Fort Monroe and advanced up the Peninsula through Yorktown, Williamsburg,
and across the Chickahominy River to Richmond. Additional supply landings were
established at West Point on the York and at Harrison's Landing on the James.

L. P. Foster to His Father

Rhappahanock Station
March 18th /62

My Dear Father,

Your are all very uneasy about me, but I have been so situated for the last week
that I could neither receive letters nor mail them. We left our camp (Orr) on Sunday
evening. I think the whole army of the Potomac moved at the same time. As to the
move, I have nothing to say except that I regard it a good measure as it will generally shorten our line and enable us to send troops to other points. We marched to

Bristoe station the first night—8 miles. The next day to Warrenton Station 10 miles & the next morning here 10 miles. Our men were very much fatigued by the march of first and 2nd day owing to their not having been drilled any in several months. I stood the march finely carried my knapsack, haversack, sword and pistol also my overcoat and on the first day two blankets and an oil cloth. I could march every time to the word <u>halt</u>, but the first two days made me very sore. I am now quite well. We sleep under but two blankets, yet I have no[t] suffered at all from cold. We have not had a tent since we left Camp Orr. Baxter has conducted the march well much better than we ever had one conducted before. A good many stores and a greatdeal of baggage was at Manassas and quantities of blankets dropped on the way. More about that anon. When we will leave here or where we will stop or whether we make our stand here are questions which I am unable to answer. I think the yanks are not following us. There was no fighting except pickets skirmishing before we left our old line. They drove in nearly all of our pickets. Killed a few of the first Maryland reg't and had a few killed by them. Our Brig and the 1st Maryland Reg't covered the retreat our reg't and the 1st Maryland in rear all the time. It is said that we are to put as an advance corps again.

Our whole comp has come up and I think the whole Reg't. Our Reg't had but few straglers in comparison with the others. There are a great many troops in this vicinity. When I will get to send this letter I know not, nor do I know where to tell you to write.

Remember me to all. yr affec son. L. P. Foster

P.S. I expect my trunk and every thin[g] in it was burned.* I have clothes enough in my knapsack to do me. My blankets safe. L P. Foster

P.S. March 19. Still here. Nothing new

L. P. Foster to His Father

Camp 5 ms from Rappadan station
March 21st, 1862

My Dear Father

I fear you are very uneasy about me as it has been near a week since I wrote. The day after I wrote, we left our camp near Rappahannock station and marched 7 miles camping in 3 ms of Culpepper C.H. The next day we were detained at Culpepper most of the day while gen'l Longstreets Division past. We camped one mile this side of Culpepper. We marched the next day about 17 miles to a camp about 2 miles this side of the Rappadan River and yesterday moved here about 4 miles. We are now some four miles from Orange C.H. We have had some rough times we

---

* His trunk was apparently shipped before Manassas Junction was burned because his Father's commission made it home. It is still in possession of the editor's family.

have had no tents since we left Bull Run and bid fair not to have any soon. We have had some very wet weather, but we stitch up our oil cloths and sleep pretty well. Last night was a very wet night. It is said we are to remain here for some ten days after which time no one seems to know what is to become of us. Some say we are to be ordered to Richmond to be mustered out of the service others that we will still be held over and others that we have been already drafted in so far without be[ing] asked to volunteer or knowing anything about it. Such a thing would raise a ruckus. As is what is to become of us I profess ignorance. I am getting anxious to start home. I have not seen a letter from any of you since I left Bull Run. There is no enemy in pursuit of us that I hear of. I have seen no papers in a long time we are just cut off from the world. Our march has been very orderly and well conducted. Four of the Tigers* were court marshalled for stealing private property and sentenced very heavily. One to 2 years imprisonment in penitentiary and during 20 days of each yr. to be limited to bread and water and after the end of the time to have his head shaved and dismissed out of the service. I have nothing new to write. Remember me to all. Write soon.

Yr affec. Son
L P Foster

In the following letter, Foster referred to Pickens' Proclamation on March 5, 1862, when Governor Pickens issued a call to respond to Jefferson Davis's request for five new regiments from South Carolina. A regiment consisted of about 1,000 troops, hence the reference to the 5,000. Men were given notice that volunteers would not be assigned to existing regiments until the five new regiments had been filled.† Foster indicates that existing troops were upset, apparently at the prospect that they would not be able to volunteer for reenlistment with their units until the five regiments were raised.

The issues of conscription and re-enlistment were discussed frequently in the following months. Because of the increasing Confederate need for soldiers, the Confederate Conscription Act was approved on April 16, 1862, replacing an earlier volunteer system. At the start of the war, local leaders had organized volunteer companies that elected officers. Men served with their friends, relatives, and neighbors for specified volunteer periods. With the Conscription Act, men were drafted and assigned to units decided by state draft officials. Many of the volunteers had enlisted in early 1861 for one-year terms, and those terms were coming to a close. This left them with tough decisions. Should they try to time their reenlistment after the five new regiments were raised so that they could stay in their units? Should they let their enlistments expire,

* The 1st Louisiana Special Battalion of Confederate Zouaves under command of Roberdeau Wheat was nicknamed Wheat's Tigers.

† Charles Edward Cauthen, *South Carolina Goes to War 1860–1865* (Columbia: University of South Carolina Press, 2005), 144.

go home, and take their chances with a draft? Uncertainty as to how the draft would be operated increased speculation and made the decisions even more difficult.

The Conscription Act allowed exemptions for certain key occupations. Those who exercised those exemptions were seen by some as shirkers, the exemptions seen as loopholes for the sons of the upper class. Those who went home after their volunteer periods ended risked being viewed as deserters of The Cause. Conscripts were in some cases viewed as rabble who lacked the courage to volunteer when the Confederacy first called for help.

Leadership issues also emerged. Foster's letters show a suspicion that the new conscript units were being created to find positions for political appointees. On the other hand, the electing of officers was said to put easygoing, undemanding officers in command.

It all added up to a confusing, uncertain, and contentious time.

L. P. FOSTER TO HIS FATHER

*Camp five miles from
Rapidan Station. March 22nd 1862*

My Dear Father,

I rec'd 6 letters from home yesterday evening. Several from you one urging me to come home as recruiting officer for my comp. Had I rec'd your letter in time to have got home by the 20th ins, I should have been disposed to have complied. I could have been furloughed as recruiting officer by promising to but I have seen and read Pickens proclamation also the instrument you sent me and think it would have been of no use since he has evidently stopped all volunteering until his 5000 are raised and we suppose from the reading of the instrument you sent me that all troops in S.C. are to be raised here after by draft. Had that system been commenced at first it would have done well, but it is sure to injure the cause among the troops here. Every body is abusing Pickens and his council. I hear some say he shall never get a chance at them. That they will volunteer in regts from other states. I think the whole plan bears but one design which is to get the appointment of officers. I think now my only chance for an office is for you to apply for an appointment for me for some office and perhaps by yr influence with gov Gist* who is in the executive council you may effect such a thing. I wrote home yesterday telling our whereabouts. No news to write.

Remember me to all.

Write soon

yr affec Son
L. P. Foster

* William Henry Gist was governor of South Carolina from 1858 to 1860.

L. P. FOSTER TO HIS MOTHER

Camp 5 miles from Rapadan
Station—March 24th 1862

My Dear Mother,

We are still here and I suppose will remain here until we start home which most of us think will be next week, Monday, and that we will remain a wk in Richmond. I think the late proclamation of the gov and council of S.C. will cause a great many to reinlist here. Men sense they shall not have a chance at them. I scarcely know what to do for if I go home I will have to enroll my name within ten days and then will not have the privilege of volunteering, but will have to await the draft. I have no news to write. The furloughed men are coming back. Col. Williams came night before last. The men serenaded him, made him give them a little speech. Gamaliel James and Anthony Shands came day before yesterday. We have had a goodeal of wet weather. There is but little sign of spring here. Clover fields & wheat fields look green but trees and shrubbery look as naked as in dead of winter. No one is planting yet.

I think I will be a[t] home by the 14th or 15th of June.

Write soon. Remember me to all.

yr affec Son
L. P. Foster

L. P. FOSTER TO HIS SISTER. PROBABLY SALLIE

Camp near Rapadan Station
March 26th 1861 [1862]*

My Dear Sister

I received yours of the 17th inst. yesterday evening. I know you were uneasy about me but could not prevent it. I have nothing more to write. We are still bivouacing here in the woods. A great many of our furloughed men and a good many recruits have come back. All look well and hearty. We are having pretty cold weather but very pleasant weather for march. We have had but very little wind. The birds are singing this morning which make me think of springs. This like most of Va that I have seen is a fine farming country and in a very high state of cultivation. Everything bespeaks of plenty. We can scarcely buy any thing owing to the no of troops camped near here. We have commenced drilling again. Have two drills a day at 9 comp drill and at 5 Bat drill. Remember me to all and write soon. yr affec brother
L. P. Foster

---

* Although dated 1861, this is certainly an error; Foster's location and content are clearly indicative of an 1862 date.

L. P. Foster to His Father

Camp Near Rapadan Station
March 27th 1862

My Dear Father,

I have no news to write you. We are still here but I think if nothing happens it will not be long before we will be moved towards Richmond. I don't think our comp can be raised here and I am at a loss to know what to do. Can I volunteer after I come home if I do not reenlist here or will I have to await my chance in the draft? Write me very soon answering these questions. I don't think any more reenlisted men will be allowed furloughs. Johnston has already refused to grant any more and our reenlisted men are down on him. 7 comps are now complete in Winders* reg't. The others will make four or five each. I have nothing more to write. Remember me to all. Write soon. yr

affec Son
L P Foster

In the following letter, Foster speculated about being sent to North Carolina. Beginning in February 1862, General Ambrose Burnside led a combined Army-Navy expedition to North Carolina. The Federals captured Roanoke Island on February 8 and took New Bern on March 14th.† The intent of these and subsequent operations was to end the ability of the Confederacy to use the North Carolina coastline for blockade running. At this time, there were no engagements as far inland as Goldsboro.

L. P. Foster to His Father

Camp 2 miles from Orange C.H.
March 29th 1862

My Dear Father,

You will see from the above that we have been on the march again. Day before yesterday evening we were ordered to be ready to march at a moments warning. Yesterday morning about 1 hr by sun we took up line of march not knowing where we were going, but all thinking that we were going to western Va to reinforce gen'l Jackson but afterward found out that we had started to N.C. but when we had marched some 4 miles we were halted and informed that the order had been countermanded. We were all in fine spirits with the idea of riding on the cars to N.C. and getting that much nearer home, but we are still here in the woods. There are

* Probably Brig. Gen. John H. Winder who commanded the Confederate Department of Henrico.
† E. B. Long, *The Civil War Day by Day* (Garden City, N.Y.: Doubleday, 1971), 168, 184.

various conjectures about the reason of our being stopped. Some say we could not get transportation. Others that the yanks are threatening in front. Others that our men have whipped the yanks at Goldsborough N.C. No one knows any thing about it. I think we will have to leave here before long. The time of service of Kershaws Reg't will expire in 10 day, ours in 16 days. Several of our comp have joined the 5 Reg't—a Reg't of 10 comps will be organized to day from the 5th & 6th Reg'ts. There are 6 comps from the 6th & 4 from the 5th Reg't—Jenkins* & Sechrist† are running for Col., Joe Walker‡ for Lt. Col, & Goss§ for Maj. Both of the latter have opponents from the 6th Reg't. I have no more news to write. Remember me to all and write soon.

Yr affec Son

L. P. Foster

P.S. 30th Nothing new. Sleet yesterday evening and last night we are all very well.

L. P. Foster

While Perrin Foster and the 3rd S.C. were marching into position along the Rapidan northwest of Richmond, his brother, Tony, was assessing his military service options. In March 1862, Jefferson Davis proposed the Conscription Act which obligated all men between ages eighteen and thirty-five to enter or to remain in the army.

Tony Foster decided to enlist in a regiment of his choosing; he joined the 13th Regiment of the South Carolina Volunteers under Col. Oliver E. Edwards. The 13th had been organized in August 1861 at Lightwood Knot Springs in Columbia, South Carolina, and had moved three months later to Pocotaligo along the South Carolina coast. The 13th was later stationed at Green Pond, South Carolina, a depot along the Charleston and Savannah Railroad. The 12th, 13th, and 14th Regiments were organized into a brigade under Brig. Gen. Maxcy Gregg. The Green Pond camp was also known as Camp Gregg. The following rail passes outline Foster's train journey to his new regiment.

TONY FOSTER'S TRAIN PASSES

The Conductor of the Spartanburg & Union Rail Road will furnish transportation for the bearer J. Anthony Foster a recruit on his way to join the 13th Reg't S.C.V.

March 17 1862.

Jn W Carlisle¶

Lieut Co. "C" 13th Reg't S.C.V.

* Col. Micah Jenkins, 5th S.C.
† Sechrist was Lt. Col. A. J. Secrest of the 6th S.C.
‡ Capt. Joseph Walker of Co. K, 5th S.C.
§ Capt. J. W. Goss of Co. A, 5th S.C.
¶ Capt. John W. Carlisle, 13th S.C.

Recruiting Officer

The Conductor of the Greenville & Columbia Rail Road will furnish transportation for the bearer J. Anthony Foster a recruit on his way to join the 13th S.C.V.

March 17 1862

Jn W Carlisle

Lieut Co. "C" 13th Reg't S.C.V.

Recruiting Officer

The Conductor of the Charleston & So. Ca. Rail Road will furnish transportation for the bearer J. Anthony Foster a recruit on his way to join the 13th S.C.V.

March 17 1862

Jn W Carlisle

Lieut Co. "C" 13th Reg't S.C.V.

Recruiting Officer

The Conductor of the Charleston & Savannah Rail Road Company will furnish transportation for the bearer J. Anthony Foster a recruit on his way to join the 13th S.C.V.

March 17 1862

Jn W Carlisle

Lieut Co. "C" 13th Reg't S.C.V.

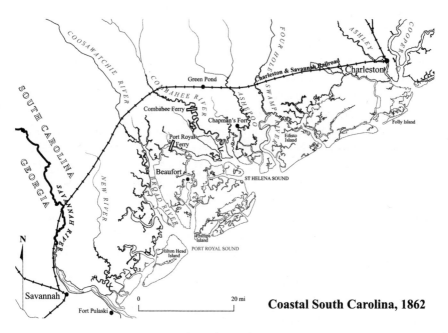

Coastal South Carolina, 1862.

Foster's letter gives a vivid description of the train journey that the Spartanburg recruits took to Green Pond. They departed Spartanburg on the Spartanburg and Union Railroad, and changed to the Greenville and Columbia Railroad in Alston. They traveled on this line to Columbia; transferred to the South Carolina Railroad; and proceeded to a major railroad junction at Kingsville, between Columbia and Orangeburg. The railroad continued through Branchville to Charleston. At Charleston, the Charleston and Savannah Railroad carried them to the depot at Green Pond.

J. A. FOSTER TO HIS MOTHER

Green Pond
March 25th 1862

My Dear Mother,

I arrived here safe this evening about three o'clock, after a long and part of the time very disagreeable ride. We got along finely until we got about a mile this side of Kingville. There the engine broke loose from the train, and stoped so sudenly that the passenger cars ran into the box cars and mashed up two of them so badly that we had to leave them. fortunately no one was hurt. I never had such a jolt in my life. We were detained there at least three hours. We then started and ran like a streak of lightning to make up lost time. until we got in about seventeen miles of Charleston where the same accident again occured with the exception that there was no injury done except to the cars which broke loose which was the one I was on. We were here again detained a considerable length of time and arrived in Charleston at half past eight o'clock, our train being due there at three. The remainder of the journey was very agreeable indeed with the exception of the last five miles, which I travelled on foot through the sand. I had a first rate view of the ocean from the steam boat on which we crossed the Ashley river. I could see the masts of the vessels in the harbour very plain. They are throwing up very strong fortifications 2 or 3 miles this side of Charleston. I saw a great many negroes at work on them. This is one of the strangest looking countries I ever saw. it is almost as level as a plank floor as far as the eye can reach. The timber is mostly long leaf pine covered with moss from three to twenty feet long. There are a great many ponds about here. I think at least one fourth of the land is covered with water or is at certain seasons of the year. The water (except the water we use) looks almost perfectly black even down to the rivers have the same black look. I have seen more ducks to day than I have ever seen in one day in my life, and more water terripins than you could count in a week. The logs in some of the ponds were covered from one end to the other. I will not attempt any farther description of the country. You can form no idea of it until you see it. There are any amount of alligators in the ponds about here, the boys had four sunday before last. I think I will like camp life first rate. It will not do for us to remain here longer that the first of April. Cousin Oliver thinks we will be

sent to North Carolina in the course of 2 weeks from this time. Captain Duncan*
& Captain Smiths† companies are out on picket. All of our friends here that are in
camp are well. I must close this. I have not slept but about a quarter of an hour since
I left Spartanburg and it is now about eight o'clock. I am well and do not feel at all
tired. Bookter‡ sends his respects to the family. We left Mr Carlisle§ in Charleston
with the provision boxes. We did not get them in time he got them on the C&S Rail
Road. He will be here tomorrow. My love to the family

Your affectionate son,
J. A. Foster

March 26th

P. S. Col Edwards thinks I had better be mustered in at once, he says he can with
the consent of the Captain, transfer me and that it will not have to go before the
Gen. Tell father to write me what he thinks about it.

J. A. Foster to His Father

Green Pond
March 28th 1862

My Dear Father:

I wrote to mother the day I got here, giving her an account of my trip here. I
had not then seen much of this country. Yesterday I went down to the Combahee
ferry 6 or 7 miles from here, where our pickets are stationed. I crossed the river on
a bridge built on flat bottom boats which rose and fell with the tide, which was a
curiosity to me as you may well know. The country between here and there is decidedly the most beautiful country I ever saw, it is perfectly level all the way, the timber
is principally long leafed pines, magnolias, and live oak. I saw the rice plantations
of Col Haywood¶ and others, they are worth looking at. I never have seen farming
carried to such perfection. These plantations which contain thousands of acres are
as nicely worked as our finest gardens. as far up and down the river as the eye can
reach these plantations are perfectly level, and I think I could see twenty miles each
way. I saw a masked battery on the way, which protects the road from this place to
the ferry. The fences down here are mostly made of wire and dirt. I saw more game
yesterday than I ever saw in one day in my life. If I had a gun I believe I would
support myself by hunting, but we are not allowed to shoot about here. I saw John

---

* Capt. David R. Duncan of Co. C, 13th S.C.

† Capt. Andrew K. Smith of Co. I, 13th S.C.

‡ Bookter Foster, son of Joel and Charlotte Foster.

§ Lt. Jno. W Carlisle of Co. C, 13th S.C.

¶ Col. Haywood—This likely refers to Col. William Cruger Heyward's Cypress Plantation
on the Combahee River.

Harmon yesterday he is looking better than I ever saw him. Wm White* and Bob Smith† got here yesterday. I must close this as the mail will soon start. I like camp life first rate. I have not drilled any yet but will commence to day. All of our men were received. I wrote to mother asking your opinion about my being mustered in. Cousin Oliver says he has the right to give me a transfer with the consent of the Captain. I am well. My love to all.

Your affectionate son

J. A. Foster

J. A. Foster to His Sister, Probably Sallie

Camp Gregg
Colleton Dist S.C.
March 30th 1862

My Dear Sister:

I have not received a letter from home since I left. This is the third letter I have written since I left home. I heard a sermon to day from an officer in Capt Hunt's‡ company. I find a great deal more strict observance of the Sabbath in camp than I had any idea I would. Not withstanding the sound of drums and the marching to and fro of armed men. The casual observer would not be at a loss to recognize the day. The longer I stay here the better I like camp life. This is a beautiful country. I find a great many curiosities here. I wish you could be here for a while. You could enjoy yourself finely by looking at the great variety of plants and trees. Every thing here is as green as in May in Spartanburg. If I get a chance I will send you a water lily. I could send you a great many curiosities if I had the chance. There are some of the most beautiful doves down here I ever saw. They are about as large as a common black bird and of a beautiful golden colour. The negroes catch them in traps and bring them to camp.§ The black birds here are almost as large as crows. There are a great many snakes here, and more alligators than you could count in a week. They are very easily caught. The get out on the logs in the ponds and go to sleep. The boys watch for them and when they see them asleep they step up and hit them on the head with a club, this stuns them and before they come too, they have them safe. I intend to skin one and send you his skin if I get an opportunity. Joe Harmon⁵

---

* Wm. White—Likely W. F. White in Company C of the 13th S.C.; Company C, the Forest Rifles, was formed by men in the Spartanburg District.

† Bob Smith—Likely Robert Smith also in Company C of the 13th S.C.

‡ Captain Isaac F. Hunt of Co. K, 13th S.C.

§ This is intriguing. Passenger pigeons, now extinct, had a beautiful iridescent bronze neck and breast. Perhaps Foster is describing Passenger Pigeons.

⁵ Joseph S. Harmon of Co. C, 13th S.C.

sent you some palmetto to day by Mr. Lamasters; he will carry it to Spartanburg for you. If you get it it will be enough to keep you busy for months. Every little pond here is full of fish. I think if I had a seign down here I could get 2 or 3 hundred at a draw. We get any amount of the finest sort of shad, and that is about all the good eatable we get. If we were allowed we could kill any amount of turkeys and deer but we are not allowed to shoot in a mile of camp. I heard heavy firing this evening in the direction of Beaufort, but that is no uncommon thing. The pickets of our company fired four or five times at some Yankees last night, but did not kill any. I am in John Harmans* mess. Wilford Harris† an old friend of mine is also in this mess. I have got so I feel perfectly at home in camp and can sleep just as well as I can at home. Col. Edwards sends his love to you all. I am well. Write soon. Your Brother.

Toney

J. A. FOSTER TO HIS SISTER, PROBABLY SALLIE

Camp Gregg Colleton Dist
April 6th 1862

My Dear Sister:

I would have answered your letter yesterday or the day before, but a letter will go from here as quick to start it tomorrow as it will if you send it on Saturday and if I had written Friday I could not have sent it until Saturday. The reason letters go as quick to send them on Monday as they do to start them on Saturday is that if you send them on Saturday they are detained a day in Charleston. I have not got but two letters from home since I came here. I have not heard a word from Perrin save what you wrote in your letter, viz that he was a Rapidan Station or in 5 miles of that place. I don't suppose he knows where I am or he would write to me. I got leave from the Capt yesterday and went a fishing in a pond about a hundred yards from camp. I saw any amount of the finest kind of pirches but could not catch any. Mr. Landrum‡ caught a very fine fish of some sort, but let it get away from him. We will be moved from this place this week to a place near the Rail Road. I have no idea when we will leave these swamps. But I expect before long. I have just got back from a little walk. I saw five alligators in a little pond. You may know from that how thick they are down here. Some of the ponds about here look very pretty, the water lilies in them have bloomed, they are very much like the bloom of the magnolias, but not so large. I drill three times a day besides dress parade. We have a brass band to play for us which I think is a great addition to the Regiment. I heard a sermon to day from Mr. Landrum, he seems to take a great interest in the Regiment and

---

* John F. Harman of Co. C, 13th S.C.

† Sergeant Wilford I. Harris of Co. C, 13th S.C.

‡ Rev. John G. Landrum was Chaplain of the 13th S.C.

the men generally like him. Mr. Walker is very popular in this company. He is not like he was when he stayed in the book store at the village, he takes a notion some times and is as lively as you please. I like camp life better and better every day. We have rough fare, but the best of appetites. I have not been sick a minute since I've been here. I can sleep just as well in my tent as I can at home in a bed. You have no idea how comfortable a tent is. Our tents are to like the one we had in the mountains; they can be closed up before and behind. I have no news to write. I suppose you have heard before this time that Robert Smith* is on his way to Richmond as he is going by home. I expect you will get to see him. [. . .]

The references to the victory in Tennessee and to General Beauregard concern the Battle of Shiloh on April 6–7, 1862. While Beauregard had inflicted severe losses to Grant on the 6th, Beauregard was unable to dislodge the Union forces from Tennessee. On the following day, Grant's attack forced Beauregard to retreat to Corinth, Mississippi; however, the Union forces were too exhausted to pursue the Confederate forces.

When Georgia seceded from the Union, Gov. Joseph E. Brown of Georgia sent soldiers to take command of Fort Pulaski. This brick-walled fort on Cockspur Island at the mouth of the Savannah River protected the entrance to Savannah. On April 11, 1862, Fort Pulaski fell to the rifled cannons used by Federals on nearby Tybee Island. These new rifled cannons were able to deliver accurate focused fire on the brick walls of Fort Pulaski. After a day of bombardment, the Federals had penetrated the fort's walls and were delivering shot close to the fort's magazines. Threatened with the complete loss of his soldiers due to a magazine explosion, Confederate commander Col. Charles H. Olmstead surrendered to Capt. Quincy Gillmore. Foster's position along the South Carolina coast near Savannah allowed him to hear the reports of this battle.

J. A. FOSTER TO HIS SISTER SALLIE

Camp Gregg Colleton Dist
April 10th 1862

My Dear Sister:

I received your letter of the 3rd last Monday. Nothing of interest has transpired since I last wrote. I find it difficult to find material for a letter. Camp life is very monotonous, and unless we are moving about I find nothing new of which to write. We expect to move our camp before long to a place near Green Pond Station. I will not be sorry for the sand flies and musketers are getting very bad here. I saw a feller the other day that had just come off of picket from the Combahee River. The sand flies and musketers had made a sad havoc of his beauty. You could not have but your finger any where on his face without puting it on a bump from their bites.

---

* Probably Robert Smith of Co. C, 13th S.C.

We expect to go next Sunday to Chishoms island* about 15 miles below here on picket. I intend to be on the <u>qui vive</u>† and see if I cant get a shoot at a yankee. We will not go over on the island but will stay in the neighborhood of it. The Yankees very frequently come up there in small squads on potato stealing expeditions. This week was our time to go up on the Rail Road and we were very anxious to go but Lieut Col. Calhoun sent another company in our place and as an officer's word is the very fiat of fate we had to succomb. We are all rejoicing here on account of our recent victory in Tennessee‡ but are fearful that it will turn out to be another Fort Donalson affair. I do not think there is any chance of a fight on the coast. I think we ought to be moved from this place to N.C. or Tenesee. I have no idea that the Yankees would risk themselves for one night in the swamps. You would be surprised to see how forward every thing is here. The leaves on the trees are almost grown. Corn has been up here for 2 or 3 weeks. You asked in your letter if I was not afraid the snakes would crawl in my tent at night. I am not at all afraid of it though such a thing is not very uncommon in the Regiment. I never think about snakes when I go to bed. There is not much danger of them unless you walk about in the woods after night. When I go out from camp I am always on the look out for them. I have long since lost my infatuated love for snake hunting and do not now turn aside from my path to hunt them, but when I do come across them I still fulfill the same tune, which says "The seed of the woman shall bruise the serpents head" & c. You ask how I get along cooking. I do not cook. We have a boy hired to cook for us at six dollars a month and as there are eleven in our mess it is cheaper than cooking ourselves. I would like much to share my shad with you. We have not had any in a good while. I reckon the time of them is most over. A recruit in Capt Smiths§ company challenged the relief gard last night in the following original manner Come up one of you and give the countersign "Halt Front Right dress."

April 11th I did not get a chance to finish this letter last night. I hear heavy firing this morning south of this place but it is no uncommon thing here. I would not be surprised though if we have to take another march today. I have nothing more to write. My love to all. Write Soon

Your Brother Tony

P.S. Joe Harmon.⁋ The palmetto he sent is for you and Sister Eunice together. TF

---

* Chisholm's Island is a neck of land on the Northeast bank of the Coosaw River at St. Helena Sound.

† <u>Qui vive: on the alert.</u>

‡ Foster is referring to Shiloh, fought on April 6–7, 1862.

§ Either Capt. A. K. Smith or Capt. S. F. Smith of Co. I 13th S.C.

⁋ Likely Joseph S. Harman of Co. C, 13th S.C.

J. A. FOSTER TO HIS MOTHER

Camp Gregg Colleton Dist S.C.
April 13th 1862

My Dear Mother,

I received sister Sallie's letter yesterday evening and was very sorry to hear of the death of Mr Smith. He will be a great loss to our church, and to the neighborhood. I dont know when I have been more surprised to hear of any one's death. We are all rejoicing here over the late news from Beauregard,* and grieving over the fall of Pulaski.† I heard most of the fight. The roar of artillery was terrible. I counted over forty rounds in about ten minutes, and the firing then had somewhat abated. Our company has gone over to the Combahee ferry on picket. They did not go as expected to Chisholm's Island. I did not go with them owing a slight accident which occurred to me the day before they started. I sprained one of my ankles in jumping. My ankle is about well, but I now have a case of mumps on hand, so you see my spraining of my ankle seems almost providential, for if I had have taken the mumps on picket it would have been bad. I have them only on one side. They do not make me sick, and I hardly know I have got them only when I go to eat any thing. My jaw is not swelled very much yet, I felt them first yesterday morning, but did not know then that it was the mumps. I dont think there is any doubt of it now. John Harmon‡ is here with me he has been very unwell for two or three days with diarrhea. Joe§ has also been sick with the same disease but has got better, and gone over to the ferry this evening. Cousin Augustus Edwards¶ has just been here teasing me about my mumps, he sends his best respects to you all. I must close this as it will soon be dark. I will take care of myself as well as I can. My love to all. Write soon.

Your affectionate son
J. A. Foster

COL. OLIVER E. EDWARDS TO BARHAM BOBO FOSTER

Green Pond
April 17 1862

Dear Barram

I was sorry I could not see you when at home on more accounts than one. I wanted to see you especially about Toney. He is here and anxious to stay & I am

---

* Refers to the Battle of Shiloh on April 6.
† Fort Pulaski, guarding the channel to Savannah, fell on April 11.
‡ John F. Harmon of Co. C. 13th S.C. was killed at Second Manassas.
§ Probably Joe Harmon of Co. C 13th S.C.
¶ Augustus Edwards, Commissary, 13th S.C., was Col. Oliver Edwards's brother.

anxious to have all such soldiers, but the thing which embarrasses him is he has not been mustered in. I hope you will consent that he be mustered at once. He will by that means get the bounty and commutation for clothing & his pay as a soldier added. As it is he is getting nothing. If he desires to be transferred to Perrin, if he makes a company, there will be no difficulty unless the law is changed. I will consent and so will his Capt. As the case stands, were he in a battle his name would only appear as a volunteer fighter. These reasons I think are sufficient aside from a sort of pride a boy has in being identified with any thing in which he is interested. Toney is a splendid boy—seems quite at home. He now has a slight touch of mumps—not sick much—was at my quarters a few minutes ago. His company on our piquettes, but he is in camp. I now have on the roll 1030 men & they are coming every day. Will Perrin come home now? I hear they are at Yorktown & will stay for three months longer. Is it so? I had an order from Richmond last night ordering that no more companies, Battallions or Regiments shall be raised without permission from War Department. Can Perrin raise a company? If so & you want Toney I have no doubt you can get him off. I am now in one mile of the R.R. We are doing piquette service for 20 miles along the R.R. & 8 or 10 miles down the river. I have no idea what will become of us. We have no information. I still think we will go away very soon unless we are to be kept for the defence of Charleston or Savannah. This may be as great preparations are going on at both places for their defence. Several large cannons are going to Savannah near our fort* and Ashpoo† has been abandoned & all pieces moved. Our country is in a great war. The trump card must be played this year—neither government can bear it longer. We will suffer for food before the year ends. My love to all the family. Write soon

Yours

O. E. Edwards

McClellan intended to take Richmond by making a shipborne landing at Fort Monroe at the end of the Peninsula formed by the York and James Rivers. He planned to move his army up the Peninsula to West Point on the York River where he would establish a supply base. From there, he would advance towards Richmond, provoke a major fight with the Confederates, decisively defeat them, and take Richmond. He landed an army of 100,000 and an immense supply of war matériel, and began moving up the Peninsula.

McClellan's advance up the Peninsula was opposed by Gen. Joseph Johnston's well-prepared defenses at Yorktown, and along the Warwick River by Gen. Magruder. These positions were manned by about 30,000 Confederate defenders. In early April,

---

* Likely refers to Fort Pulaski.

† Apparently refers to Fort Chapman, an earthen works battery on the Ashepoo River near Green Pond.

McClellan determined that moving up the Peninsula would require a siege of Yor-ktown. Over the next several weeks, he began positioning his siege artillery for the attack on Yorktown; firing had begun. By the end of April, McClellan was ready. On May 4, Johnston evacuated the Yorktown lines, spoiling McClellan's plan for a bril-liant victory.

Magruder's headquarters during the defense of Yorktown were at Lee Hall, a plantation house a couple of miles above the Warwick River, the main Confederate

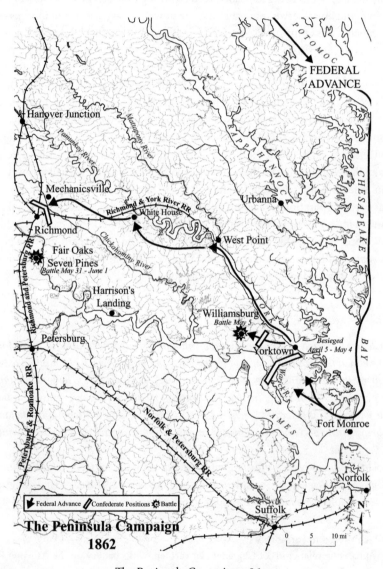

The Peninsula Campaign, 1862.

defensive line. Foster's letters indicate that they were encamped on the Lee plantation property. The letters of April 16 and 18 describe the engagement at Dam No. 1 on the Warwick River. A Union probe on April 6, 1862 alerted both the Federals and the Confederates of weakness in this segment of the Confederate line. Magruder quickly began reinforcing the defenses at Dam No. 1. McClellan determined that strengthening this point could interfere with siege works construction intended to reduce the Yorktown defenses and instructed Brig. Gen. William F. Smith to stop the Confederate strengthening of this position. On April 16 the Federals attacked at Dam No. 1 and managed to get four companies across the river. The Federals failed to reinforce this advance force and the Confederates counterattacked, driving the Federals back across the river. The Federals suffered about 165 casualties; the Confederates about 75.

L. P. Foster to His Father

Camp near York Town
April 10th 1862

My Dear Father,

We are still here. I wrote yesterday telling you that we came here two days since and were expecting a big fight. I doubt whether that letter went and don't think this will. The fight has not yet come off yet last night the yankees seemed to have but whether for good or not we can not tell. I don't think we will have any fight here. I think the Yankees are scared off by our reinforcements and the fight in the west. You know I can not write you any thing with certainty. I am well. Remember me to all and write soon.

yr affec Son
L. P. Foster

The next two letters refer to the engagement at Lee's Mill, also known as Dam No. 1, on the Warwick River.

Lewis Perrin Foster to His Father

Lees Farm 7 miles from York Town
April 16th 1862

My Dear Father.

We arrived on the peninsula on the 6th. Since that time I have written home 3 times, but have no idea that you have or will receive either of them. I hope you will get this as Col Baxter has offered to send it in the genls mail Our time (as you know) was out on the 14th—but in compliance with a request from genl McGruder, we have nearly all agreed to remain with until the 1st May or until the fight is over. I don't think 50 men from our Brigade have gone off. The beat of the enemies drum and roar of his cannon and crack of his musketry are music to which I may march forward but never wish to march backward. The battle has actualy begun—there has been more or less firing every day since I came here—yesterday there was a good deal of cannonading and this evening the roar of the musketry and incesant peals of artillery is terriffic. It is now nearly sun down and it rages with unabated fury. I trust in god for success and have perfect faith in our success. I don't think the enemy have done us any material injury yet. I don't know the enemys loss. I am about two miles from the scene of action. We are under arms awaiting orders and ready for the fray. Many of us may pay the price for our victory—but the sacrifice must be made. I trust we can make it cheerfully.

When we get home S. M. Lanford and I will try to raise our company. Do all you can for us.

My love to all the family.

. Write soon.

Yr affec son L P Foster

P.S. Tell Billy Wofford that his sons are well. Also Harvey Wofford. Tell any of the friends of your company that you see that we are well and in fine spirits.

LPF

P.S. April 17th. All was quiet last night and remains so this morning. The enemy was repulsed at every point yesterday.

LPF

L. P. Foster to His Mother

Lees Farm 6 Miles from York [Town]
April 18th 1862

My Dear Mother,

I got Col Baxter to send a letter out for me yesterday directed to Father. We are here on the Peninsula and have no mail facilities. I have been here now nearly two wks and have not rec'd a letter from home yet. It can not be [any time] until the great battle now pending is decided. I will write every chance and hope you will not be uneasy about me, but bear all cheerfully. I wrote to father concerning our operations here also telling him something of the battle of day before yesterday. Since that time all has been quiet save a little skirmish last night. In which it is said the Enemy were repulsed. In the battle of day before yesterday we lost 20 men killed. The Enemies loss was much greater. Our men held every point. The Enemy charged our breast works 3 times but were repulsed every time. Over two of their comps about 170 men succeeded in crossing Warwick river (a little stream in front of our breast works, and even mounted our breastworks but all were shot down but 13 and they were captured. Their comrades would not follow them across the river or they would have shared the same fate. All is quiet now. Both armies are large and very near each other. We can not tell what a day may bring forth; I think our army here larger than any I have been in yet and feel confident in success. All the S.C.s are here except the 1st Reg't. In my last letter I said some of our men had started home [. . .] returned to the Reg't and [. . .]. You will have seen that Va conscription act has past congress. Also that the 12 ms troops are held 90 days longer. What effect it will have on us I can not say. Our time was out before it passed and we are remaining here merely as independents. If we are enrolled for the war I shall serve cheerfully. I have as many ties of affec[tions] and endearing recollections call me home as any one and am as anxious to see home as any one yet I will willingly forego all for the present to serve my country. Many here condemn the action of the gov as unjust and some profess [to] have not confidence in it. Not with me. I think in many respects the government acted unwisely yet I know not under what circumstances it has acted and must believe it has acted in good faith. Look [on] the bright side of the picture. Dont suffer your mind to despair. Rather see in the justice of our cause a path for gods mercy and in the determined spirit which rules our men their ultimate independence. I think the time has arrived when the war must assume a desperately active shape. When yankeedom will put forth its entire strength to crush us and when the south must strike to her might. God grant we may arise from the storm in triumph. Our comp generally well. I was sorry to hear through a letter from Robt Smith* of Mr. Enoch Smith's death.†

Remember me to all the family. Write soon directing to York Town or Williamsburg. I have as many clothes as I can take care of at present.

Yr affec Son

L. P. Foster

L. P. FOSTER TO HIS FATHER

Lees Farm

April 22nd / 62

My Dear Father

I rec'd three letters from home yesterday evening the first I have rec'd since I left Richmond. I have written home several times lately and given you all the points I could. I have nothing new to write. Things are as quiet as the nature of the case will permit—the two armies being so very near each other. There is more or less picket firing every day and some one killed almost every day. Yet there has no fight since the one mentioned in my two previous letters. Some think there will be no fight here, that McClellan will withdraw but I think that Johnson will attack him if he

---

* Lt. Robert M. Smith of Co. K, 3rd S.C. was the son of Enoch H. and Nancy Smith from the Glenn Springs area of Spartanburg County.

† Landrum, *History of Spartanburg County*, 280–281.

attempts it. Our comp are generally well. We have had some very pleasant weather lately, very warm, trees are beginning to look green.

Johnny and Jimmy Beard are well. The enemy attempted to shell York Town yesterday but their shells fell short. We will have to reorganize our comp in a few days. I hope we will have enough men to be held as a comp. I think we are all in for the war from what I can learn from the conscription act.

Remember me to all and write soon.

Yr affec son
L. P. Foster

P. S. 23rd. Nothing new.

Sallie Foster to Her Cousin, Elizabeth Cothran

Glenn Springs
May 9th, 1862

My stock of patience having become complet[ely] exhausted waiting for my dear Lizzie to answer my letter, and feeling very uneasy about your remaining silent so long, have concluded to write to you, hoping to hear very soon from you. Three long weary months have passed since I have heard one word from you, and I cannot endure it much longer. I fear something unusual has occurred preventing you from writing.

There has been a great deal of sickness in our settlement this year. Pneumonia and Typhoid fever have been the prevailing diseases, and hardly a family in the settlement has escaped and there are still some cases of typhoid fever. Hanna Montgomery, Sallie's sister, is very low with it. Mrs. Lancaster, our nearest neighbor died April last with bilious colic,* leaving an infant only three days old. We all hated very much giving her up for she was such a kind good neighbor. Sister Eunice and Jennie were quite sick last week with fever, sore throat and such, but they are now better, though still complaining. Last week was spent in the deepest anxiety about our friends and the fate of the battle at Richmond,† and I feel truly thankful that our men were again victorious, but it is perfectly awful to think of the suffering of our poor wounded soldiers. There were a great many wounded and several killed in the two companies from the village. Oh! When will this dreadful and unjust war end? It seems to me it has already lasted a century—but it is far preferable to a Yankee despotism, and I never have thought the South could be conquered. Brother Tony came home the 27th of April on sick furlough, and had a severe spell of sickness. When he first came home he could not walk alone, he was so weak. He had mumps, took cold with them and then took camp diarrhea, which reduced

---

* Bilious colic manifested in severe stomach pain and was associated with liver disease.
† The reference is to the Battle of Williamsburg on May 5, 1862.

him a great deal, but he has recovered now and looks stout and well. He has been expecting to start to camp every day, for the last two weeks, but is waiting for Lieut. Cunningham* to start, who is out recruiting for the Blackstocks company. Tony has been transferred from the 13th Regt. to the 3rd. He was very anxious indeed to be with Brother Perrin, and I am delighted that they will be together. I think Tony will certainly get off this week.

Cousin Lou Carlisle† came down yesterday and intends staying with us some time. She is very sad and low spirited. Her little boy, only two months old, died the 31st of May. He is far happier than he ever could be in this world, but the circumstances under which he died are distressing. Mr. Carlisle being from home in the army and had never seen his little boy, although had applied repeatedly for a furlough to come home.

We received a letter from Brother Perrin Saturday, dated June 1st.‡ He was quite well and wrote very cheerfully.

Where are Cousins Wade and Sam?§ We have heard nothing from them in a long time. I suppose Dr. Hearst is at home now. I heard of his being on the way. Father is a great deal better—has improved a great deal since he came home, but he is far from being stout—almost any little exposure makes him sick. He frequently speaks of going to the army again.

Now dear Lizzie, you must write to me very soon. If you could imagine how anxious I am to hear from you, you would certainly answer this immediately.

Give my best love to Auntie.¶ Mother and Father send love to all. Excuse defects and write soon.

Your ever devoted
Cousin Sallie A. F.

The following poem was found among the Foster papers. Based on the author's name, "Law," this may have been written by James Wardlaw Perrin or Lewis Wardlaw Perrin.

DO NOT DESPAIR
BEZER GROVE MAY THE 9TH 1862
LAW

---

* Lt. James Henry Cunningham of Co. K, 3rd SCV.

† Louisa Bobo, the daughter of Simpson Bobo, was married to Captain John Wilson Carlisle who served with Company C of the 13th SCV. Landrum, *History of Spartanburg County*, 524–525.

‡ June 1 is an incorrect date.

§ Samuel Gaines Cothran served in the South Carolina Coastal defenses early in the war.

¶ Elizabeth Lee Perrin Cothran.

Do Not Despair

-1-

My Country! my country! do not despair;
Though millions may threaten to lay thee bare,
Thy sons will be faithful, their hearts are brave,
And, God is on their side, their Country they'll save.

-2-

Thou hast Beauregard, Johnson, noble Lee,
And hosts of freemen contending for thee;
Yes freemen! Not base slaves, who fight for gain,
And freemen they'll be, or lie with the slain.

-3-

Though Northern hosts all thy armies defeat,
Still spurn submission, the cowards retreat;
Though all thy cities be razed to the ground,
Louder let the freeman's paean resound.

-4-

We will not be conquered, we can not be.
They cannot be conquered, who will be free.
Our all's at stake, and bravely we'll defend,
The rights, for which freemen only contend.

-5-

Our number are thousands, our hearts are one,
We'll ne'er cease fighting till the victory's won.
No, Land of the brave! We'll ne'er forsake thee,
Until ourselves are slain or thou art free.

Johnston continued his withdrawal up the Peninsula and established Richmond's defenses behind the Chickahominy River. McClellan, after occupying the abandoned Yorktown defenses, had continued his slow progress up the Peninsula. Finally, Federals and Confederates faced each other at the Chickahominy.

Foster's letter reveal his insight into McClellan's strategy and the Confederate response that would be needed to counter it. McClellan had very methodically and thoroughly prepared his artillery, siege guns, supply lines, and superior forces for his assault on Richmond. Given enough time to prepare those massively superior resources and troop numbers, McClellan would surely prevail and Richmond fall. Foster was correct in his assessment of McClellan's strategy. The safety of the Confederate capital depended on Confederate action before McClellan executed the battle on his terms.

The letter below describes the Battle of Williamsburg on May 5, 1862 and related actions. On May 3, Johnston's forces left Yorktown and marched to Williamsburg. The

3rd S.C. began marching to Williamsburg that night and arrived there on the morning of the 4th. About midday on the 4th, the 3rd S.C. was ordered back in the direction of Yorktown to help Gen. Paul J. Semmes's Brigade cover the retreat against McClellan's pursuing cavalry.* General Stuart's Confederate cavalry protecting the retreat skirmished with Union Gen. George Stoneman's cavalry on the same day.† McClellan's advancing army, intending to attack Johnston's retreating rear guard, found that the Confederates had stopped outside Williamsburg and were waiting for the Federal advance. A sharp day-long battle ensued, resulting in some 2200 Federal and 1700 Confederate casualties.

The letter goes on to describe Union General William B. Franklin's amphibious landing at West Point on May 6th. This landing was met by Confederates under Gen. John Hood's Brigade and Hampton's Legion in an action on May 7th known variously as West Point, Barhamsville, and Eltham's Landing.

L. P. Foster to His Father

Camp 5 Miles from Chickahominy
May 11th 1862

My Dear Father

  I know you are all very uneasy about me for it has been more than a week since I have had any chance to write to you and during that time our army has had several fights with the Enemy. Our Brig has not yet been actively engaged. We left Custis farm and camp near York Town. Last night was one week since.‡ Our Brig and gracy's Bat.§ bring up the rear guard that we marched to Williamsburg 14 miles, about 12 Oclock were ordered to march forward but did get half through the town before we were about faced and ordered to meet the yankys.¶ We were thrown in position to support our batteries and our cavalry of Hamptons Legion ordered to charge their artillery and cavalry. The Enemy gave away at the first charge, our men capturing a good many prisoners and horses also 2 pieces of artillery and 3 caisons, but as the Yankees cut the throats of the horses to one gun they had to leave it spiked on the field. About 20 of our regt fired at one yanky but did not kill him. On the same

---

* Wyckoff, *Third South Carolina*, 40.

† Stephen W. Sears, *To the Gates of Richmond, The Peninsula Campaign* (New York: Ticknor and Fields, 1992), 69.

‡ On the evening of May 3, the 3rd S.C. left Yorktown marching toward Williamsburg.

§ Gracy's Battalion refers to Archibald Gracie's Alabama Battalion attached to Kershaw's Brigade in McLaws's Division in Yorktown.

¶ The 3rd arrived at Williamsburg in the morning of May 4. About midday they were ordered to march back to assist Gen. Semmes Brigade cover the retreat. The letter describes the skirmish with the pursuing Federals.

evening Gen'l Stuart had a fight with them at McClouds Mill near Williamsburg. They cut off one of his Reg'ts and 2 pieces of artillery and surrounded it but he cut his way out bringing the artillery with him and suffering no loss.* A good many shells bursted over our Regt but none were hurt. After night we were ordered on the march. Marched 3 miles and camped. The next morning† marched forward some 6 miles and were ordered back two. That morning the big fight commenced at Williamsburg which lasted all day. We had 29 Reg't engage & the yanks about 50. Our men repulsed them and held the field, removed our wounded to the hospital, but as it was necessary to continue our retreat that night many of our wounded were left there in charge of our surgeons. The yanky loss was much greater than ours. If you will look on the map you will immediately see the necessity of our leaving Williamsburg a river on either side and gun boats in them. 5 S.C. Regts were engaged in the fight at Williamsburg. Jenkins, Giles 4th 6th and Brattons Bat.‡ The 4th and 6th suffered most heavily.

On Tuesday§ the Yankees run their gun boats up to West Point and land troops ahead of us but they were met by the Legion and a Texas Brig and were badly whipped.⁵ Our Brig has not been engaged yet. We are now in 20 miles of Richmond. I am [. . .]

yr affec Son L. P. Foster

my love to all.

In April 1862, many of the one-year volunteer enlistments were coming to an end, causing a significant crisis in obtaining re-enlistments, with many deciding to let their enlistments expire and return home. With McClellan inexorably moving up the Peninsula toward Richmond and a major engagement in the offing, this was a difficult time for enlistments to run out and for the Confederate army to go through a reorganization. Civil War units retained a decidedly local orientation. Officers were not always appointed by a central command, particularly during periods of organization. Units were frequently formed by an individual who was then typically elected as captain of a company or as colonel at the regimental level. Company lieutenants, regimental lieutenant colonels, and other intermediate positions were also elected. The next few letters discuss the election of officers in the Blackstock Company K.

* On May 4, Stuart's cavalry engaged pursuing Federal cavalry under Gen. George Stoneman. Foster identifies the location of this action as McCloud's Mill.

† May 5, The Battle of Williamsburg.

‡ John Bratton commanded the 6th S.C. Infantry regiment beginning March 1862.

§ On Tuesday, May 6, Union General William B. Franklin landed his division at West Point.

⁵ This engagement, on Wednesday, May 7, was variously known as West Point, Barhamsville, or Eltham's Landing. Sears, *To the Gates*, 85–86; Burke Davis, *Jeb Stuart, The Last Cavalier* (New York: Bonanza, 1957), 99–100.

For a Company like the Blackstocks which was quickly organized and enlisted en masse, the end of the enlistment period could challenge the existence of the unit. In the case of the Blackstocks (Company K), Capt. Benjamin Kennedy decided to return home upon the end of his enlistment. Adjutant of the 3rd Regiment, William Drayton Rutherford wrote Col. James Nance concerning the reenlistment problems. In this letter, Rutherford refers to Captain Kennedy as "Aunt Ben" and, based on a conversation with B. B. Foster, predicted that the company would dissolve if Kennedy left.*

Another account of Kennedy's resignation was recorded from a 1917 interview with Thomas Hyatt of Company K. in which Mr. Hyatt said: "at the end of the first 12 months a period of first enlistment, Capt. Benj. Kennedy of Co. 'K' 3rd S.C. Vol. or ('Blackstocks Company') told the men that he did not want to be an officer any longer and requested that he not be re-elected."

"I have seen Capt. Kennedy take a man's gun and walk post on line of pickets for he was too good a man to be an officer. He would let men impose on him for fear that he would be to severe on them."†

Having reached the end of his twelve-month volunteer term,‡ Capt. Benjamin Kennedy resigned his commission§ on May 13, 1862, and briefly returned home to the family farm before reenlisting.¶ On May 13, the regiment elected and promoted Seaborn M. Lanford to captain of Company K. Perrin Foster was elected and promoted to first lieutenant of Company K at the same time.** Other election results are accurately described in Foster's letters.

L. P. FOSTER TO HIS FATHER

Camp 5 miles from Chickahominy
May 12, 1862

My Dear Father,

I wrote you a very hurried letter yesterday but had time to do no better. I am in fine health. We are encamped about mid way between the head of York

---

* Wyckoff, *Third South Carolina*, 39.

† Albert Gibert Kennedy, Sr. unpublished interview with George Thomas Hyatt and J. N. McArthur (May 5, 1917).

‡ As a matter of interest, Captain Kennedy's monthly pay was $130 as recorded in his end-of-service statement of account preserved in the S. C. Archives.

§ South Carolina Archives, "Confederate Archives, Chapter 1, File No. 81, page 473," Columbia, S.C.

¶ Kennedy returned to active duty in November 1862 and fought until the end of the war.

** South Carolina Archives, "Commissioned Officers, Present and Absent Accounted for by Name," of Company K, 3rd Regiment for the Month of May 1862, Columbia, South Carolina.

and Chickahominy Rivers awaiting the approach of the Enemy. It is said that they are landing in five miles of us in heavy forces, but I fear they will not attack us. They have already been whipped 4 times on this retreat and are getting cautious. Besides the late victories of genl's Boureguard* and Jackson† will influence the[ir] movements. It is said here that Jackson has been reinforced to 60,000 men and is driving the enemy before him with orders to cross the river and carry the war into Maryland. I hope it is true. I hope the dawn of a brighter day is at hand. The policy of fighting gun boats has been given up and our army withdrawn from the coasts to the interior where we will easily whip them. They can take every place which can be approached by gun boats, Charleston will fall whenever they try it. I am sorry our people are trying to defend it. Rather send the soldiers some where else. If they could pass forts Jackson and Philip‡ they can pass any forts which we have. Our policy is to whip them with small armies. We are not even throwing up a breast work—expect to whip them in the open field. Every soldier is confident of success. You would think that so much retreating would discourage them but not so. They are more exasperated than ever and wish for the Enemy to come on in all his strength. And when he comes we will whip him easily. Each army has a river at its back and retreat will be difficult. The line we left on Warwick River§ was the most thoroughly fortified I ever saw yet the most dangerous for a large army owning to the narrowness of the peninsula here and the facility which the rivers on either side furnished the Enemy for running troops to our rear and cutting us off. Gen'l Johnson opposed taking the army there from the start and thinks after he saw it never thought of defending it at all if he could get away. If you will just examine your map you think it at most a miracle that we escaped so large an army in such a place. Gen'l Johnson is the man. The retreat was difficult in every respect. The march was hard. Three times the whole army was ordered back to support the rear guard. Our brigade was rear guard most all the time. During one whole day we marched in line of battle with a line of skirmishers deployed in our rear more than a mile long From the time we left Custis farm on Saturday night until we reach this place last Friday we drew 2 days rations. I did not suffer from hunger but felt it more than ever before. We had meat most of the time but no [bread] for most of the time. It could not be avoided—corn was issued to some of the troops, yet our men were all willing to fight Yankees and endure all cheerfully. I have often heard

* Refers to Shiloh.

† Jackson's Shenandoah Valley Campaign.

‡ In April, David Farragut made his famous run past Fort Jackson and Fort Phillip on the Mississippi to take New Orleans.

§ The small Warwick River ran in front of the defensive work the Confederates built at Yorktown to face McClellan's advance.

them say they would live on half rations if they could get to fight Yankees. We are better now and will receive full rations as soon as this post ever be supplied from Richmond which is only 10 miles. We have no tents yet and don't want any our reg't is healthier without them by for I think the war is hastening to a close. You have seen accounts of our fights in the papers. They do not give our loss or the Enemies at Williamsburg near large enough. I think we there lost at least 1000 men in killed & wounded and the enemy twice that number. Col Mott* of the 12 Miss Reg't was killed Gen'l Early severely wounded.† I can give details all the 6 Regts engaged did well. I rec'd yr letter of April 28 and Mothers of the 4 May this morning. I was sorry to hear of Toney's illness also of Mrs. Lancasters death. Tell Toney that our comp will reorganize tomorrow. I am a candidate for Lt., Wofford‡ and Lanford for Capt' It was the desire of comp that Sebe should run against Wofford. So I yielded. I have no opposition as yet for my office but think Dr. Young§ will run. My friends & I think I will be elected. Yr friends well. William Lancaster is with us again came last night. Capt Nance is running against Col. Williams for Col and I hope and believe will be elected. The other candidates have not declared them selves. The election will come off day after tomorrow.

Remember me to all and write soon.

yr affec Son
L. P. Foster

L. P. Foster to His Sister, Sallie

Chickahominy River
5 miles from Richmond
May 18th 1862

My Dear Sister,

I wrote to Nunie yesterday. I rec'd a letter from you bearing date 24th Apl. on yesterday. The first I have received for some time. We came here yesterday on picket. Our men are bathing this morning in the river. It is a clear and very pretty stream with hundreds of acres of fine bottom land on either side. This is a level pretty country. The peninsula is by far the finest farming country I ever saw. The land is very rich and very level. Soil sandy but stiff with lime and all under laid

---

* Col. Christopher H. Mott of the 19th Mississippi Volunteers was killed at Williamsburg.

† Brig. Gen. Jubal Early.

‡ Probably John Young Wofford of Co. K, 3rd S.C. but other Wofford men of Co. K are possibilities.

§ William H. Young was elected lieutenant of Co. K, 3rd S.C. on May 13, 1862.

with marl.* We see every where fine wheat, oat, clover and corn fields. Here the principle woods growth is pine. On the peninsula there was a great deal of hommock† land covered as thick as could be with gum and cypress. The wild onions grow all over the fields here and on the peninsula. I have seen them as thick as the wheat. They do very well to eat and are recommended by our surgeons. I found them very palatable on the retreat. I have no news to write. The Enemy seems to be remaining behind, it is said they are landing troops on the other side of James River and that we will be sent over the rivers between Richmond and Petersburg to meet them. There are 2000 or 3000 hands at work on our batteries on and obstructions in James River. If they succeed in making them strong enough to prevent the gun boats from passing up the River we can defend Richmond and Petersburg both. I have no idea that the city will be surrendered. If the Yankees take it I think they will have to burn it from their gun boats. Our men are well and in fine spirits, well pleased with their Col.‡ He does all he can for our comfort and requires every man to do his duty. I will give you a list of the Cols of our Brigade—2nd Reg't Col. Jno Kennedy (an old classmate of mine),§ Lieut Col. Goodwyn⁋ of Columbia. Maj Gilliard** 7th Reg't Col. Aiken,†† Lt. Col. Bland‡‡ Maj. White§§ 8th Reg't Col. Hennigan⁋⁋—don't know the others.

We have beautiful weather. I am well.

My love to all.

yr affec Brother

L. P. Foster

---

* Marl is a soil material made from shell. It is a clay-like material used as fertilizer. Apparently naturally occurring in the Peninsula.

† A hommock, normally called a hammock or hummock, is a small, usually conical, eminence, typically rising out of a wetland.

‡ James Drayton Nance was elected colonel of the regiment in the May 13 elections. Benjamin Conway Garlington was elected lieutenant colonel. Seaborn M. Lanford was elected captain of Co. K; James Henry Cunningham was promoted to lieutenant of Co. K the same day.

§ Col. John Doby Kennedy, 2nd S.C. He attended from South Carolina College with the class of 1857, a year ahead of Perrin Foster. Moore, *Roll of Students*, 27.

⁋ Lt. Col. A. D. Goodwin, 2nd S.C.

** Lt. Col. Frank Gailliard, 2nd S.C.

†† Col. D. W. Aiken, 7th S.C.

‡‡ Lt. Col. Elbert Bland, 7th S.C.

§§ Major W. C. White, 7th S.C.

⁋⁋ Col. Jno. W. Henagan, 8th S.C.

L. P. Foster to His Mother

Camp of 3rd S.C. Reg'mt
1½ miles from Richmond
May 20th 1862

My Dear Mother,

I have but little of interest to write you we are camped here in the woods and know but little of the plans of either army. I get the papers every morning, but the Editors like every one else are ignorant of gen'l Johnsons plans. Nothing indicates a battle soon. Every thing indicates that a desperate one, perhaps a regular siege is to be entered here in the course of 6 wks or 2 mos. I think the Enemy will advance very slowly and fortify as they come. We drill 5 hrs per day from 6 to 7 and from 9 to 11 A.M. and from 3 to 5 p.m. We have a Col. who will make his reg't one of the first in the service and be very popular. Recruiting officers are to be sent home in a short time to raise our comps to 125. As J. H. Cunningham is a married man he will be sent from our camp. I would [like] to have the place but as I have no wife I have no chance. You see wives control almost every thing. I went to Richmond yesterday. Things are very high. I bought two [colored] Shirts for which I had to pay $4.00 each. I have plenty of shirts in my trunk, but it is at Lynchburg and I can not get there. I had a change (which is all that we can carry) with me but the Zouaves [. . .] took them from me—when they intend I gave them possession hence had to buy more. We are faring very well now. We can buy some vegetables, onions, cabbage and Irish potatoes of the last yr crop. Gen'l McGruder* issued an order yesterday ordering that details should be made from camps to go into the gardens and get vegetables also in the fields to gather Lambs quarter,† Poke salad and wild onions to prevent scurvy. I don't [think] we have any of it in our Reg't yet we have been without antiscorbutic‡ so long that there is danger of it. We have very warm weather. I am glad we are off the peninsula as think this weather would have produced chills and fever. Tell Father that Y. J. Pope§ has been appointed Adjt of our Reg't and Tom Moorman Elected OS of the Quitman Rifles.

The non commissioned officers of our comp are

Jno. P. Robuck O.S.
Wm Beardon 2nd Srgt¶

---

* Maj. Gen. John G. Magruder.
† Lamb's Quarter is another name for Birthroot in the Trillium plant family.
‡ An antiscorbutic is a food or agent to prevent scurvy.
§ Adjutant Young John Pope of the 3rd S.C.
¶ William S. Bearden, Co. K, 3rd S.C.

Jno Beard 3rd Seargt

D. S. Bray 4th Seargt.

G. W. James 5th Seargt

Wm. B. Wofford 1 Corpl

C. P. Varner 2nd Corpl*

W. A. Smith 3rd Corpl[†] and

J. A. Thomas 4th Corpl.[‡]

Nunies letter of the 15th inst is at hand, before this time you have rec'd several letters from me and know why I did not write as I have written very often lately. Tell Tony that I say if he does not see any of Kershaws Brig in Richmond [when] he gets there to leave a letter in the P.O. for me and I will come for him. We are very near the Fairfield Race Course.[§]

If he has not left when this [reaches] you tell him get me a small valise in Columbia or some where else and bring [it]. If you can get any oil cloth please make me a Haversack and send me. Sew the bottom in so that it will hold four or five days rations let the strap broad. Father knows how it should be build. But the casing buttoned in so that it can be washed. Tell Father that Tony is O.S. of Capt McGowans Comp.[¶] Is T. J. West well. If so he has to return to his reg't as Col. [. . .] will soon take steps to get all the members of his reg't here. He has been reported as absent without leave. The fact that his time of service had expired does not excuse him.

My love to all yr affec Son
L. P. Foster

Tell Nunie that I say if I was a molasses generator I could get rich.

May 22nd I am well. Nothing New.

L. P. Foster to His Sister, Probably Sallie

Fairfield Race Course
2½ miles from Richmond
May 23rd 1862

My Dear Sister,

I wrote to mother day before yesterday giving her all the news and now have but little to write. We are still at our first camp in this vicinity drilling, equipping

---

* Capel Perry Varner, Co. K, 3rd S.C.

† William A. Smith, Co. K, 3rd S.C.

‡ John Alexander Thomas, Co. K, 3rd S.C.

§ The Confederates had a headquarters located at the Fairfield Race Course northeast of Richmond, just outside the city along the Mechanicsville Turnpike. Douglas Southall Freeman, *R. E. Lee, A Biography, Vol. II* (New York: Scribner's, 1934), 58.

¶ Homer Leonidas McGowan, Co. F, 3rd S.C.

ourselves with knapsacks, canteens, haversacks &c. I wish our company was full as we are now have a fine chance to drill recruits. I am looking for Tony every day. Will he have to go to the 13th Reg't before he joins ours. If he has ever been mustered into the service he will have to get a transfer.

Eight of his Reg't were taken prisoner a short time since our picket. They were green. They were taken by cavalry. Bennett and Tollinson* have moved to Petersburg, and I wish they were over the Potomac. This said they have made a fortune. They sold at most exhorbitant prices. Check cotton shirts with cost more than 2½ yards to the shirt $3.00, other things in proportion. They merit the contempt of their country. I don't know when our recruiting officers will get off. If you have not time to make any haversacks before Tony leaves make and send it by Lt. Cunningham. Has Henry Barnett got home? I suppose he has and is quite a hero. Our men generaly well.

Remember me kindly to all.

yr affec Brother
L. P. Foster

The following note is a continuation of the above letter.

My Dear Father

I would like for you to look around and see if you can find a boy to hire who has some idea of cooking. Our mess need and wish to hire one.

yr affec Son
L. P. Foster

L. P. Foster to His Mother

Camp 3rd Regt Chickahominy River
May 29th 1862

My Dear Mother

We came out here on picket day before yesterday about 6 miles from Richmond. When we came here there was plenty of them in sight and yesterday our boys were climbing trees nearly all day looking at their camps. They were about 1 or 1 1/2 miles from us. Yesterday evening they sent up two balloons to make observations on our line. Capt Kemper† fired a few shots from a rifle piece at one and made him come down in a hurry. the other was too far off. Their balloons are perfectly beautiful, but I would not give one good man with a musket and 40 rounds for all of them.

---

* Bennett and Tollinson were apparently merchants.

† Kemper's Battery of light artillery, from Alexandria, Virginia, founded by Captain Dell Kemper and attached to Kershaw's Brigade. Dickert, *History of Kershaw's Brigade*, 54.

This morning no yankees are in sight. I think they moved up on our left wing where they had a severe fight yesterday.* I have not heard from it, but the roar of musketry for four or five hours yesterday was almost continuous. There was but little artillery. We thought that our men were successfull from the fact that the sound of the musketry gone away on the enemys side and got farther from us. Everything here indicates a great fight before very long. McClellan seems to be trying to cut off our retreat seems to think that we have no idea of fighting him here. He seems to be sending troops around the city and if I mistake not, he will before long find his line badly cut to pieces. I have not a doubt of whipping. In Fathers last letter he seemed to think Richmond would fall because we had been retreating so much. If he had been with us or could now be with us and see how confidant our troops are of success and how much confidence they have in Genl Johnson he would not think so. Our retreats have all been necessary and will result in good to the cause. They have exhibited more generalship than any battle which has yet been fought and the troops have more confidence in Johnson now than ever before. I think we will have to attack the enemy here for McClellan will not attack us until he has fortified every place strongly and largely reinforces his present army. Fathers letter said that Toney would be in Richmond tonight or tomorrow night. I will try to get off this evening and meet him. Capt Lanford saw a letter from W. S. Bearden yesterday evening saying that he had been discharged also that Benj M Smith (Mr William Smiths son) died at Chimborazo hospital on the 9th last We did not know where he was when we left Orange C.H. he was left at Gordonsville as a baggage guard. Albert Smith with him. When the guard was released Albert came to the Regt. some 10 days after we arrived at Yorktown and told us that Benjamin had been sent to the hospital sick. I sympathize deeply with Mr Smith and family. I am well. Our camp generaly well. Scott Mayes[†] was sent to the hospital the other day. Wm. J. Mayes[‡] Wm. H. Lancaster[§] are at the hospital. We like our Col[¶] better every day. he is one of the prettiest drill officers I ever saw. Every moves on quietly and even those who took the most decided stand against him are silent He sends the kindest regards to father my love to all

yr affec son

L P Foster

* There was no major action on the Confederate line on May 28th. That does not mean there was not a burst of firing as Foster reports.

† Samuel Scott Mayes of Co. K, 3rd S.C.

‡ William J. Mayes of Co. K, 3rd S.C.

§ William Henry Lancaster of Co. K, 3rd S.C.

¶ James Drayton Nance was elected as Colonel of the 3rd S.C. on May 13, 1862.

L. P. Foster to His Sister, Probably Sallie

Camp of the 3rd S.C. Reg't
6 miles from Richmond
May 30th 1862

My Dear Sister,

Yours of the 22nd came yesterday. I was glad to hear that Capt Kennedy was to see you. I fear that he unnecessarily alarmed you about our clothes. When he left we were dirty and ragged but since we have bought under clothes and Col Nance has made arrangements to get a uniform for us from the Q. M. department. I have clothes in my trunk at Lynchburg but I am not likely to see it soon. I have a Confederate uniform making in the city and have bought some shirts and drawers. I will need no more except the shirts and drawers which I wrote to mother so send me by Tony. I was glad to hear that Tony was coming on to our comp. I rec'd a letter from Father a few days since saying he would be in Richmond on his way to the 13th Reg't last Wednesday or Thursday evening. I went to Richmond to meet him Wednesday night. I expect the 13th Reg't now quartered near Richmond as I hear that the army of the Rhappahannock was fallen back to this point. I was sorry to hear of the illness of Mrs Montgomery's family. Remember me to them. You have seen an account of the skirmish near Hanover* in [which] our men whipped the yanks badly capturing about 70 prisoners and according to the account of the prisoners killing and wounding nearly all of the Reg't. You have also seen an account of a fight near Ashland† on the same day in which the Editor of the dispatch says we were whipped but his account shows that he knew nothing about it. We had but one Regt engaged and it was merely a skirmish and I think accounts to nothing. There are skirmishes almost every day and our men invariably repulse the yanks and take some prisoners. We have been here on picket near the Chickahominy river for four days. The yanks have made no demonstration at this point until this morning about 10 oclock. They marched two or three Regt down to the river as if they intended to try to cross. Col Nance ordered us to get under arms and formed in line of battle to await them but Capt Kemper fired 20 or 30 shots at them and they run. I think they merely wished to find out whether we had any artillery here or not.

You have seen accounts of Jackson's victory.‡ They are fully confirmed. It is now reported and accredited that he has crossed the Potomac and is now in Maryland

---

* There was fighting at Hanover Court House on May 27th as Brig. Gen. Fitz John Porter protected McClellan's flank against a Confederate force under Brig. Gen. Lawrence Branch.

† On May 28th, there was an engagement at Ashland, Virginia, resulting in the destruction of Confederate supplies.

‡ This letter references Jackson's victory at the Battle of Winchester on May 25th in which Jackson attacked Nathaniel Banks's retreating forces.

near Frederick Town with 42,000 men.* The cry for an onward movement is now greater than ever. I am willing to await genl Johnsons time, yet believe we can whip them now. Jackson has rendered his name immortal. If he has crossed in to Maryland we will have no fight here.

I am well. Write soon.

My love to all

Yr affec Brother

L. P. Foster

On May 30, 1862, a violent thunderstorm caused the Chickahominy to flood. McClellan faced Richmond with three of his five corps on the north side of the river and with Gen. Samuel P. Heintzelman's and Gen. Erasmus D. Keyes's corps south of the river. McClellan was in a vulnerable position with two corps isolated by the swollen river, and the flooding threatened to take some or all of the Union bridges out of service. On the morning of the 31st, Gen. Joseph Johnston struck Heintzelman and Keyes on the south bank of the Chickahominy. Due to poor execution of the battle plan, the Confederates were unable to focus their superior numbers in a decisive blow. McClellan was able to get Gen. Edwin Vose Sumner's Corps across the river to bolster the two isolated corps, and the Battle of Seven Pines or Fair Oaks was fought to a draw. The Confederates suffered 6000 casualties to the Union's 5000. The action served to delay McClellan's advance on Richmond by three weeks. General Johnston was severely wounded in the battle and was replaced by Gen. Robert E. Lee. While the 3rd S.C. did not participate in this action, Foster's letter attests to the desperate fighting and to his loss of friends in the 5th S.C.

L. P. FOSTER TO HIS FATHER

———————

Camp 3rd S. C. Regt
6 miles from Richmond
June 3rd 1862

My Dear Father

The excitement of the last battle is over. Calm deliberation has taken its place. One can look upon the picture unmoved but our men gained a decided victory. Whipped them from the field but at fearful loss. I think not greater than the enemys. They fought the enemy at great odds and in a fearfully superior position The enemy were in redoubts behind breastworks and fallen timbers yet our men drove them before them steadily 4 miles and held the field. You have seen from the papers how

---

* Jackson reached and skirmished near Harpers Ferry from May 27 to May 30, but did not cross the Potomac into Maryland. He commanded closer to 17,000 men, not the 42,000 reported by Foster.

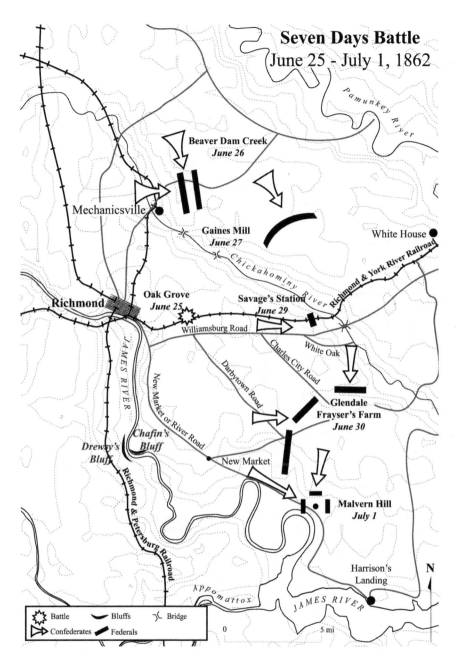

The Seven Days' Battle, June 25–July 1, 1862.

severe our loss is, & how stoutly the S. C. Regts fought. I think no men ever fought more desperately. The S. C. troops suffered severely. The Spartan Rifles lost 3 killed and 24 wounded. Alfred Fosters* comp 22 killed and wounded. Jno Evins[†] was shot in the arm since been amputated. Jim Moore[‡] and Houghston[§] were killed. John White[¶] shot in the hand. Hank Landrum wounded. Elias Gentry wounded. Warren Drummond** shot through the calf of the leg. Sam Miller[††] wounded. Major Bill Foster[‡‡] wounded. Maj. Mattison[§§] of the 4th S. C. Regt wounded. Capt Carpenter[¶¶] killed. Capt Camp*** wounded. genl Hampton[†††] wounded in the foot. Col. Giles[‡‡‡] killed. The brig under command of Col Jenkins shot 30 rounds. You can judge of the fight. Our wounded are being as well cared for as possible. The ladies of Richmond married and single nurse them in person. The yanks threw shell at our pickets and Kershaw has answered a few times to day. aside from this things are quiet. I am well.

Remember me to all

Your affec Son L P Foster

PS. has Toney left home I have not seen him. He [may] be at Richmond waiting to learn my whereabouts LPF

June 4th Nothing new.

heavy rain last night and still raining

L. P. FOSTER TO HIS MOTHER

Camp 6 miles from Richmond June 7th 1862

My Dear Mother

Our company came off post this morning nothing of great intrest is passing. all here seems dull. The yanky shells whistle over us occaisionally and arouse us. It is strange that this place, about which the whole world seems excited & to which our whole people are looking with almost frantic anxiety and interest should seem so

---

* Captain Alfred Harrison Foster of the Morgan Light Infantry (Company F) of Micah Jenkins's 5th S.C. Regiment.

† Jno Evins was Captain John Hamilton Evins of Co. K, 5th S.C.

‡ James A. Moore of Co. K, 5th S.C.

§ George N. Hughston of Co. K of the 5th S.C.

¶ Likely John Warren White—Co. K, 5th S.C.

** Warren S. Drummond of the 5th S.C.

†† Possibly Samuel W. Miller of Co. K of the 5th S.C.

‡‡ Maj. William Moultrie Foster, Co. C, 5th S.C.

§§ Maj. C. S. Mattison of the 4th S.C. Infantry.

¶¶ Capt. Jacob Quickle Carpenter of Co. G of the 5th S.C.

*** Capt. W. D. Camp of Co. I of the 5th S.C.

††† Gen. Wade Hampton, commander of Hampton's Brigade.

‡‡‡ Col. John R. R. Giles of the 5th S.C.

dull. yet such is the case. It arises not from any lack of interest in the cause for all are ready and watching for the important hour but from the force of habbit we are thrown in close contact with the enemy so much & hear so much of their shelling that the scene now fails to exite us. Yesterday morning a brisk duel commmenced between our batteries and the enemys which last for some two hours but with little injury to either side. We had four men and some horses killed. It is said the enemy also lost several men but I could not tell as we were not allowed to show ourselves. They threw one shell at the point of woods in which our company was stationed. it struck the ground some 50 or 100 yds in front of us but did not explode. The enemy are busy along the line building roads bridges redoubts what policy our genls intend to pursue is a mystery to me. Sometimes I think it certain that we will fight here then perhaps in less than a day something will happen which will make me think that genl Johnson* will in a short time will have us on the "git up and git" again. I am ready for anything I have implicit confidence in his judgement and am willing to obey. Be ready for anything & if Richmond should fall, don't be at all discouraged. The same god rules everywhere and I still firmly believe that our course is just and will finaly be successfull. I also believe that we can end the war sooner by giving up Richmond than if we fight here for owing to the situation of the Chickahominy River and the swamp to the York and James Rivers where their gun boats and batteries stand in readiness. It will be almost impossible to route their army we may fight and repulse them every day but they have only to retire behind their batteries and cross the river and the battle must stop until they chose to come again. besides it is almost impossible to fortify Richmond to our advantage since the hills on the north and east side are higher than those on S. & W. These are merely my own notions. others think otherwise and seem to think it certain that we will have a battle here. Capt Kemper has just raised a little muss with the yanks they exchanged several shots I don't know with what effect. one of our recruiting officers has returned. Says he saw Father in Columbia last monday that he was well. Where is Toney—I suppose he has determined to work for Lt. Cunningham. Marshalls Regt† is about 3 miles above us on the river I [am] very anxious to go to it to see uncle James‡ and the Abbeville boys, but it is allmost impossible to get leave of absence and justly. Our company generaly well. Wm Lancaster is with us again. It has been several days since I have heard from Louie. You have heard that genl Bourguard has evacuated Corrinth. I am glad of it since I think it time for us to quit lying behind breast works. Some think he will turn up here others say 20,000

---

* Gen. Joseph E. Johnston.

† Col. Jehu Foster Marshall of Orr's 1st S.C. Rifles. Marshall was elected colonel following Orr's resignation and election to the Confederate Congress.

‡ Col. James Monroe Perrin was in the 1st S. C. Rifles in Gregg's Brigade.

of his troops have already passed through Lynchburg on their way to join Jackson. If so, I think Maryland will be ours or this army leave.*

My love to all

yr affec Son

L P Foster

L. P. Foster to His Sister, Probably Sallie

Camp 3rd S.C. Reg't 6 miles from Richmond
June 8th 1862

My Dear Sister,

Another Sabbath has come. You are by this time starting to Philadelphia[†] to church to hear Mr. Barnett or some other minister expound the word of life. O that I could be there too. What joy would it afford me to meet my friends at our beloved church, to meet the Sunday school in which I still feel great interest but a duty as stern and imposing as Lycurgan Laws[‡] holds me here a duty owed to every thing I hold dear on this earth. Aye! A duty to my God, but however dark and furious the present storm may become, still the Christians light of hope shall ride in brilliant glory above the tempest with power to rule and controll it and <u>will</u> <u>rule</u> it to their <u>eternal</u> <u>good</u>. Let the faint-hearted despond. I know not the feeling as yet.

How is the Sunday school getting on. Who is superintendent, who are teachers, are any of my class there and in charge of whom? I have but little news to write you. Things here move much in the same channel as when I last wrote. Nothing but occasionally picket firing disturbs the quiet. I have entirely lost sight of the plans of our genl's. How long these two armies are to sit here and watch each other I am unable to say. Some think they are waiting for Bouregard to join Jackson who we hear has had another fight and whipped Shields capturing 700 prisoners,[§] but I can not vouch for the truth of the report. Some of the men saw it on the Bulletin board at Richmond. I saw Tom Quarles yesterday evening. Wade C. was elected Capt of

---

* On May 29th, Beauregard's army evacuated Corinth, Mississippi, toward Tupelo, escaping Halleck's much larger force. No transfer of forces as described by Foster from Beauregard to the Virginia theater occurred. Foster's incorrect information that Jackson was north of the Potomac in great force led to his hopes that McClellan would be forced to withdraw to protect Washington.

† Foster is referring to Philadelphia Baptist Church in Glenn Springs, South Carolina.

‡ Lycurgan Laws were strict laws promulgated by Lycurgus in ancient Sparta.

§ The reference is to the Battle of Cross Keys, Virginia. Richard Stoddart Ewell, under Jackson's command in the Valley Campaign, repulsed an attack by John C. Fremont on June 8. James Shields was leading a column of Federals advancing toward Jackson from the north, but did not participate in the action. On June 9 Jackson defeated Shields at Port Republic.

their comp without opposition notwithstanding considerable efforts by Capt Bradley and Dr. Hearst to the contrary. Wade is at home sick. Tom has been sick but looks better now. He complains of yr not writing to him. I have not seen any of our friends in Marshalls Reg't but know they are well. Tom Chiles* went to see them a few days since. You said in yr last letter that Father was trying to by a colts rifle for Tony. I fear he will not be allowed to use it since it has no bayonet and is not of the same caliber as our muskets, hence he can not draw ammunition for it. Tell him to be sure to bring an oil cloth. I rec'd a note from Father written in Columbia in which he said he expected to come to see us when his harvest was over. I would like very much to see him. Yet if he is not stout would advise him not to come as we have to take things as they are. Nothing more of interest to write. My love to all. Tell Jones I have not seen a Va. Girl that I liked well enough to marry and if I had she would have to come to here and bring the preacher with her since I cant get away. Yet I will come as soon as we whip out these Yankees.

yr affec Brother

L. P. Foster

L. P. FOSTER TO HIS MOTHER

Camp 3rd Reg't S.C. Volunteers
Near Richmond
June 9th 1862

My Dear Mother,

I have nothing of interest to write you. Every thing here is as quiet as the nature of the call will permit. How long this state of suspense is to last I can not tell. John Gentry† went to see his Brother Elias yesterday. He is seriously wounded in the left shoulder but his physician thought he would be well enough to go home in two weeks. He was shot by a Minnie ball after he had shot 43 rounds. When shot he went to the rear and seeing a company of men thought them our men, but they were yanks and all fired at him a very short distance, but no one hit him. I write this letter to get the ladies of our settlement to make some under clothes, shirts, drawers, socks for our comp. We have deferred writing for some time owing to the uncertainty of getting things here but Col. Nance thinks it better to have them made at home than pay the present prices here. As soon as I can I will send a list of articles needed. Our company goes on picket post in the morning. I fear Old

---

* Likely either Thomas W. Chiles or Thomas Milton Chiles of Co. C (from Abbeville, South Carolina) in the 7th S.C. Both are listed as "Childs" in the 7th S.C. rosters. However, Chiles was a common name in the Perrin family and is likely the correct name.

† John L. Gentry of Co. K, 3rd S.C.

Pickens will not allow Tony to come on with Cunningham since he has stopped one already who was coming on with Capt. Langston.*

My love to all—write often.

yr affec Son

L. P. Foster

How is the wheat crop—we hear a bad account of it.

L. P. Foster to His Mother

Camp 3rd S.C. Reg't 4 miles from Richmond
June 13th 1862

My Dear Mother,

The morning after I wrote to Father we left our camp and march back here some 2 miles in rear to rest by drilling 5 hrs per diem but don't understand me to mean that I dislike to drill. I have long since learned that as soon as any corps ceases to drill it begins to loose energy—sluggishness marks their course and want of efficiency is seen in every thing they do. Our reg't has suffered enough already from a want of drill, but Col Nance is beginning anew. Commencing in the school of the soldier and I hope soon to see our reg't well drilled. We will now be released from picket duty for a while and I think it time for we have been out on the post only 18 days. I saw the infantry of H. Legion† this morning. Their ranks are very much thinned. The 7 comps did not look as large as two good companies. They were very badly cut up in the late fight. Hampton has been appointed to Brigadier gen'l but is not able to assume his command. I have not seen Uncle James or any of our S.C. relations yet, though they are camped very near us. I will get my new uniform of confederate grey this evening and will go up to see him in a few days if he we remain here for two or three days. Every thing has been very quiet on the line. It is reported that McClellan has withdrawn some of his forces which think quite probably since he will be compelled to stop Jackson which has been largely reinforced recently and will doubtless whip the Enemy out of the valley. Now we don't realy believe that there will be any fight here at all. McClellan has already shown that he intends going to Richmond not by the bayonet but by the spade and before he [can] get ¼ of a mile at his slow rate our generals [can] reinforce Jackson so strong as to make him either give up Maryland or leave here and go to defend it. We have very warm weather. We have just got off from drill.

---

* Capt. David Mason Henry "Mase" Langston of Co. I, 3rd S.C.

† Hampton Legion suffered high casualties at the Battle of Seven Pines on May 31, and Gen. Wade Hampton was wounded in the fight.

Remember me to all. Write soon.

Yr affec son,

L. P. Foster

P.S. June 14th changed camp again moved yesterday evening ½ mile.

L. P. Foster to His Sister, Probably Sallie

3rd S.C. Reg't Near Richmond
June 15th 1862

My Dear Sister,

Yours of the 9th inst came yesterday evening. I never rec'd a telegram from Father. Capt. Carpenters* is indeed a melancholy case. Johnny Foster[†] an old scholar of mine son of William Foster Esq. was severely wounded and has never been heard from. The members of his comp (Morgan Light Infantry) hunted for him but could not find him. I suppose he is in the hands of the enemy. He was his Fathers only Son. I was glad to hear from Tony as I have been looking for him for sometime. I heard day before yesterday that he was at Richmond under arrest but did not believe it. I am sorry that Cunningham could get no recruits. I think there are men there who are showing very dastardly. I wish I could have been at Philadelphia at yr last preaching day. [I] have written to Mrs. Clopton, but hope that Mother answered her letter. Did she? Mrs. Clopton has been a very kind friend to me. No one could have taken more interest in my welfare.

Yr Bill of Fair was quite in accordance with my taste, yet as I had some important business to attend could not attend yr dining I went to the 13th Reg't yesterday was there some time, saw our relations and many friends. Cousins Oliver, Bookter—Augustus, Jno Carlisle and Ed Leitner[‡] all look very well and seem to be enjoying the camp finely. Some Lt. Carlisles mess say that he can eat 1½ lbs salt bacon at any time. He looks very hearty. So tell Cousin Lou[§] not to be uneasy about. Jno Harmon & Berry have both gone to the hospital with measles. Joe looks a little puny A great many of their reg't have camp diarrhea owing (I suppose) to change of water. They have a very large reg't but their men do not look near as rough and stout as our men and notwithstanding they have [200] or 300 men more than we have. Yet I don't think they can turn more men for heavy duty than we can. They think they have seen rough times but I have traveled the path they are now traveling

---

* Captain Jacob Quickle Carpenter of Co. G of the 5th S.C. who was killed at Seven Pines.

† Likely John A. Foster in the Morgan Light Infantry, Co. F, 5th S.C. He was hospitalized in Charlottesville in July 1861. Tedards, *History of the Fifth South Carolina*, 181.

‡ Ed Leitner served in Co. C of the 13th S.C.

§ Cousin Lou—Louisa Bobo Carlisle.

and know what is in store for them. They show they have never been very near the Enemy before and remind me of our reg't when at Fairfax. Was amused at Col. Edwards speaking of the close proximity of the pickets he said they were in rifle range 1000 yds of each other. I told him that we had not picket any further from the Enemy in a long time and often closer. Bookter send his love to you all. He seems quite lively. Gus looks as lazy as ever. Dr. Kilgore and Kennedy* looks finely. Mr. Landrum also looks well. I heard him preaching some time before I reached the camp and knew his voice. I said he had preached every Sunday since he joined the Reg't except one. Marshalls Reg't will move down near us to day. It has been attached to Gregg's Brig. Which now consists of 5 S.C. reg't 1st Orrs 12th 13th 14th. A very fine Brigade. There are enough S.C.s here now to make a fine division & I wish they would put us all together. I understand that Gov. Brown† and Jeff Davis have raised a row about the conscription Act. They would do well to send along the mc‡ and let nice points be considered after the fighting has been done.

Remember me to the family also Cousin lou.

Write soon yr affec Brother
L. P. Foster

The skirmish described in this letter occurred at Fair Oaks east of Richmond on June 18, 1862. Gen. Lafayette McLaws ordered Kershaw to send a probing force to identify enemy positions. Units of the 2nd and 3rd S.C. Infantry were ordered to advance along the Nine Mile Road toward Fair Oaks where they encountered Union pickets supported by Federal batteries behind entrenchments. The firing of canister and shell by the Federals revealed their strong position.§

L. P. FOSTER TO HIS SISTER, PROBABLY SALLIE
———

Camp Jackson June 19th 1862

My Dear Sister,

I expect our Reg't is entirely convinced that it has seen the Elephant. We were in the closest place yesterday evening that we have been in. The Yankees for a few days past have been firing vollies into our pickets very unexpectedly. Yesterday evening they tried the same game and our Brigade was ordered to the front we marched in line of battle through thickets and felled timber, marshes, ponds &c until we came very near the Enemys pickets. When the rifle companies of each reg't were deployed to the front to drive in the enemys picket, they did not get 200 yds before

* L. C. Kennedy, surgeon of the 13th S.C.
† Governor Joseph E. Brown of Georgia, who opposed the Confederate Conscription Act.
‡ The abbreviation "mc" might mean military conscripts.
§ Wyckoff, *Third South Carolina*, 45.

they stirred up the yanky picket and raised a row with them. The firing was brisk. The yanky picket fell back and a battery of several guns opened on our pickets in the front with shell grape and canister shot. The Battery was almost 50 yds in front of our line of skirmishers. The skirmishers were in pines. We in the open field in rear. They raked the pines and fell every where around us. We lay flat—very flat down [. . .]. They threw canister all around us, rolled grape between our ranks & bursted bombs over us. It was the worst place I ever was in—yet every one stood to his post manfully & no one could discern any excitement. I did not ly down until I saw several grape shot fall in front and whissing through the ranks. We remained there 15 or 20 minutes [. . .] our officers seeing our very imminent danger and seeing several men wounded moved us by the right flank under cover of pines some 100 yds to the right. We had one member of our comp wounded—John Stallions* little finger shot off with piece of shell. I was lying near Joe McArthur† when a grape shot struck his cartridge box and glanced just off Lt. Youngs‡ head in his rear. I was struck on the calf of the leg by a spent canister shot but not hurt, it felt about like some one had shot a marble against my leg. 7 of our Reg't were wounded. Capt Walker§ of Cross Anchor comp wounded twice in right arm with canister shot one while being borne from the field flesh wounded. Dr. Thompson⁵ hospital clerk was wounded in the thigh with a shell died this morning at 4 oclock. 2 of the S. Rifles** were very slightly wounded. 2 of Capt Todds†† men were wounded, one in the ear slightly the other canister shot in arm, flesh wound but pretty severe. Many others of the Reg't were struck but not hurt. I can not describe to you our position unless you know what canister shot are and how they whistle. They are musket balls about a hat full of them or more are put in a wooden canister or box that rammed down the gun and when the box bursts and scatters the balls every where. I think they would have killed or wounded more of our men if we had been standing up. Every time their guns fired I could hear a perfect storm of balls going over my head and the way I lay close to the ground we remained in our new position until about dark when we returned to camp delighted with the coolness of our field officers but not all in love with skirmishing especially in such thick woods. I dont know the casualties of the other reg't but two or three in this reg't wounded severe enough to keep them from duty for any length of time. I regret Thompson's death very much but

---

* John M. Stalions of Co. K, 3rd S.C.

† Joseph M. McArthur of Co. K, 3rd S.C.

‡ Lt. William H. Young of Co. K, 3rd S.C.

§ Capt. F. N. Walker of Co. D, 3rd S.C. was permanently disabled from this wound.

⁵ Dr. William Henry "Willie" Thompson of Co. E, 3rd S.C. was the first man in the regiment to be killed in action. Wyckoff, *Third South Carolina*, 304.

** Spartan Rifles, Co. K of Jenkins's 5th S.C.

†† Capt. Rutherford Pressley Todd of Co. G, 3rd S.C.

think we should be thankfull to god that things are no worse for I can not see how we escaped so well.

Nothing more of interest to write. Remember me to all. Write soon.

I am well

Yr affec Brother L. P. foster

Tom Quarles's letter informed the Foster family that Tony Foster was able to transfer from his cousin Col. Oliver Edwards's 13th S.C. to the 3rd S.C. with his brother and neighbors, and that he had arrived in camp in the Richmond defenses.

Quarles refers to Gen. J. E. B. Stuart's ride with cavalry completely around McClellan's army on June 12–15, which was recognized as an important accomplishment. It demonstrated to Lee that McClellan's right flank was severely exposed just east of Mechanicsville, vulnerable to a flanking attack. Lee intended to deliver that attack with Jackson's troops arriving from the Shenandoah Valley campaign combined with Longstreet's and D. H. Hill's divisions.

TOM QUARLES TO HIS COUSIN SALLIE FOSTER

Camp of the 7th S.C. Regt.
June 22nd 1862

My Dear Cousin Sallie

Having heard yesterday that Tony was over in the 3rd Regt.* I immediately called on him and was very glad to see that he had come with the intention of remaining. He is looking very well indeed. I can to some extent conceive your feelings upon giving him up, and could my sympathies assist you in this trial of yours you should have them will all my heart. But alas! 'tis not in my power thus to aid you. Remember too, dear cousin, that I am in the same situation as Toney, having left my dear mother, Sisters, Brothers and many dear relations which has, indeed tried my soul. Consider but for one moment! I have not been home since June 1861 over one year since I have seen my mother. Do you not think Cains expression— This is more than I can endure—applicable to my case? Verily it is hard but I will not go so far as Cain did, ah! No. I hope & trust that I am more thankful than to make us of such an expression for although it is disagreeable and very unpleasant to be thus separated from my dear relations & friends. Yet it might be much worse with me than it now is. I am blessed with good friends and many more conveniences than some soldiers and have endured hardships of camp life remarkably well, far better than I ever expected. Taking all these things into consideration I have concluded to content myself with the present state of affairs hoping for better

---

* Perrin Foster's brother, Tony Foster, joined Company K of the 3rd S.C. on June 19th. Wyckoff, *Third South Carolina*, 255.

times in future. Be ye thus consoled, as regards Toney. I know he will do well no matter where he goes. He gave me a letter written by you something which I have long looked for. It is needless for me to say that it was acceptable since you know that I am ever anxious to hear from you. Had I known why you did not write to me after I left Manassas, I would certainly have written to you informing you of my whereabouts, but this I did not know, hence the reason I did not write sooner. You speak of being astounded because I wrote as though I thought you desired to extinguish our correspondence when you never had thought of such things. I am truly glad to hear that you had no such intentions, though during your long silence I must say, that I could not think otherwise just put this question to yourself. If I had postponed answering your letter three or four months what conclusions would you have come to? I can guess you would have either thought me very sick very busy or very careless, and when you did hear from me, that friendly quarrel would have been commenced. Would I were with you this evening I would be willing for us to quarrel some. Not too much, however but as I am not with you I will not commence our quarrel. Cousin Wade is now with us looking much better than I expected to see him. He was quite sick for a while. He says as you were sorry for him before when he was sick, you will have to get sorry again for he is getting sick again. Cousin Wade is very popular in our company. I am glad to hear that Uncle Foster* is well. I will be glad to see him, I saw Toney & Cousin Perrin yesterday. Cousin Perrin† was complaining some. Though he was looking very well. They gave me some cake which came from your house. I appreciated it very much as I knew it was made by my own relations and perhaps by yourself. 'Twas very nice in so much that I came very near making myself sick by eating so much of it. I got a letter from Sis Sarah‡ the other day. She was braging considerably on her four boys. Just to think I have four nephews and 1 niece. That looks like I am growing old, but I can not realize that I am anything but a little boy. Bud, I understand is quite as large as myself. Nancie is nearly grown oh how I would like to see them. I suppose you have heard before this of the skirmish which the 2nd & 3rd Regts had with the yanks.§ The 7th was very near them ready to support them in a case of immergency, but they had no trouble to drive them before them. So we had nothing to do but stand in hearing of the muskets and a wait the issue. We are daily expecting a big battle here, that circuit which Genl Stuart took in rear of the enemy was one of the most brilliant things of the war. We had three cousins in that affair. All Perrins sons of old Cousin Abner Perrin.¶ They all came through safely. Uncle James company is

---

* Barham Bobo Foster.
† Lewis Perrin Foster.
‡ Sarah B. Quarles, daughter of Agnes White Perrin and R. P. Quarles.
§ The skirmish took place at Fair Oaks on June 18th.
¶ General Abner Perrin of the 14th S.C.

stationed very near us now. Toney & I are going over to see him and our Cousins Lou,* Will† and Wardlaw.‡ We have no very arduous duties to perform. Nothing to do but drill and work on breastworks. We are at last relieved from pickett duty. Having given you all the news that a monotonous camp life can afford I will close. In conclusion however I will simply ask you to answer this letter immediately after you receive it. I suppose I must again pardon you for your long silence before, but remember Cousin Sallie that if I have to write twice to you once again I will be very apt to pick a friendly quarrel with you. Now I must bid you adieu!! Cousin Wade joins me in much love to you all. In ten days I shall expect an answer to this

Your devoted Cousin—Tom

L. P. FOSTER TO HIS FATHER

Camp Jackson June 22, 1862

My Dear Father,

Toney wrote his letter yesterday morning but neglected to send it to the office so I will add a few lines. Toney came to us whilst on the picket line as a reserve Thursday evening. Loring came from Richmond without a pass and flanked all the pickets. I was looking for him that day. He said he got through "Right side up." He seems well pleased and looks well. I have nothing new to write. Tom Q. was over yesterday evening. He is well. I was a little unwell yesterday and day before from camp diarhea, but I am better now & think I have it stopped. I am senior officer of the entrenching detail to day.

Remember me to all. Tell mother that my things all suited me well and I am much obliged for them also the cake.

Yr affec son. L P Foster

J. A. FOSTER TO HIS MOTHER

Camp Jackson
June 26th 1862

My Dear Mother,

I would have written to you before this but things have been so unsettled here ever since I came, and there is so much to do that I can scarcely find time to write.

---

* Lewis Wardlaw Perrin, son of Thomas Chiles Perrin served in Co. B of the 1st S.C. Rifles, Orr's Regiment.

† William H. Perrin, son of Thomas Chiles Perrin served in Co. B of the 1st S.C. Rifles, Orr's Regiment.

‡ James Wardlaw Perrin, son of Thomas Chiles Perrin served in Co. B of the 1st S.C. Rifles, Orr's Regiment.

Perrin has written to you all several times this week. I have been well ever since I came here. I think this country will agree with me finely. We live pretty badly, but as far as eating is concerned as well as we did on the coast. I have slept out without shelter several nights since I have been here, and find that I can sleep just as well that way as any other. I have learnt the whistle of the shell, and I think I can say with others that I will never forget the sound. The yankees throw shells at us every day, but generaly throw them too high or miss the range, as they are shooting many by guess. They threw some over this morning that I think must have come from a new fashioned gun or from a great distance, as we did not hear the report of the gun at all. There was heavy skirmishing on our right yesterday, we know none of the particulars.* When the fight will take place here I can not tell nor have the most remote idea. We are prepared to meet them at any time, and I think will be sure to whip them. I have heard several skirmishes since I have been here, and could hear our men charge, and generaly when our men make a charge the fight stops. I have not yet had an opportunity of trying my gun. If I could get it through Richmond I would send it home by Mr Roundtree, as I will have to keep a musket or be account-able for one on all parades. All our friends here are well as far as I know. I saw Tom Quarles & Wade Cothran last week, Tom has got fat on the war. Perrin is well, he has been unwell since I came here, but is well now and looking as well as usual. You must make Berry take good care of the puppies. Excuse this badly written letter. We have no writing conveniences at all. Give my love to all.

Your affectionate son

J. A. Foster

Robert E. Lee replaced Joe Johnston who was severely injured from a shell fragment on May 31st at Seven Pines. Lee faced McClellan's 105,000 fighting effectives with only about 50,000; Jackson was positioned near Charlottesville with about 35,000 soldiers, ready to continue his campaign against Federals in the Shenandoah Valley or move to support Richmond. Lee formulated a battle plan for the defense of Richmond intending nothing less than the destruction of McClellan, his army, and the possible end to the war. Gen. John Magruder was assigned to man the Richmond defenses with a thin force of 25,000 facing McClellan's immediately available 75,000. His role was to make a large demonstration before McClellan; and, holding McClellan's attention, to keep the Union forces unaware of how weakly Richmond was defended. Lee planned to move his remaining forces north to McClellan's right flank coordinated with the arrival of Jackson's 35,000, and to hit McClellan's exposed right flank while the Union general was occupied with Magruder's demonstration at his front.

The Seven Days Battle opened on June 25 with a Federal attack at Oak Grove. This minor battle resulted in a Federal advance of about 600 yards.

---

* This likely refers to the Battle of Oak Grove, the opening battle of the Seven Days Battle.

The fighting continued on June 26th at 3:00 P.M. when A. P. Hill marched through Mechanicsville and attacked Gen. Fitz John Porter's Union position at Beaver Dam Creek on McClellan's right. This frontal attack on a strong Federal position was premature; Jackson's forces had not yet arrived, and the Confederates were not available to deliver a coordinated attack on the Federal right flank. The Federals repelled Hill's attack with heavy Confederate losses.

On the morning of the 27th, McClellan withdrew Porter on his right flank through Gaines's Mill to a position that could defend his supply line to White House Landing on the Pamunkey River. Even now, McClellan could easily have broken through Magruder's weak lines and taken Richmond. Magruder's show of force and McClellan's natural instincts, however, combined to make this an impossible choice. Kershaw's Brigade, including the Foster boys in the 3rd S.C., was assigned to Magruder's defense of the Confederate capital. Lee attacked Porter on June 27th at Gaines's Mill and late in the day, collapsed Porter's line. On the 28th, after the Gaines's Mill defeat, McClellan evacuated his supply base at White House, moving it to a new supply base at Harrison's landing on the James River, and ordered a retreat to that new base.

On the morning of the 29th, Magruder's forces, including the 3rd S.C., moved out of their defensive positions in the direction of Savage's Station along the Richmond and York River Railroad. After crossing abandoned or lightly defended Federal earthworks, the Confederates proceeded through thick undergrowth toward Savage's Station, eventually encountering Federal fire. With the 3rd S.C. in the Confederate center, Kershaw's Brigade launched a charge against the Federal lines, driving them across the field up a hill where they were able to rally. The Federals received reinforcements, and the Confederates lost their numerical advantage. Further, the Confederates lost momentum when an unknown officer gave the 2nd and 3rd S.C. orders to withdraw. The Federals counterattacked, driving the Confederates back. Finally, darkness ended the action.

The press on the Union army continued on the 30th at the Battle at Glendale (Frayser's Farm) in Lee's attempt to stall the Federal retreat to Harrison Landing on the James River. Fighting desperately, the Federals were able to maintain their retreat to the relative safety of the covering artillery placed on Malvern Hill a few miles to the south. Meanwhile, Kershaw's Brigade marched toward Richmond, and then turned back to the south, following McClellan. Marching through the night, they came upon the Glendale battlefield on the morning of July 1* and continued to Malvern Hill.

At Malvern Hill, the beleaguered Federal Army established a strong defensive position. The Confederates suffered severe casualties in repeated assaults on Malvern Hill. The 3rd S.C., positioned on the Confederate left, advanced until it was pinned down directly in front of the Federals. In this place they were subject to raking cannon and musket fire from the Federals on the hill. After remaining in this untenable position for about an hour, the Carolinians were able to withdraw from the battlefield.

---

* Wyckoff, *Third South Carolina,* 57.

The Seven Days Battle ended with McClellan's army confined to a defensive position at Harrison's Landing under the protection of Federal gunboats, Richmond preserved, and Robert E. Lee leading the Army of Northern Virginia.

The letter below describes the Battle of Mechanicsville, launched by A. P. Hill on June 26th on McClellan's right flank. The strong fortifications discussed probably refer to Fitz John Porter's position at Mechanicsville where the Confederates were repulsed on the 26th. Jackson's forces arrived on June 27th at the Battle of Gaines's Mill. The reference to Jackson having cut off their retreat probably refers to control of the Richmond and York River Railroad line that connected McClellan's forces to his supply depot on the Pamunkey River at White House. The 28th was the quietest day of the Seven Days Campaign, as McClellan continued his retreat from Richmond and Lee prepared for his next attack.

L. P. FOSTER TO HIS FATHER

Camp Jackson June 28th 1862

My Dear Father,

Before this reaches you, you will have heard that our troops have fought another great battle and won another great victory. I know but little about the fight except what I see in the papers & hear from notes from our genls to the cols of this Brig. Our Brig was not engaged. The fight occurred on the extreme right of the Enemy's line but in hearing of us.* We had to hold the center.† The 5 S.C. Regts of Greggs Brig were engaged also Andersons Brig‡ and perhaps two others. The fight was a complete success. The Enemy entirely retreated and many prisoners and a quantity of artillery and other military stores fell into the hands of our men. Jackson came in the fight yesterday.§ The S.C. Regts under Gregg are said to have suffered severely. They were ordered to charge a strong fortification which proved too strong for them. They were repulsed twice and the battery was then taken by gen'l Pender¶ of N.C. other troops having attacked it in the rear. All agree that Greggs men fought desperately. Col Marshall was killed.** Col McGowan wounded.†† I heard from

---

* Mechanicsville on June 26th.

† The 3rd S.C. was part of Gen. John Magruder's thin demonstrating defensive line between McClellan and Richmond.

‡ Gen. Joseph R. Anderson's 3rd Brigade in A.P. Hill's Division.

§ Gaines's Mill on June 27th.

¶ General William Dorsey Pender, commanded a brigade in A. P. Hill's Light Division.

** Foster is probably referring to Lt. Col. Jehu Foster Marshall of Orr's 1st S.C. Rifles. Col. Marshall was not killed in this engagement.

†† Col. Samuel McGowan, 14th S.C., was wounded at Gaines's Mill.

Duncans Company* this morning. He had but one man killed. James White† was shot through the breast but was not dead. I have not heard from uncle James. Cousin Oliver was not hurt. It is said that Jackson has succeeded in cutting off their retreat and that they will have to give us battle. How it is I can not tell. He still has a strong force on this side the river. We were on the line yesterday and last night as a picket reserve. There was heavy skirmishing all along the line several times during the day and night. Our post not attacked but those on the right and left of ours were. In the evening 2 regts of our Brig, the 7th and 8th were sent to the front to feel of the Enemy and see if he was still in position. They drove in the Enemys picket and had a brisk skirmish. One man of the 7th killed and one of our reg't wounded by a shell in ankle. Our reg't did not advance yet they threw their shells over us. Thomas Lake‡ of the Q. R.s§ formerly a member and Seargt. of Capt Nunamkers Company.⁑ His wound is not serious. Toney thin[k]s this a warm country but takes the shelling very coolly. He is well.

My love to all—write soon. yr affec Son

L. P. Foster

29th 6400 prisoners have been sent to Richmond also 2 genls. The news gets better.

Perrin Foster's letter describes the Battle of Savage's Station on the 29th, burying the dead, and marching on the 30th to the battlefield of Glendale (or Frayser's Farm), and arrival at Malvern Hill on the morning of July 1st.

At Malvern Hill, McClellan concentrated his army into a very strong defensive position supported with artillery and fire from gunboats on the James River. This position protected his retreat route to Harrison's Landing where he could evacuate the Peninsula and hold a fortified position under cover of Federal gunboats. Malvern Hill was the only Union victory in the Seven Days Battle. Lee repeatedly sent brigades up the slope into the face of overwhelming artillery fire. Finally night fell on thousands of dead and wounded men, the Federals still holding their position on the hilltop. Kershaw's Brigade with the 3rd S.C. was positioned between the fork created by the Carter's Mill Road and the Willis Church Road directly in front of the Federal Forces at Malvern Hill.

* Captain W. H. Duncan's Company was Co. E of the 1st S.C. Rifles, Orr's Regiment.

† Possibly James White in Co. G of the 14th S.C. "The South Carolina Civil War Soldiers Index," http://www.researchonline.net/sccw/index/index253.htm#.V6t762X9OUc (accessed August 10, 2016).

‡ Thomas Marion Lake of the Quitman Rifles (Co. E) of the 3rd S.C.

§ Quitman Rifles.

⁑ Company H of the 3rd S.C.

Savage's Station, Union Field Hospital, with wounded from the June 27 Battle at Gaines's Mill. Courtesy, Library of Congress, Prints and Photographs Division, LC-B811–491. James F. Gibson, photographer. "Savage Station, Va. Field Hospital after the battle of June 27th." Library of Congress, Prints and Photographs Division, Washington, D.C., Reproduction number LC-B811–491. June 10, 2008.

L. P. FOSTER TO HIS FATHER

Battle field July 3rd 1862

My Dear Father

I have sent two telegraphic dispatches recently but had no paper & hence could only send such a dispatch as a friend would remember—hence I hope the friends of our company will not think me careless of their anxieties. Our army has been fight[ing] up to yesterday for 8 days. We have been successful on every field but at immense loss. Our Brig was first engaged on Sunday evening* last pursuing the Enemy for several miles we caught up with them near dispatch depot York River R. Road his artillery opened on us their battery supported by a Brig or legion of regulars was ordered to be charged by 3 regts of our Brig the 2nd 3rd & 7th the

---

* The 3rd Regiment engaged the Federals late in the day on June 29th at Savage's Station.

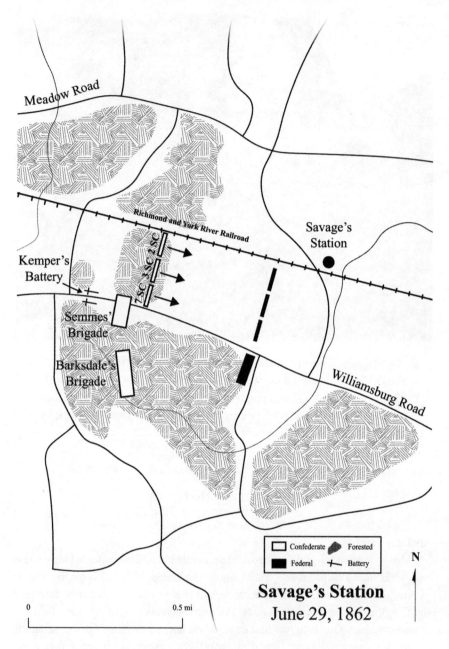

The Battle of Savage's Station, June 29, 1862.

artillery retreated but the infantry awaited our approach in the edge of a thick wood neither side fired until within 15 or 20 paces of each other where 2 or 3 murderous rounds were fired by each where our men again charged in a sheet of fire. The Yankees gave away & near there the order cease firing was given by some officer under the impression that we were killing our own men. This created confusion it was dark and our Brig drawn off. We killed a great many of them many more than they killed of our men but had i[t] not been for that order we would have killed many more since they were running not 50 yds by us. They retreated under cover of night leaving their dead on the field. I will give you a list of casualties in our company* killed Corpl W. A. Smith & Private J. L. Gentry-Wounded Capt Lanford wounded in leg has since died. Lt Young flesh wound in leg. Corpl Varner wounded in leg. Havner† in arm and shoulder dangerously. Levi Hill‡—flesh wound in leg—G. T. Hyatt§ very slightly in breast. W. J. Mayes flesh wound in arm—J. S. Roundtree¶ flesh wound in leg—B. A. Shands** flesh wound in thigh. James Storey severely in shoulder. A. C. Stripling†† flesh wound in leg—E. E. Smith slightly in hand. W. T. Wofford flesh wound in leg. Besides a good many were struck but not sent off. I was struck full in the breast was stunned a little not hurt by the ball. The next day after detailing here to bury our dead, marched over here near James River.‡‡ Our men were fighting when we got here and whipped the yanks badly.§§ Day before yesterday¶¶ we found them again in positions near James River. Our men attacked them they huddled 36 pieces of artillery together on a high hill*** and supported them by a very strong infantry force. Our men made several unsuccessfull attempts to take it. The cannonade was the most terrific by far I ever heard in my life. Late in the evening we were ordered up to support a column attempting to charge their batteries. We marched a mile in the heaviest fire of shell cannon balls grape canister and rifle balls I ever saw. We met the column coming back. Made them lie down and marched over there. We got near the battery were made to lie down in a

---

* The listed casualties are from Co. K, 3rd S.C.

† J. P. Havner, Co. K, 3rd S.C. His wound was mortal.

‡ Levi Hill, Co. K, 3rd S.C.

§ George Thomas Hyatt, Co. K, 3rd S.C.

¶ J. S. Rountree, Co. K, 3rd S.C.

** B. A. Shands, Co. K, 3rd S.C.

†† A. C. Stripling, Co. K, 3rd S.C.

‡‡ On June 30th Kershaw's Brigade marched to the Glendale battlefield, arriving early on July 1.

§§ On June 30th the Battle of Glendale (Frayser's Farm) was fought.

¶¶ July 1st; the "positions" were on Malvern Hill.

*** Malvern Hill.

road under cover of a bank at which their whole fire artillery and infantry seemed to be directed. After lying there a while gen'l Kershaw came to the conclusion that it was impossible for us to pass the bank and live and withdrew us. That place was the most perfect pandemonium I can imagine. We did not fire a gun. Our men fought them until night at other positions. After night the yanks retreated. Loss on both sides heavy and about equal. We had lost one man killed in our regt and but few wounded. We had a wound in our comp—G. W. James* severely in knee bone not broken. Corpl J. A. Thomas flesh wound in leg. W. [. . .] in foot. Toney was struck twice with spent balls once with a splinter but not hurt at all. The yanks have retreated across James River and it is said are going to attack Richmond on the Petersburg side. We have captured a great many prisoners we should be truly thankfull to god. The loss of our regt in the Sunday evenings fight was very heavy for the time we were engaged not more than ½ hr. We lost in killed and wounded 133 men—Col. Garlington was killed shot through. As he fell he exclaimed "forward my brave boys. Never give it up." Will Perrin† was killed last Friday in the fight on the other side of the Chickahominy. Our other friends safe. Uncle James carried 45 men in that fight and brought out 21. Don't believe the tales you hear about regts being cut up. I am disgusted at them. Every Col. seems to wish to claim the post of danger since the reports arise I can not give you a account of all the battles fought lately. Let the friends of our company know how things are. Tony and I are well. Capt Lanford was wounded in front of his comp when gallantly doing his duty. We regret his loss very much as of all our men yet they fell as the price of liberty. William Smith was shot through the head. Jno Gentry through bowels. Jim and Reid Tinsley‡ were wounded on Sunday evening. Our men have quantities of trophies. On Monday evening our men took 33 pieces of artillery. The whole country will be a grave yd. Our men not yet done burying. Small arms scattered every where. Tony and I are well. Remember me to all. Write Soon.

yr affec Son

L. P. Foster

Anthony Foster's letter below describes his experiences at the Battle of Savage's Station on June 29th and at Malvern Hill on July 1st. His brother, Perrin Foster, was promoted from lieutenant to captain of Company K following the death of Captain Seaborn Lanford, killed leading the charge at Savage's Station. Foster's letter was written from the battlefield at Malvern Hill.

* Gamaliel W. James, Co. K, 3rd S.C. The wound was mortal.
† This is William H. Perrin of Co. B, 1st S.C., Orr's Rifles, Lewis Perrin Foster's cousin who was killed at Gaines's Mill.
‡ James L. Tinsley and A. Reid Tinsley of Co. K, 3rd S.C. Reid was mortally wounded.

J. A. Foster to His Mother

Battlefield of the 1st July
July the 4th 1862

My Dear Mother:

As everything is again quiet and I know you are very anxious to hear from us I will write you this morning. Perrin and I are both safe, which you have heard by this time if you received Perrin's telegram to father. I know you will expect me to give you a description of the battles of Sunday and Tuesday. I can give you perhaps a vague idea of them, but it is beyond any power to describe them. Late Sunday evening we came up with one of the enemy's batteries.* They immediately commenced shelling us, and we were ordered to get in position to charge the battery, but while we were moving around to get our position Col. Kemper† turned loose on them an soon silenced their battery and compelled them to fall back. We then advanced again, and about an hour and a half by sun we came in range of them again. We remained under their fire about one hour, and were again ordered to charge the battery we raised a yell and put out at double quick through the woods, after advancing about three or four hundred yards we came in about ten steps of the enemy, they fired a deadly volley on us, we returned the fire with such deadly effect and so rapidly that they took to their heels and ran with all their might down the hill but soon rallied and oppened on us with more terrible effect that ever. It was then and not till then that I witnessed all the horror of a battle. I had been under fire numbers of times before, but not until then had I ever had an idea of a battle. I have often since I have been in the army pictured battles in my mind but never until then did I have a correct idea of one. It was nothing like I expected. I was perfectly cool and took as deliberate aim at them as I ever did at anything in my life. The killed and wounded fell all around me; and the groans of the wounded and dying were perfectly awful. One poor fellow turned over and raised up on his elbows and looked very pitifully at me and said "I am wounded in the side, dreadfully wounded, see here what a hole the ball has made, wont you take me off of the field?" You know how badly I felt especially when I was compelled to refuse him as we were expressly forbid to leave ranks to carry off any dead and wounded man, and if it had not have been against orders it was perfectly out of my power to carry him off without help. Capt Lanford fell in front of his company bravely leading them to the charge. I was by his side just before he fell and told him to watch or he would be shot by his own

* Sunday, June 29th, the Battle of Savage's Station.
† Capt. Dell Kemper's Battery of light artillery, from Alexandria, Virginia, was attached to Kershaw's Brigade.

men as they were firing from behind, he fell as nobly as did Bartow* or Bee.† Perrin immediately sprang out and took command of the company, and rallied them now falling back. You must not think that Black Stocks‡ were the only company that fell back the whole regiment gave way under the terrible fire, but soon rallied and it was with difficulty that the commanders could get them to retreat. Now the reason why we retreated was we were ordered to cease firing, and this confused the ranks, and we fell back to form again. We were ordered to cease firing because our commanders thought there was danger of our firing into a Miss Reg. I think there was at least 20 balls passed through a little bush just in front of me, and yet strange to say and not strange either I was not touched, one ball passed through my coat, but did not touch the skin. I have entered more into particulars than I expected to when I began this letter. I will now skip over the time from the Sunday's§ fight until the Tuesday's¶ fight. We were under fire from about 2 O'clock in the evening until 9 or 10 at night. It would be vain for me to attempt a description of this fight. Gen. Kershaw in the midst of the engagement said it was a perfect pandamonium, and that expression describes it better than any I know of. It did not seem to me that anything could escape the fire was so terrific. You could not distinguish the report of the cannons at all it was one continual roar. Men never were exposed to a more terrible fire. We marched over three columns of our troops lying down that had backed out from the fight, and could not be urged forward at all even after we took the lead. I think they were N. Carolinians but am not certain. We marched up in about four hundred yards of the battery, if such it was. (for there were 36 pieces of artilery playing on us) and ordered to ly down in the road. This we did and

"Then shook the hills with thunder riven
Then rushed the steeds to battle driven,
And louder the bolts of heaven
Far flashed the red artillery."**

The scene was magnificently grand, and terrible beyond description. Our Genls. said that if we had have advanced 50 yds farther, not a man of us would have escaped. We were therefor ordered to fall back. Col. Nance rallied his Reg.†† five

---

* Col. Francis S. Bartow commanding the 8th Georgia Volunteer Infantry was killed at First Manassas.

† Gen. Barnard E. Bee was killed at First Manassas commanding the Third Brigade.

‡ The Blackstocks was the original name of the Spartanburg County unit that became organized into Company K of the 3rd S.C.

§ Sunday's fight, June 29—Savage's Station.

¶ Tuesday's fight, July 1—Malvern Hill.

** Quoted from the poem, "Hohenlinden" by Scottish Poet Thomas Campbell.

†† The 3rd S.C.

Telegraph from L. P. Foster to B. B. Foster. From the editor's collection.

times in falling back. The retreat was more terrible to me than the advance. We fell back to an open field, and Col. Nance displayed his Reg as skirmishers to stop stragglers. We were marched about eleven o'clock out into a piece of woods and stayed there during the night. I was struck twice by spent balls but they did not hurt me. I must close this letter as I have no more paper here. We are now on the battle field how long we will stay here I can not tell. Perrin and I are both well. Your aff son Tony

A few days after the battle, Perrin Foster was able to dispatch a telegram to his father, with the most critical news of the battle.

TELEGRAPH FROM L. P. FOSTER TO HIS FATHER

Received at Columbia July 6, 1862
By telegraph from Richmond 3 to Lt Col. Foster
Glenn Springs, SC

Tony & I are unhurt. been hard times, killed Capt Landsford. J L Gentry Corpl W A Smith

L P Foster

L. P. Foster to His Father

Camp on the Battle field Crews farm
July 6th 1862

My Dear Father,

We are still here on the battle field. The excitement has all died away and now there is room for calm reflection. Our fight on Tuesday* was a draw fight for the time. The Enemy did not leave the field until dark. I am now satisfied that no battle ever was poorly managed so far as our corps of the army was concerned. It is the impression of every one that McGruder was drunk and I hear has been relieved of his command.† Our artillery did no good at all. There was but one or two places where it could be brought to bear on the Enemy and the first battery that was sent forward opened immediately, thus drawing the fire on that position so that the others could not get in position. We had plenty of artillery unengaged. McGruder threw forward Brigade after Brigade to the front when neither the Brigadier genls or he know any thing of the position of the Enemy except his direction. Since much confusion ensued and Brigades overlapped each other. It is said that the forces on the Enemies flanks did not get in position before McGruder commenced the fight. I said it was a draw fight. I suppose I could not call it such since our men killed as many as we lost or more and the enemy retreated at night with much signs of disorder. Our men captured a good many prisoners. What I meant was that when the firing ceased both armies had held their ground. We captured some of their artillery. I wish you were here to see the field and all the other fields. The Enemy was completely routed and many prisoners and much artillery taken. On Friday evening our men were not done burying the Enemys dead on the battle fields of Monday & Tuesday evening.‡ The plan of battle as laid by genl Lee I think was fine and contemplated the capture of most of McClellans army and I believe would have succeeded had all officers done their duty. The Enemys infantry did but little good but their artillery was well arranged and managed.

On Friday evening§ late we rec'd orders to pack up for a rapid march of 6 miles and it was said we were going down to Shurly⁋ to take some arms left by the Enemy. We march about 7 miles that night down James river and camped until day [. . .] morning. We sent some cavalry [. . .] to the place which was [. . .] on the river

---

* The Battle of Malvern Hill.

† Gen. Magruder was recalled to Richmond and transferred to the Texas coast defenses.

‡ Monday, June 30th, the Battle of Glendale (Frayser's Farm) and Tuesday, July 1, Malvern Hill.

§ July 4.

⁋ Probably refers to the area around the Shirley plantation a few miles south of Malvern Hill.

[. . .]. the gun boats were there finding them absent [. . .]. Marched [. . .] our forces consisting of 13 comps from our Brig & the 9th Ga. Reg't under command of Col Nance. The[re] were guns ammunition, tents, and almost every thing else scattered every where. We each now got two fine rifles besides his own and came away in quick time carried back a mile to our wagons and loaded them up 15 number but left many there as we were afraid to remain long so near their gun boats. There every thing presented the appearance of a disorderly retreat. Things were scattered every where and roads barricaded. We got one prisoner—quite an intelligent old Englishman. We treated him very kindly and he seemed well satisfied. He seemed to be an honest and truthfull man and remarked not long after we had taken him whilst we were eating breakfast that he heard no swearing in our army & that it was very different from theirs. He said that thousands of McClellans army were sick and great numbers had straggled off that their men were loosing confidence in success and were tired of the war. That man had joined his army because they could not get employment at home. Said he who had seen the English army was disgusted with the rabble of McClellan. He seemed anxious to get to England. I was sorry for him. He reminded me very much of Dr. Artis. It is said th[at] most of McClellans army have crost the river and gone to West Point. Some are still on this side about 13 miles below here. None near here. It is 16 miles from here to Richmond. Our men well but generally very tired. Our waggons are behind and I have to use such papers as I can get. You I have written on a morning report of the Enemy. I don't think McClellan can fight us again soon unless he is reinforced. You can not imagine the horrible sights through which we have passed. I have seen dead men and heard the groans of the wounded until I thought nothing could be more horrible. Remember me to all.

Yr affec Son L. P. Foster

P.S. Yrs of the 22nd June has just been rec'd. Our men say that their folks at home have clothes ready made for them but have not had a chance to send them. I will therefore only mention a few would not likely to have them. George Simmons 1 shirt 1pr drs 1 pr socks. Joe Chumley* 2 shirts 2 pr drs 2 pr socks. George Chumley† [. . .] James Riddle [. . .]. If you can have them boxed up at Glenns and sent to us by any one we will be much obliged. We will soon get uniforms but as you say will need clothes. So buy wool for [. . .] us if you think the parents of the members of our comp have none and we will pay for it. Have me a heavy pr army shoes made No. 6 ½, thick bottom, heels raised on insole. I have good shoes now but will need them before winter.

Yr affec son
L. P. foster

* Joseph Chumley of Co. K, 3rd S.C.
† George W. Chumley of Co. K, 3rd S.C.

L. P. Foster to His Mother

Camp 5 miles from Richmond
July 9th 1862

My Dear Mother

We are back at our old camp. Revilie was beat at our camp in James River 12 miles below here this morning at 2½ Oclock and we packed up and left before sun up. We reached this place about 12 pm. Why we left I know not. Some say to draw the Enemy from their gun boats. It may have been to get from the battle field which was by no means a pleasant place since the stench arising from dead horses, shallow graves & unburied men was very offensive indeed & would have created fear and the yanky camps on this side were so filthy we could not have stopped in them. I do not wonder at the sickness of McClellans army having seen the filth of his camps which exceeded anything of the kind I ever saw any where. It was very disagreeable to march through. We got new uniforms to day and are now a decent looking lot. They are made of grey cloth. The coats on close jackets on the whole look very well. They cost $11.50 per suit. I heard from uncle James a few days since. He was not hurt in the fight. Tom Quarles is at Richmond in the hospital. He was shot through the rist below the bones on the 29th June. His wound not serious. I have nothing more to write.

Remember me to all. Write soon.

yr affec Son
L. P. Foster

P.S. 10th Nothing new.

J. A. Foster to His Sister, Sallie

Camp Jackson
July 13th 1862

My Dear Sister:

I wrote to you last week but we had to move and I did not get to send it as Mr. Gwin is going to start home tomorrow. I will write again today. I have just heard a sermon from the Rev. A. W. Moore; it was a first rate war speech and if he had not have taken a text would have been openly applauded. He is a very fine speaker. I have not received a letter from any of you since I have been in Virginia. I can not think so hard of you as to believe you have not written. Therefore must think your letters have been misplaced or delayed through the negligence of post-masters. I heard yesterday that it was reported at home that I was killed in the Sunday's or Tuesday's battle. I was very sorry to hear it for I knew if such a report has reached you, you have suffered a good deal of uneasiness about me. How such a report got out I can not say. I was not touched in the Sunday's fight, a ball passed through my coat but did not touch me at all. The report may have got out in the Tuesday's fight* from some cowardly scoundrel who backed out of the fight. I did fall once in the Tuesday's fight but it was to dodge a thirty pound bomb shell which would have taken off my head if I had not dodged it. I was hit twice, as I told mother in my letter to her but by spent balls both times. Neither of which hurt me. I must conclude that some fellow put out the report to create a disturbance or for the sake of lying. I understand that the Guardian† says Kershaw's brigade ran like turkeys. They never did any such a thing. We never retreated until Kershaw gave the order himself. Gen. McLaws‡ said the Sunday§ fight was the most desperate he ever saw. It don't look much like we ran when we marched upon in 15 feet of the enemy without firing a gun and received their whole broad side without flinching, though it told with deadly effect upon our ranks and layed many a brave soldier low. We did not even stop only to load our guns. I wish the editor of the Guardian if he did publish such a thing could be in the place we were in for just ten minutes. I think it would satisfy him. I have some beautiful little rocks I got out of a little branch running through the battle field of the 1st of July¶ in the absence of something better. I will enclose some of the smallest of them in this for yourself, sister & Eunice & Jennie. If I could have had any chance I would have sent you a great many relics of the battle fields. You may form some idea of the immensity of the slaughter in the Tuesday's battle when I tell you that there were dead men lying on the field one week after the battle. I have seen so many dead men that I can hardly tell a sleeping man from a dead one. You may think strange of this nevertheless it is so. What do you all think of the late battles any how? I would like to know. Do you think foreign intervention will now take place. I think it would if foreign powers could get at the truth. But that is the rub. Virginia is a nasty, wet, muddy country if it is all like this. We have good spring water here but very hard to get there are so many men about here. It is one of the greatest farming countrys I have ever seen. We have to give the most extravagant prices here for every thing we get. We even have to give 25 cts for one onion. Perrin went to Richmond yesterday and got some mutton, coffee, and cabbages, so we are living finely to day. I had the best diner to day I have had since I have been here. I would like very much to have a good dinner of beans, Irish potatoes and corn bread, and would not object to a little butter milk, but I expect it will be many a long day before I enjoy many of the luxuries of life. We have a plenty of plane healthy food and can not complain. I have not been sick a day since I have been here and I think as stout as I ever was in my life. I stood all our marches as well

* Tuesday's Fight was Malvern Hill.
† *The Daily Southern Guardian*, a Columbia, South Carolina, newspaper.
‡ Gen. Lafayette McLaws.
§ Sunday, June 28, was the Battle of Savage's Station.
¶ Malvern Hill.

as any of the Reg except for the last days march. I did not fall out of ranks (a great many did) but I never was so hot and tired in my life. We were scarce of water part of the time could not get any at all. I never knew till then what it was to suffer for water, at times on the march I would have given everything I was worth almost for one drink of good cool water. It was the best for us though that we did get much. A man don't know what he can stand until he stands it. We are having an easy time now, easier than it has been since I have been here. When is father coming out. All the boys here say they would be very glad to see him. If you know how many times I have been asked when he was coming out. I am very well pleased with our field officers. Col. Nance is as cool a man in a fight as any body I ever saw. Now I know you are anxious to know just how I felt while in battle. I don't know as I can tell you exactly, but I think I can say and tell the truth that I was not scared a bit. I was as cool as I ever was in my life, and never felt more determined to do or die, but at the same time I could not but feel that my life was not in my hands nor in the hands of the Yankees, I felt that a higher power than man then reigned supreme.

The Yankees fight well at long range but when ever we get close up we can whip them three to one. They are certainly a great deal better artillerists than our men and would whip us all day in a cannon fight. I am convinced that the changing policy is the best for us. They cant stand cold steel nor even the thought of it for they run before our men can get close enough to apply it unless they greatly out number us. Gamaliel James is dead and died from a wound received in the Sunday's fight I fear from wont of attention. I don't know this to be the case, but his wound was not considered dangerous. We have lost many valuable men in the last battles. The destination of human life is awful to think of. All our neighbors boys that are in camp are well as far as I know. Give my best respects to Maj. Lancaster. I would like to be at home if the war was over but not as it is. Give my love to all and write soon.

Your affectionate brother

Tony

On July 15, the Confederate gunboat CSS Arkansas *steamed from the Yazoo River down the Mississippi. En route, it encountered and attacked two Federal gunboats, the* Carondelet *and the* Tyler, *and the ram* Queen of the West. *The* Arkansas *badly damaged the two gunboats and fought her way through the remaining Union fleet to the safety of Vicksburg's cannons. In August, the* Arkansas *suffered a mechanical breakdown during an engagement with the Union ironclad* Essex *and drifted ashore. The Confederates burned her to prevent her capture.*

The reference to the account of the discovery of a salt lake in Alabama is interesting. Salt was essential for preserving food and as a nutrient. The Federals recognized its importance and raided salt works throughout the war. In May 1862, a significant deposit of rock salt on Avery Island, Louisiana (also named Petite Anse Island), gave the Confederacy a new source of salt. This may be the discovery mentioned by Foster.

Avery Island provided salt to the Confederacy until it was lost to advancing Feder-als in 1863. *

L. P. FOSTER TO HIS SISTER

Camp Jackson July 17th/62

My Dear Sister,

Yours of the 23rd June came yesterday. It seems that we can not of late get a letter from home before it is over three weeks old. This is annoying and I can see no sense in it or cause for it. Pray there is not anything wrong at Jonesville. I hear not a word of complaint in other companies. The papers contain an account of a naval victory at Vicksburg achieved by the Arkansas a vessel which at the time of . the taking of Memphis was in an unfinished state and sent up the Yazoo River for completion. Report says she attacked the federal fleet of 26 vessels captured sunk and burned 9 & the rest ran. I know not whether I believe or not. It is hard to get the truth now. I only hope it is so for Vicksburg certainly deserves defense. She had acted more noble and honorably than any state city in the south & I sincerely hope she may never be found to yield to the tyrants will.

Things are quiet here. I don't know what either the enemy or our generals are doing. We do nothing but drill. Col Nance keeps at that with a close hand and our Regt has improved very much in that respect. We had a review day before yesterday evening. We had on our new uniforms and I thought presented a fine appearance. I don't recollect to have told you that we have again got new tents for the whole Regt. We have been without them a long time. They are much longer than our old tents and I like them much better.

Our wounded were doing well at last accounts. A good many have gone home. Some will soon return to the Regt. We have had beautifull rains lately. We had a heavy rain yesterday evening. We have a perfect host of flies. They seem to have forsaken the deserted yanky camps and will come over to our side and are realy tormenting.

You all must dry all the fruit you can. Save all the sour crout & pickles you can and every thing else in the shape of an antiscorbutic for if we have to go into winter quarters this winter we will need them. It will be hard to keep down scurvy. Cabbages are worth in Richmond from 50 to 75 cts per head onions 15 cts a piece and fresh potatoes 50 cts a quart. Everything else in proportion. I buy vegetables every chance I get which is not often. There are any amount of huckle berries around our camp & some black berries. We could have pies if we could get sugar but sugar is worth from 75 cts to $1.00 per lb in Richmond & we cant by much. Molasses 5

* Eugene W. Hilgard, *Geology of Lower Louisiana and the Salt Deposit on Petite Anse Island* (Washington, D.C., Smithsonian Institution, 1872), 1.

dollars per gallon. Have you seen any account of the discovery of a salt lake in Ala When the discoverer is making 2 bushels per day to the land and it is not enough can be more there to supply the confederacy. So goes the report Capt Del Kemper* has been promoted to Maj of Artillery and placed in command of the reserved corps of our division. I have nothing more to write.

My love to all. Write Soon yr

Affec Brother L P Foster

SALLIE FOSTER TO HER COUSIN, ELIZABETH COTHRAN

Glenn Springs
July 18th [1862]

My Dearest Lizzie,

Only a few evenings since your much appreciated letter was received and I was delighted to hear from you again, for had rather receive a letter from you than anyone else, and while reading a letter from you feel almost as though you had been sitting by me talking. You know I had rather be with and talk to you than any other creature, my sweetheart not excepted. Oh! I was thinking of former years, entirely forgetting that I am minus a sweetheart these days. You need not fear that anyone can persuade me out of the notion of being an "old maid," so let me beseech you not to suffer any uneasiness on that score. But I do fear that some of the many wounded soldiers returning almost daily from camp will elicit your sympathies and you will conclude to change your name, giving up all ideas of being an "old maid."

I was very sorry indeed that Tom Quarles was wounded,[†] but delighted to hear of his coolness and bravery. I hope sincerely he will speedily recover from his wounds, but being in the rist, I fear it is very severe. I would like so much to see Tom, and wish he would come up while absent from the army.

It is distressing to hear of our poor wounded soldiers, just think of them suffering, and it is awful to hear of the killed—but they have died in a noble and righteous cause. A grateful people will ever remember them. many families in our neighborhood are left to mourn the departure of husbands and sons killed in the late battles. Mr. Zimmerman[‡] had a son killed in one of the early battles near Richmond. They all take his death so hard & the whole family seemed devoted to him, for he was the only steady & promising one of the boys. He was engaged to be married. I do feel so much for them all. We surely are truly sorry and much grieved to hear

---

* Dell Kemper was promoted from Captain of Artillery in Brig. Gen. Robert Toombs's Brigade to rank of major in McLaws's Division.

† Tom Quarles, of the 7th SCV was wounded in the wrist at Savage's Station on June 29th.

‡ This may refer to John Zimmerman of Co. K, Palmetto Sharpshooters, who was killed at Frayser's Farm. Landrum, *History of Spartanburg County*, 704.

of Cousin Will's* death. It was such a shock for I never once thought he would be killed. I feel to thankful, my dear Lizzie, that our brothers were spared, but my brothers made some very narrow escapes. Brother Perrin was struck in the center of the breast with a spent ball, which stunned him very badly for awhile, but did not hurt him. Tony was struck three times with spent balls but was not hurt, had a hole shot though his coat.

I received a long letter from Tony last night giving me a description of the fight, and how he felt, etc etc. which was very interesting. He sent me also some relics from the battlefield. The Capt of the Blackstock Company was killed† while in front of his company gallantly leading them on to the charge. Oh! It is so sad and melancholy to hear of any soldier being killed, but more particularly of those of our friends and acquaintances. The week of the battle was one of deep anxiety to me. I never did spend such a time in my life. I look back on it with horror, hoping to be spared from another such scene. When will this wicked war end? It is heart aching to think of it, but I trust that a higher power than here below reigns supreme and that He will direct all for our good.

Rain is needed very much. The corn is suffering for it. We had some refreshing showers today, but the wind soon dries it off and leaves no trace of rain.

Father has been for the past week very unwell, though not confined, today he is much better. Sallie Montgomery had a little sister almost scalded to death—she lived two weeks in intense agony.

Margaret, our seamstress and house maid died last Sunday, leaving a little babe only eleven days old. She is a great loss and I will miss her so much for she did a great deal of the sewing. Her little baby is living and doing very well.

Mrs. Lancaster's little babe died last Friday with diarrhea.

I expect to spend next week at the village with Anna. The young ladies at the village gave a concert and tableaux not long since for the benefit of the sick and wounded soldiers. I have not heard how much they made.

I would like right well to see Lou Smith. How does she stand the war? You must not, my dear Lizzie, be mad with me for not going down to see you last winter, for I tried faithfully to go and it was not my fault that I did not go.

Now, dear Liz, do come up this summer, do dont disappoint me. I would be perfectly delighted to have you come. Tell Auntie‡ to please consider the matter again and conclude to come, for by so doing she will gladden many a heart among us, for we are all so anxious for you to come.

Letter paper is getting very scarce & hard to get, so I have adopted the plan of writing crosswise and thick together, so that it will not take so much paper, but I

---

* William H. Perrin of Co. B, 1st S.C., Orr's Rifles, son of Thomas Chiles Perrin.
† Captain Seaborn M. Lanford of Co. K, 3rd S.C.
‡ Elizabeth Lee Perrin Cothran.

have not learned to write very straight across the lines yet. I have written several letters this way and most always turn envelopes and return them.

All join me in sending my best love to you and Auntie. Excuse mistakes and bad writing. Hoping to hear from you soon, I remain as ever your devoted

Cousin Sallie

Do write very soon.

L. P. Foster to His Father

Camp 3rd S.C. Regt July 22nd/62

My Dear Father

It has been some time since I rec'd a letter from any of you. Tony has not rec'd a letter from home since he has been here. We write almost every day. There is something wrong in our mail arrangements somewhere.

We moved our camp yesterday morning. We are now camped near the 9 mile road about one mile nearer Richmond. We have a very pleasant camp in a open field near an excellent spring. We have [. . .] above in front of our tents and all fixed up much after Flint Hill stile. Our last camp was in a low wet place, and our water very bad. The 17th Miss is on one side of us & the 18th Miss on the other. I saw George Shuford yesterday evening. He passed through the battles unhurt and is quite hearty. I saw more in their camp just from Panola. He saw Uncle Anthony a short while since. He was quite well and went back to Arkansaw. Mr Timms family are in Panola county.

I did not hear anything from Uncle Calvin.* I went to Richmond yesterday to draw money for some of the wounded members of my company and succeeded. Three have returned to camp ready for duty E. E. Smith, G. T. Hyatt and B. A. Shands. The rest all gone home except J. P. Havener and C. P. Varner. C. P. Varner will return to camp in a short time. J. P. Havener is finally disabled. He was shot through the arm about 3 in below the right shoulder. The ball passing under the shoulder and out the shoulder blade. His arm was not amputated but an incision made and about 3 inches of the bone [was] taken out. He has a very severe wound and can not turn at all on his bunk yet he bears all with great fortitude and I hope will get well. He said he knew he killed one yankee for he was not more than 6 or 8 [steps] from him when he shot.

Tony has gone to Richmond to day. He is as stout as [I] ever saw [him] in my [life].

[. . .]

---

* Calvin Foster was Barham Bobo Foster's brother. He was a first lieutenant in Co. C of the 5th S.C. until the reorganization in spring of 1862.

On my under jaw between the corner of my mouth & my chin. I hope it will come to a head in a short time. We have nothing new. My love to all. Write soon your affec Son

L. P. Foster

L. P. Foster to His Sister, Probably Sallie

Camp near Richmond July 24th 1862

My Dear Sister,

It has been quite a time since I have received a letter from home. It has been I think two weeks since I received a letter from any of you. in the mean time I have [written] regularly. Of course I am at a loss to know why I do not hear from you. I get letters of other portions of the state. I suppose our mail arrangements are defective at some points and here the anxiety we suffer originates. I have but little to write you. I wrote you som[e] time since that Will Perrin was killed in the fight across the Chickahominy. I have to day learned that Will Wardlaw* was wounded in the right lung in the same fight. Frank Wardlaw† died at Manchester hospital of typhoid fever about the same time. Will Wardlaw is at Manchester and is doing well. Every where I go I seem to hear of some friend who had been killed or wounded. The list of our killed and wounded is a fearfully long one. Yet nothing to the yanky loss and will get to make them acknowledge that there is such a government as the Southern Confederacy. We must only exercise energy and patience and trust to god who has scattered the Enemy before us so often.

Every thing here is quiet. I saw George Shuford to day he is totally well. Uncle Anthony is in command of 1000 Arkansas guereillas. I expect you will be apt to hear from him. Barham Bobo‡ is in cavalry service. Uncle Calvin is at home. David Bobo was slightly wounded in one of the late fights and has gone home on furlough. I see some men who want to go home badly that I believe they are sorry they were not wounded. I am not one. I am anxious to get home but not to bear a wound. These six months sores are terrible. July 25th nothing new. The rising on my jaw is very sore. Toney well.

My love to all write soon. No letter from home yet. yr affec Brother

L. P. Foster

* Will Wardlaw is likely related to Foster through his aunt Jane Eliza Wardlaw Perrin, wife of Thomas Chiles Perrin.

† Frank Wardlaw is also likely related to Foster through his aunt Jane Eliza Wardlaw Perrin.

‡ There was a Barham Bobo in the 28th Regiment, Mississippi Cavalry. This is likely the person referred to in Foster's letter.

L. P. Foster to His Mother
_____

Camp McLaws July 27th 1862

My Dear Mother,

Yours of the 16th June to Toney and myself came 2 days ago. Sallies of July 12th to me of July 18th to Toney & Fathers of July 10th to Toney came yesterday. All were read eagerly being the first we had rec'd in some time. I was glad to hear that all were well. I regretted to hear of the death of Margaret. I have not much news to write you. J. P. Havener a wounded member of my company I suppose is dead by this time. Lt. Brandon went to Richmond yesterday and saw him. He told him to tell us all "good bye" Said he had more peace with his god. Had been baptized. I saw him here a week ago. He was then doing very well but recently had two hemorrhages in his wound and his surgeon says can not live. His surgeon had him baptized. I suppose he died cheerfully. He was a fearless and faithfull soldier. I shall miss him very much, as I do all our brave men.

July 28th 1862. Tom Gray* came to see us a short while yesterday evening. Jno Chiles† is out here now. I suppose only on a visit as he has been pronounced physically unfit for the duties of a soldier some time ago by an army surgeon. Three new S.C. Reg'ts have just come on the 15th 18th & Holcomb Legion. They join Longstreets command. Their rest days are over. I think our brig will be thrown in reserve. I rec'd a note from Ed yesterday evening. He was here at Richmond but expect to move [too] on the Charles City road this morning. I expect they moved last night as night is our time for moving here. The yanks thought we used our whole strength, conscripts and all in the recent battle. You spoke of Franklin Smith coming on to nurse Rufus White. Lt. Bearden saw Cal [. . .] day before yesterday who told him he was dead. I don't know when he died. We have beautiful weather. Fine rains. Remember me to all yr affec Son.

L. P. Foster

_____

*Probably Thomas C. Gray of Co. C, 7th S.C.

† Probably John C. Chiles of Co. C, 7th S.C. He was a relative of Eunice Chiles Perrin, Foster's Grandmother.

CHAPTER 7

Maryland Campaign

The Third Sight of the Elephant

Robert E. Lee's job was to demonstrate in 1862 that the Federals could not defeat the Confederacy. Lee rolled back McClellan's Peninsula Campaign in the Seven Days Battle, and by the end of August, he had defeated Gen. John Pope at Second Manassas. In September 1862, Lee planned to take the war into Maryland, which would move the war out of Virginia, give the Confederacy a respite, and demonstrate their ability to threaten Washington. Lee's plan was apparently to draw McClellan into another battle on his own soil and destroy his Union army there.

The Third South Carolina continued recovering from the recent battles and participating in movements to ensure no further threat developed from the remaining Federals still at Malvern Hill. Perrin Foster developed severe abscesses that prevented him from marching; he was forced to stay convalescing in the Richmond area while Kershaw's Brigade left for a September appointment in Sharpsburg, Maryland.

J. A. FOSTER TO HIS FATHER

Camp McLaws
August 1st, 1862

My Dear Father:

I received a letter from you this week written the second of July, and one last week written the 10th. I can not imagine why it is that your letters do not come more regularly. Sometimes we get them very early and sometimes a month after they are written. Everything on this line seems perfectly quiet now, and if I were to judge from appearance I would say there would be no more fighting here soon. We heard very heavy firing last night in the direction of Drurys Bluff.* I expect it was our batteries there and the enemies gun boats. I think the next battle will

---

* Drewry's Bluff, located seven miles downstream from Richmond on the James River, was important to the defense of the Confederate capital. By fortifying this bluff, the Confederates were able to keep Federal gunboats and troops from steaming directly up to Richmond's

be fought soon in the valley between Jackson and Pope, Greggs brigade has been ordered there. I dont think our brigade will be moved. I am not as keen myself for a third sight of the elephant as I was for the first. Besides the dangers of a battle, it is tremendous labour. I am rather inclined to think that the war is near its end. I hope so at least. I am affraid there will a good many of our Regiment enlist for the regular service, and it is so small that we have not a man to spare. I suppose you have heard that Capt. Todd has been sent to Columbia for conscripts. I hope he will bring a crowd of them. Scott Mayes died at the brigade hospital day before yesterday morning. His father tried to get a discharge for him when he was out here but was refused. it is a pity he did not get it. I think the most of our surgeons need hanging. They have no more sympathy for a man than they do for a brute. and I am affraid it is not much better with our generals. some of them at least. We have a great many drills and inspections now and are kept busy the most of our time. When are you coming out. I would like very much to see you out here, if you think you are able to stand the trip. The 17th Miss. Reg. is camped in a hundred yards of ours. George Shuford is in it we see him very frequently. John Chiles was here to see us the other day, he looks perfectly natural. I wish you would get Roger to make me a heavy pair of army shoes. I do not need them now, but if we stay here I will need them after a while, and we can not buy a good pair of shoes in Richmond for less than 15 dollars, and I am determined not to give that if I can help it. If Richmond was not our capital I would say let the yankees have it, for it is one of the worst sinks of iniquity in America. The merchants there trade in dollars and no matter what little thing you get you have to pay a dollar for it. Tell mother I want her to make me a pair of suspenders and sent them to me as soon as possible. I must close this, as the mail will leave directly. Write soon. My love to all.

Your affectionate son
J. A. Foster

P.S. Perrin and I are well.

Greed found a roost in wartime scarcity, as evidenced by Tony Foster's above letter. Had Foster gone home that summer, he would have found some of the same profiteering in Spartanburg that he experienced in Richmond.* As the war continued, the stealing of food and killing of farm animals became a growing problem in Spartanburg; sometimes deserters and roving soldiers were blamed.† In the brothers' letters, Tony Foster and Perrin Foster attributed some of the local thefts to a Dick Lee and a Gaston Fleming, describing them as an armed gang. Their condemnation of Lee

---

wharves. At the Battle of Drewry's Bluff on May 15, Federal gunboats were prevented from moving past the bluff to Richmond. I found no record of action at Drewry's Bluff on July 31.

* Racine, *Living a Big War*, 33.

† Racine, *Living a Big War*, 36.

and Fleming included a call for extralegal justice, not uncommon in the culture of upcountry South Carolina. *

J. A. Foster to His Mother

Camp McLaws
August 3rd 1862

My Dear Mother,

I received your and Father's letter of the 23rd day before yesterday. Your letters have been coming much more regularly lately. Capt Mays† is here; he got here yesterday. Came to carry his son home, but got here too late, as his son had been dead two or three days when he came. He will not take his remains home. I will send my gun by him. I find that it will not pay to keep two guns, so I will send mine home. I could sell it for $100.00 but would not near take that for it. It is not a very good gun to fight in line with, it is so short that it will burn the men unless you are very particular. Sister Sallie asked if I used it in the fights. Tell her yes. I was rather surprised to hear of Dick Lees & Gaston Flemings break. I think it is not only the privilege, but the duty of the neighbors to shoot them down whenever they see them. I believe they are the spring and meat house robbers. I would shoot one of them myself quicker than I would a yankee. Uncle Anthony‡ is doing the business right. It is no use to be squeamish about it in these sort of times. I would like very much to have some of Mr. Lancasters cider and some of your peaches, but I dont expect to get any this season. You said Father was going to build you a fruit kiln if he does dry all the fruit you can. It is one of the best things we have in camp, and if we go into winter quarters this winter we would like very much to have some from home. I am rather inclined to think the war will not last longer than this fall, but I can not tell anything about it. We have no news to write. Camp life, when we are stationary, is very monotonous. Perrin has a rising on his arm that pesters him a good deal, otherwise he is well. I have enjoyed good health the better part of the time since I have been in Virginia. I have had camp diarrhea since I have been here, but am well again. We have splendid water at this Camp, a large cool spring. I must close as I have nothing more to write. Tell Jennie she must make haste and learn how to write so she can write to me. Give my love to all and write soon.

Your affectionate son,
J. A. Foster

* Eelman, *Enterpreneurs*, 90.
† Captain Mayes, father of Samuel Scott Mayes.
‡ In Lewis Perrin's letter of July 24, 1862, he refers to Anthony Foster leading a band of guerilas in Arkansas.

L. P. Foster to His Mother

Camp McLaws Aug 4th 1862

My Dear Mother,

I am trying to write you, but my right arm is so sore & swollen tha[t] I can not do much at it. The rising on my chin is well but something has got the matter of my right arm just above the elbow on the under side. Dr. Dorrah says it is going to be a rising. Dr. Hunter our assistant surgeon says if it is a rising he can not tell it. My arm is very much swollen & very sore from it. I may have hurt it but fear it may be rheumatism. I am quite [well] in other respects. Toney is well. Our new assistant surgeon (Dr. Hunter) is from Princess Ann county, Va. And seems to be a very clever man and an intelligent gentleman. Dr. Dorrah has resigned, but has not heard from his resignation. Col Nance has rec'd some blankets and clothing for us from the ladies of Newberry. Some of the "Patus Conscription" are in Richmond now but have not yet been assigned to reg'ts.

Toney is well. We [are] doing very well.

yr affec Son
L. P. Foster

August 5th

My Dear Mother

As we have moved our camp since this was written I will add a post script. We are at a very pretty [field] on Mr. Christian's farm. I think we will stay here some time. Perrin's arm is still swollen but not so painful I think as it had been. I do not think it is a rising. He either hurt it some way or it is rheumatism. I have no news to write. Times are rather dull in camp. I am getting anxious for the war to end. Give my love to all and write soon.

Your affectionate son
J. Anthony Foster

On July 14, 1862, Gen. John Pope issued orders that in areas of the Confederacy behind Federal lines, citizens who would not sign an oath of loyalty were to be arrested and sent off to prison. The populace would be held accountable for guerrilla activity, and the army would take whatever it needed from the occupied populace. In retaliation, Jefferson Davis issued a proclamation that Pope and certain of his subordinates would not be accorded rights of prisoners of war if captured.

On August 5, General McClellan advanced forces from Harrison's Landing to Malvern Hill in a feint to force Lee's Army of Northern Virginia back. McLaws's, Jones's, and Longstreet's divisions were marched to meet McClellan.* The Federals evacuated from the area and no fight developed.

* Dickert, *History of Kershaw's Brigade*, 138.

L. P. FOSTER TO HIS MOTHER

Mr. Christians Farm Aug 5th 1862

My Dear Mother

I received three letters from home yesterday evening. One from father one from Nunie & one from you. I was very glad to hear that you had fine rains and hope they may continue. I suppose there has been no need of rain [in] this state but in several of the states I suppose crops will be quite short. In Miss & Ala there has been very little rain. I am sorry to hear of so much house breaking & stealing in our neighborhood but am not surprised. When the men of any settlement suffer such men as Dick Lee and Gaston Fleming to ly out in armed defiance of the laws of their country they can not expect any better. The citizens ought to hunt them down and hang them or if they prefer to resort to a legal method let them be reported to the governor of the state & he proclaim them Enemies of their country and call upon all good citizens to shoot them wherever and whenever seen. I w[ish] they would send me & 2 or 3 men of my comp home to disperse the gangs. I would make the work short. I hope the citizens will rise and put it down. It is a disgrace to the Dist and State. We moved yesterday to this camp about 2 miles a little nearer Richmond and in ¾ mile of the Chickahominy river. It is a nice place on a high hill. good water but plenty of mosquitoes. My arm is better. Dr. Hunter says it is inflammatory Rheumatism. I think it will be well in a short time. You spoke of my getting a furlough and coming to the association. Such a thing as getting a furlough is almost impossible even on Surgeon Certificate and quite impossible for pleasure. You may be sure that if I ever get a chance to get a furlough I will do it and let you know immediately for I don't think you can want to see me much more than I wish to get home. Toney is quite well. Gen'l Kershaws wife has come You have seen Jeff Davis proclamation in which he declares he will not treat Genl Pope or any of the officers of his command as prisoners of war. I think it just and right. I could not describe to you their cruelty to the citizens of Va. Even women. A southern man who would not fight his arm is cowardly beyond description.

I have nothing more of interest to write.

Remember me to all. Write soon.

yr affec Son L. P. Foster

P.S. Aug 6th. The Regt was ordered to White Oak Swamp last night our forces had a skirmish at Malvern Hill yesterday morning. Two Reg't so the Brig have been ordered back. I therefore think there will be no fight and look our Reg't back soon. My arm better but I have a boil on my lip and could not march.

L. P. F

J. A. FOSTER TO HIS FATHER

Christian's Farm
August 9th, 1862

My Dear Father,

I have got back to camp again after some very hard marching. Tuesday evening* about sun down we were ordered to get ready to move, (we knew not where) and at 8 o'clock were put on the march. We marched all night and about day break were halted at White Oak Swamp. The enemy had been driving in our pickets there and we were sent to support them. We remained there all day, and during the day took in a good many deserters and stragglers. Wednesday night at 10 o'clock we were put on the march again to a place on the Charles City road, to get to which we had to march about 3 miles between ours and the enemy's picket lines. It was about the stillest march I ever saw. If the enemy had have known we were there they could have bagged the whole of us. We arrived at our place of destination on the Charles City road about sunup, remained there all day and night, and the next day (yesterday) we set out for camp and got here about 12 o'clock. We had to live on but little all the time we were out. Perrin was not with us he remained at camp, as he was not able to march. His arm is no better that I can see and he has a large carbuncle on his lip. I am afraid he will have to leave camp. I cant imagine what is the matter with his arm, but I am inclined to think it is inflamatory rheumatism. He is able to be up and about. If he does not get better soon, I will try to persuade him to go to a private house in Richmond and stay until he gets better. I know this letter will make you uneasy, but I don't think you need be. If Perrin knew what I was writing he would stop me. Our conscripts came in yesterday. Perrin had over 50 applications to join his company, but was not allowed to take but 25. John Hutchings† and black John Harmans‡ sons are in this company. There were only 210 conscripts for the Reg

I have nothing more of interest to write. You get all the news we have in the papers. I am well and hearty and can stand about as much marching as any of them.

Give my love to all and write soon.

Your aff son
J. A. Foster

P.S. I sent my gun home by Capt May.§ I wish you would write whether he got it through safe or not.

J. A. F.

* Tuesday evening—August 5.

† John F. Hutchings of Co. K, 3rd S.C.

‡ Eliphus Harmon, James Harmon, John Harmon, and William Harmon all enlisted July 1, 1862 from Spartanburg County and were enrolled in Co. K of the 3rd S.C. One or more of these men, and possibly all four, might be John Harmon's sons.

§ Captain Mayes, father of deceased Samuel Scott Mayes.

Perrin Foster moved into a boarding house in Manchester, outside of Richmond, while the abscesses he suffered healed. He remained there until October 18th.

L. P. FOSTER TO HIS FATHER

Richmond Va Aug 10th 1862

My Dear Father,

Yesterday evening about night our regt got orders to move the next morning at 6 A.M. to Chafins Bluff a point on James river opposite to Drurys Bluff. As I could not march owing to the abseses on my arm and lip I got our surgeon to send me here and this morning turned out to hunt boarding. I am boarding a very nice place in Manchester at Mr. Brandens near the Manchester hospital. I could not wish a nicer place. Rob Wardlaw is here sick of typhoid fever but is better. I dont think the expection of a fight caused our reg't to move. The whole division moved carrying everything. Toney was well. Our conscripts had come 215 for our reg/t 25 to my comp. I regret not being able to be there to drill them. My arm is better today. The absess on my lip is larger an sore. I have no Rheumatism in my arm. It has proved to be an absess, I think from a hurt. This is a cool quiet place in 100 yds of James River. Dr Owens of Charleston S.C. is my surgeon.

Remember me to all. Write to Capt. L. P. Foster
Richmond
Va,

Yr affec Son L. P. Foster

L. P. FOSTER TO HIS MOTHER

Manchester Aug 11th 1862

My Dear Mother,

Again I am trying to write to you—before this reaches you, you will have [heard] of another glorious victory achieved by Stonewall—1 genl 33 officers and 700 men have arrived here as prisoners taken in the fight.* The officers being from Popes army were hand cuffed and placed in a dungeon.† My arm & li[p] does not hurt me so much. Dr Owens is trying to scatter them and I hope will succeed. He is a very fine physician and very kind.

I am well placed with my boarding house, our fair is very fine but there are no ladies here. Mr. Brandus is a widower and he loves the army. Rob Wardlaw is getting

---

* Stonewall Jackson's victory at Cedar Mountain on August 9, 1862.

† This was in retaliation for Pope's orders for harsh treatment of civilians behind federal lines.

better, I think getting well. I have not heard from the Reg't since I left in but know all is quiet. My love to all. Write soon.

yr affec Son

L. P. Foster

L. P. FOSTER TO HIS SISTER

Manchester Aug 13th 62

My Dear Sister,

You see I am writing left handed not because I can not write with my right hand but the Dr. says I ought not to use it. My lip seems better. My arm is much as it was when I last wrote. It is very much swollen and at times very painful. It is sluggish and stubborn, seems slow to do any thing. Mr. Brandus is very kind. You must be content with a short letter.

My love to all. Write soon. yr affec Brother

L. P. Foster

The 3rd S.C. marched to Chaffin's Bluff and Drewry's Bluff, opposing high points, seven miles south of Richmond on the James River, to prepare for any possible move by McClellan up the James or along the Peninsula. Foster's letter a few days later, on August 19th, has a tense feel about it. He was correct in his expectation of impending troop movement. The 3rd S.C. was going to Gordonsville, on its way to engage the Federals at Harpers Ferry.

J. A. FOSTER TO HIS SISTER, PROBABLY EUNICE

Camp 3 miles from Drewry's Bluff
August 13th 1862

My Dear Sister:

We left our old camp last Sunday for this place, and got here about 3 o'clock P.M. It was a very hard march at one time the whole regiment fell out without orders. I stood it finely myself. Three men died on the road from sun stroke, but neither one from our Regiment. I would have written to you yesterday but we were ordered off early in the morning to meet the enemy reported to be advancing by way of Malvern Hill. We went about 4 miles below here and remained until late in the evening then returned to Camp. I suppose it was a false alarm as every thing is now quiet. Perrin is in Richmond at a private house. He was not able to march with us when we left camp and therefore went to Richmond. He is at Mr. Brandus' house. I suppose the same Brandus that H. Barnett staid with. I had a letter from him day before yesterday evening. He said he was doing very well had splendid fare and other accommodations as good as he would wish. I am in hopes he will soon be able to return to camp. If his arm does not get well soon I will try to persuade him to get a furlough and go home. I think it is rheumatism the matter with it and if he had some bare-foot to rub it with, it would soon be well.* I will try to get a pass to go to see him. It is only 5 or 6 miles from here to Richmond. I do not know the name of this place. We have not named our camp yet. I sent my gun home by Cap. Mayes. I would like very much to know whether he got it home safe. I reckon by the time you get this you will be fixing for the association. By the way there is some body in the <u>old</u> <u>third</u> that would like to be there monstrous well. Give my love to all. Your affectionate brother.

J. A. Foster

J. A. FOSTER TO HIS MOTHER

Camp Near Chafin's Bluff
August 15th 1862

My Dear Mother,

I received a letter from Father to Perrin yesterday. I would have liked very much for Father to come with Mr. Beard. I would like so much to see somebody from home. Mr. Beard has not got here yet, we are looking for him every day. I had a letter day before yesterday from Perrin. He says he is doing very well his arm is better, but his Doctor says will not be well in some time yet. He says he has splendid fare and other accomodations as good as he could wish. I wrote to you that he was in Richmond, it is a slight mistake, he is in Manchester. A much prettier place than Richmond. He is about 100 yds from the Petersburg R.R. bridge at a Mr. Brandus.

Robert A Wardlaw is at the same house sick with typhoid fever. Things about here look less like a fight than ever. I think McClellan has withdrawn his main force from James River and left a small force there to annoy us to keep us from sending reinforcements to Jackson. But if I am allowed to judge he is very much mistaken in his notions. I think our Brigade will remain some where on this line. I have almost dispaired of foreign intervention. I think we will have to fight it out ourselves. I have no news to write. Give my love to all. Tell Jennie she must write to me.

Your affectionate son,
J. A. Foster

---

* Bears Foot was used as an herbal remedy to rheumatism. Bears Foot, also called Lion's Foot is most commonly known as Lady's Mantle (Alchemilla Vulgaris). Jethro Kloss, *Back to Eden* (Coalmont, Tenn.: Longview, 1950), 538.

J. A. Foster to His Mother

Camp 5 miles above Malvern Hill
August 19th /62

My Dear Mother:

We have just got back from a trip to Malvern Hill, and as we are under marching orders, and expect to leave very soon for Gordonsville I will write you a few lines. McClellan has left is nowhere to be found. So the siege of Richmond has ingloriously ended. Now foreign powers may see whether McClellans falling back was a change of base or not. I think he has fallen back, or sent off his army to reinforce Pope, in order to protect their own capital. I do not know when we will leave here our orders are to be ready at a moments warning. I suppose we will go to Richmond and take the cars there. I received your letter to Perrin written August 13th, day before yesterday owing to our having to go Malvern Hill yesterday I did not get to send it to him. I had a letter from him written the 15th his chin was then better, arm no better. I get your letters regularly now, the last one came in 3 days from Glenns Springs. You must not be surprised if you do not get a letter from me in some time. I do not know that we are to go to Gordonsville, I only give you my opinion, and the general of the Reg. as to that we are never told where we are going but can generally guess pretty well. Still direct your letters to Richmond. In your letter to Perrin you asked what division we were in. We are in McLaws division. Give my love to all and write soon.

Your affectionate son
Toney

On August 23rd, there were a series of minor engagements near Rappahannock Station, Virginia, as Lee prepared for an attack on Pope at the Battle of Second Manassas. The reference to the big battle probably refers to these skirmishes.

J. A. Foster to His Sister, Probably Sallie

Camp 2 miles above Hanover Junction*
Saturday August 23rd 1862

My Dear Sister

I have just received your letter to the 12th and Father's to Perrin of the 15th. I am sorry to hear of the death of Caroline. It seems as if there is a greater fatality among the negroes this year than usual. I would have written to you sooner, but we have been very unsettled for the last week. We left our camp on the new Market Road

---

* Hanover Junction was about twenty miles north of Richmond where the Virginia Central Railroad and the Richmond, Fredericksburg & Potomac Railroad intersected.

below Richmond last Wednesday morning, and came to Richmond that evening, encamped or bivouacked that night in the suburbs of the city went to the Central depot early next morning, stayed there nearly all day waiting to get off, got off about sundown or a little before and came in Hanover Junction that night. We came to this place (2 miles above the Junction) this morning and are now encamped in a very pretty place. I heard from Perrin as we came through Richmond. He had been before the board of examination and had a recommendation for a furlough, but did not get it then. I expect he is on his way home by this time and if he has no bad luck will get there before this reaches you. I would have went to see him while we were in Richmond but could not get off. I tried to go to see him before we left camp sent up a pass but did not get it signed, consequently could not go. Passengers on the trains from Gordonsville state that a big battle is going on up there today. I hope Jackson will whip them. I don't know what we are stationed here for unless it is to act as reserves. I hope we will get to stay here some time and rest. The old 3rd has been on the trot ever since I have been in Va. and I think it is time for it to rest some. The country up here is very like that around Richmond. We have very good water at this place. I saw Joe Harmon and Kennedy Barnett in Richmond. They both look badly. Joe worse that I ever saw him, he is going to try to get a discharge. I think he ought to have it. Kennedy Barnett thought he would be able to return to his Reg in a few weeks. I also saw Mr. White in Richmond. I gave him 3 little books to take home to Jennie when he went. I reckon you are all having a good time at home now attending the association. If the war was over I would like to be there myself. But I am afraid we are a going to have a very long war yet. Tell cousin Carrie, if she has not gone, that there is no chance now for me to send her my picture nor no chance to get it taken. I have nothing more to write. Tell father to send my shoes by the first opportunity, I would like for you to make me some flannel shirts. If we stay here this winter I will need them. I speak in time so you can have them ready. If it could be got here I would not trouble you. Write soon and send all the news. Give my love to all.

Your affectionate Brother

J. A. Foster

August 24th/62

P.S. Nothing new. It rained very hard here last night. I am well.

J. A. Foster

L. P. FOSTER TO HIS FATHER

Manchester Aug 24th 1862

My Dear Father,

I wrote you a few days ago saying that I had applied for a furlough, but owing to an error in my certificate failed to get it. I have sent in another & think I will get it this evening as the Surgeon General has ordered it. If so, I will start for home tomorrow evening (Monday). My chin is nearly well but my arm is much the same as when I last wrote.

I have not heard from the Regiment since it left for Gordonsville.

I have heard no news to day.

Remember affectionately to all.

Your aff son

L. P. Foster

A series of engagements and movements beginning at Cedar Mountain on August 9th ended on August 30th with Lee and Jackson defeating Gen. John Pope at Second Manassas. Pope did well to escape complete destruction and was able to retreat to Centreville. On the heels of McClellan's Peninsula Campaign, Lee continued to attempt to prove to Europe that the Federals were incapable of defeating the Confederacy. Jefferson Davis's one real hope for Southern independence counted on England and France reaching a point where their textile industries could no longer stand the disruption of cotton. These European powers would have to intervene on the Confederacy's behalf. Lee intended to complete this picture by defeating McClellan in Maryland, on Union soil, and then threatening Washington.

Before he initiated his contest with McClellan in Maryland, he needed to dispatch a Federal force at Harpers Ferry that would threaten his rear in a march into Union soil. Lee divided his army, sending Jackson along with Gen John G. Walker's and Gen. Lafayette McLaws's divisions from Longstreet's Corps to take Harpers Ferry. Jackson looped to the north to attack from the west, Walker approached from the south, and McLaws approached from the east. McLaws was directed to take Maryland Heights, the commanding heights across the Potomac from Harpers Ferry.

On September 12, McLaws ordered Kershaw to lead a direct attack up the back slope of Maryland Heights. Gen. William Barksdale's brigade was added to Kershaw's brigade for this assault. The Confederates advanced up the slopes and stopped before the Federal abatis* and breastworks. Darkness fell and the Confederates spent a restless night on the mountain.

On the morning of the 13th, the Carolinians advanced up the slope, led by the 7th S.C. Under fire, they cleared the abatis, followed by the 2nd and 3rd S.C. regiments. The Union defenders retreated to a stronger set of breastworks protected by a second abatis. The Confederates continued the advance to the second abatis where the 3rd S.C. replaced the 2nd S.C. At the abatis, the Federals opened a tremendous volley with deadly effect, killing Tony Foster and many of his fellow soldiers. The Carolinians were unable to advance through the abatis under such concentrated fire and the

---

* Abatis: defensive works of sharpened sticks.

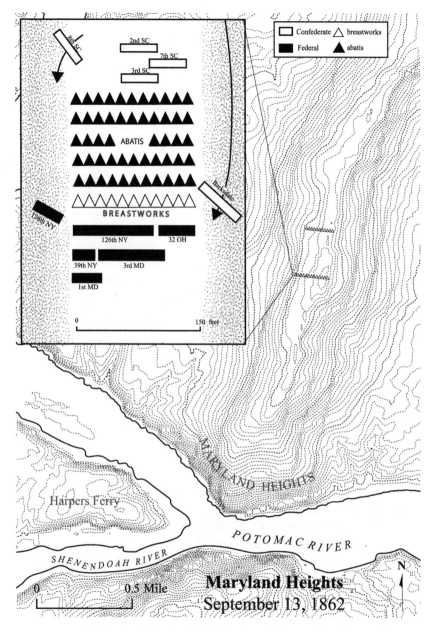

The Battle of Maryland Heights, September 13, 1862. The
units, positions, and movements are from Wyckoff.*

* Mac Wyckoff, *A history of the Third South Carolina Regiment: Lee's Reliables* (Wilmington, N.C.: Broadfoot Publishing Co., 2008), 96.

*action settled into an exchange of gunfire. This situation was relieved when the 8th S.C. flanked the Union right and drove them in a panic from the breast works.**

Lee's Maryland Campaign ended a few days later along Antietam Creek. The Confederate battle plans fell into Union possession, McClellan seized the initiative, and the battle was prematurely drawn at Sharpsburg, Maryland, along Antietam Creek. The 3rd S.C. was ordered from Harpers Ferry with McLaws's Division to join Jackson in the West Woods by the Dunker Church.† *At Sharpsburg the Federal and Confederate forces fought to a bloody draw in the Cornfield, at Dunker Church, Antietam Bridge, and the Sunken Road. Lee moved his army to safety across the Potomac on September 19th and, over the next few weeks, down the Shenandoah to recuperate. The 3rd S.C. camped in Berryville (called Berrietown in these letters) near Winchester.*‡ *Perrin Foster returned to his Company on the 27th. On November 9th, the brigade moved into camp near Culpeper.*§

Perrin Foster had been granted leave and had returned to South Carolina on August 25th. He was at home when his brother was killed. At the end of his furlough, he returned to the private home in Manchester, Virginia, where he lived while he recovered. He rejoined his unit in Berryville, Virginia.

Lt. William Bearden to B. B. Foster

Camp near Winchester Va.
Oct 9th 1862

Col. B. B. Foster

Dr. Sr. I should have written to you immediately after your son was killed but had no opportunity of doing so until several days afterwards. And I knew then that some few others had written to your neighborhood with instructions to inform you of his death. H. M. Cunningham¶ was one of the first to write from the company & he wrote to his Brother to see you & let you know what had become of Toney. I saw Lt. Carlisle** of Spartanburg as we passed Harpers Ferry on the 16th Sept. & he said he would write if he could find any way to send a letter to you from there as they were going to remain there a day or two. Toney was killed in the battle on the Maryland Heights on the 13th of Sept. while we were advancing on the Enemy breast works. He was shot through the boddy & fell dead when we were about 40 or

* Wyckoff, *Third South Carolina*, 69–71.
† Wyckoff, *Third South Carolina*, 74–76.
‡ Dickert, *History of Kershaw's Brigade*, 165.
§ Dickert, *History of Kershaw's Brigade*, 166.
¶ Henry M. Cunningham of Co. K, 3rd S.C.
** Probably John W. Carlisle of Co. C, 13th S.C.

50 yds from the works. I & Sergt Bray* went to him when the fight was over which was but a short time, and straightened him out. The ground was covered with fallen timber & very difficult to get through. As we came near the Enemy works they left & the fight ended that day & we remained on the heights till Monday morning when Harpers Ferry was surrendered. H.M.C.† attend the burying of Toney & marked his grave with a plank having his name, Company & Reg't lettered on it which was the best we could do under the circumstances.‡ I think he fell conscious of doing his duty to his country & to his God. The first thing I saw of him the morning before he was killed he was reading his Bible as soon as it was light. We were all much fatigued & worn down by our long march & having to do without much to eat after we started. The report of all the late battles have been sent on & I expect the last will reach you before this letter. We had the hardest fought battle at Sharpsburg Md. on the 17th of Sept. that we have been in yet. Our Division was marched all night before the battle and crossed the Potomac before day & went on & was carried into the battle immediately after we got there. The Enemy was driving our men back when we got there but the tide was soon changed when McLaws Division went but the extreme right & left not being able to drive the Enemy from his position we could do no more than retake the ground our men had lost—we fought on the ground where they had been fighting all the morning & about 11 a.m. we got possession of all that portion of the battle field the Enemy fell back to a strong position & shelled us the ballance of the day. The next morning they sent a flag of truce to get off their wounded which we agreed & all that was done that day was to take care of the wounded & dead. The wounded on our side have most all been taken care of the evening before and during the night. Our line was amongst the thickest part of the dead & wounded Yankees. There were as many as 8 or 10 of them killed to one of our men as far each way as I saw but I suppose this was not the case all along the line. The next morning the 19th we recrossed the river at Shepherdstown our mission then being accomplished to relieve Longstreet & D. H. Hill who had been hard pressed for Boonsboro from Sunday to that time & were not likely to get over the River. They brought up the rear from Fredricktown as the rest of our columns marched on Harpers Ferry & had they got along without being pressed on the last fight in Md. would have been in my rear. William has been unwell ever since we first went into Md. But is some better now & would soon be well I think if he could have a little better care taken of himself. I think of sending him home

---

* Sergeant D. S. Bray of Co. K, 3rd S.C.

† Henry M. Cunningham.

‡ Toney (Tony) Foster's remains were later transferred to Hollywood Cemetery in Richmond.

by Majr. W.M. Foster* who will leave day after tomorrow as I don't know not when the Capt.† will return & I don't wish to have the responsibility of taking [. . .] upon myself here. We flung away every thing we had on the march except one suit of clothes & I cant get him any thing more unless I could get back to Richmond, in fact the [. . .] of the men are no better off than he is except they most all have a blanket & oiled cloth. They most all sent their knap sacks back & all the extra baggage was left at Rapidan. Tell the Capt. we have had the hardest time we have ever had since he left us. Tell him to write if he don't return soon. very truly yours

W. Bearden

I have no stamps & have to trunk my letter.

L. P. FOSTER TO HIS FATHER

Manchester Oct 17th 1862

My Dear Father

We arrived here late this evening. I would have arrived one day sooner had I not remained in Columbia one day longer than I expected. I am at Mr. Brandus. He is quite well, but one of his sons very sick of typhoid fever. He seems very glad to see me, and is very kind. Nothing of interest occured on the road. Before this reaches you will have heard of Genl Braggs great victory. The enemys loss is estimated at 25,000, and the army driven across the Potomac.‡ Also of the fight at Perryville where our men captured 5,500 prisoners.§ Mr Brandus thinks the tales we have heard as to the suffering conditions of our army are false. He thinks it in as good condition now as it was at this time last yr, which I suppose is true. Henry Barnett went to see his father and mother tonight. I have not seen either of them yet. I expect to have this medly of confusion day after tomorrow. I went to Genl G. W. Smiths⁋ office to night and he gave me permission to remain here 10 days. He is now commandant of this post. I am quite well. My love to all. Write to me soon. Direct to Winchester Va

yr affec Son L P Foster

* Major William M. Foster of the 5th S.C.

† Refers to Capt. L. P. Foster, recuperating from abscesses on his elbow and chin in Richmond.

‡ Very confused news must have reached Richmond. Gen. Braxton Bragg was busy retreating from Kentucky to Knoxville at the time and had achieved no victory. The reference to the Potomac is simply in error if it refers to any action associated with Bragg in Kentucky.

§ The Battle of Perryville, Kentucky between Gen. Braxton Bragg and Maj. Gen. Don Carlos Buell on October 8, 1862 ended the Confederate offensive into Kentucky.

⁋ General G. W. Smith temporarily replaced Gen. Joseph E. Johnston when he was wounded at the Battle of Seven Pines. Smith's inability to press the attack on the Federals led to his replacement by Robert E. Lee.

L. P. FOSTER TO HIS MOTHER
_____

Monticello House. Richmond Oct 18th 62

My Dear Mother,

I wrote home last night but as I have found out my destination & will leave in the morning at 6 oclock, I write again. I have been ordered by Col H. H. Walker* to take charge of a company in a detachment which leaves in the morning for Winchester. I will, I suppose, have to march from Staunton. We are ordered to go on the cars to Staunton, then take line of March at rate 18 miles per diem which will take us 6 days to get to our Regts.

Ed† saw Mr. Landrum yesterday on his way home. He has William in his charge. Williams unwell & I suppose my mess sent him home. I did not get to see him.

Ed has been ordered to report at Camp Lee to carry exchanged prisoners to their respective Regts.

I left Mr. Brandus this evening. He kindly offered to receive anything sent to me. He is a kind hearted man and Christian gentleman.

Kennedy Barnetts better getting well. I saw Mr. Barnett to day.

I am well. Remember me to all. yr affec son.

L. P. Foster

SERGEANT DAVID S. BRAY TO MRS. B. B. FOSTER
_____

Camp near Winchester, Va.
Oct 22nd /62

Mrs. Foster

I received your letter yesterday requesting me to give you particulars of your son; whose death I lament and do truly sympathize with you and family. I intended writing to Capt Foster some time ago concerning Tonys death, but on account of our unsettled state was unable to do so. So soon as we became settled Lieut Bearden wrote to Col Foster saying that he stated the particulars. Tony wrote you a letter and the last on, the 5th Sept while at Leesburg Va. after which time we crossed into Maryland and were deprived of the opportunity of sending letters. He would often express his anxiety to send a letter home. He was very cheerful while on the march until about the 8th Sept when he complained of being unwell and was unwell the morning the battle but would not give up, went into the engagement very cool and deliberate. The evening 12th Sept we anticipated an engagement with the Enemy early next morning, he and I were to one side sitting by our little fire conversing when the subject arose concerning our feelings before going into and in the

_____
* Col. Henry Harrison Walker of the 49th Virginia Infantry, later promoted to General.
† Edwin Henry Bobo.

midst of battle, he says "I go trusting to the kind hand of Providence, if it is his will for me to fall I will fall otherwise I will not" told me that he was not afraid to die. The morning the 13th the battle commenced. Our Regiment was ordered into the engagement about 9 oclock we fought some ¾ of an hour. Tony was shot ¼ of an hour before we drove the Enemy from their fortifications. Our company was greatly exposed to the enemy so much so that we would have to ly down at times. Tony was on his knees in the act of getting up when a ball struck him centerally in the body entering his cap box and passing through him. As soon as he was struck he clapsed his hand upon his wound and said I am killed, the last words he was heard to speak. So soon as the firing had ceased I went to him, but was too far gone to speak he only drew a few breaths, he looked very calm just as if he had fallen asleep, only lived about 15 minutes after he was shot. Our mess intended burying him to himself, but before we had time to bury our dead, we were ordered forward, a detail of one man from each company being left to bury. Mr. Cunningham* saw him buried he was buried in a grave with four. Mr. C cut his name upon a board and placed it at his head.

Tonys death was much regretted by the company, not only the comp, but by all who knew him in the Regiment, he was a good soldier always at his post and per-formed all his duties cheerfully. He was not only a good soldier battling in defense of his country, but a soldier of the cross a follower of Christ. I believe him to be a Christian, he was very attentive to his bible on the march. I must close as I have given you all the particulars. Please remember me kindly to Col Foster.

No more

Your friend. D.S. Bray

Jno. W. Carlisle† to B. B. Foster

(Berkley County)
Camp near "Bunker Hill"
Army of Northern Va.
Sunday October 26th 1862

Col B. B. Foster

We are now bivouacked near Bunker Hill half way between Martinsburg & Winchester 11 miles from each place—last week we were engaged in tearing up the Baltimore & Ohio Rail Road—our Division tore up the track in sight of Harp-ers Ferry in full view of the Federal Tents on Loudon Heights—the Enemy did not molest us & we returned to our present camps on last Thursday—when in full

---

* Henry M. Cunningham of Co. K, 3rd S.C.

† John W. Carlisle of Co. C, 13th S.C. Carlisle was Toney Foster's recruiter earlier in the year.

view of the Maryland heights my thoughts wandered back to the time when they echoed to the sound of artillery & I thought of the noble spirits that poured out their blood for their Country on that rugged mountain. I thought of your noble son just stepping into manhood offering himself up as a sacrifice for his Country, his career was brief but brilliant—he fell fighting for his Country, the Country that gave him birth the Country that contains the graves of his Ancestors who could not who would not fight in such a cause. I saw Tony only once since he came to us—few days after the fights around Richmond were over. I met him with his Regt going to James River to gather up some arms that the Enemy had left there. I saw him but for a few moments & little did I think that that would be the last time that I would look upon his manly honest face—we parted then never to meet again on Earth. A noble old roman once said he would not give his dead son for all the living sons in Rome—but it was left for a Christian Father to say the Lord gave & the Lord taketh away blessed be the name of the lord. Toney fills a soldiers grave on Maryland heights near by the beautiful Potomac & within sight of the lovely Shenandoah & tho' they may roll by many a soldiers grave they murmur over no grave that holds a lovelier Patriot—his life was short but he did more than many who live to three score & ten years—he died like a soldier he died at his post—what more could He have done—He fell like a Christian Hero—he fell in the discharge of his duty—his Country demanded the sacrifice & Tony did not falter—it is hard to give up one so lovely & so young yet his death should teach us this lesson—to discharge our Duty tho' we fall in the effort. Peace be to his ashes—you have my sympathies but I know they avail nothing in such a case.

Tell Mr. Harmon that his son John* was a good soldier & was very popular in the company we all miss him much. I saw him when he was shot—he was shot in the lower part of the abdomen & lived some 3 or 4 hours. I went up to see him after he was shot—he seemed perfectly resigned. I had a short conversation with him while the Bullets were flying thick around us. The last words he said to me were Lieutenant I think the Genl kept us at that place too long. He spoke calmly & mildly & seemed perfectly aware of his condition. He was taken to the rear & in a few hours died. I did not have any conversation with Robt Smith† he was carried to the rear immediately to the hospital & the living had to press on in their work of death—Robt died that night. We had not time to attend to their burial even—we were in line of Battle until we marched away (Sunday) but a burial party was left behind. Marion Thomas‡ was killed almost instantly—their families have the sympathies of our whole company.

---

* John F. Harmon of Co. C, 13th S.C. was killed at Second Manassas.
† Robert Smith of Co. C, 13th S.C. was killed at Second Manassas.
‡ Marion L. Thomas of Co. C, 13th S.C. was killed at Second Manassas.

Col Edwards* has gone home—he is troubled with his old complaint—we miss him very much—he behaved most gallantly in all the engagements & is very popular with his Regt. My health is fine—fattening every day. I have escaped unhurt through all the Battles that our Brigade has been engaged in—at Sharpsburg my hat band was cut through—that was a most terrific battle our Division marched 15 miles that day & got into the fight about 3 oclock P.M. just in time to save the right wing of our army—we fought until dark drove the Enemy back to the mountains & slept on our arms all night. We have had rest from fighting ever since the 20 septr, the battle of Shepherdstown†—at which time & place we drove the Enemy in great confusion across the Potomac capturing some 3 or 400. Longstreets Corps is between us & Winchester some 4 miles from us. I suppose Perrin & Edwin‡ have both got to their Regts tho' I have not heard from them yet.

I wish you could see "Stonewall" on his Maryland steed charging by his troops & his troops shouting & waving their hats—it is a grand sight—no genl creates the enthusiasm that he does—when Genl Lee rides by, the soldiers gaze at him in silent admiration, but whenever Jackson is seen every soldier's mouth flies wide open—you can always tell when Stonewall is coming. Genl Stuart also creates a considerable enthusiasm he is about your size wears a large black feather in his hat & very frequently a large bunch of flowers stuck in his bosom—his raid into Penn astonished the Yankees very much—but of all the genls I think Genl Lee by far the most superior—he has no equal in this continent in my estimation.—our Gen'l (A. P. Hill) is a small man—looks something like W. C. Kilgore—he is a good fighter & is making for himself quite a reputation.

We have had several good frosts—today is cool & drizzly. I rec'd a letter from Lou 17th. Give my respects to your family. May god spare you your only son & may he be a comfort & an honor to you.

yours Jno W. Carlisle.

L. P. Foster to His Father

Berrietown Oct 27th 1862

My Dear Father,

I am at last with my company. We reached Winchester morning before last having had a very pleasant 6 days march through the prettiest country I ever saw anywhere. We were not relieved of our command until yesterday. We brought our

---

* Col. Oliver E. Edwards of the 13th S.C.

† The campaign ended at Shepherdstown on September 20 when A. P. Hill fought pursuing Federals, forcing them to fall back.

‡ Edwin Bobo.

men through safely. I reached our Regt encamped about 8 miles from Winchester on the road to Charlestown yesterday morning. All of our boys are well. Every man in our company reported for duty this morning. Col Nance well. Our men generaly well clothed and shod. Some need shoes and blankets. Reserves in our company moved right barefooted. got scared at Sharpsburg & run and left every thing behind Lt Beardon had written all the particulars of Toneys death. He was shot at Maryland Heights about 15 minutes before our right took the yanks breast works. He had kneeled to load his gun and was raising to shoot when the ball struck him and passed through his cap box and body. He spoke but once "Said I am killed" and died in a very few minutes. He was in the front rank and amongst the foremost men—not more than seventy paces from the yankees. He was buried there with three others of my company and his soldiers grave marked by H. M. Cunningham with a head board. His things were sent home by Mr Landrum. He told David Bray before he went into the fight that he did not fear death and felt as safe on the battle field as anywhere. He died bravely as ever man died. All our men testify of the coolness and gallantries of Col Nance both at Maryland Heights and Sharpsburg and say that genl Lee himself could not have done better. Also to the desperate bravery of Genl Kershaw Bravery of the men at both places shot away all their ammunition they claim victories in every battle say they killed more yanks in every fight ran them off and held the field.

Col Rutherford* was left behind sick and captured.—has since been paroled. We have very cold weather. A great many ask about you. I am quite well. Remember me to all and write soon.

Yr Affec Son

L P Foster

Among the papers of Albert Gibert Kennedy, Sr. of Union, South Carolina, the editor found a record of his meetings with two surviving Confederate veterans from the Foster's Co. K of the 3rd S. C.,† which included a description of Tony Foster's final moments and death.‡ The reference to the head wound is likely incorrect; witnesses described no such wound. George Thomas Hyatt, a Private in Co. K., was wounded at Savage's Station and at Fredericksburg. He was captured at Lynch Creek, imprisoned, and paroled on June 13, 1865. J. N. McArthur, a Sergeant in Co. K, was wounded at Maryland Heights and Chickamauga, and was paroled in Greensboro, N.C.

Kennedy's note records:

* Lt. Col. William Drayton Rutherford of the 3rd S.C.

† Wyckoff, *Third South Carolina*, 267, 276.

‡ Albert Gibert Kennedy, Sr. unpublished interview with George Thomas Hyatt and J. N. McArthur, May 5, 1917.

Mr. G. Thomas Hyatt of Co. K 3rd S.C. Volunteers made the following statement May 5th, 1917.

Anthony "Toney" Foster, a Corpl. in said Co. had the following conversation about twenty minutes before he was killed with Mr. Hyatt. When we were marching up Maryland Heights he came up to me and offered to give me his haversack with his rations and said to me that he would never have any use for them. I took the haversack, but never could eat the rations. One of the hospital men told me that Tony Foster was killed by a bullet wound in the head. His skull in the top of his head was split open, and his brains could be seen where the skull was shot away. This was at the battle of Harper's Ferry, Va.

Note. In conversation Mr. J. N. McArthur told me [A. G. Kennedy] that he saw Tony Foster my uncle fall at the battle of Maryland Heights.

CHAPTER 8

Marye's House

Last Sight of the Elephant

In the weeks following Antietam, Lee's wounded army recuperated, reinforced, and resupplied. Meanwhile, Lincoln tried in vain to get McClellan to press his advantage against Lee with his larger, better-equipped army. McClellan slowly refurbished his army, and, in late October, crossed the Potomac and began glacial movements towards Warrenton, Virginia. To counter this move and protect Richmond, Lee promptly marched his army to Culpeper. Lincoln had had enough. On November 7, Lincoln replaced McClellan as commander of the Army of the Potomac with Ambrose Burnside.

L. P. FOSTER TO HIS MOTHER

Berrietown Burkly Co. Va
Oct 28th 1862

My Dear Mother,

I wrote to Father yesterday giving him all the points I then had. We have clear pleasant weather, very cold nights, ground froze last night & water froze in our canteens but the atmosphere is pure and open. We had a battalion drill yesterday evening. Our regt has improved very much in drilling. Every man now steps and moves himself like a soldier. I did not think Col Nance could have made such a change in so short a time. The whole regt seem to take a pride in drilling and being considered the finest regt in our division which is now given up. I wish you could see our men on drill. They move like machinery. We have now the best band we have ever had. It consists of 1 base drum 1 kettle drum and a fife. We have a splendid fifer & two good drummers. Frank Pettit* is our base drummer. Our Regt has over 500 men for duty. The Seventh Regt has a right new uniform and look more like a regt of Yankees than I ever saw any regt. Their pants blue & coats almost black. I have just been to see the grand mounted. It is mounted with music and all military

---

* B. F. Pettit of Co. K, 3rd S.C.

ceremony and it a pretty thing. Tell Rufus Lancaster that his son William is with the company and looks better than I ever saw him in my life. Albert Smith looks very well. All our boys stout and ready for duty. Ed Bobo is with his company. They are camped almost two miles from here. We are now in Longsteets army corps. Dr. Evans* is our surgeon. The boys do not like him. He is too <u>cross</u>. I have just come off company drill. Gen'l Lee is to review us this afternoon at 1 oclock. The whole division I suppose will [. . .]. our men will need bed clothing this winter, also socks. The ladies of our community—I hope will commence at once to make comforters woolen or cotton, also to knit socks wool or cotton. They will also need shirts and drawers. I think the government will furnish over clothes and perhaps shirts and drawers. We have plenty of fine beef and & flour and our mess bought the finest mutton horn yesterday I ever saw weighing 15 lbs. There is a branch which heads a very large spring about one & half miles above here and has between here and its head three mills & a factory. This is a fine country but I would not like to live in it. It is too near out of the world and too cold for me. Our boys were not pleased with the Marylanders. Say the majority of them are union men and have no sympathy for us, closed up their stores & would not sell to our men. I have not heard from home since I left.

Remember me to all
yr affec son L. P. Foster

Many Carolinians paid close attention to the South Carolina elections in 1862. Following the Federal occupation of Port Royal, Governor Pickens was viewed as ineffectual. The Secession Convention, still in existence, convened and in December 1861 established an Executive Council to provide governance. South Carolina was now under two governments, the Governor and Legislature established by the Constitution of 1790, and the Executive Council established by the Secession Convention.† By August 1862, South Carolinians were ready to end the Executive Council. The Convention convened and the Executive Council was dissolved in September 1862 pending agreement by the legislature, which was having an election in October. Dissolution of the Executive Council was still an issue. This is likely why we see the reference to the election in the following letter. The legislature abolished the Executive Council on December 18, 1862.‡

---

* Dr. James Evans, 3rd S.C.

† Walter Edgar, *South Carolina, A History* (Columbia: University of South Carolina Press, 1998), 361.

‡ Cauthen, *South Carolina Goes to War*, 158–161.

L. P. Foster to His Father

Berrietown Oct 30th 1862

My Dear Father,

Your letter of the 21st came yesterday. The first I have recd from home since I left. I was glad to hear that you were all well. I had heard from the election and I assure you that I was gratified with the result of the senatorial election & I am satisfied with the other. There is no danger of being captured in marching from Staunton to Winchester. The troops march the road without arms. I have written you the conditions of my camp. They need shoes and blankets worse than anything else. They will need clothes of all kinds this winter. I think however that we can draw our clothes except overcoats from the government. That is Col Nance's notion. If you can buy the leather on a credit and have shoes made for our company we will pay for them and be much obliged to you. I will send the numbers as soon as I can. In the mean time get the leather and workmen, say leather enough for 40 prs stout shoes. Lts Bearden and Cunningham wrote to Jim Hill and engaging the making of 33 prs. See if he has had them made, if so we will not need to many. Tell the ladies to make under clothes for us, also. Comforting Knit socks, cotton if not wool. Col Nance has advised me to this course. Elija Smith is much better. Our other neighbors well. Nothing new to write.

I am quite well. I add Nance begs to be remembered to you.

My love to all

Yr affec son
L P Foster

Tom Moorman is absent sick I expect gone home.

L. P. Foster to His Mother

Camp 3rd S.C. Regt.
Nov 4th 1862

My Dear Mother

The "Old 3rd" is on the trot again and has been most of the time since we came to Va. We left our Camp at Berrietown 8 miles beyond Winchester last Friday morning and that day marched in the direction of Front Royal 22 miles. The next day we marched about 10 miles crossed the north and south Shenandoah rivers, fording both of them. I forded the first bare footed but the rocks hurt my feet so that I tried the other shoes on. We would have marched further but had to wait for our wagons to cross the river. I was put in command of a detail from our brig to have wagons pushed up the hill on this side of the river. We march that night 3 miles on this side of Front royal and campt in the mts on the Chester gap. The next day we marched through the Mts about 13 miles and camped near Perryville in Rhappahannock Co. and yesterday marched to this place about 20 miles. Our march was almost all of the way on a uncorduroyed road* and our feet are very sore. Yesterday we marched 7 miles in quick time without a halt and in 2 hrs—is that not equal to Jacksons ft cavalry? Our men have stood it well. Every man in my company for duty this morning. One man David Bryce† (a conscript[)] slipt off from me on the first days march on the road and I fear has deserted. L. H. Vaughn‡ broke out with measles on the road and I turned him over to the surgeon. Vaughn is no account and I don't care if I ever see him again. Our regt in fine health. We are now in 3 miles of Culpepper C.H. camps. Longstreets Corps is here I don't know where we are going. Some say to some place to take up [. . .] others say to Petersburg, others say our brig is going to Charleston, that genl Bouregard has made a special requisition for it.

Jackson's Corps it is said has come down through the Perryville gap nearer the Potomac & had a fight a few days since with Siegls Corps and whiped it.§ The Holcomb Legion is camped in 100 yds of us. I have seen Burnwell and Ed Bobo, both well. I hear no more about small pox, but our surgeons have been vaccinating all our men. It will not take in my arm. I have seen more Mts since I left Staunton than in all my life before. Try to urge the people to prepare winter bedding and under clothes for our men. I have nothing more of interest to write. I am well. Our boys well. My love to all. Write soon

I cannot tell you where to write unless to Richmond.

Yr affec Son L. P. Foster

L. P. Foster to His Mother

Camp 3rd S.C. Regt near Culpeper
Nov 14th 1862

My Dear Mother

We are still in the vicinity of Culpeper and wont be surprised if we spent our Christmas here. We move our camp day before yesterday evening to this place about one mile from our old camp. We moved on acct of wood. We have plenty of wood here and water convenient. I get but few letters from home. I have rec'd

---

* Corduroyed roads were roads built from logs laid crossways. While more passable than mud, they were rough and especially miserable for wounded men in wagons.

† David P. Brice of Co. K, 3rd S.C.

‡ L. H. Vaughan of Co. K, 3rd S.C.

§ I find no engagement that matches this information. There were several skirmishes in Virginia in early November and one of these may be the source of Foster's report. The reference is to Gen. Franz Sigel who commanded the Union XI Corps at this time.

but four since I left home and none from you. I can not see why they do not come regularly now as we are in three miles of the R.R.

We have very pleasant weather and I am quite comfortably fixed, but several of my mess are without shoes and there is not the least chance to get them here. I suppose we have to wait until we can get them from home. They also still need blankets, socks, under clothes, I hope our people are exerting themselves to supply them—without this and more our men cannot be comfortably clad. Our government must have acted very corruptly with the hides of cattle slaughtered for this war or they could have furnished shoes with abundance. The idea of foreign intervention has crippled the energies of our people from the beginning and even now that lurking hope renders useless many an arm. I think in many instances cowardice produces such hopes. Men have not the nerve to meet the scenes and acts of this day and hope for other shoulders to bear their burthens—sooner or later they must feel this way and I for one am opposed to any armistice until the north offers terms of peace to we can honorably acceed. Jackson it is said is at Martinsburg & A. P. Hill at Charles Town.* They (it is said) have had a fight with the enemy and captured a large am't of Q'master & commissary stores. We have reports of the recognition the C.S. of America by France & Eng by I don't credit them.† We are now passing through just what we had last fall in that respect. The people had better go to work and let England France alone. Draytons Brigade‡ is camping very near us. We had a review and a rigid inspection yesterday by gen'l McLaws. Our regt was lightly complimented by one of McLaws aids. Direct to Culpeper C.H. I am quite well. I have a sore arm from vaccinations but it does not hurt me much. My love to all.

yr affec son.

L. P. Foster

L. P. FOSTER TO HIS FATHER

Camp Near Culpeper
Nov 16th 1862

My Dear Father,

I have nothing of interest to write you. I have received no letters from home recently but have heard from home through Tom Wofford & my recruitment who came in last night. My wounded men are coming in rapidly. I have near 60 men present and only 3 off duty from sickness. They are only unwell. Dr Young and Jas

* At this time, Lee's army was divided. Jackson's corps was in the Shenandoah Valley and Longstreet was at Culpepper, Virginia. The fight may refer to an action at Snicker's Gap, Virginia, on November 5, 1862.

† Foster probably meant to say, ". . . but I don't credit them."

‡ Gen. Thomas F. Drayton commanded a brigade in Longstreet's Division.

Hill* are on the way and I suppose will soon be here. I received a note from Miss Sallie Montgomery sec. of the philadelphia L.A.L.† informing me of that the L.A.L. had sent me certain articles for my company. I am very much obliged for them and am anxious to acknowledge through the paper their receipt but am not certain as to the name of the county, please inform me as to that point. The box has not yet come but I suppose Lieut Young will bring it. Everything is quiet. Nothing indicates a fight soon. There was a short cannonade yesterday morning in the direction of Hazel River, but I suppose merely a picket skirmish. I have heard that a fight is daily expected at Charleston S.C. but suppose it is sinsation. I have not been able to learn anything from Uncle James at last accounts A. P. Hills Division was at Strasburg on the Perryville turnpike which is in the valley of Va. below Front Royal. We do little of anything but drill fortifying seems to have gone out of date. We have Batallion drill in the morning and Brigade drill in the evening. We had a pretty brigade drill yesterday evening. Genl Kershaw gave the command 1. to Form Squares on 2nd Batallion. 2nd Left Wing forward. Right Wing about face. 3rd Form Echelon at 100 paces. and stumped the party at first but when he explained it we performed it. We have quite cool weather and it looks like snow urge the friends of my company to send on their clothes shoes and blankets or comforters very soon. It is time that our people had ceased to rely upon vessels running the blockade and determine with their own resources to do for themselves They are continuously looking just ahead to time when England and France will aid them. Thus in their very actions acknowledging our imbecility calculated to unnerve many an arm and criple our efforts The war is not over depend upon it. More effort is necessary than our people have yet made. I am well. My love to all.

Write often

Yr affec Son
L P Foster

L. P. Foster to His Mother

Camp 3rd S.C. Regt near Culpeper
Nov 17th 1862

My Dear Mother,

We have a wet bad morning, yet are ordered to be in readiness for a fight; I have just been drawing & distributing 40 rounds of cartridges to my men. I think there will be no fight but perhaps a move somewhere. Where I can not tell. We have had the same order so often and done nothing that I think little of them more than to

---

* Jas Hill—probably James C. Hill of Co. F, 3rd S.C.
† Probably refers to a Ladies Aid society associated with the Philadelphia Baptist Church.

obey them—which you know is the part of every officer. Everything seems quiet &
see nothing which indicates a fight; yet I can not tell when one may come. I know
of no Enemy moves and the order to keep my men in camp this morning and see
that they had 40 rounds ammunition took me rather by surprise. Sometimes these
orders are given much to keep us in readiness.

One case of small pox was reported in our regt yesterday morning. Whether it
was small pox or not I can not tell. It was a [. . .]. I am not at all afraid of it. I have
just had a sore arm from vaccination and nearly all of my company have been vac-
cinated, so don't be uneasy about. I write because I know you will hear it—perhaps
much magnified. I rec'd a letter from Belle Perrin yesterday. Anna Nickolson is married to an old widower with two sons in the army. The women will marry—won't
they? Wade C. at home. Tom Q better. My men genly well. I must go to breakfast.
Write soon. My love to all.

yr affec son

L. P. Foster

*When Gen. Ambrose Burnside replaced McClellan as commander of the Army of the
Potomac on November 7, 1862, he had 120,000 fresh troops. A thirty-mile march to
Fredericksburg would put the Federal army closer to Richmond than Lee's army at
Culpeper. Burnside moved quickly. By November 14th, Burnside had White House
approval for his plan to move against Richmond and force the much smaller Confederate army to fight him in defense of the capital. On the 17th, the Army of the Potomac
was positioned at Falmouth, ready to cross the Rappahannock into Fredericksburg;
Burnside needed only the previously arranged arrival of the pontoons and materials
needed to construct bridges across the river into Fredericksburg. Delays in the arrival
of the bridging materiel, however, prevented Burnside from crossing the river until
December 11th.* *

*Lee recognized the threat to the Richmond and quickly moved the Army of North-
ern Virginia into defensive positions at Fredericksburg. Foster's company's preparations
on the 17th were for real this time. McLaws's Division marched for Fredericksburg on
November 18th, arriving in Chancellorsville just west of Fredericksburg on the 19th.†
By December 11th both Longstreet's and Jackson's Corps were in strong defensive positions in Fredericksburg. Kershaw's Brigade with the 3rd S.C. was positioned at about
the center of Lee's long defensive line along Telegraph Road.*

---

* Bruce Catton, *Never Call Retreat* (Garden City, N.Y.: Doubleday, 1965), 15–16.

† Wyckoff, *Third South Carolina*, 82.

L. P. FOSTER TO HIS FATHER

Camp 3rd S.C. Reg't near Fredericksburg
Nov 24th 1862

My Dear Father

I had no chance to write to any of you yesterday of day before. The day before that I wrote informed you as to our march to this place. We arrived here Thursday night and Friday night we were sent on picket in the city along the river. Our whole brigade went. The 2nd and 7th were put on post and our reg't put in an old ware house where we remained all night without fire. We had forded a creek and our feet & legs were very cold. I was afraid to pull off my wet shoes and socks as we were in 300 yds of the Enemy and slept with them on. The next morning we built fires in the house on piles of dirt on the floor but they were too small to do much good. We could see the yanks plainly. [Their] pickets were on one side of the river and ours on the other in 100 yds of each other both with arms stacked and talking very friendly to each other. Burnsides seem to have changed the way in that respect. The pickets do not pretend to shoot. Gen'l Kershaw & Col Nance rode in 50 yds of them and were not fired at. About 11 Oclock we moved out one division at the time and marched thence down on a street near the river and remained there until last night when we returned to Camp. The yanks had a cannon bearing on every street in the place which ran towards the river but did not fire on us though we were in less than half a mile of their guns. They first gave the terms until friday morning to surrender or be shelled. A comitty of citizens went over and were given until yesterday eleven Oclock to get the women and children out and men also [with] assurance that the town would not [be] shelled except in combat. I think there will be no fight since they are afraid to cross the river and afraid to remain where they are lest Jackson should come down in their rear and catch them between the Potomac and Rhappahannock rivers a neck of country not more than 10 miles wide for 20 miles down to Chesapeake bay. It was thought last night that they were leaving. The citizens of the city were all leaving on Saturday. They were very kind to us gave us freely of what they [. . .] shoes shirts socks & books. It is truly a secesh town. The prettiest & most loyal town to the south that I have seen in Va. The citizens took many of us to their houses to eat and warm. If you had been there and seen the yanks walking in crowds on the other side of the river & our men in crowds on this side you might have guessed that both sides belonged to the same army. I could not understand it & could not help wishing to tell our men to shoot the scamps.

Two conscripts from Spartanburg Dist in the 7th Reg't from the Rolling Mill settlement named Mathers deserted a few nights since & went to the yanks. Some of our men knew them well.

I fear we will not get the box you sent [. . .] brought the box to Gordonsville and left it there and came on here when he got sick we were in line of battle down in the city and [. . .] at the place satisfied fine he left [. . .] not seeing any one except the sick in camp or even detaining has [. . .]

My love to all. Write soon. L. P. Foster

L. P. Foster to His Father

Camp 3rd S.C. Regt near Fredricksburg
Nov 30th 1862

My Dear Father,

Yr letter of Nov 24th and Nunies of Nov 17th came last night. I was very glad to hear that you had more arrangements to have our shoes made. We have rec'd some shoes from the government recently and our men are better shod, but the shoes are of a very inferior quality and will not last any length of time. Our men are also better clothed than they were. The boxes sent by Dr. Young and turned over by him to Ransply have not reached us. They are said to be at Gordonsville. Ransply acted badly. I hope they may conscript him and put him some place where he can get accustomed to the sight of artillery.

I remarked some time since that I had almost as soon have one well drilled & disciplined Regt for active service as all the reserves of S.C. & I think from the start the 7th Regt has made I did not underrate their effectiveness. Certainly it should have been celebrated and appropriate speeches made. Feasts g[iven] in honor of the gallant union the appealing smiles of friends, wives, & children. Some temple of Janus should be erected in Spartanburg in which could be hung the spoils and relicks of the memorable 7th Reg't and now that their families rest in peace and security they have in many hard fought fields discomfited and routed the Enemy— and driving back the dark clouds of before which have so long hung threateningly over our misery stricken country and allowed rays of the sun of peace to enliven the thresholds once more—its door should be closed for another war.

They have at last invited a burlesque on S. C. Chivalry—burlesque of truth.

Whenever men who having friends and relations are in the field fighting for their liberties and hard men hesitate, falter, & fail to take their post when called on such a flimsy pretext as the one they allege their patriotism or their bravery one of the two must be at a low ebb and I much fear both. Oh for a propitious wind to swell the once buoyant but now subside shorn of patriotism and bravery in S.C. You will recollect when we were called to turn our service to Confederate States service in Columbia, it was said that if we failed the old men of the country would take our arms. Yes our fathers and uncles would step in our shoes and fight the war leaving us to sing lullabies & rock the babies, but now when the time of need has come, when a bleeding suffering country asks them to fill up our thinned ranks merely to take the guns of our gallant boys who have bravely fallen they stand aghast and like McBeth see a bloody "dagger of the mind" which they cannot clutch and with one hand grasping their pocket books drop down to their pockets and the skin hung mournfully about their mouthes. See them turn their backs on the Enemy and lend a deaf ear to their country's call. Tis the same S.C. which they took from the Union and vowed to protect with lifes richest blood in the stormy days of parades and patriotic buttons when no guns alarming soon had started the inflated storm of patriotism now that gun has been fired and a safety valve is found through which its waters have passed. The appointment of officers by government I must fear then the gurgling in the stream patriotism was one froth. To a man who has seen men endure, patiently endure as much as I have seen them endure such an excuse without even a trial to help us is flimsy and worse than nothing. It seems strange that we should have found so much privation and they revolt at the first bone of it. You are at liberty to read this to any of them. [I] came off picket last night all is quiet no news I am well. My love to all

Yr affec son L. P. Foster

L. P. FOSTER TO HIS SISTER, PROBABLY EUNICE

Camp near Fredricksburg
Dec 2nd 1862

My Dear Sister

    I fear you think I have forgotten you but not so for I am trying to write you a letter now. I would have written to you before but most of my letters home have been on errands to which you could not attend, but this morning I feel easier than at anytime lately. If you were here this morning you would not see a barefooted & ragged set of soldiers. You would see every man in Comp K with a pretty good pr of shoes, one or two good blankets and generaly very well clothed. Nearly half having good overcoats and I hope soon to see all of them have good overcoats. The government has done wonders lately. They have given us a good many shoes & blankets, overcoats & I drew 23 blankets 11 overcoats and 17 pr socks for my company yesterday. So you can tell the people to dry up about the "poor b-a-r-e footed soldiers" in our brig. for I don't suppose there is a barefooted man in it. This morning we have a bright pleasant day. our men quite well. only 29 in the Regt off duty & none bad sick. If you were here I could show you a yanky camp from where I am writing. Their tents look white and pretty. I have been busy for some distributing clothes to my company, but have got through with it. We have also bread and beef. My commisary is cutting up and distributing another days rations of beef. Our brig had been considerably enlarged the 15th S.C. Regt and James Batalion* have been annexed to it. you must write to me soon and give me all the news.

My love to all yr affec
Brother L P Foster

My Dear Father

My company is at last shod. The shoes will do for awhile until we get those you are having made. most of the shoes we have rec'd from the government are inferior pairs from 4 1/2 to 10 dollars per pr. The last we got were home made pegged and stitch down shoes at $10.00 per pr. I sent Mr Beard a certificate yesterday from Col Nance.

I am well.

yr affec son
L P Foster

L. P. FOSTER TO HIS SISTER, PROBABLY SALLIE

Camp near Fredricksburg
Dec 3rd 1862

My Dear Sister,

Your home missive of Nov 25th has been read with interest I have little material here to make a letter interesting. I keep the tablet of memory pretty well drained by writing so often. Scarce a day passes without my writing home. I enjoy no pleasure here so much as reading the letters of my friend and relations. I wrote to Anna and Jolla more than six weeks since & have never received an answer from them. I am not sorry that I wrote to them since I thusly fulfilled a promise, but had I thought that my letters would have elicited no answer, I should not have promised to write to them. I have no doubt but that the dish presented by my pen was rough and insipid perhaps to much so for the dainty taste of college young ladies—perhaps it was presumption in me to offer the dish. If so I ask their pardon. I received a long and very interesting letter from one of my Columbia correspondents last night. We are here doing very little of anything. We rise at reveille attend roll call then get breakfast, drill in school of the company from 10 to 11 a.m. have roll call and inspection at 1 p.m. then some eat dinner, our generally eat twice a day—at sundown we have retreat or dress parade at 8 p.m. tattoo and then to bed. The intermediate time is taken up with getting wood making details, cooking etc. It is a dull life in some respects. Intellectually it is very dull. We have but little to read. Seldom even get a

---

* James's Battalion was the 3rd Infantry Battalion, also called the Laurens Battalion. It was commanded by Lt. Col. William G. Rice at Fredericksburg. This unit was named for Lt. Col. George S. James who organized the battalion.

paper. I bought two books when in Fredricksburg and have reading one entitled Life and Thought Memorials of Mrs Dison.* It is interesting—composed principally of extracts of her diary and letters. The religious tone of her letters is very fine. I have another The Great Tribulation† which I have not yet read. We have quite cold weather and smoky fires. I have been scratching terribly lately on account of the itch & souaves but am about well of the former ailment. It has never made me sick but is no little annoyance. So are the sooves,‡ but I know no remedy for them. I was very sorry to hear of George Shufords§ death. When will the terrible and bloody history of that awfull field cease to be revealed to me. Every wk I hear of some friend who fell there. Truly the scourge of Civil War is awfull. We have felt it near two yrs and who in our broad land that is true to his country has not been a sufferer When will the [. . .] will this country have paid the terrible sacrifice of liberty. When will the angel of peace over this misery stricken country and speak peace and give it to our troubled country. Who would not welcome the glad appearance of his bright prospect. Every thing here is quiet. The two armies come far out—each other rec'd there may be a fight at any time but I don't think one probable. I delivered Dick Lees bundle to Ed Bobo who was going [. . .] to take to him with instruct care that if he did not see him to leave it [. . .] & Tollersons. He promised me to do it.

My love to Cousin Carrie. Tell her I can not attend her wedding until after the war ends & think she had better promenade her [. . .] to go long and help end it if she wants me there. Then tell father please to [. . .] my suspend in from John [. . .] and send [. . .] by Mr. Beard. Please send me some towels and a handkerchief also some [. . .] papers. Don't send the comforts until I write for them.

I am quite well. My love to all.

Write Soon

Yr affec Brother
L. P. Foster

L. P. FOSTER TO HIS MOTHER

Camp near Fredricksburg Dec 7th 1862

My Dear Mother,

I have been thawing my ink for some time, but find it a rough business. Have broke one vial. I never felt much colder weather than we now have. The ground

---

* *Life and Thought or Cherished Memories of Julia A. Parker Dyson* by E. Latimer. Dyson (1818–1852) was a teacher and writer.

† Probably *The Great Tribulation or Things Coming on the Earth* (1860), by John Cumming.

‡ The meaning of "souaves" and "sooves" is unclear. Perhaps he means salves.

§ George Shuford of Co. H in the 17th Mississippi Infantry was killed in action at Sharpsburg on September 17, 1862.

is covered with snow and froze perfectly hard. Went on picket day before yesterday evening. It was then snowing very fast. Went down on the river below Fredericksburg. My comp was on the reserve which was stationed at the house of an old woman who had little enough feeling to attempt to keep us out of her farm house but it was no use. We went in and piled down on her hay and slept finely until morning. The next morning I rose quite early every thing was white and the sun rise in the sheet of white to the east was very pretty. We built warm fires and spent the day pleasantly. Had a man told me before this war broke out that I could have endured at all what I endure with comfort I would have believed him a fool, a maniac or a columinator. I can not say that I have yet suffered in this war badly. Some from sickness and I feel gratefull for the fine health I now enjoy. I never enjoyed better health than I have since I returned to the army. When on picket we saw the yanky sentinels passing their lines in the snow without fire. Everything seems quiet. Gen'l McClellan and gov Leamore are said to be under arrest with charge of treason. It is the statement of a boy escaping from the yanky lines to genl Lee. Our box sent by your society and vicinity has at last reached us. We are very grateful to you all for the shirts, socks and drawers and appreciate the difficulties under which you labor. I will acknowledge the receit as soon as I can. I have nothing more to write. My love to all.

yr affec son

L. P. Foster

L. P. FOSTER TO HIS FATHER

Camp near Fredricksburg Dec 8th 1862

My Dear Father

This is another very cold morning. The ground still covered with snow and hard frozen. We are standing it very well but one man in my company W. J. McAbee* has pneumonia and I suppose he will be sent to the hospital this morning. He is a recruit and this weather is hard on him. You wrote me to send Bro. Tonys account of pay and clothing. We have been ordered to send the pay amount of all deceased members of our Company to the 2nd Auditors office, Richmond Va. Where they will be audited and await there yr call or the call of your attorney. I will send Bro. Tonys in a few days. All is quiet. Yr letter of Dec 1st has been rec'd and I am much obliged for your trouble about our shoes. I think the society had better withhold the comforts until I order them. [Since] it is not all certain that we are stationary. We may move from here at any time and the men could not carry comforts. Whenever I think we are settled for any length of time I will order them. Our men are now in very good condition as to shoes and clothes. We are much better as to blankets. Tell

---

* W. J. McAbee of Co. K, 3rd S.C.

mother please to send me two each of cotton socks, two worsted [. . .] if she can buy them. I find my wool socks sweat my feet too much. Nothing more to write. My love to all.

Yr affec son

L. P. Foster

P.S. Lt. Bearden says request you to go to Capt Cotes and get a pr of pants out of his trunk and send them if you have an opportunity

L. P. F.

Enclosed I send you a short acknowledgement of the receipt of the clothing sent by the soldiers aid Society at Philadelphia.* You may publish it if you think it appropriate. It may be too short but I was fearful of making it clumsy.

L. P. F.

L. P. Foster to His Mother

Camp near Fredricksburg Dec 10th 1862

My Dear Mother,

We moved our camp about 1 mile yesterday morning to this place to be more convenient to wood and were all day yesterday fixing up our shanty. We have it now quite comfortable. We have one log laid on the ground at our head and small poles the length of a man laid one end on this and the other on the ground. On these fine cedar brush and on these we spread our blankets, covering the whole with our oil cloths, placed on poles set over it slanting so as to trim the water. Imagine a large fire just in front and you have the hd qrs of comp (k). I am sitting on my valise writing to you. Jno Wofford† is frying some meat to get grease to make up some bread for breakfast. The others sitting around assisting in getting breakfast. The sun is just rising you see we rise early. Your letter of the 20th Nov. came last night. We have had but one case of small pox since I first wrote of it. That case came from the hospital and was sent back immediately on the appearance of the disease. I have no idea that it will spread. Have you received matting. You ask me if I would like to have a comfort. I suppose I can have one hauled. I wrote to you some time since, not to send the comforts until I ordered them. Our men can not carry them and can not get them hauled and I don't think we will stay here very long. I would be much obliged to you to send me one. I have already written for all that I wanted except a pr of pants and suppose you can not get the cloth to make them so will have to send to Richmond after a while for a pr.

I don't know whether uncle Jas has gone home or not. Gregg's Brigade is camped now in about 6 miles of us. Jacksons Corps I hear came in about one wk

---

* Philadelphia Baptist Church in Glenn Springs, South Carolina.

† Either John Henry Wofford or John Wesley Wofford of Co. K, 3rd S.C.

since.* I have seen Pickins message and think it very good. I have no hope of foreign intervention, but don't fear reconstruction. There is too much voting strength in the army to permit such a thing. I would prefer that our government would join any government known than again unite with the United States. I never could again bear willing allegiance to that government & sincerely hope I may never have it to do nor not [now] see what would make me do it.

I have written to Father to have me a pr of shoes of boots made. My shoes are very good yet. I wrote for a heavy vest which I need more than anything else.

Everything here is quiet. I am quite well. All my company well. We have very cold weather, but not quite so cold as we have had. The ground still pretty much covered with snow. We drew bacon last night. The third time since I came to the Regt. I hope we may draw it for a few days, but don't want it too long as it will give one Scurvy in less than two weeks. One who has had scurvy will like it very quick. Lt. Col Goodwin has just past riding and carrying his crutch. He can not walk. I suppose is merely on a visit to the army.

My love to all. Write soon

Yr affec Son
L. P. Foster

In mid-November, Gen. Ambrose Burnside received permission from Lincoln to move his army through Fredericksburg and capture the Confederate capital. His rapid advance soon slowed due in large part to logistical problems and by December 13th his army of approximately 120,000 faced a well-positioned army of somewhat more than half that size.

On the morning of December 13th, the Confederates were in strong defensive positions along Marye's Heights just to the west of the center of Fredericksburg with the front line of Confederate forces arrayed behind a stone wall along Telegraph Road at the base of Marye's Heights. Artillery and additional units were positioned on the Heights. Marye's House, located to the Confederate left, became a major battlefield landmark. Units of Longstreet's Corps extended and connected with Jackson's Corps, forming a long battle line stretching south along the heights above the Richmond, Fredericksburg, and Potomac Railroad Line. On the morning of December 13th, Kershaw's Brigade, including the 3rd S.C., was in defensive positions along the battle line next to Telegraph Road about ½ mile south of the Stone Wall.

Gen. Burnside opened the battle in mid-morning with a direct assault by William H. French's Division directly at the Confederate positions along the Stone Wall. This attack was repulsed and followed at 1:00 by a second attack by Gen. Winfield Hancock's brigades.

---

* Jackson's Corps arrived in Fredericksburg on December 1st.

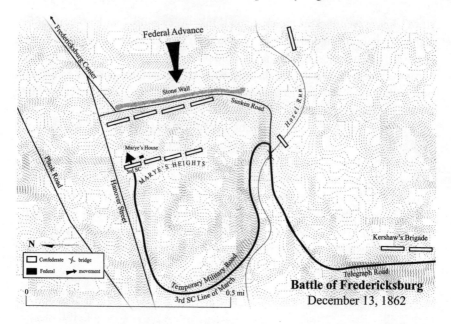

The Battle of Fredericksburg, December 13, 1862.

About an hour later Col. Nance received orders to reinforce Marye's Heights. The 3rd S.C. marched along Telegraph Road from their right flank position and crossed Hazel Run. They then followed a road recently built to facilitate troop movements behind Marye's Heights. The 3rd S.C. followed this new military road behind Marye's Heights and took a position behind the knoll just to the left of Marye's House.

The 3rd S.C. formed a battle line and marched over Marye's Heights to a position over knoll to the left and ahead of Marye's House. On this exposed position, the 3rd immediately took casualties. Col. Nance, recognizing the dangerous position his soldiers were in, directed their movement back to a more protected position in front of the Marye House. Officers and men continued to fall in the hail of bullets.*

In the first few minutes, Col. Nance, Lt. Co. Rutherford, and Maj. Maffett were severely wounded. Capt. William W. Hance fell, mortally wounded. Capt. John C. Summer fell with a mortal head wound. Capt. Lewis Perrin Foster fell, shot through the forehead.† Capt. Jonathan Nance commanded the regiment through the rest of the fight.‡ Fighting ended with the growing darkness. The 3rd S.C. advanced to new positions on the Stone Wall to wait out the freezing miserable night filled with the groans of the wounded and dying.

* Wyckoff, *Third South Carolina*, 86–93.
† Graydon, Graydon, and Davis, *McKissicks*, 176.
‡ Dickert, *History of Kershaw's Brigade*, 187.

Marye's House, Showing Rifle Pits, Fredericksburg, Virginia. Courtesy,
Library of Congress, Prints and Photographs Division, LC-USZ62–53709*

*Although Fredericksburg was a major Confederate victory, the Third South Caro-
lina paid heavily for its role in the battle, especially in losses of officers. The report of
casualties in McLaws's division identified the loss of five officers in the 3rd S.C.† Col.
Nance, in his December 24, 1862 report on his regiment's actions in the Battle of Fredericksburg, stated in part: "Capt. John C. Summer, a most successful officer; Capt. L.
Perrin Foster, an efficient, zealous, and conscientious officer; and Lieutenants [James]
Hollingsworth and [James C.] Hill, both young lieutenants of promise, were killed."*
*Marye's House was located on the left of the Confederate lines and faced the Fed-
eral advance towards the sunken road and the Stone Wall running at the base of this*

* James B. Gardner, photographer. "Fredericksburg, Va. Marye House, with Rifle Pits in
Front." Library of Congress, Prints and Photographs Division, Washington, D.C., Reproduction number LC-USZ62–53709. June 10, 2008.

† United States War Department, *War of The Rebellion: The Official Records of the Union
and Confederate Armies*, Series I, Vol. 21 (Washington, D.C.: Government Printing Office,
1888), 583.

hill, in the approximate position of the photographer. The 3rd S.C. approached the battle from the left, crossed behind Marye's House, and emerged on the battlefield on the right side of the house, as seen from the photographer's position. As they positioned themselves partway down on the right in a very exposed position, they came under intense Federal fire that killed many of the officers and enlisted men. Capt. Foster fell to the right front of the house. Col. Nance, although seriously wounded, continued to direct his regiment, moving his men to a less exposed position in front of the house.

On May 15, 1917, Albert Gibert Kennedy of Union, South Carolina, met with Thomas Hyatt, a surviving Civil War veteran who served in Co. K of the 3rd South Carolina. Kennedy recorded the following from that meeting:*

> Mr. G. Thomas Hyatt of Co. K 3rd S.C. Volunteers made the following state-ment May 5th, 1917.
>
> Mr. Hyatt said that he helped bury Captain L. Perrin Foster and also helped his father, Lt. Col. B. B. Foster take up his body when he came for it. Capt. Perrin Foster was shot in the head at the battle of Fredericksburg, Va. at the Brick House which his command was guarding a battery."
>
> Mr. Hyatt in the same conversation said that Co. "K" 3rd S.C.V. went from Sptg. To Cola. April 14th, 1861 with 96 men. At the close of the war, only 8 of the 96 original men returned with the company. A few were trans-ferred and not all killed.

Sallie Foster was visiting Lizzie Cothran at Millway in Abbeville District. Eunice wrote her about the death of their brother.

Dec. 19th 1862

Dear Sister,

I would fain put off writing this evening, but Mother bids me to write and tell you that Father is too unwell to go for you. He is going on to Va. as soon as he is able for the remains of our only Brother. Oh, Sister, Mother says get some of the relatives, Uncle Samuel[†] or someone to bring you home.

Poor Mother, this last blow is too much for her, and Father almost sinks under it. We know none of the particulars—we only know that both are now in heaven. I would that I were there. I cannot trust myself to write, I feel like shrieking now.

Come as soon as possible.

Sister Eunice

---

* Albert Gibert Kennedy, Sr. unpublished interview with George Thomas Hyatt and J. N. McArthur, May 5, 1917.

† Samuel Perrin.

I suppose there is no end to the ways that war inflicts pain. Mrs. John R. Little of Spartanburg, S.C. recalled after the war, "We had during the war a Ladies Aid Society. Mrs. B. B. Foster, whose husband was a colonel, was the president. I was the secretary. Mrs. Foster had two sons killed in the war. We sent boxes of clothing to her son, Captain Perrin Foster, in Virginia. As I was secretary, I wrote a letter with the box of clothing. He received the box and the letter and wrote me a beautiful letter. Before he could mail it he went into a battle and was killed. The letter was sent me and on its pages were spots of blood. It was read to the Society and his mother was present. His body was brought home and buried in the family burying ground near Spartanburg."*

CARRIE ZIMMERMAN TO SALLIE FOSTER

My Dear Sallie

How deeply do we sympathize with your family in your sad and crushing affliction! Truly the black cloud of sorrow has overshadowed your once happy household. May our Heavenly Father lift your hearts up to him and sanctify unto you this great sorrow. I know full well the agony of your loving hearts. I know what it is to be torn suddenly from those we dearly love, and I know full well the agony and struggle it costs to say, "Thy will O Lord be done." But who shall dare complain? The Lord reigneth without or against Him we can do nothing. Let us therefore in meekness and resignation bow to His decrees and gather consolation from its only true and unfailing source: faith in the blood of the Lamb. God has mercifully relieved your brother from many toils and troubles to come. He has been plucked from the contaminating influences of this vile and deceitful world, unbespotted and unsullied by vice or crime! Except his mere departure you and your family have nothing to lament for his translation is a gain to him which you may well envy but should not deplore! How sweet dear Sallie is your sorrow for both of your dear brothers to know that you mourn for yourselves and not for them. How many mothers have to give up their only child and how many have to mourn without hope! When I think of such sad cases I feel, dear Sallie, that our afflictions are light in comparison. My mother sends her kindest love and sympathy to your mother and says she never bows her head in prayer but what she remembers her afflictions. May God give you the comfort which you so much need dear Sallie for "vain is the help of man"! My sisters send much love and sympathy to you and your sisters and also to

---

* United Daughters of the Confederacy, South Carolina Division, *Recollections and Reminiscences 1861–1865 Through World War I, Vol. I* (South Carolina: S. C. Division, United Daughters of the Confederacy, 1990), 352.

your dear mother. Try and come to see us we would be so glad to have you spend a few days with us.

Yours most affectionately

Carrie Zimmerman

Rose [...]

Dec 26th 1862

JENNIE McGREGOR TO MRS. B. B. FOSTER

Columbia Jan 4th 1863

My Dear Mrs. Foster

You will no doubt be surprised at receiving a letter from me, as it has never been my pleasure to see you or even to exchange a word of conversation with any of your family save your noble brave son who has so recently fallen in the defence of our rights to liberties. God has seen fit in his all wise Providence to lay his afflicting hand heavily upon you during the year that has just passed. I know that you are one of His children. I trust His grace will be your great sufficiency in this your hour of deep afflictions. I am one of His professed disciples & feel that all His followers are my brothers & sisters in Christ. Our blessed Savior has told us to "weep with those who weep to rejoice with those that rejoice."* I feel it no common privilege to be permitted to mingle my tears with you over the bier of your dear Son who was one of my most honored & esteemed friends. It was my privilege to become acquainted with him while at Camp Johnston near our city & after he went to Virginia we carried on a friendly correspondence which culminates with his last letter to me written from Fredericksburg Nov 27th. Could you see this letter my dear friend no doubt could arise and your mind as to the devoted piety of your loved son. I feel that I have been permitted to enjoy an uncommon privilege in being one of his correspondents. I believe I am a better Christian from reading his pious letters. I could not believe that he had fallen when I first heard of his death & [...] not until I knew it to be so. I received a letter from Captain Douglass† who knew him, he says "Among the honored noble spirits who have fallen is Capt Foster" "He fell nobly doing his duty & urging his men on to meet the foe" His death in lamented by all who knew him." Weep not dear friend over your noble dead. He fell just when he would have wished to fall, if fall he must. He fills a patriot & a hero's grave & long long shall his memory be enshrined in the hearts of his country men & country women. His name shall be on the honored list of those heroes who have given their precious lives in behalf of Southern liberty & independence. Again you have much to comfort you in the blessed knowledge that your Son was

* Romans 12:15.

† Probably Captain James T. Douglass from Union County with the 5th S.C.

a true soldier of the cross of Christ. He is now a glorified spirit & with his noble brother who fell only a few short months ago is an inheritor of a crown of unfading glory. We know they can never return to us, but hence as consolation we can go to them in the language of another. You can say with reference to your lost loved ones. "Farewell saved spirit. Thou shalt ever be a star to guide one up to Heaven & thee." We will not weep for this! Thou are free. Thy tools and cares are over and thou art an angel of light and immortality! We will not weep for thee but for ourselves for the great loss we have sustained by thy death. We weep not as those without hope, for we hope to meet the on the "Shining shore" no more to part where "Soul springs to soul & heart united to heart."*

I heard that Col Foster had gone on to Richmond. I hope he has accomplished the object of his visit & that you have the comfort of having your dear Sons remains among you. I have never heard any of the particulars of his death and as he was a young man in whom I felt a deep interest & with whom I have had such pleasant intercourse. I naturally feel an anxiety to hear anything concerning him. I have never seen his equal. I have never before met with a young gentleman so pious, so sincere, so brave and noble in all respects. All his friends in Columbia feel that they in common with your afflicted family have sustained an irreparable loss, but we know that your loss is his everlasting gain. Try then dear friends tho' your hearts are bleeding over your severe loss try to say with God's servant of old, "Tho' He slay me yet will I trust in Him" Thy will oh God not mine be done" & with meek submission to God let the language of our hearts be "The Lord hath given "& the Lord hath taken away, blessed be the name of the Lord." May His grace be sufficient for you all in this trying hour is the prayer of your sympathizing

The unknown friend.
Jennie G. McGregor

Columbia, S.C.

My kind regards to your husband & all of your family. Tell Miss Sallie I know her by reputation & will be delighted to know her personally. Ask her to write to me when she can trust her feelings to do so. I would have addressed this to her but thought I ought to write to the Mother of my dear & lamented friend first.

J. G. McGregor

JENNIE McGREGOR TO MRS. B. B. FOSTER

Columbia Feb 17th 1863

My very dear Friend,

Your sweet kind letter to me was received a few days since, and was read by me with feelings that words unclear fail to express. How thankful I feel to be assured by

---

* From "Repose in Faith" by E. Bulwer Lytton.

you that my letter was a source of comfort to you! It is a command of our blessed Lord "to rejoice with those who rejoice & to weep with those that weep."* I delight to share the happiness of my friends nor do I find less satisfaction in sharing, as far as I can, their sorrows. Thank God that he has so constituted me!

You said in your letter to me my dear friend that you "could not ask me to write to you." Why not! If my feeble efforts to comfort you have been blessed with success and my letters have been so much appreciated by you believe me it will be a great source of pleasure and gratification to write to you as often as I can. Do not for a moment think it would be any but a delightful task for me to do! I know it must have been a trial to you to write to me about your dear sons. I thank you for your kindness. Oh! What [. . .] patriots have you given to your country! I did not know your younger son but read his obituary in the Southern Guardian.† He must have been a treasure to you. God has only removed your dear son to that better home dear Friend and oh! What a strong link have you made to him, your spirit to the heavenly world! Your dear ones are only asleep in Jesus. Their precious dust alone remains on earth. Their glorified spirits are happy with God and one no doubt hovering around the dear ones at home very very often for I believe that God permits the spirits of loved ones who have passed from earth away to a better world to be ministering spirits to the loved ones on earth. No doubt they know what is transpiring below & no doubt your dear angel sons would beseech you not to grieve too much for them, could they speak to mortals with their spirits voices! I have to think this, I have to think that God's children in earth, tho' bittered by earthly cares and earthly sorrows can with the eye of faith look away from scenes of earth and can hold sweet converse with their dear departed ones. Some might call such a theory visionary. Is it visionary to you dear Friend? I think not and I have written thus because I believe your nervousness in your letter to me accord such for you said you were comforted with the thought that your dear son "Perrin" would, could he see you grieving at his body say to you "Oh! Mother dear master don't take my leaving you so hard"! Then listen to the whisperings of your angel sons and be comforted dear Friend. They are happy with God in heaven and are waiting the arrival of their loved ones on the "shining shore." Do you not thank your God, that He gave you strength and grace to bring you dear sons up in the "nurture and admonition of the Lord." Oh! It was indeed a hard trial to give them up though you were assured that your loss was their eternal gain but [. . .] would it have been if they had had no hope in Christ! Let me quote a verse which I have found in the Charleston Courier in an obituary. It will be comforting to you because it [is] all true concerning your dear departed ones.

---

* Romans 12:15.
† *The Daily Southern Guardian*, a Columbia, South Carolina, newspaper.

"Think oh ye who fondly languish
O'er the grave of those you love
While your bosom throbs with anguish
They are singing hymns above
While your silent steps are straying
Lonely thro' nights deepening shade
Glory's brightest beams are playing
Round the happy Christian's head
Light and peace at once desiring
From the hand of God must heigh
In his glorious presence living
They shall never never die
Cease then mourners cease to lament
O'er the graves of those you love
Pain and death, and night and anguish
Enter not the world alone"!

I send you also a few lines of my own composition which I could not refrain from putting on paper and sending to you as they were my thoughts in reading the beautiful passages of scripture from which your dear sons funeral sermon was preached.

"Let me die the death of the righteous"* and may my last end be like his! That I may with his dear parents and sisters meet him in heaven.

My kind regards to your husband and my love to your daughters. Nothing would give me more pleasure than to gain the acquaintance of your whole family. May the comforts of God's spirit be vouchsafed to you and all your afflicted family in the prayers of your sincere and sympathetic friend.

Jennie G. McGregor

Perrin Foster's body was brought back to Spartanburg and is in the family graveyard behind the old Foster home. Tony Foster never quite made it home. He rests in Hollywood Cemetery in Richmond.† A monument to both sons was placed at Perrin's grave. The inscription reads, "To live in hearts one leaves behind is not to die."

---

* Num. 23:10.
† Graydon, Graydon, and Davis, *McKissicks*, 175.

Epilogue

Combat was over for the immediate Foster family, but the war ran its course. B. B. Foster joined the Home Guard, a militia of older men and others who were not suitable for military service. These Home Guard units provided protection and civil order for their local communities. Foster managed his struggling plantation and served as a representative from Spartanburg to the S.C. state legislature from 1864 to 1865.* His wife, Mary Ann, was president of the Ladies Aid Society in Spartanburg,† a group that made clothes and food boxes for soldiers on the front.

The few remaining Foster family wartime letters attest to their worry and grief as the war claimed more and more casualties.

Sallie Foster wrote to her sister Jenny on May 28, 1863 saying, "Bennie Chiles came home last night, he is severely wounded in the breast. A prayer book saved his life. I am going up to see him today and will write more particularly about him." Benjamin Chiles, a relative, was in Company B of Orr's Regiment. He was apparently wounded at Chancellorsville on May 1–3, 1863.

Sallie's letter continues, "Cousin Jimmie Cothran is wounded in the face and they are looking for him home." Lt. James S. Cothran of Company B in Orr's Regiment was also wounded at Chancellorsville.

Chancellorsville took the life of Col. James Monroe Perrin of Orr's Regiment in Greggs Brigade. He was B. B. Foster's brother-in-law. Thomas Samuel Perrin, Sallie Foster's cousin, was also killed at Chancellorsville, serving in the same regiment. The impact of their deaths are felt in the following letter.

Col. Oliver E. Edwards had very close ties to his Foster cousins, especially Sallie. On May 3, at Chancellorsville, he assumed command after General McGowan was wounded leading the capture of Union breastworks. During a countercharge, Edwards was walking on the breastworks encouraging the brigade when he was wounded.‡ His wife, Jane Gary Edwards, attempted to get him back to his Spartanburg home, but he weakened on the journey, was taken off the train in

* Landrum, *History of Spartanburg County*, 649.

† United Daughters of the Confederacy, *Recollections*, 352.

‡ H. P. Griffith, *The Life and Times of Rev. John G. Landrum* (Philadelphia: H. B. Garner, 1885), 89.

Goldsboro, North Carolina, and died there in his wife's care on June 21, 1863.*
Word of Edwards's death had not made its way to Glenn Springs at the time of the
following letter.

SALLIE FOSTER TO HER COUSIN, ELIZABETH COTHRAN

Glenn Springs
June 22nd [1863]

Little did I think, my dearest Lizzie, when your kind letter was so joyfully received
that it would remain unanswered until now. Really I feel badly about this delay
and regret very much having been unable to reply sooner, but I have had company
and various causes have prevented my doing so, though let me assure you my dear
Lizzie, often, very often you are the subject of my thoughts, and each day closes
with the ungratified wish that my home was nearer yours. The greatest pleasure I
have now is receiving your letters and it would be such a pleasure and comfort if I
could only see you frequently, but I trust this separation will soon be at an end, for
I hope to welcome you soon to my own dear home, even the thought of this makes
my heart bound with pleasure. Mother told me that you said you would be up the
last of the summer, so don't put it off and come as soon as possible. Father and
Mother arrived home safely Saturday morning after they left Abbeville and you may
be sure I was delighted to see them. Jennie and I did finely while they were away.

Troubles indeed, my dear Lizzie, come not singly, but crowd up on one—our
tears for one loved one are scarcely dry before there is another to weep for. There
were few such men as Uncle James, so noble and patriotic and his last moments will
testify that his walk was none other than that of a pure Christian. It is hard, very
hard to give up those we do dearly love, and I feel that his loss is irreparable. Had
his life been spared, what a comfort he would have been to his wife and dear little
children. But twas not thus, God gave [. . .] and sealed his fate, Heaven—and oh!
is it not consoling that he is now dwelling in the home of the pure and blest and
that his trials are forever at an end.

Poor Tom, his career was short and tis very sad to think one so very young
should have been made so early a tenant of the tomb.† The last battle of Fredricksburg brought so vividly the remembrance the first great battle there when at one
blow was withered all that seemed to brighten my pathway and created within my
heart an aching void that time nor change can ever fill. There is always so much
connected with victory to make one feel sad and melancholy for so many are left
to mourn the departure of precious ones. When I see how hard our beloved country struggles for independence, and think how much we have suffered and how

* Landrum, *History of Spartanburg County*, 513.
† Thomas Samuel Perrin of the 1st S.C. Rifles (Orr's Brigade) was killed at Chancellorsville.

cruelly and outrageously the Yankees have treated our ladies, their steps marked by cruelty and desolation, I feel like taking the sword that my dear brothers can no longer wield and defend my country to the last. This feeling, dear Lizzie, may be wrong, but I cant help it. I feel very anxious indeed about the fate of Vicksburg. The Yankees seem determined to take the place, but our men seem equally determined to defend to the last and I don't believe Vicksburg will fall. I liked Pemberton's address to his army very much. I am very sorry Tom* did not succeed in getting an office in the war department, for I don't believe he is able to endure the hardships of camp now.

Anna Bobo came down to see me last week, returned to the village Saturday. Howard Bobo† expects to join the army next month. They are making up his clothes. His mother will not consent to his being mustered into the service, for he will not be seventeen (17) until next September, but is willing for him to try it awhile.

We have any quantity of elegant cherries. I wish you were here to help us eat them. Now if sugar was not so scarce, what nice preserves I could make, but as it is don't expect to have any.

We have had a great deal of rain lately, which I fear has injured the wheat to some extent. The crops generally up here are looking finely. Mother's garden is late and I think good, though we are having all the vegetables now except tomatoes and okra, but I am almost ashamed to tell you about our garden when Auntie's is so far ahead of us.

Mr. Anderson opened the hotel at Glenn Springs Saturday at $3.00 per day. He has three or four boarders.

Col. Edwards is improving, it is thought now that he will recover. He is at Goldsboro, N.C. at Cousin Anna Leitner Davis‡—he applied for a furlough, and was refused but succeeded in getting a transfer to Columbia and I suppose is trying to get there. It will be a long time before he can return to the army, and I think it an injustice to keep him in the hospital. How is Cousin Wade getting? I feel anxious about him and trust he may be entirely restored.

Do, my dear Lizzie, write to me very soon, for I am getting terribly anxious to hear from you. Please don't retaliate, but be a good child and write to me soon. Excuse bad writing and these scraps of paper. I am entirely out of letter paper. I am afraid you will be troubled to decipher the crossed part.

* Sergeant Thomas P. Quarles was in Co. C of the 7th S.C.

† Howard S. Bobo, Co. C of the 13th S.C. He was killed in action on Aug. 16, 1864 in the defense of Petersburg and Richmond.

‡ Col. B. B. Foster's sister, Elizabeth, was married to E. C. Leitner. Anna Leitner Davis was probably his sister.

My best love to Auntie and accept the love of your devoted cousin—Mother sends love to you & Auntie.

Sallie A. Foster

The following letter describes Oliver Edwards's funeral.

SALLIE FOSTER TO HER COUSIN, ELIZABETH COTHRAN

Glenn Springs
July 2nd [1863]

How shall I attempt to express thanks to my dearest and best cousin for replying so soon to my very poor letter, when I had [. . .] receive your letter yesterday, although you did not scold me, or say to me one harsh word, still your kindness in writing to me and kind letter was a sufficient rebuke.

This has been rather a busy week with me, have been trying to finish up most of the sewing before the heat sets in, when we feel like doing nothing but sleeping, eating, etc., etc. By the by, has not this been a delightful summer? We have not had any very warm weather. For the last two weeks the weather has been cool, damp, showery and some hard rains, which we hope has not injured the wheat, but fear it has, for tis all in the field, though cut. Never before this year have I taken such an interest in the crops and provisions generally, for the salvation of our country depends so much upon a sufficient supply of provisions. I still feel anxious about the fate of Vicksburg, though have felt confident all the while that victory would be ours. And I feel very anxious to know where our noble Lee's [. . .] remain ignorant as to his movements until they are carried out or until Lee chooses to divulge them. It is so strange how his movements are kept so secret. It is one of the greatest mysteries of the day, not even the prying editors can definitely locate him, but enough.

It would be so much better for Tommie Quarles if he could get a position in the War Department and I earnestly hope he will succeed in doing so. What has become of Jimmie Quarles?* Was he in the cavalry fight recently where Co. Butler was wounded?†

We regret the death of Col. Edwards exceedingly and we will long miss him for he was a kind, good cousin and we all loved him. He lived a pious devoted Christian life and except his mere departure we have nothing to lament for his transition is his eternal gain, which we may well envy. He bid adieu to this deceitful world, unspotted and unsullied by vice or crime. The Baptist Church at Spartanburg has truly lost one of its best members for he was the pillar of that church. It makes me

---

* James W. Quarles was in Co. I of the 2nd Regiment, S.C. Cavalry, Hampton's Legion.

† Col. Matthew Calbraith Butler commanded the 2nd Regiment, S.C. Cavalry, Hampton's Legion. On June 9, 1863 he was wounded at the Battle of Brandy Station, losing a foot.

sad to think of that church now, for I can safely say there is not a member that can take his place. His death was unexpected to us for all the time we had been hearing such favourable reports. All the attention and honor that could be paid to anyone, Cousin Oliver's remains received. He was buried in the village graveyard the 25th of last month with Masonic and military honors. We all went up to the funeral, and burial, and I have never seen such a large assemblage of people. Col. Edwards' wife seems almost crushed, it is heart-rending to hear her sighs and moans. I do feel so sorry for her. Witnessing such a scene of distress brought so vividly to remembrance my own great sorrow, but I thank God that I mourn not as those without hope.

I am glad that Cousin Wade is improving. Tell him I would and all of us would be glad to have him and family pay us a visit, perhaps breathing our fresh mountain air would be beneficial. I am more than willing to do anything in my power to alleviate his suffering.*

Your paying me that visit is uppermost in my thoughts. Oh, I do, Cousin Lizzie, think of it so much and you and Auntie must be sure and come.

Mother sends best love to Auntie and yourself and says you must be certain and come. Father, I know, would send many messages about it if he were here, but he spends a large part of his time at the plantation.

As regards Belle's being engaged to John Watts, it is no more than I expected when she went to Laurens and was rather surprised that her Father would allow her to go while J.W. was at home.

There are about ten or twelve boarders at Glenns and one cabin recently occupied. I know very little about the place now for I very seldom ever visit the place.

It is reported up here that Mr. Seyman (the Rev. sir teaching at Liberty Hill) is engaged to be married to Miss Maggie Walker of Cedar Springs, who is a graduate of Limestone and took first honor. I cant tell you how much of this is true or how much false. I only tell you what I heard. Do, my dear Lizzie, excuse this mixed up poor letter and write to me very soon.

My love to inquiring relatives.

Mother joins me in sending love to you and Auntie.

As ever, your devoted cousin
S. A. F.

---

* Capt. Wade Elephare Cothran of Co. C, 7th SCV was wounded in both thighs at Maryland Heights in 1862. He was discharged from the service at nearby Harpers Ferry; apparently, he was still recovering from his wounds. H. T. Cook, *The Hard Labor Section* (South Carolina Magazine of Ancestral Research, 1993), 44; Glen Allen Swain, Sr., *The Bloody Seventh* (Wilmington, N.C.: Broadfoot Publishing, 2014), 475.

The war ended in April 1865 and the occupation of the Confederacy by the Federals began. The early months of the occupation were a period of uncertainty and economic insecurity; homes were pillaged by lawless individuals including Federal soldiers. A letter from Mary Eunice Perrin Harrison to Sallie Foster on July 4, 1865, describes Eunice's fear and helplessness when her home was pillaged by Federal soldiers; the horses were taken, and the house was set on fire in an attempt to force the disclosure of hidden silver and gold.*

In a letter dated July 10, 1865, Ann Beaufort Sims wrote to Harriet Palmer that her sister, Leora (Babe) Sims, had recently left to spend the summer with the Fosters in Spartanburg.† Lewis Perrin frequently visited with the Sims family while his regiment was organizing in Columbia and he corresponded with Babe Sims while in Virginia. In a subsequent letter, dated November 3, 1865, Sims offers insight into the Foster family during this period. Three years after the deaths of her sons, and now preparing for Sallie Foster's upcoming marriage to Isaac Going McKissick, Mary Ann Foster was described as depressed.‡

Sarah (Sallie) was married on September 28, 1865 to Col. Isaac Going McKissick. McKissick was a Colonel in the Seventh South Carolina Calvary Regiment and was twice wounded, leading charges at Williamsburg and Cold Harbor.§ He had been the Clerk of Court of Union County before the war, but was not allowed to seek public office under the rules of surrender.

Sarah was unable to purchase wedding clothes, so she created a wedding suit from her fiancé's gray, Confederate uniform. For years her friends thought that the suit had been storebought. She bore her husband eight children; four died in infancy and she raised four to adulthood.¶

Foster's future son-in-law and first captain of the 3rd S.C., Benjamin Kennedy, had left the regiment in May of 1862, no longer wanting to serve as an officer. He joined the 7th Regiment, S.C. Reserves, under Col. William Blackburn Wilson in 1862 and was the acting adjutant for several months. The reserves were called up for duty from Nov. 6, 1862, to Feb. 11, 1863, serving at Mt. Pleasant, South Carolina. On February 20, 1864, Kennedy enlisted as a private in Company A of the 18th S.C. Infantry a few days before the 18th was sent to Florida to reinforce Confederate units protecting that major source of food supplies. In May 1864, the 18th was transferred to the Petersburg trenches and was near the center of the mine explosion at the Crater. At least

---

* Harrison, *Thomas Chiles Perrin*, 21–23.

† Towles, *World Turned Upside Down*, 477.

‡ Towles, *World Turned Upside Down*, 490.

§ Graydon, Graydon, and Davis, *McKissicks*, 18–24.

¶ Graydon, Graydon, and Davis, *McKissicks*, 37.

Col. Barham Bobo Foster during the years he was living in
Jonesville, South Carolina. From the editor's collection.

twenty-four soldiers in his company were killed in the explosion. Kennedy nearly
lost his life there.*

*Because he owned a horse, Kennedy was transferred to the 5th. S.C. Cavalry on
November 15, 1864. He served with Gen. Joe Johnston through the remainder of the*

---

* "Eighteenth South Carolina Infantry, Company A, Union County, S.C." http://freepages
.genealogy.rootsweb.com/~york/18thSCV/A.html (accessed May 30, 2005).

war; fought in the last major engagement of the war in Bentonville, North Carolina; and surrendered with Johnston's forces at Hillsboro, North Carolina, on April 28, 1865.

Eunice Foster married Captain Benjamin Kennedy on October 26, 1869, and went to live on the Kennedy farm near Jonesville, South Carolina. They had seven children over the next seventeen years.

Jane Eliza (Jennie) Foster married James Andrew Thompson on December 21, 1871. The Thomsons farmed in Jonesville and Pacolet in South Carolina.

The Foster family immediately lost a substantial portion of their wealth with emancipation. After the war, the South Carolina Reconstruction government raised taxes on land, and all over the state, lands were sold at auction to raise money for the new land taxes. * *B. B. Foster was forced to declare bankruptcy on February 28, 1868. Foster lost his home, property, and all his possessions including livestock, horses, carriages, and furniture to the bankruptcy auctioneer to pay his taxes. His daughter, Eunice, was saddened by and always regretted the sale of Dinah, her Father's parade horse, in the tax auction. She never reconciled with the man who bought Dinah.*† *Foster's bankruptcy was declared in Final Discharge on January 13, 1870.*‡

In 1867 Barham Bobo Foster moved to Jonesville, between Spartanburg and Union, and set up a grocery and dry goods business. Foster operated the merchandise business until 1884,§ *but it eventually failed. Lacking money at one point, he sent his gold watch to a man in Philadelphia to whom he was indebted. The watch was returned with the message that the creditor would not take a man's watch.*¶

Jonesville, South Carolina, was incorporated in 1876, ** *and the town organized into a town council, four aldermen, and an intendent or mayor.*†† *Barham Bobo Foster, a temperance advocate as "the leader of the dry ticket" was elected the town's first mayor.*‡‡ *Over the years, Foster served in other government functions. In 1877*

---

* Edgar, *South Carolina*, 394.

† Albert Gibert Kennedy III, unpublished interview with Barham Foster Kennedy II, August 24, 2003, concerning conversations he had with his father, Albert Gibert Kennedy, Sr., Barham Bobo Foster's grandson.

‡ "Final Discharge of Bankruptcy" document in possession of A. Gibert Kennedy, III of Aiken, South Carolina. May 30, 2005.

§ Jesse Calvert III, *History of Jonesville* (publisher and date not recorded. From internal evidence, the history was published about 1970), 5; Dickert, *History of Kershaw's Brigade*, 101.

¶ Albert Gibert Kennedy III, unpublished interview with Barham Foster Kennedy II, August 24, 2003, concerning conversations he had with his father, Albert Gibert Kennedy Sr., Barham Bobo Foster's grandson.

** Allen Charles states the incorporation date as 1876; Calvert claims 1878.

†† Calvert, *History of Jonesville*, 4.

‡‡ Allan D. Charles, *The Narrative History of Union County South Carolina* (Spartanburg, S. C.: Reprint, 1987), 276.

Advertising Poster from B. B. Foster's store. From the editor's collection.

*Foster was a trial justice for the state of South Carolina; he was the Union County treasurer for many years.**

Foster was devoted to the Christian faith, and he was the prime mover in building the Jonesville Baptist Church in 1876. The church was built in six weeks and was dedicated by the Reverend J. G. Landrum, a lifelong friend of B. B. Foster. Foster and his wife pledged as charter members, and Foster was chosen as a deacon along with Thomas Belue and H. G. Coleman. Reverend George Anderson from West Springs was the first pastor. He served until 1881.†

On October 29, 1886, B. B. Foster lost his wife, Mary Ann. The night before her death, she was receiving an overnight visit from her daughter, Sallie, and her husband, Isaac McKissick. Mary Ann Foster went to bed in apparent health. At about four o'clock in the morning, B. B. Foster awoke to hear her coughing, as if strangling. He called his daughter in to help, but Mary Ann took only a few breaths after Sallie got to her bedside. The newspaper reported, "A mother in Israel has fallen."‡

On June 6, 1894, Eunice Foster's husband, Benjamin Kennedy, died in his home in Jonesville after an illness of two weeks. He was buried at Fair Forest Cemetery in Union County, South Carolina, leaving behind Eunice and seven children. The family's struggle to continue to operate the farm is evident in Eunice's letter of July 26. Her

* Based on papers in personal possession of A. G. Kennedy and from the McKissick Papers in the South Carolina Caroliniana Library. Dickert, *History of Kershaw's Brigade*, 101.

† Calvert, *History of Jonesville*, 12–13.

‡ These details come from a newspaper obituary clipping. The name of the newspaper and date were not preserved. The clipping is in the possession of the editor.

Mary Ann Perrin Foster. From the editor's collection.

sons Arthur Bienaime and Barham Foster (Banny) were twenty-one and seventeen years old, respectively, when they had to assume responsibility for providing for the family by successfully operating the farm.

EUNICE FOSTER KENNEDY TO HER FATHER, B. B. FOSTER

Home
July 26 [1894]

My Dear Father,

I have been waiting for every body to be well again before writing to you, but it seems that is not to be soon. So I'll write, for you will be anxious anyway. I was sick for two weeks with dysintery don't know when I ever suffered more; before I felt able to write Banny* broke down, from overwork, the Dr. said & when he got up May took sick.† She has what the Dr. says is known as walking typhoid fever. does not seem to be much sick but has a slight continuous fever. She has been sick about nine days is not closely confined to bed, but keeps one always anxious. If the covers ever get able to send off I'd be so thankful. The others were all up and going to church. Mr. Senish is having a protracted meeting at Sulphur [. . .] to keep but Arthur. Banny was elected deacon in his father's place last Saturday, will be ordained this meeting.‡ Wish you could see it. Andrew was elected at the same time. Jennie & Bess have been chilling, but both are attending the meeting. I have not seen Jennie but once since you left. Andrew called a few moments on his way from town but did not come in the house.

The boys have a fine crop. Dr. Littlejohn says he never saw a finer prospect for corn than they have on the bottoms. Father, he has been so nice to me, he comes over generally to tell me not to run the estate and ministered on, said it was a needless expense & as he was the only one interested he would never press us, but always be glad to help the crop if he could. We all acknowledged Banny as man of the farming interest, even Arthur does not issue orders without first consulting Banny & he seems to manage well and gets on pleasantly with the hands. Arthur is generaly our ho[u]sing agent & does the hard work of the concern. They all work harmoniously & well. They have lain by the corn & are waiting for the ground to get dry enough to put the center furrow to the cotton & plow the peas which will finish the laying by. Since taking the stumps and racks off the hay earned money for the mower. They have planted about eight acres in peas. They have made the orchard pig right & cord high & we have a fine lot of pigs & lots of nuts to feed them on.

Arthur has an offer of $25.00 each for the corn mill stones & spindle & wants to take it as he needs the money much wishes to settle with his hands whose times expired. Capt. K always said he intended to sell them & buy a better set if he ever rebuilt the mill.§ I advised Arthur to see Mr. Harper & ask him what they were worth. We need the money badly right now. I wrote & asked Eddie to lend it to me until fall, but he could not spare it so I know of no better way than to sell the stones.

* Barham Foster Kennedy (1876–1938), son of Eunice and Benjamin Kennedy, nicknamed Banny; he was seventeen years old at the time.

† Mary (May) Perrin Kennedy (1871–1954), daughter of Eunice and Benjamin Kennedy preferred to be called May.

‡ Benjamin Kennedy served as a Deacon at Sulphur Springs Baptist Church for many years. When he died suddenly, Banny assumed his Father's church leadership role.

§ Benjamin Kennedy ran a corn mill near his family home outside of Jonesville, South Carolina. By the time of his death, he had apparently ceased active mill operations and was considering refurbishing the mill. A painting of the mill can be seen on page 233 of Albert M. Hillhouse's *Pierre Gibert, French Huguenot, His Background and Descendants.*

Eunice Foster Kennedy. From the editor's collection.

Mr. Booth helped Mr. Humphries in a meeting at Jonesville last week, they had a good meeting & among the others Tom Coleman joined. I do pray it is the beginning of a better life for him. Sandys wife is very bad with typhoid fever & Sandy has the poorest crop he ever had.

May sends love & says tell you she doesn't think she is much sick.

What will it cost to send her to Cedar Mountain?* How could we go through the country, via Hendersonville or in Greenville? Dr. thinks a trip through the country as soon as she could stand it would get her & Banny both up.

* At this period, B. B. Foster was staying at Cedar Mountain, North Carolina, located near present day Caesar's Head State Park in South Carolina. His directions, written on the back of the envelope said, "Let them go to Elijah Wrights first day. Then to Greenville from there to mountain fifteen miles above Greenville. Then to Cedar Mountain 16 miles. They will strike the Jones Gap turn pike. Have the buggy harness runs and holding back straps made strong."

Sarah Agnes (Sallie) Foster McKissick in De Land, Florida,
March 9, 1916. From the editor's collection.

I hope you are improving & having a good time generally. Tell sister I'll write her a long letter soon & try to repay for those she has written me. I hope she is getting strong & well. I am glad to think you all are so pleasantly situated. I have not written a letter, save one to Eddie since you left & I have a pile to answer, friends have been kind to remember me.

I think I've written you all the home news & I have to go off the place to learn any other.

With a heart full of love.

Your stricken
Daughter

B. B. Foster never seemed to look back with regret on his decision to vote for secession, despite the tremendous personal cost to himself and his family. Today, nearly 150 years of history shape our perception of the United States as a single entity. The Foster family is an example of the people who remained devoted and loyal to their state, and whose devotion was given to the Confederacy.

Rion McKissick, son of Sallie Foster and Isaac Going McKissick, grandson of Lt. Col. Foster, and a former president of the University of South Carolina, described his memory of his grandfather in Men and Women of South Carolina *in 1948:*

> *The Confederacy was never forgotten in our home. My father and maternal grandfather Foster had been lieutenant-colonels respectively of cavalry and infantry. The former had a brother and the latter two sons killed in battle. The old men almost every night after supper sat opposite each other by the fire and talked about the war, never tiring of the subject. My grandfather Foster was a signer of the Ordinance of Secession from Spartanburg county. Pictures, some of them Currier and Ives prints, of Lee, Jackson, Johnston, Preston Brooks, John C., Breckenridge, and others, hung from the walls in several rooms. When my father was made a brigadier-general of the United Confederate Veterans he chose his official staff with the utmost care. He read the list to my mother who emphatically disapproved of the habits of one man, and said so. My father replied, "But Sally, he was a good, true soldier." For him that settled it.**

In his later years, Foster went to live with his daughter, Sarah McKissick in Union. He joined the Baptist Church in Union and represented that church at every association and union meeting.†

In 1895, B. B. Foster suffered a paralyzing stroke. In June 1897, while visiting his daughter Eunice Kennedy, he suffered a second stroke of paralysis and lingered until June 9. He was buried at the old Fair Forest cemetery in Union near the grave of his son-in-law Benjamin Kennedy who preceded him in death by three years. At the twilight funeral‡ in a quiet country graveyard, the Reverend A. A. James,§ a fellow Confederate soldier, spoke, "The descendents of this grand old man ought to catch the inspiration of this moment. His greatest loyalty to the South and his faith in the hereafter was that he never murmured, but bore with marvelous fortitude the terrible blow

---

* Rion McKissick, *Men and Women of South Carolina* (Columbia: University of South Carolina Press, 1948), 38.

† Landrum, *History of Spartanburg County*, 433.

‡ Eunice Kennedy marked Romans 3:10 in B. B. Foster's Bible as the text used in the preaching at Foster's funeral. The verse is "As it is written, there is none righteous, no not one."

§ Rev. A. A. James was chaplain of the 18th S.C. Infantry.

Col. B. B. Foster in old age. From the editor's collection.

that came to him when his two children gave up their lives for the cause for which he had fought and lost everything but honor. No greater page of honor did he ever wish or crave than that it should be known that he was a Confederate soldier, and that he gave his all to save his State."

Looking back on these people through the lens of our early 21st century beliefs and attitudes, it is easy and, perhaps, tempting to judge them; to judge the wisdom or foolishness of their actions; to judge the morality of their lives as slaveholders. Despite

* Landrum, *History of Spartanburg County*, 434.

their faults, they left a legacy of letters that are a testament to their resilience, sense of duty, and courage. They lost friends and family on the battlefield. They fought and died for a cause they believed in.

Following the Civil War, my ancestors rebuilt their lives at a time in life when people typically retire. Their sons were killed, but the daughters married and had families, raising children who grew up to become successful doctors, lawyers, judges, captains of the textile industry, professors, a president of the University of South Carolina, farmers, ministers, engineers, and businessmen.

These people live on in the hearts of those they left behind.

BIBLIOGRAPHY

Government Documents

Brady-Handy Collection. *"Centreville, Va. Confederate Winter Quarters."* Library of Congress, Prints and Photographs Division, Washington, D.C., Reproduction number LC-DIG-ppmsca-32991. January 24, 2017.

Barnard, George N., photographer. *"Centreville, Va. Confederate Winter Quarters South View."* Library of Congress, Prints and Photographs Division, Washington, D.C., Reproduction number LC-B817–7212. January 24, 2017.

Barnard, George N., photographer. *"Centreville, Va. Fort on the heights, with Quaker guns."* Library of Congress, Prints and Photographs Division, Washington, D.C., Reproduction number LC-B811–334A. January 24, 2017.

Barnard, George N., photographer. *"Manassas, Va. Orange and Alexandria Rail Road wrecked by retreating Confederates."* Library of Congress, Prints and Photographs Division, Washington, D.C., Reproduction number LC-B817–7197. June 10, 2008.

Gardner, James B., photographer. *"Fredericksburg, Va. Marye House, with Rifle Pits in Front."* Library of Congress, Prints and Photographs Division, Washington, D.C., Reproduction number LC-USZ62–53709. June 10, 2008.

Gibson, James F., photographer. *"Savage Station, Va. Field Hospital after the battle of June 27th."* Library of Congress, Prints and Photographs Division, Washington, D.C., Reproduction number LC-B811–491. June 10, 2008.

Archival Sources

Foster, Lewis Perrin, *Letter to Mrs. Barham Bobo Foster dated September 14, 1861* (South Caroliniana Library, James Rion McKissick Collection, P Box 1).

South Carolina Archives, "Commissioned Officers, Present and Absent Accounted for by Name," of Company K, 3rd Regiment for the Month of May, 1862, Columbia, S.C.

South Carolina Archives, "Confederate Archives, Chapter 1, File No. 81, page 473," Columbia, S.C.

Articles

Chadwick, Thomas W., Ed., "The Diary of Samuel Edward Burges, 1860–1862," *The South Carolina Historical and Genealogical Magazine*, LXVIII, no. 1, January (1947).

Wooster, Ralph, "Membership of the South Carolina Secession Convention." *The South Carolina Historical Magazine*, LV (1954).

Books

Calvert, Jesse, III. *History of Jonesville*. (Publisher and date not recorded; from internal evidence, the history was published about 1970.)

Catton, Bruce. *Never Call Retreat*. Garden City, N.Y.: Doubleday, 1965.

Catton, Bruce. *Terrible Swift Sword*. Garden City, N.Y.: Doubleday, 1963.

Cauthen, Charles Edward. *South Carolina Goes to War 1860–1865*. Columbia: University of South Carolina Press, 2005.

Charles, Allan D. *The Narrative History of Union County South Carolina*. Spartanburg, S.C.: Reprint Company, 1987.

Cothran, Thomas Perrin. *The Perrin Family*. Greenville, S. C.: Privately printed by the Peace Printing Company, 1924.

Davis, Burke. *Jeb Stuart, The Last Cavalier*. New York: Bonanza, 1957.

Davis, William C. *Battle at Bull Run*. Garden City, N.Y.: Doubleday, 1977.

Dickert, August D. *History of Kershaw's Brigade*. Newberry, S.C., n.p., 1899; reprint, Dayton: Morningside Press, 1988.

Edgar, Walter. *South Carolina, A History*. Columbia: University of South Carolina Press, 1998.

Eelman, Bruce W. *Enterpreneurs in the Southern Upcountry*. Athens: University of Georgia Press, 2008.

Everson, Guy R. and Edward W. Simpson, Jr. *Far, Far from Home*. New York: Oxford University Press, 1994.

Foster, Billy Glen. *The Foster Family of Flanders, England, and America*. Bryan, Texas: Insite, 1990.

Freeman, Douglas Southall. *R. E. Lee, A Biography Vol. II*. New York: Scribner's, 1934.

Graydon, Nell S., T. Graydon, and Margaret McKissick Davis. *The McKissicks of South Carolina*. Columbia, S.C.: R. L. Bryan, 1965.

Green, Edwin L. *A History of the University of South Carolina*. Columbia, S.C.: The State Company, 1916.

Griffith, H. P. *The Life and Times of Rev. John G. Landrum*. Philadelphia: H. B. Garner, 1885.

Harrison, Thomas Perrin. *The Honorable Thomas Chiles Perrin of Abbeville, South Carolina, Forebears and Descendants*. Greenville, S.C.: A Press, 1983.

Hilgard, Eugene W. *Geology of Lower Louisiana and the Salt Deposit on Petite Anse Island*. Washington, D.C.: Smithsonian Institution, 1872.

Hillhouse, Albert M. *Pierre Gibert, French Huguenot, His Background and Descendants*. Danville, Ky.: Bluegrass, 1977.

Kloss, Jethro. *Back to Eden*. Coalmont, Tenn.: Longview, 1950.

Landrum, J. B. O. *History of Spartanburg County*. Atlanta, Ga., n.p., 1900; reprint, Spartanburg, S.C.: Reprint Company, 1985.

Lesley, J. P. *Iron Manufacturer's Guide to the Furnaces, Forges and Rolling Mills of the United States*. New York: John Wiley, 1859.

Long, E. B. *The Civil War Day by Day*. Garden City, N. Y.: Doubleday, 1971.

May, John Amasa and Joan Reynolds Faunt. *South Carolina Secedes*. Columbia: University of South Carolina Press, 1960.

McKissick, Rion. *Men and Women of South Carolina.* Columbia: University of South Carolina Press, 1948.

Mills, Robert. *Statistics of South Carolina.* Charleston, S.C.: Hurlburt and Lloyd, 1826.

Moore, Andrew Charles. *Roll of Students of South Carolina College 1805–1905.* Columbia, S.C.: no publisher listed, 1905.

Moore, John Hammond. *Columbia and Richland County.* Columbia: University of South Carolina Press, 1993.

Morison, Samuel Eliot, Henry Steele Commager, and William E. Leuchtenburg. *The Growth of the American Republic, Vol. I.* New York: Oxford University Press, 1969.

Racine, Phillip N. *Living a Big War in a Small Place.* Columbia: University of South Carolina Press, 2013.

Sears, Stephen W. *To the Gates of Richmond, The Peninsula Campaign.* New York: Ticknor and Fields, 1992.

Simkins, Francis Butler and Robert Hilliard Woody. *South Carolina during Reconstruction.* Chapel Hill: University of North Carolina Press, 1932.

South Carolina Daughters of the Confederacy. *Recollections and Reminiscences 1861–1865 Through World War I, Vol. 3.* Daughters of the Confederacy, 1992.

Stone, DeWitte Boyd, Jr. *Wandering to Glory, Confederate Veterans Remember Evans' Brigade.* Columbia: University of South Carolina Press, 2002.

Sturkey, O. Lee. *Hampton Legion Infantry C.S.A.* Wilmington, N.C.: Broadfoot Publishing, 2008.

Swain, Glen Allen, Sr. *The Bloody Seventh.* Wilmington, N.C.: Broadfoot Publishing, 2014.

Tedards, Rosalind Todd. *A History of the Fifth South Carolina Volunteers.* Wilmington, N.C.: Broadfoot Publishing, 2013.

Towles, Louis P. *A World Turned Upside Down, The Palmers of South Santee, 1818–1881.* Columbia: University of South Carolina, 1996.

United Daughters of the Confederacy, South Carolina Division. *Recollections and Reminiscences 1861–1865 Through World War I, Vol. I.* South Carolina: S. C. Division, United Daughters of the Confederacy, 1990.

United States War Department. *War of The Rebellion: The Official Records of the Union and Confederate Armies, Series I, Vol. 21.* Washington, D.C.: Government Printing Office, 1888.

Wyckoff, Mac. *A History of the Second South Carolina Infantry: 1861–65.* Wilmington, N.C.: Broadfoot Publishing, 2011.

Wyckoff, Mac. *A History of the Third South Carolina Infantry, 1861–1865.* Fredericksburg, V.A.: Sergeant Kirkland's Museum and Historical Society, 1995.

Wyckoff, Mac. *A History of the Third South Carolina Regiment: Lee's Reliables.* Wilmington, N.C.: Broadfoot Publishing, 2008.

Internet Sources

"Descendants of George Bulman II, http://www.genealogy.com/ftm/i/b/e/Linda-J-Iben/BOOK-0001/0006-0003.html (accessed September 29, 2016).

"Descendants of Unknown Wofford," http://www.genealogy.com/ftm/w/o/f/Melinda -M-Wofford/GENE5–0008.html (accessed August 10, 2016).

"Eighteenth South Carolina Infantry, Company A, Union County, S.C." http://freepages .genealogy.rootsweb.com/~york/18thSCV/A.html (accessed May 30, 2005).

"Guide to the Ghost Towns of South Carolina," http://freepages.history.rootsweb .com/~gtusa/usa/sc.htm (accessed March 10, 2005).

Minutes of the Forty Second Anniversary of the State Convention of the Baptist Denomination in S.C. (Columbia, S.C.: E. R. Stokes, 1862), p. 176 (Call No. 4384, Rare Book Collection UNC-CH. http://docsouth.unc.edu/imls/scbc1862/scbc1862 .html) (accessed August 10, 2016).

Overton and Jesse Bernard Diaries #62-z, Southern Historical Collection, Wilson Library, University of North Carolina at Chapel Hill. Folder 3, dated June 14, 1861. http://blogs.lib.unc.edu/civilwar/index.php/page/141/ (accessed August 10, 2016).

"Person Sheet," http://homepage.mac.com/bfthompson/Miller_family/ps02_378.html (accessed July 20, 2004).

"The Charleston Fire," http://www.sonofthesouth.net/leefoundation/civil-war/1861/ december/charleston-fire.htm (accessed May 10, 2005).

"The South Carolina Civil War Soldiers Index," http://www.researchonline.net/sccw/ index/index253.htm#.V6t762X9OUc (accessed August 10, 2016).

"Virginia Earthquake History," USGS, http://earthquake.usgs.gov/earthquakes/states/ virginia/history.php (accessed August 10, 2016).

"Winder Hospital," http://www.mdgorman.com/Hospitals/winder_hospital.htm (accessed August 10, 2016).

"Winthrop University Digital Commons @ Winthrop University, The Lantern, Chester S.C.—March 19, 1907, http://digitalcommons.winthrop.edu/cgi/viewcontent.cgi ?article=1017&context=chesterlantern1907 (accessed September 7, 2016).

INDEX

Page numbers in italic type refer to illustrations or maps.